I0528489

שמות

THE
ISRAEL
BIBLE

EXODUS

EDITED BY

Rabbi Tuly Weisz

ISRAEL 365

The Israel Bible: Exodus

First Edition, 2021

The Israel Bible was produced by Israel365 in cooperation with Teach for Israel and is used with permission from Teach for Israel. All rights reserved. The English translation was adapted by Israel365 from the JPS Tanakh. Copyright © 1985 by the Jewish Publication Society. All rights reserved.

Cover image used under license from Shutterstock.com

ISBN 978-1-957109-27-5

A CIP catalogue record for this title is available from the British Library

The Israel Bible: Exodus is a holy book that contains the name of God and should be treated with respect.

Table of Contents

Introduction

The Hebrew Bible is commonly known as the *Tanakh* which stands for *Torah* (the Five Books of Moses), *Neviim* (the Prophets) and *Ketuvim* (the Writings). The *Tanakh* consists of 24 books that are considered by Jews to be the word of God. While these books have been referred to as the "Old Testament," many Jews reject this label since it implies the replacement of the Hebrew Bible with something newer and prefer the more authentic Jewish name.

The *Tanakh* is not only the most important book known to man, it is God's word that is perfect and absolute. It is therefore a daunting undertaking to publish an edition of the *Tanakh*, and the responsibilities are awesome. There is no room for error or carelessness in dealing with the eternal word of God. Further, upon embarking on such a serious initiative, we ask ourselves if our efforts are gratuitous. Considering the many editions of the Bible in print, is there truly a need for yet another one?

While there are numerous Bibles in circulation today, its most central aspect – the Land of Israel – has often been overlooked. References to Israel appear on nearly every page, and the city of Jerusalem is specifically referred to hundreds of times throughout the Bible. The essential link between Israel and *Torah* is emphasized repeatedly in verses such as, "For instruction (*Torah*) shall come forth from *Tzion*, the word of *Hashem* from *Yerushalayim*" (Micah 4:2).

The miraculous return of the People of Israel to the Land of Israel in our own generation provides the perfect moment for a new volume to fill this void in biblical literature. *The Israel Bible* includes many special features elucidating God's focus on Israel throughout *Tanakh* and there are many additional, multimedia features available on our website **www.theisraelbible.com**.

Ordering and Presentation – In presenting *The Israel Bible*, our goal is to spread awareness of the biblical significance of the Land of Israel as well as the Jewish people's eternal connection to the land, based on the text of the *Tanakh*, the Hebrew Bible. We aim to honor "the God, the People and the Land of Israel" from an Orthodox Jewish perspective. To that end, *The Israel Bible* follows the traditional Jewish ordering of the books and the customary Hebrew division of chapters. Therefore, for example, we count 24 books of *Tanakh* with *Sefer Divrei Hayamim* (Chronicles) appearing last. It is our hope that our rich content will speak to all Jews and non-Jews who appreciate Israel as the God given land of the Jewish people.

English Translation – Throughout history, Jews have studied the Bible in Hebrew, as any form of translation would miss much of the nuance of the original holy tongue in which *Torah* has been transmitted since the days of Moses. However, as many Jews settled in America in the 19th Century, the need for an English translation became necessary. To be sure, there were already English translations prepared over the centuries by Christians, but in the words of the original editors of the Jewish Publication Society (JPS), "The Jew cannot afford to have his Bible translation prepared for him by others. He cannot have it as a gift, even as he cannot borrow his soul from others."

JPS set out in the late 1800s to publish an authoritative English translation "in the spirit of Jewish tradition." It was compiled over decades by some of the leading Jewish scholars of the time. They formed committees and subcommittees to compare existing English versions, considering medieval and modern Jewish commentators. The monumental JPS translation, originally published in 1917, has been updated in recent years, and *The Israel Bible* is proud to utilize the 1984 New Jewish Publication Society (NJPS) version with its modern, clear language, as well as its wide-ranging acceptance as an accurate and high-quality translation. We applied the NJPS translation verbatim, except for a select list of nouns which we replaced with their traditional Hebrew names. This is true even when we found the NJPS translation to be different than the popular translation of a word or phrase and when the NJPS switched the order of the text for the sake of clarity (see, for example, Ezekiel 24:22–24).

Hebrew Transliteration – To give our readers an authentic *Tanakh* experience, every verse that has commentary is transliterated from Hebrew into English. The Hebrew alphabet chart includes our standards for transliteration and pronunciation of Hebrew verses, enabling readers of *The Israel Bible* to decipher key biblical passages in the holy language. Readers can hear the entire Bible read in Hebrew on our website **www.theisraelbible.com**.

There are various standards when it comes to transliterating Hebrew words into English letters. While we have relied primarily on the classical Hebrew transliteration, we have occasionally deviated for the sake of simplicity, clarity and to reflect common usage.

In addition to whole verses, we have also transliterated many proper nouns in the English translation so that our readers can learn the names of key biblical figures and locations in their Hebrew form. As a rule, we chose to transliterate names of people that were central in the establishment and functioning of the nation of Israel, as well as significant places in the Holy Land. Therefore, regarding Adam's sons, for example, only *Shet* (Seth) is transliterated since it was from him that *Noach* (Noah), and ultimately *Avraham* (Abraham), descended. For this reason, there might be verses or sections of *The Israel Bible* that contains multiple names and only some of them are transliterated.

For the same reason, we have transliterated the names of the books of *Tanakh* when referring to them in our introductions and commentary. When referencing a specific chapter or verse, however, we use the English names of the books in our citations for clarity. We also transliterated ideas and concepts that are central to Judaism such as *Shabbat* (Sabbath), the names of the Jewish holidays and the *Beit Hamikdash* (Temple), as well as biblical measurements. Finally, the name of God is transliterated. Out of respect, Orthodox Jews generally refer to the Lord as *Hashem*, which literally means 'the Name.' Referring to God as *Hashem* reminds us that we feel close to Him but also recognize our distance at the same time. To stress this moniker, we transliterated both the Tetragrammaton as well as the name *Elohim* as *Hashem*.

Study Notes – Our unique commentary was compiled by Orthodox Jewish scholars who live in Israel. It is an anthology in the sense that most of the commentary is not original, but draws from traditional teachings of early Jewish Sages and modern rabbinic commentators. We also include quotations from individuals who have played a significant part in the past century of modern Israeli history including Israeli prime ministers, poets and military leaders.

Our commentary can be broken into four categories, three of which are identified by an icon at the beginning of the study note:

 Israel lessons are indicated with an icon bearing the map of Israel and focus on the Land of Israel and the modern State of Israel.

 Jewish lessons are indicated with a *Torah* scroll and teach a concept in Judaism or a classic idea from rabbinic thought.

 Hebrew lessons are represented by an icon bearing the letter *aleph* and focus on the meaning of a Hebrew word or phrase.

All other comments are considered general comments and are not assigned an icon.

Supplemental Material – In addition to our unique translation and original commentary, *The Israel Bible* offers supplementary material to enrich the learning experience of our readers. Before every book of *Tanakh*, we provide an introduction, as well as information, generally in the form of a map, a chart or a list, which is central to the specific book.

Maps – As the purpose of *The Israel Bible* is to highlight the biblical significance of the Land of Israel, significant time was spent researching and preparing maps to bring the physical contours of the holy land to life with great accuracy. However, since there is a lack of information regarding the precise locations of certain ancient cities, some of the places on our maps are approximate or subject to debate. In these cases, we followed the opinion that we are most comfortable with, but acknowledge that there is room for disagreement. We continue to produce new maps, which are available on our website **www.theisraelbible.com/maps**.

Torah **Readings** – The *Torah* is not just a work that is studied privately, it is also read out loud in synagogue. Every *Shabbat* and holiday a portion of the *Torah* is read, as well as a related section from *Neviim*, the prophets, called the *haftarah*. We included the blessings recited before and after the reading of the *Torah*, a list of the weekly *Torah* portions and their corresponding *haftarot*, and a chart of the *Torah* readings for special days with their corresponding *haftarot*. Readers can always find the current week's *Torah* portion by visiting **www.theisraelbible.com/weekly-torah-portion**. In this volume, we indicate where a new *Torah* portion begins by highlighting the Hebrew verse number with a gray box so readers can follow along with the communal *Torah* readings. Furthermore, we have included prayers for the State of Israel and the soldiers of the Israel Defense Forces (IDF) that are generally recited following the *Torah* reading in synagogue. It is our constant prayer that God watch over the State of Israel and the members of the IDF, who defend Israel every hour of every day.

In 1948, the State of Israel was created providing a modern answer to Isaiah's ancient question, "Is a nation born all at once?" (Isaiah 66:8). *The Israel Bible* was first published in the 70th year of God's miraculous restoration of the People of Israel to the Land of Israel. Jewish wisdom teaches that 70 is a significant number: *Moshe* (Moses) translated the *Torah* into 70 languages for all 70 nations of the world. From our very origins, the Jewish people were meant to be a light unto the 70 nations, spreading God's truth to the masses.

In the seven decades since the modern rebirth of the State of Israel, God's plan has been unfolding with unprecedented speed, dramatic highs and heartbreaking lows. Never has Israel been at the forefront of the world's attention as it is in our generation. Efforts to vilify the Jewish State seem to spread every day across the globe. At the same time, so does the growing movement of millions of non-Jewish biblical Zionists who stand with the nation of Israel as an expression of their commitment to God's word. As we seek to understand the clash of these two conflicting worldviews, the need for *The Israel Bible* has never been so important.

Standing on the great shoulders of those who came before us and emanating from the land that has always served as the birthplace for the Bible, we conclude with a heartfelt prayer: May the Almighty bless our efforts in offering this *Tanakh* to influence the hearts, minds and actions of its readers. In this way, it is our hope to spread God's name so that the publication of *The Israel Bible* brings us one step closer to the final redemption of Israel and the entire world.

Rabbi Tuly Weisz
Editor, *The Israel Bible*

Foreword

The mandate to study God's word daily is interestingly not found in the Five Books of Moses (Pentateuch), but rather in the first book of our prophetic writings: "Let not this Book of the Teaching cease from your lips, but recite it day and night, so that you may observe faithfully all that is written in it. Only then will you prosper in your undertakings and only then will you be successful" (Joshua 1:8). Charged with bringing the Israelites into the land covenantally promised to Abraham, Isaac and Jacob, God ensures Joshua of His protection if the nation observes His ways as dictated in the Divine constitution known as the *Torah*.

In Jewish tradition, Joshua (1:8) is directly linked with Deuteronomy (11:14), "You shall gather in your new grain and wine, and oil."[1] Our Sages deduced from this scriptural combination the importance of merging *Torah* study with a profession. Completely dedicating oneself to the study of *Torah* without having the financial means to sustain this lifestyle can lead one to eventually straying from observance of God's will. Poverty and crime can have an intimate relationship.

We must also be careful that our work does not affect our daily study of Scripture. The addiction of becoming a workaholic and not making *Torah* study a priority can also lead one into temptations that can violate our personal relationship with Him as well as our fellow human beings. The goal is to achieve a healthy balance between our study of God's word and our daily work.

The Deuteronomic verse quoted above is part of the second section of the Shema[2] that discusses the concept of reward and punishment. Sanctifying God by fulfilling His commandments results in the Land of Israel practically benefitting from rains that occur in the right season and reaping the abundance from the fields. However, if the nation follows pagan gods and practices, the consequences are devastating – famine and death. The Land of Israel is intrinsically linked with the keeping of the *Torah*. Covenant Land comes with covenant responsibility.

---

1. Talmud Bavli Berachot 35b
2. Consisting of three sections within the Five Books of Moses (Deut. 6:4–8; 11:13–22 and Numbers 15:37–42), the *Shema* is proclamation of accepting God's Kingdom in our lives, loyalty to His commandments and remembering His redemptive act of liberating us from Egypt. Jews recite the *Shema* twice a day as stated in Deut. 6:7.

Born into slavery, Joshua is now leading His people into the Promised Land. More than 500 years separates him from his ancestral forefather Abraham. The historical narratives that took place between Abraham leaving everything behind to follow God in Genesis 12 and the death of Moses in the last chapter of Deuteronomy are filled with intrigue, suspense, joy, sorrow and hope. What began as a family is now a nation actualizing its mission to be a kingdom of priests to the world. However, for the Israelites to succeed in the Land of Israel, they must see the *Torah* as the only compass to direct their lives.

The biblical episodes after our first entry into the land are well known. Our ancestors' triumphs and sins are all on public record. We learned the harsh reality of Leviticus (18:28) "So let not the land spew you out for defiling it as it spewed out the nation that came before you." Twice, we lost the privilege to be stewards of the Land of Israel and to fulfill our nation state mandate to be a light to the world. However, when the annals of history were ready to archive the Jewish people after the Holocaust, God kept His covenantal promise and gathered us from the four corners of the globe to come home. The year 1948 was a game changer. Biblical prophecies were and are being realized. We are now living in the birth pangs of the messianic era.

In our morning prayers, we recite a series of blessings over the *Torah* that include petitioning God to have a sweet tooth for His word, to study it without any ulterior motive and to have Him to teach it to us. They are some congregations that invoke the following liturgical prayer after the completion of these blessings: *May the Torah be my faith and El Shaddai my help. Blessed be the name of His glorious kingdom forever and all time.*

According to Jewish tradition, the neglect of not blessing the *Torah* before engaging in its study was one of the reasons for the destruction of the Temple.[3] This is deduced from the redundancy of words in Jeremiah (9:12) that talks about Israel not following God: "...Because they forsook the teaching I had set before them. They did not obey Me and they did not follow it [did not make a blessing before studying it]." Our inability to properly cherish God's greatest gift to the world, the *Torah*, led to our eventual exile from our land.

On Israel's Independence Day, Jews around the world recite Psalms 113–118 to express our gratitude to God for His Divine hand in helping establish the State of Israel. We have learned from our past and realize the privilege to see firsthand the land, people and *Torah* operating all together in our generation.

---

3.   Babylonian Talmud Nedarim 81a

When Rabbi Tuly Weisz approached me about his intent to publish *The Israel Bible* that would highlight commentary about the special relationship between the land and people, I saw this project as another way to publicly demonstrate our appreciation to God for having the State of Israel. In addition, it is another educational tool to ensure biblical literacy. If we are to truly enjoy the Land of Israel, it is incumbent upon us to continually study the *Torah*. Isaiah once prophesied that the Jewish people would return to Zion with songs, "crowned with everlasting joy" (35:10). *The Israel Bible* provides us the lyrical content to express our joy in living in the land that God calls holy.

Rabbi Shlomo Riskin
Chief Rabbi of Efrat
Founder of the Center for Jewish-Christian
Understanding & Cooperation (cjcuc)

Introduction to Sefer Shemot
The Book of Exodus

Introduction and commentary by Rabbi Tuly Weisz

Location and geography are central to *Sefer Shemot* (Exodus). Ancient Egypt and the barren wilderness form the essential backdrop to the drama which unfolds in the second book of the Bible. While all of the events recorded in *Sefer Shemot* take place outside of the Land of Israel, this does not mean that *Eretz Yisrael* is unimportant in this book. On the contrary, the Land of Israel is a central theme and primary focus of *Sefer Shemot*.

The Hebrew name for the Book of Exodus is *Sefer Shemot*, the 'Book of Names,' taken from the opening words of the first verse. Continuing the narrative from the point where *Sefer Bereishit* (Genesis) ended, it transitions from a family's individual story to the birth of an entire nation. The opening chapters of *Sefer Shemot* describe the trials experienced by the Children of Israel in the fiery furnace of slavery. This brutal oppression in a foreign land has been explained by Jewish commentators as a process of national purification, necessary in order to prepare the Israelites for entry into the "land flowing with milk and honey" (Exodus 3:8).

Sefer Shemot goes on to describe the exodus from Egypt and offers timeless insight into God's loving relationship with humanity as their ultimate Redeemer. With each step they take in the wilderness, the Israelites are marching towards, and getting closer to, *Eretz Yisrael*, which becomes the ultimate ideal for which they strive.

It is no wonder then, that the Book of *Shemot* has served throughout the ages as an inspiration for those who have longed for *Eretz Yisrael*. Wandering through the bitter exile, Jews have always seen themselves as following in the footsteps of the ancient Israelites. In the darkest moments of Jewish history, we have borne the burden of persecution with the knowledge that we are always getting closer to deliverance and redemption, and to Israel. *Sefer Shemot* causes us to realize that the destiny of the People of Israel always leads towards the Land of Israel.

Map of the Journey from Egypt to Mount Sinai

This map traces the journey of the Children of Israel from Egypt to Mount Sinai as described in *Sefer Shemot* (12:37–19:2).

1. The Children of Israel leave Egypt from **Ramses** (Exodus 12:37).

2. The first stop on their journey is **Succoth** (Exodus 12:37).

3. From Succoth they travel to **Etham** (Exodus 13:19). II Kings

4. They camp between **Midgol** and the sea while the Egyptian army pursues them (Exodus 14:1–14).

5. The **Sea of Reeds** splits, allowing the Jews to cross on dry land (Exodus 14:15–31).

6. The people travel to **Marah** where they find bitter water (Exodus 15:23–26).

7. In **Elim**, they find 12 springs of water and 70 palm trees (Exodus 15:27).

8. In the **wilderness of Sin**, they complain about the lack of food (Exodus 16:1–36).

9. They again lack water in **Rephidim**. God provides water from a rock and Amalek attacks (Exodus 17:1–16).

10. From Rephidim, they travel to **Mount Sinai** (Exodus 19:1–2).

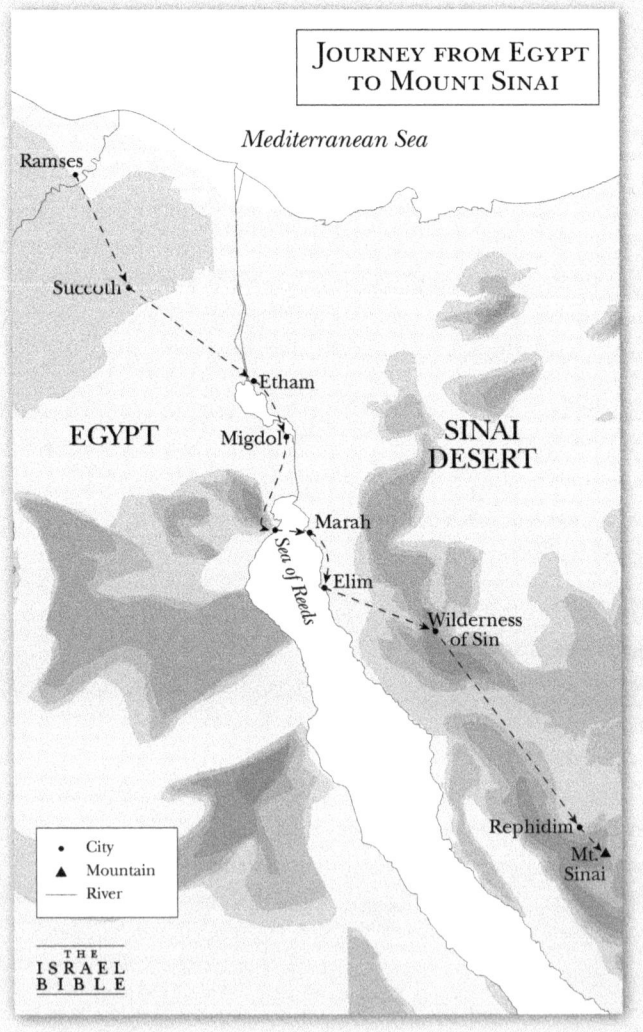

1 **1** These are the names of the sons of *Yisrael* who came to Egypt with *Yaakov*, each coming with his household:

א וְאֵלֶּה שְׁמוֹת בְּנֵי יִשְׂרָאֵל הַבָּאִים מִצְרָיְמָה אֵת יַעֲקֹב אִישׁ וּבֵיתוֹ בָּאוּ:

v'-AY-leh sh'-MOT b'-NAY yis-ra-AYL ha-ba-EEM
mitz-RA-y'-mah AYT ya-a-KOV EESH u'-vay-TO BA-u

2 *Reuven, Shimon, Levi,* and *Yehuda;*

ב רְאוּבֵן שִׁמְעוֹן לֵוִי וִיהוּדָה:

3 *Yissachar, Zevulun,* and *Binyamin;*

ג יִשָּׂשכָר זְבוּלֻן וּבִנְיָמִן:

4 *Dan* and *Naftali, Gad* and *Asher.*

ד דָּן וְנַפְתָּלִי גָּד וְאָשֵׁר:

5 The total number of persons that were of *Yaakov*'s issue came to seventy, *Yosef* being already in Egypt.

ה וַיְהִי כָּל־נֶפֶשׁ יֹצְאֵי יֶרֶךְ־יַעֲקֹב שִׁבְעִים נָפֶשׁ וְיוֹסֵף הָיָה בְמִצְרָיִם:

6 *Yosef* died, and all his brothers, and all that generation.

ו וַיָּמָת יוֹסֵף וְכָל־אֶחָיו וְכֹל הַדּוֹר הַהוּא:

7 But the Israelites were fertile and prolific; they multiplied and increased very greatly, so that the land was filled with them.

ז וּבְנֵי יִשְׂרָאֵל פָּרוּ וַיִּשְׁרְצוּ וַיִּרְבּוּ וַיַּעַצְמוּ בִּמְאֹד מְאֹד וַתִּמָּלֵא הָאָרֶץ אֹתָם:

8 A new king arose over Egypt who did not know *Yosef.*

ח וַיָּקָם מֶלֶךְ־חָדָשׁ עַל־מִצְרָיִם אֲשֶׁר לֹא־יָדַע אֶת־יוֹסֵף:

9 And he said to his people, "Look, *B'nei Yisrael* are much too numerous for us.

ט וַיֹּאמֶר אֶל־עַמּוֹ הִנֵּה עַם בְּנֵי יִשְׂרָאֵל רַב וְעָצוּם מִמֶּנּוּ:

10 Let us deal shrewdly with them, so that they may not increase; otherwise in the event of war they may join our enemies in fighting against us and rise from the ground."

י הָבָה נִתְחַכְּמָה לוֹ פֶּן־יִרְבֶּה וְהָיָה כִּי־תִקְרֶאנָה מִלְחָמָה וְנוֹסַף גַּם־הוּא עַל־שֹׂנְאֵינוּ וְנִלְחַם־בָּנוּ וְעָלָה מִן־הָאָרֶץ:

11 So they set taskmasters over them to oppress them with forced labor; and they built garrison cities for Pharaoh: Pithom and Raamses.

יא וַיָּשִׂימוּ עָלָיו שָׂרֵי מִסִּים לְמַעַן עַנֹּתוֹ בְּסִבְלֹתָם וַיִּבֶן עָרֵי מִסְכְּנוֹת לְפַרְעֹה אֶת־פִּתֹם וְאֶת־רַעַמְסֵס:

12 But the more they were oppressed, the more they increased and spread out, so that the [Egyptians] came to dread the Israelites.

יב וְכַאֲשֶׁר יְעַנּוּ אֹתוֹ כֵּן יִרְבֶּה וְכֵן יִפְרֹץ וַיָּקֻצוּ מִפְּנֵי בְּנֵי יִשְׂרָאֵל:

13 The Egyptians ruthlessly imposed upon the Israelites

יג וַיַּעֲבִדוּ מִצְרַיִם אֶת־בְּנֵי יִשְׂרָאֵל בְּפָרֶךְ:

ואלה

1:1 **These are the names** *Sefer Shemot* starts with the letter *vav* (ו), which signifies the conjunction 'and,' thus connecting it to the end of *Sefer Bereishit.* In fact, the passages beginning with *Shemot* 1:1 and *Bereishit* 46:8 are practically identical, each containing a list of *Yaakov's* descendants who accompanied him to Egypt. The end of *Sefer Bereishit* describes the children of *Yaakov* leaving their homeland and descending to Egypt. *Sefer Shemot* continues the story of the exile and the subsequent miraculous redemption, and is therefore a direct continuation of *Sefer Bereishit.* However, the story does not end with the conclusion of *Sefer Shemot.* While the slavery itself comes to an end with the exodus from Egypt, the ultimate redemption comes only with the reunification of the Children of Israel and their homeland, as described in *Sefer Yehoshua.*

New immigrants arriving in Israel, 1950

Exodus

14 the various labors that they made them perform. Ruthlessly* they made life bitter for them with harsh labor at mortar and bricks and with all sorts of tasks in the field.

יד וַיְמָרְרוּ אֶת־חַיֵּיהֶם בַּעֲבֹדָה קָשָׁה בְּחֹמֶר וּבִלְבֵנִים וּבְכָל־עֲבֹדָה בַּשָּׂדֶה אֵת כָּל־עֲבֹדָתָם אֲשֶׁר־עָבְדוּ בָהֶם בְּפָרֶךְ:

15 The king of Egypt spoke to the Hebrew midwives, one of whom was named Shiphrah and the other Puah,

טו וַיֹּאמֶר מֶלֶךְ מִצְרַיִם לַמְיַלְּדֹת הָעִבְרִיֹּת אֲשֶׁר שֵׁם הָאַחַת שִׁפְרָה וְשֵׁם הַשֵּׁנִית פּוּעָה:

va-YO-mer ME-lekh mitz-RA-yim lam-ya-l'-DOT ha-iv-ri-YOT a-SHER SHAYM ha-a-KHAT shif-RAH v'-SHAYM ha-shay-NEET pu-AH

16 saying, "When you deliver the Hebrew women, look at the birthstool: if it is a boy, kill him; if it is a girl, let her live."

טז וַיֹּאמֶר בְּיַלֶּדְכֶן אֶת־הָעִבְרִיֹּות וּרְאִיתֶן עַל־הָאָבְנָיִם אִם־בֵּן הוּא וַהֲמִתֶּן אֹתוֹ וְאִם־בַּת הִיא וָחָיָה:

17 The midwives, fearing *Hashem*, did not do as the king of Egypt had told them; they let the boys live.

יז וַתִּירֶאןָ הַמְיַלְּדֹת אֶת־הָאֱלֹהִים וְלֹא עָשׂוּ כַּאֲשֶׁר דִּבֶּר אֲלֵיהֶן מֶלֶךְ מִצְרָיִם וַתְּחַיֶּיןָ אֶת־הַיְלָדִים:

18 So the king of Egypt summoned the midwives and said to them, "Why have you done this thing, letting the boys live?"

יח וַיִּקְרָא מֶלֶךְ־מִצְרַיִם לַמְיַלְּדֹת וַיֹּאמֶר לָהֶן מַדּוּעַ עֲשִׂיתֶן הַדָּבָר הַזֶּה וַתְּחַיֶּיןָ אֶת־הַיְלָדִים:

19 The midwives said to Pharaoh, "Because the Hebrew women are not like the Egyptian women: they are vigorous. Before the midwife can come to them, they have given birth."

יט וַתֹּאמַרְןָ הַמְיַלְּדֹת אֶל־פַּרְעֹה כִּי לֹא כַנָּשִׁים הַמִּצְרִיֹּת הָעִבְרִיֹּת כִּי־חָיוֹת הֵנָּה בְּטֶרֶם תָּבוֹא אֲלֵהֶן הַמְיַלֶּדֶת וְיָלָדוּ:

20 And *Hashem* dealt well with the midwives; and the people multiplied and increased greatly.

כ וַיֵּיטֶב אֱלֹהִים לַמְיַלְּדֹת וַיִּרֶב הָעָם וַיַּעַצְמוּ מְאֹד:

21 And because the midwives feared *Hashem*, He established households for them.

כא וַיְהִי כִּי־יָרְאוּ הַמְיַלְּדֹת אֶת־הָאֱלֹהִים וַיַּעַשׂ לָהֶם בָּתִּים:

22 Then Pharaoh charged all his people, saying, "Every boy that is born you shall throw into the Nile, but let every girl live."

כב וַיְצַו פַּרְעֹה לְכָל־עַמּוֹ לֵאמֹר כָּל־הַבֵּן הַיִּלּוֹד הַיְאֹרָה תַּשְׁלִיכֻהוּ וְכָל־הַבַּת תְּחַיּוּן:

---

* "the various labors that they made them perform. Ruthlessly" moved up from the end of the verse for clarity

1:15 The Hebrew midwives The identity of these 'Hebrew midwives,' *meyaldot haivriyot* (מילדות העבריות), is debated by Rabbinic commentators. Many have assumed, as the literal reading implies, that they were Jewish women. But other commentators, such as the *Abrabanel*, suggest that the midwives Shiphrah and Puah were Egyptians. This interpretation is primarily based on the use of the phrase "fear of God," a phrase often used to describe the behavior of exceptional gentiles, in reference to their heroic actions. According to these interpreters, the phrase *meyaldot haivriyot*, 'Hebrew midwives,' is deliberately ambiguous, and it actually refers to the "midwives for the Hebrew women." If so, Shiphrah and Puah were the first gentiles in history to risk their lives in order to rescue a Jew. Israeli Bible scholar and teacher *par excellence*, Nechama Leibovitz, remarked about this passage, "If we accept that the midwives were Egyptian, a…very vital message becomes apparent. The *Torah* indicates how the individual can resist evil. He need not shirk his moral responsibility under cover of 'superior orders'… Neither moral courage nor sheer wickedness are ethnically or nationally determined qualities. Moab and Ammon produced a Ruth and Naamah respectively; Egypt two righteous midwives."

Nechama Leibowitz
(1905–1997)

2 ¹ A certain man of the house of *Levi* went and married a Levite woman.

ב א וַיֵּלֶךְ אִישׁ מִבֵּית לֵוִי וַיִּקַּח אֶת־בַּת־לֵוִי:

² The woman conceived and bore a son; and when she saw how beautiful he was, she hid him for three months.

ב וַתַּהַר הָאִשָּׁה וַתֵּלֶד בֵּן וַתֵּרֶא אֹתוֹ כִּי־טוֹב הוּא וַתִּצְפְּנֵהוּ שְׁלֹשָׁה יְרָחִים:

³ When she could hide him no longer, she got a wicker basket for him and caulked it with bitumen and pitch. She put the child into it and placed it among the reeds by the bank of the Nile.

ג וְלֹא־יָכְלָה עוֹד הַצְּפִינוֹ וַתִּקַּח־לוֹ תֵּבַת גֹּמֶא וַתַּחְמְרָה בַחֵמָר וּבַזָּפֶת וַתָּשֶׂם בָּהּ אֶת־הַיֶּלֶד וַתָּשֶׂם בַּסּוּף עַל־שְׂפַת הַיְאֹר:

⁴ And his sister stationed herself at a distance, to learn what would befall him.

ד וַתֵּתַצַּב אֲחֹתוֹ מֵרָחֹק לְדֵעָה מַה־יֵּעָשֶׂה לוֹ:

⁵ The daughter of Pharaoh came down to bathe in the Nile, while her maidens walked along the Nile. She spied the basket among the reeds and sent her slave girl to fetch it.

ה וַתֵּרֶד בַּת־פַּרְעֹה לִרְחֹץ עַל־הַיְאֹר וְנַעֲרֹתֶיהָ הֹלְכֹת עַל־יַד הַיְאֹר וַתֵּרֶא אֶת־הַתֵּבָה בְּתוֹךְ הַסּוּף וַתִּשְׁלַח אֶת־אֲמָתָהּ וַתִּקָּחֶהָ:

⁶ When she opened it, she saw that it was a child, a boy crying. She took pity on it and said, "This must be a Hebrew child."

ו וַתִּפְתַּח וַתִּרְאֵהוּ אֶת־הַיֶּלֶד וְהִנֵּה־נַעַר בֹּכֶה וַתַּחְמֹל עָלָיו וַתֹּאמֶר מִיַּלְדֵי הָעִבְרִים זֶה:

⁷ Then his sister said to Pharaoh's daughter, "Shall I go and get you a Hebrew nurse to suckle the child for you?"

ז וַתֹּאמֶר אֲחֹתוֹ אֶל־בַּת־פַּרְעֹה הַאֵלֵךְ וְקָרָאתִי לָךְ אִשָּׁה מֵינֶקֶת מִן הָעִבְרִיֹּת וְתֵינִק לָךְ אֶת־הַיָּלֶד:

⁸ And Pharaoh's daughter answered, "Yes." So the girl went and called the child's mother.

ח וַתֹּאמֶר־לָהּ בַּת־פַּרְעֹה לֵכִי וַתֵּלֶךְ הָעַלְמָה וַתִּקְרָא אֶת־אֵם הַיָּלֶד:

⁹ And Pharaoh's daughter said to her, "Take this child and nurse it for me, and I will pay your wages." So the woman took the child and nursed it.

ט וַתֹּאמֶר לָהּ בַּת־פַּרְעֹה הֵילִיכִי אֶת־הַיֶּלֶד הַזֶּה וְהֵינִקִהוּ לִי וַאֲנִי אֶתֵּן אֶת־שְׂכָרֵךְ וַתִּקַּח הָאִשָּׁה הַיֶּלֶד וַתְּנִיקֵהוּ:

¹⁰ When the child grew up, she brought him to Pharaoh's daughter, who made him her son. She named him *Moshe*, explaining, "I drew him out of the water."

י וַיִּגְדַּל הַיֶּלֶד וַתְּבִאֵהוּ לְבַת־פַּרְעֹה וַיְהִי־לָהּ לְבֵן וַתִּקְרָא שְׁמוֹ מֹשֶׁה וַתֹּאמֶר כִּי מִן־הַמַּיִם מְשִׁיתִהוּ:

va-yig-DAL ha-YE-led va-t'-vi-AY-hu l'-vat par-OH vai-hee LAH l'-VAYN
va-tik-RA sh'-MO mo-SHEH va-TO-mer KEE min ha-MA-yim m'-shee-TI-hu

The Sea of Galilee

משה

2:10 She named him *Moshe* *Moshe* was the greatest of all of Israel's leaders, who is known with affection in Jewish tradition as *Moshe Rabbeinu* (משה רבינו), '*Moshe* our Teacher.' Although *Moshe* speaks directly with *Hashem*, he is identified as the most humble person to ever live (Numbers 12:3). The name *Moshe* is a constant reminder of his modest origins. According to the Sages of the *Midrash*, *Moshe* actually had ten names, but out of appreciation to Pharaoh's daughter who saved him, he is referred to by the name she gave him: *Moshe*, which means 'I have drawn him from the water.'

11 Some time after that, when *Moshe* had grown up, he went out to his kinsfolk and witnessed their labors. He saw an Egyptian beating a Hebrew, one of his kinsmen.

יא וַיְהִ֣י ׀ בַּיָּמִ֣ים הָהֵ֗ם וַיִּגְדַּ֤ל מֹשֶׁה֙ וַיֵּצֵ֣א אֶל־אֶחָ֔יו וַיַּ֖רְא בְּסִבְלֹתָ֑ם וַיַּרְא֙ אִ֣ישׁ מִצְרִ֔י מַכֶּ֥ה אִישׁ־עִבְרִ֖י מֵאֶחָֽיו׃

12 He turned this way and that and, seeing no one about, he struck down the Egyptian and hid him in the sand.

יב וַיִּ֤פֶן כֹּה֙ וָכֹ֔ה וַיַּ֖רְא כִּ֣י אֵ֣ין אִ֑ישׁ וַיַּךְ֙ אֶת־הַמִּצְרִ֔י וַֽיִּטְמְנֵ֖הוּ בַּחֽוֹל׃

13 When he went out the next day, he found two Hebrews fighting; so he said to the offender, "Why do you strike your fellow?"

יג וַיֵּצֵא֙ בַּיּ֣וֹם הַשֵּׁנִ֔י וְהִנֵּ֛ה שְׁנֵֽי־אֲנָשִׁ֥ים עִבְרִ֖ים נִצִּ֑ים וַיֹּ֙אמֶר֙ לָֽרָשָׁ֔ע לָ֥מָּה תַכֶּ֖ה רֵעֶֽךָ׃

14 He retorted, "Who made you chief and ruler over us? Do you mean to kill me as you killed the Egyptian?" *Moshe* was frightened, and thought: Then the matter is known!

יד וַ֠יֹּאמֶר מִ֣י שָֽׂמְךָ֞ לְאִ֨ישׁ שַׂ֤ר וְשֹׁפֵט֙ עָלֵ֔ינוּ הַלְהׇרְגֵ֙נִי֙ אַתָּ֣ה אֹמֵ֔ר כַּאֲשֶׁ֥ר הָרַ֖גְתָּ אֶת־הַמִּצְרִ֑י וַיִּירָ֤א מֹשֶׁה֙ וַיֹּאמַ֔ר אָכֵ֖ן נוֹדַ֥ע הַדָּבָֽר׃

15 When Pharaoh learned of the matter, he sought to kill *Moshe*; but *Moshe* fled from Pharaoh. He arrived in the land of Midian, and sat down beside a well.

טו וַיִּשְׁמַ֤ע פַּרְעֹה֙ אֶת־הַדָּבָ֣ר הַזֶּ֔ה וַיְבַקֵּ֖שׁ לַהֲרֹ֣ג אֶת־מֹשֶׁ֑ה וַיִּבְרַ֤ח מֹשֶׁה֙ מִפְּנֵ֣י פַרְעֹ֔ה וַיֵּ֥שֶׁב בְּאֶֽרֶץ־מִדְיָ֖ן וַיֵּ֥שֶׁב עַֽל־הַבְּאֵֽר׃

16 Now the priest of Midian had seven daughters. They came to draw water, and filled the troughs to water their father's flock;

טז וּלְכֹהֵ֥ן מִדְיָ֖ן שֶׁ֣בַע בָּנ֑וֹת וַתָּבֹ֣אנָה וַתִּדְלֶ֗נָה וַתְּמַלֶּ֙אנָה֙ אֶת־הָ֣רְהָטִ֔ים לְהַשְׁק֖וֹת צֹ֥אן אֲבִיהֶֽן׃

17 but shepherds came and drove them off. *Moshe* rose to their defense, and he watered their flock.

יז וַיָּבֹ֥אוּ הָרֹעִ֖ים וַיְגָרְשׁ֑וּם וַיָּ֤קׇם מֹשֶׁה֙ וַיּ֣וֹשִׁעָ֔ן וַיַּ֖שְׁקְ אֶת־צֹאנָֽם׃

18 When they returned to their father Reuel, he said, "How is it that you have come back so soon today?"

יח וַתָּבֹ֕אנָה אֶל־רְעוּאֵ֖ל אֲבִיהֶ֑ן וַיֹּ֕אמֶר מַדּ֛וּעַ מִהַרְתֶּ֥ן בֹּ֖א הַיּֽוֹם׃

19 They answered, "An Egyptian rescued us from the shepherds; he even drew water for us and watered the flock."

יט וַתֹּאמַ֕רְןָ אִ֣ישׁ מִצְרִ֔י הִצִּילָ֖נוּ מִיַּ֣ד הָרֹעִ֑ים וְגַם־דָּלֹ֤ה דָלָה֙ לָ֔נוּ וַיַּ֖שְׁקְ אֶת־הַצֹּֽאן׃

va-to-MAR-na ish mitz-RI hi-tzi-LA-nu mi-YAD ha-RO-eem
v'-GAM da-LO LA-nu va-YASHK et ha-TZON

20 He said to his daughters, "Where is he then? Why did you leave the man? Ask him in to break bread."

כ וַיֹּ֥אמֶר אֶל־בְּנֹתָ֖יו וְאַיּ֑וֹ לָ֤מָּה זֶּה֙ עֲזַבְתֶּ֣ן אֶת־הָאִ֔ישׁ קִרְאֶ֥ן ל֖וֹ וְיֹ֥אכַל לָֽחֶם׃

21 *Moshe* consented to stay with the man, and he gave *Moshe* his daughter *Tzipora* as wife.

כא וַיּ֥וֹאֶל מֹשֶׁ֖ה לָשֶׁ֣בֶת אֶת־הָאִ֑ישׁ וַיִּתֵּ֛ן אֶת־צִפֹּרָ֥ה בִתּ֖וֹ לְמֹשֶֽׁה׃

2:19 An Egyptian rescued us from the shepherds Based on this verse, the Sages of the *Midrash* contrast *Yosef* and *Moshe*. *Yosef* identified himself with *Eretz Yisrael*, as he says, "I was kidnapped from the land of the Hebrews" (Genesis 40:15), whereas *Moshe* does not protest when Jethro's daughters refer to him as an Egyptian. *Yosef* therefore merits to be buried in the Land of Israel, while *Moshe* does not. Rabbi Zalman Sorotzkin points out that *Moshe*'s behavior is understandable, as he was not born in Israel nor had he ever been there. However, once *Hashem* had promised *Avraham* that his descendants would inherit the land, it became their homeland. No matter where in the world a Jew may find himself, he is called upon to identify with *Eretz Yisrael*.

Yosef's tomb in Shechem

²² She bore a son whom he named *Gershom*, for he said, "I have been a stranger in a foreign land."

כב וַתֵּלֶד בֵּן וַיִּקְרָא אֶת־שְׁמוֹ גֵּרְשֹׁם כִּי אָמַר גֵּר הָיִיתִי בְּאֶרֶץ נָכְרִיָּה:

²³ A long time after that, the king of Egypt died. The Israelites were groaning under the bondage and cried out; and their cry for help from the bondage rose up to *Hashem*.

כג וַיְהִי בַיָּמִים הָרַבִּים הָהֵם וַיָּמָת מֶלֶךְ מִצְרַיִם וַיֵּאָנְחוּ בְנֵי־יִשְׂרָאֵל מִן־הָעֲבֹדָה וַיִּזְעָקוּ וַתַּעַל שַׁוְעָתָם אֶל־הָאֱלֹהִים מִן־הָעֲבֹדָה:

²⁴ *Hashem* heard their moaning, and *Hashem* remembered His covenant with *Avraham* and *Yitzchak* and *Yaakov*.

כד וַיִּשְׁמַע אֱלֹהִים אֶת־נַאֲקָתָם וַיִּזְכֹּר אֱלֹהִים אֶת־בְּרִיתוֹ אֶת־אַבְרָהָם אֶת־יִצְחָק וְאֶת־יַעֲקֹב:

²⁵ *Hashem* looked upon the Israelites, and *Hashem* took notice of them.

כה וַיַּרְא אֱלֹהִים אֶת־בְּנֵי יִשְׂרָאֵל וַיֵּדַע אֱלֹהִים:

3 ¹ Now *Moshe*, tending the flock of his father-in-law Jethro, the priest of Midian, drove the flock into the wilderness, and came to Horeb, the mountain of *Hashem*.

ג א וּמֹשֶׁה הָיָה רֹעֶה אֶת־צֹאן יִתְרוֹ חֹתְנוֹ כֹּהֵן מִדְיָן וַיִּנְהַג אֶת־הַצֹּאן אַחַר הַמִּדְבָּר וַיָּבֹא אֶל־הַר הָאֱלֹהִים חֹרֵבָה:

² An angel of *Hashem* appeared to him in a blazing fire out of a bush. He gazed, and there was a bush all aflame, yet the bush was not consumed.

ב וַיֵּרָא מַלְאַךְ יְהֹוָה אֵלָיו בְּלַבַּת־אֵשׁ מִתּוֹךְ הַסְּנֶה וַיַּרְא וְהִנֵּה הַסְּנֶה בֹּעֵר בָּאֵשׁ וְהַסְּנֶה אֵינֶנּוּ אֻכָּל:

³ *Moshe* said, "I must turn aside to look at this marvelous sight; why doesn't the bush burn up?"

ג וַיֹּאמֶר מֹשֶׁה אָסֻרָה־נָּא וְאֶרְאֶה אֶת־הַמַּרְאֶה הַגָּדֹל הַזֶּה מַדּוּעַ לֹא־יִבְעַר הַסְּנֶה:

⁴ When *Hashem* saw that he had turned aside to look, *Hashem* called to him out of the bush: "*Moshe*! *Moshe*!" He answered, "Here I am."

ד וַיַּרְא יְהֹוָה כִּי סָר לִרְאוֹת וַיִּקְרָא אֵלָיו אֱלֹהִים מִתּוֹךְ הַסְּנֶה וַיֹּאמֶר מֹשֶׁה מֹשֶׁה וַיֹּאמֶר הִנֵּנִי:

⁵ And He said, "Do not come closer. Remove your sandals from your feet, for the place on which you stand is holy ground.

ה וַיֹּאמֶר אַל־תִּקְרַב הֲלֹם שַׁל־נְעָלֶיךָ מֵעַל רַגְלֶיךָ כִּי הַמָּקוֹם אֲשֶׁר אַתָּה עוֹמֵד עָלָיו אַדְמַת־קֹדֶשׁ הוּא:

⁶ I am," He said, "the God of your father, the God of *Avraham*, the God of *Yitzchak*, and the God of *Yaakov*." And *Moshe* hid his face, for he was afraid to look at *Hashem*.

ו וַיֹּאמֶר אָנֹכִי אֱלֹהֵי אָבִיךָ אֱלֹהֵי אַבְרָהָם אֱלֹהֵי יִצְחָק וֵאלֹהֵי יַעֲקֹב וַיַּסְתֵּר מֹשֶׁה פָּנָיו כִּי יָרֵא מֵהַבִּיט אֶל־הָאֱלֹהִים:

⁷ And *Hashem* continued, "I have marked well the plight of My people in Egypt and have heeded their outcry because of their taskmasters; yes, I am mindful of their sufferings.

ז וַיֹּאמֶר יְהֹוָה רָאֹה רָאִיתִי אֶת־עֳנִי עַמִּי אֲשֶׁר בְּמִצְרָיִם וְאֶת־צַעֲקָתָם שָׁמַעְתִּי מִפְּנֵי נֹגְשָׂיו כִּי יָדַעְתִּי אֶת־מַכְאֹבָיו:

⁸ I have come down to rescue them from the Egyptians and to bring them out of that land to a good and spacious land, a land flowing with milk and honey, the region of the Canaanites, the Hittites, the Amorites, the Perizzites, the Hivites, and the Jebusites.

ח וָאֵרֵד לְהַצִּילוֹ מִיַּד מִצְרַיִם וּלְהַעֲלֹתוֹ מִן־הָאָרֶץ הַהִוא אֶל־אֶרֶץ טוֹבָה וּרְחָבָה אֶל־אֶרֶץ זָבַת חָלָב וּדְבָשׁ אֶל־מְקוֹם הַכְּנַעֲנִי וְהַחִתִּי וְהָאֱמֹרִי וְהַפְּרִזִּי וְהַחִוִּי וְהַיְבוּסִי:

9 Now the cry of the Israelites has reached Me; moreover, I have seen how the Egyptians oppress them.

ט וְעַתָּה הִנֵּה צַעֲקַת בְּנֵי־יִשְׂרָאֵל בָּאָה אֵלָי וְגַם־רָאִיתִי אֶת־הַלַּחַץ אֲשֶׁר מִצְרַיִם לֹחֲצִים אֹתָם:

10 Come, therefore, I will send you to Pharaoh, and you shall free My people, the Israelites, from Egypt."

י וְעַתָּה לְכָה וְאֶשְׁלָחֲךָ אֶל־פַּרְעֹה וְהוֹצֵא אֶת־עַמִּי בְנֵי־יִשְׂרָאֵל מִמִּצְרָיִם:

11 But Moshe said to Hashem, "Who am I that I should go to Pharaoh and free the Israelites from Egypt?"

יא וַיֹּאמֶר מֹשֶׁה אֶל־הָאֱלֹהִים מִי אָנֹכִי כִּי אֵלֵךְ אֶל־פַּרְעֹה וְכִי אוֹצִיא אֶת־בְּנֵי יִשְׂרָאֵל מִמִּצְרָיִם:

12 And He said, "I will be with you; that shall be your sign that it was I who sent you. And when you have freed the people from Egypt, you shall worship Hashem at this mountain."

יב וַיֹּאמֶר כִּי־אֶהְיֶה עִמָּךְ וְזֶה־לְּךָ הָאוֹת כִּי אָנֹכִי שְׁלַחְתִּיךָ בְּהוֹצִיאֲךָ אֶת־הָעָם מִמִּצְרַיִם תַּעַבְדוּן אֶת־הָאֱלֹהִים עַל הָהָר הַזֶּה:

13 Moshe said to Hashem, "When I come to the Israelites and say to them, 'The God of your fathers has sent me to you,' and they ask me, 'What is His name?' what shall I say to them?"

יג וַיֹּאמֶר מֹשֶׁה אֶל־הָאֱלֹהִים הִנֵּה אָנֹכִי בָא אֶל־בְּנֵי יִשְׂרָאֵל וְאָמַרְתִּי לָהֶם אֱלֹהֵי אֲבוֹתֵיכֶם שְׁלָחַנִי אֲלֵיכֶם וְאָמְרוּ־לִי מַה־שְּׁמוֹ מָה אֹמַר אֲלֵהֶם:

14 And Hashem said to Moshe, "Ehyeh-Asher-Ehyeh". He continued, "Thus shall you say to the Israelites, 'Ehyeh sent me to you'".

יד וַיֹּאמֶר אֱלֹהִים אֶל־מֹשֶׁה אֶהְיֶה אֲשֶׁר אֶהְיֶה וַיֹּאמֶר כֹּה תֹאמַר לִבְנֵי יִשְׂרָאֵל אֶהְיֶה שְׁלָחַנִי אֲלֵיכֶם:

15 And Hashem said further to Moshe, "Thus shall you speak to the Israelites: Hashem, the God of your fathers, the God of Avraham, the God of Yitzchak, and the God of Yaakov, has sent me to you: This shall be My name forever, This My appellation for all eternity.

טו וַיֹּאמֶר עוֹד אֱלֹהִים אֶל־מֹשֶׁה כֹּה־תֹאמַר אֶל־בְּנֵי יִשְׂרָאֵל יְהוָה אֱלֹהֵי אֲבֹתֵיכֶם אֱלֹהֵי אַבְרָהָם אֱלֹהֵי יִצְחָק וֵאלֹהֵי יַעֲקֹב שְׁלָחַנִי אֲלֵיכֶם זֶה־שְּׁמִי לְעֹלָם וְזֶה זִכְרִי לְדֹר דֹּר:

16 "Go and assemble the elders of Yisrael and say to them: Hashem, the God of your fathers, the God of Avraham, Yitzchak, and Yaakov, has appeared to me and said, 'I have taken note of you and of what is being done to you in Egypt,

טז לֵךְ וְאָסַפְתָּ אֶת־זִקְנֵי יִשְׂרָאֵל וְאָמַרְתָּ אֲלֵהֶם יְהוָה אֱלֹהֵי אֲבֹתֵיכֶם נִרְאָה אֵלַי אֱלֹהֵי אַבְרָהָם יִצְחָק וְיַעֲקֹב לֵאמֹר פָּקֹד פָּקַדְתִּי אֶתְכֶם וְאֶת־הֶעָשׂוּי לָכֶם בְּמִצְרָיִם:

17 and I have declared: I will take you out of the misery of Egypt to the land of the Canaanites, the Hittites, the Amorites, the Perizzites, the Hivites, and the Jebusites, to a land flowing with milk and honey.'

יז וָאֹמַר אַעֲלֶה אֶתְכֶם מֵעֳנִי מִצְרַיִם אֶל־אֶרֶץ הַכְּנַעֲנִי וְהַחִתִּי וְהָאֱמֹרִי וְהַפְּרִזִּי וְהַחִוִּי וְהַיְבוּסִי אֶל־אֶרֶץ זָבַת חָלָב וּדְבָשׁ:

va-o-MAR a-a-LEH et-KHEM may-o-NEE mitz-RA-yim el E-retz ha-k'-na-a-NEE v'-ha-khee-TEE v'-ha-e-mo-REE v'-ha-p'-ree-ZEE v'-ha-khi-VEE v'-hai-vu-SEE el E-retz za-VAT kha-LAV ud-VASH

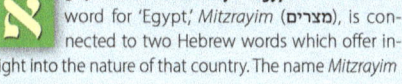

3:17 Out of the misery of Egypt The Hebrew word for 'Egypt,' Mitzrayim (מצרים), is connected to two Hebrew words which offer insight into the nature of that country. The name Mitzrayim is related to the Hebrew word tzara (צרה), meaning 'tragedy' or 'distress.' This connection teaches that Egypt was a land of suffering for the Children of Israel, who suffered in slavery for hundreds of years before being re-

מצרים

Exodus

18 They will listen to you; then you shall go with the elders of *Yisrael* to the king of Egypt and you shall say to him, '*Hashem*, the God of the Hebrews, manifested Himself to us. Now therefore, let us go a distance of three days into the wilderness to sacrifice to *Hashem* our God.'

19 Yet I know that the king of Egypt will let you go only because of a greater might.

20 So I will stretch out My hand and smite Egypt with various wonders which I will work upon them; after that he shall let you go.

21 And I will dispose the Egyptians favorably toward this people, so that when you go, you will not go away empty-handed.

22 Each woman shall borrow from her neighbor and the lodger in her house objects of silver and gold, and clothing, and you shall put these on your sons and daughters, thus stripping the Egyptians."

4 1 But *Moshe* spoke up and said, "What if they do not believe me and do not listen to me, but say: *Hashem* did not appear to you?"

2 *Hashem* said to him, "What is that in your hand?" And he replied, "A rod."

3 He said, "Cast it on the ground." He cast it on the ground and it became a snake; and *Moshe* recoiled from it.

4 Then *Hashem* said to *Moshe*, "Put out your hand and grasp it by the tail" – he put out his hand and seized it, and it became a rod in his hand

5 "that they may believe that *Hashem*, the God of their fathers, the God of *Avraham*, the God of *Yitzchak*, and the God of *Yaakov*, did appear to you."

6 *Hashem* said to him further, "Put your hand into your bosom." He put his hand into his bosom; and when he took it out, his hand was encrusted with snowy scales!

יח וְשָׁמְעוּ לְקֹלֶךָ וּבָאתָ אַתָּה וְזִקְנֵי יִשְׂרָאֵל אֶל־מֶלֶךְ מִצְרַיִם וַאֲמַרְתֶּם אֵלָיו יהוה אֱלֹהֵי הָעִבְרִיִּים נִקְרָה עָלֵינוּ וְעַתָּה נֵלֲכָה־נָּא דֶּרֶךְ שְׁלֹשֶׁת יָמִים בַּמִּדְבָּר וְנִזְבְּחָה לַיהוה אֱלֹהֵינוּ:

יט וַאֲנִי יָדַעְתִּי כִּי לֹא־יִתֵּן אֶתְכֶם מֶלֶךְ מִצְרַיִם לַהֲלֹךְ וְלֹא בְּיָד חֲזָקָה:

כ וְשָׁלַחְתִּי אֶת־יָדִי וְהִכֵּיתִי אֶת־מִצְרַיִם בְּכֹל נִפְלְאֹתַי אֲשֶׁר אֶעֱשֶׂה בְּקִרְבּוֹ וְאַחֲרֵי־כֵן יְשַׁלַּח אֶתְכֶם:

כא וְנָתַתִּי אֶת־חֵן הָעָם־הַזֶּה בְּעֵינֵי מִצְרָיִם וְהָיָה כִּי תֵלֵכוּן לֹא תֵלְכוּ רֵיקָם:

כב וְשָׁאֲלָה אִשָּׁה מִשְּׁכֶנְתָּהּ וּמִגָּרַת בֵּיתָהּ כְּלֵי־כֶסֶף וּכְלֵי זָהָב וּשְׂמָלֹת וְשַׂמְתֶּם עַל־בְּנֵיכֶם וְעַל־בְּנֹתֵיכֶם וְנִצַּלְתֶּם אֶת־מִצְרָיִם:

ד א וַיַּעַן מֹשֶׁה וַיֹּאמֶר וְהֵן לֹא־יַאֲמִינוּ לִי וְלֹא יִשְׁמְעוּ בְּקֹלִי כִּי יֹאמְרוּ לֹא־נִרְאָה אֵלֶיךָ יהוה:

ב וַיֹּאמֶר אֵלָיו יהוה מזה [מַה־] [זֶּה] בְיָדֶךָ וַיֹּאמֶר מַטֶּה:

ג וַיֹּאמֶר הַשְׁלִיכֵהוּ אַרְצָה וַיַּשְׁלִכֵהוּ אַרְצָה וַיְהִי לְנָחָשׁ וַיָּנָס מֹשֶׁה מִפָּנָיו:

ד וַיֹּאמֶר יהוה אֶל־מֹשֶׁה שְׁלַח יָדְךָ וֶאֱחֹז בִּזְנָבוֹ וַיִּשְׁלַח יָדוֹ וַיַּחֲזֶק בּוֹ וַיְהִי לְמַטֶּה בְּכַפּוֹ:

ה לְמַעַן יַאֲמִינוּ כִּי־נִרְאָה אֵלֶיךָ יהוה אֱלֹהֵי אֲבֹתָם אֱלֹהֵי אַבְרָהָם אֱלֹהֵי יִצְחָק וֵאלֹהֵי יַעֲקֹב:

ו וַיֹּאמֶר יהוה לוֹ עוֹד הָבֵא־נָא יָדְךָ בְּחֵיקֶךָ וַיָּבֵא יָדוֹ בְּחֵיקוֹ וַיּוֹצִאָהּ וְהִנֵּה יָדוֹ מְצֹרַעַת כַּשָּׁלֶג:

A narrow street in the Old City of *Yerushalayim*

deemed by the Almighty. And the word *Mitzrayim* (מצרים) is also connected to the word *tzar* (צר), meaning 'narrow.' On a metaphorical level, a person is enslaved when he feels constricted and limited, and thereby unable to actualize his unique potential.

7 And He said, "Put your hand back into your bosom." – He put his hand back into his bosom; and when he took it out of his bosom, there it was again like the rest of his body.

ז וַיֹּאמֶר הָשֵׁב יָדְךָ אֶל־חֵיקֶךָ וַיָּשֶׁב יָדוֹ אֶל־חֵיקוֹ וַיּוֹצִאָהּ מֵחֵיקוֹ וְהִנֵּה־שָׁבָה כִּבְשָׂרוֹ:

8 "And if they do not believe you or pay heed to the first sign, they will believe the second.

ח וְהָיָה אִם־לֹא יַאֲמִינוּ לָךְ וְלֹא יִשְׁמְעוּ לְקֹל הָאֹת הָרִאשׁוֹן וְהֶאֱמִינוּ לְקֹל הָאֹת הָאַחֲרוֹן:

9 And if they are not convinced by both these signs and still do not heed you, take some water from the Nile and pour it on the dry ground, and it – the water that you take from the Nile – will turn to blood on the dry ground."

ט וְהָיָה אִם־לֹא יַאֲמִינוּ גַּם לִשְׁנֵי הָאֹתוֹת הָאֵלֶּה וְלֹא יִשְׁמְעוּן לְקֹלֶךָ וְלָקַחְתָּ מִמֵּימֵי הַיְאֹר וְשָׁפַכְתָּ הַיַּבָּשָׁה וְהָיוּ הַמַּיִם אֲשֶׁר תִּקַּח מִן־הַיְאֹר וְהָיוּ לְדָם בַּיַּבָּשֶׁת:

10 But *Moshe* said to *Hashem*, "Please, O *Hashem*, I have never been a man of words, either in times past or now that You have spoken to Your servant; I am slow of speech and slow of tongue."

י וַיֹּאמֶר מֹשֶׁה אֶל־יְהוָה בִּי אֲדֹנָי לֹא אִישׁ דְּבָרִים אָנֹכִי גַּם מִתְּמוֹל גַּם מִשִּׁלְשֹׁם גַּם מֵאָז דַּבֶּרְךָ אֶל־עַבְדֶּךָ כִּי כְבַד־פֶּה וּכְבַד לָשׁוֹן אָנֹכִי:

11 And *Hashem* said to him, "Who gives man speech? Who makes him dumb or deaf, seeing or blind? Is it not I, *Hashem*?

יא וַיֹּאמֶר יְהוָה אֵלָיו מִי שָׂם פֶּה לָאָדָם אוֹ מִי־יָשׂוּם אִלֵּם אוֹ חֵרֵשׁ אוֹ פִקֵּחַ אוֹ עִוֵּר הֲלֹא אָנֹכִי יְהוָה:

12 Now go, and I will be with you as you speak and will instruct you what to say."

יב וְעַתָּה לֵךְ וְאָנֹכִי אֶהְיֶה עִם־פִּיךָ וְהוֹרֵיתִיךָ אֲשֶׁר תְּדַבֵּר:

13 But he said, "Please, O *Hashem*, make someone else Your agent."

יג וַיֹּאמֶר בִּי אֲדֹנָי שְׁלַח־נָא בְּיַד־תִּשְׁלָח:

14 *Hashem* became angry with *Moshe*, and He said, "There is your brother *Aharon* the Levite. He, I know, speaks readily. Even now he is setting out to meet you, and he will be happy to see you.

יד וַיִּחַר־אַף יְהוָה בְּמֹשֶׁה וַיֹּאמֶר הֲלֹא אַהֲרֹן אָחִיךָ הַלֵּוִי יָדַעְתִּי כִּי־דַבֵּר יְדַבֵּר הוּא וְגַם הִנֵּה־הוּא יֹצֵא לִקְרָאתֶךָ וְרָאֲךָ וְשָׂמַח בְּלִבּוֹ:

15 You shall speak to him and put the words in his mouth – I will be with you and with him as you speak, and tell both of you what to do

טו וְדִבַּרְתָּ אֵלָיו וְשַׂמְתָּ אֶת־הַדְּבָרִים בְּפִיו וְאָנֹכִי אֶהְיֶה עִם־פִּיךָ וְעִם־פִּיהוּ וְהוֹרֵיתִי אֶתְכֶם אֵת אֲשֶׁר תַּעֲשׂוּן:

16 and he shall speak for you to the people. Thus he shall serve as your spokesman, with you playing the role of *Hashem* to him,

טז וְדִבֶּר־הוּא לְךָ אֶל־הָעָם וְהָיָה הוּא יִהְיֶה־לְּךָ לְפֶה וְאַתָּה תִּהְיֶה־לּוֹ לֵאלֹהִים:

17 and take with you this rod, with which you shall perform the signs."

יז וְאֶת־הַמַּטֶּה הַזֶּה תִּקַּח בְּיָדֶךָ אֲשֶׁר תַּעֲשֶׂה־בּוֹ אֶת־הָאֹתֹת:

18 *Moshe* went back to his father-in-law Jether and said to him, "Let me go back to my kinsmen in Egypt and see how they are faring." And Jethro said to *Moshe*, "Go in peace."

יח וַיֵּלֶךְ מֹשֶׁה וַיָּשָׁב אֶל־יֶתֶר חֹתְנוֹ וַיֹּאמֶר לוֹ אֵלְכָה נָּא וְאָשׁוּבָה אֶל־אַחַי אֲשֶׁר־בְּמִצְרַיִם וְאֶרְאֶה הַעוֹדָם חַיִּים וַיֹּאמֶר יִתְרוֹ לְמֹשֶׁה לֵךְ לְשָׁלוֹם:

19 *Hashem* said to *Moshe* in Midian, "Go back to Egypt, for all the men who sought to kill you are dead."

יט וַיֹּאמֶר יְהוָה אֶל־מֹשֶׁה בְּמִדְיָן לֵךְ שֻׁב מִצְרָיִם כִּי־מֵתוּ כָּל־הָאֲנָשִׁים הַמְבַקְשִׁים אֶת־נַפְשֶׁךָ:

Exodus

20 So *Moshe* took his wife and sons, mounted them on an ass, and went back to the land of Egypt; and *Moshe* took the rod of *Hashem* with him.

כ וַיִּקַּח מֹשֶׁה אֶת־אִשְׁתּוֹ וְאֶת־בָּנָיו וַיַּרְכִּבֵם עַל־הַחֲמֹר וַיָּשָׁב אַרְצָה מִצְרָיִם וַיִּקַּח מֹשֶׁה אֶת־מַטֵּה הָאֱלֹהִים בְּיָדוֹ:

21 And *Hashem* said to *Moshe*, "When you return to Egypt, see that you perform before Pharaoh all the marvels that I have put within your power. I, however, will stiffen his heart so that he will not let the people go.

כא וַיֹּאמֶר יְהוָה אֶל־מֹשֶׁה בְּלֶכְתְּךָ לָשׁוּב מִצְרַיְמָה רְאֵה כָּל־הַמֹּפְתִים אֲשֶׁר־שַׂמְתִּי בְיָדֶךָ וַעֲשִׂיתָם לִפְנֵי פַרְעֹה וַאֲנִי אֲחַזֵּק אֶת־לִבּוֹ וְלֹא יְשַׁלַּח אֶת־הָעָם:

22 Then you shall say to Pharaoh, 'Thus says *Hashem*: *Yisrael* is My first-born son.

כב וְאָמַרְתָּ אֶל־פַּרְעֹה כֹּה אָמַר יְהֹוָה בְּנִי בְכֹרִי יִשְׂרָאֵל:

v'-a-mar-TA el par-OH KOH a-MAR a-do-NAI b'-NEE v'-kho-REE yis-ra-AYL

23 I have said to you, "Let My son go, that he may worship Me," yet you refuse to let him go. Now I will slay your first-born son.'"

כג וָאֹמַר אֵלֶיךָ שַׁלַּח אֶת־בְּנִי וְיַעַבְדֵנִי וַתְּמָאֵן לְשַׁלְּחוֹ הִנֵּה אָנֹכִי הֹרֵג אֶת־בִּנְךָ בְּכֹרֶךָ:

24 At a night encampment on the way, *Hashem* encountered him and sought to kill him.

כד וַיְהִי בַדֶּרֶךְ בַּמָּלוֹן וַיִּפְגְּשֵׁהוּ יְהוָה וַיְבַקֵּשׁ הֲמִיתוֹ:

25 So *Tzipora* took a flint and cut off her son's foreskin, and touched his legs with it, saying, "You are truly a bridegroom of blood to me!"

כה וַתִּקַּח צִפֹּרָה צֹר וַתִּכְרֹת אֶת־עָרְלַת בְּנָהּ וַתַּגַּע לְרַגְלָיו וַתֹּאמֶר כִּי חֲתַן־דָּמִים אַתָּה לִי:

26 And when He let him alone, she added, "A bridegroom of blood because of the circumcision."

כו וַיִּרֶף מִמֶּנּוּ אָז אָמְרָה חֲתַן דָּמִים לַמּוּלֹת:

27 *Hashem* said to *Aharon*, "Go to meet *Moshe* in the wilderness." He went and met him at the mountain of *Hashem*, and he kissed him.

כז וַיֹּאמֶר יְהוָה אֶל־אַהֲרֹן לֵךְ לִקְרַאת מֹשֶׁה הַמִּדְבָּרָה וַיֵּלֶךְ וַיִּפְגְּשֵׁהוּ בְּהַר הָאֱלֹהִים וַיִּשַּׁק־לוֹ:

28 *Moshe* told *Aharon* about all the things that *Hashem* had committed to him and all the signs about which He had instructed him.

כח וַיַּגֵּד מֹשֶׁה לְאַהֲרֹן אֵת כָּל־דִּבְרֵי יְהוָה אֲשֶׁר שְׁלָחוֹ וְאֵת כָּל־הָאֹתֹת אֲשֶׁר צִוָּהוּ:

29 Then *Moshe* and *Aharon* went and assembled all the elders of the Israelites.

כט וַיֵּלֶךְ מֹשֶׁה וְאַהֲרֹן וַיַּאַסְפוּ אֶת־כָּל־זִקְנֵי בְּנֵי יִשְׂרָאֵל:

30 *Aharon* repeated all the words that *Hashem* had spoken to *Moshe*, and he performed the signs in the sight of the people,

ל וַיְדַבֵּר אַהֲרֹן אֵת כָּל־הַדְּבָרִים אֲשֶׁר־דִּבֶּר יְהוָה אֶל־מֹשֶׁה וַיַּעַשׂ הָאֹתֹת לְעֵינֵי הָעָם:

Father and son at the Mediterranean coast

4:22 My first-born son God refers to the Children of Israel as His first-born son. A firstborn is not the only child, yet his status is unique and therefore carries extra responsibility. Similarly, all nations of the world are *Hashem*'s children; anyone can form a meaningful relationship with Him. However, He chose the Jewish people as a "firstborn" to fulfill a unique role; to be His representatives to bring Godliness into this world. Similarly, He also chose *Eretz Yisrael* as the place where they are to fulfill that responsibility.

³¹ and the people were convinced. When they heard that *Hashem* had taken note of the Israelites and that He had seen their plight, they bowed low in homage.

לא וַיַּאֲמֵן הָעָם וַיִּשְׁמְעוּ כִּי־פָקַד יְהוָה אֶת־בְּנֵי יִשְׂרָאֵל וְכִי רָאָה אֶת־עָנְיָם וַיִּקְּדוּ וַיִּשְׁתַּחֲוֽוּ׃

5 ¹ Afterward *Moshe* and *Aharon* went and said to Pharaoh, "Thus says *Hashem*, the God of *Yisrael*: Let My people go that they may celebrate a festival for Me in the wilderness."

ה א וְאַחַר בָּאוּ מֹשֶׁה וְאַהֲרֹן וַיֹּאמְרוּ אֶל־פַּרְעֹה כֹּה־אָמַר יְהוָה אֱלֹהֵי יִשְׂרָאֵל שַׁלַּח אֶת־עַמִּי וְיָחֹגּוּ לִי בַּמִּדְבָּֽר׃

² But Pharaoh said, "Who is *Hashem* that I should heed Him and let *Yisrael* go? I do not know *Hashem*, nor will I let *Yisrael* go."

ב וַיֹּאמֶר פַּרְעֹה מִי יְהוָה אֲשֶׁר אֶשְׁמַע בְּקֹלוֹ לְשַׁלַּח אֶת־יִשְׂרָאֵל לֹא יָדַעְתִּי אֶת־יְהוָה וְגַם אֶת־יִשְׂרָאֵל לֹא אֲשַׁלֵּֽחַ׃

va-YO-mer par-OH MEE a-do-NAI a-SHER esh-MA b'-ko-LO l'-sha-LAKH et yis-ra-AYL LO ya-DA-tee et a-do-NAI v'-GAM et yis-ra-AYL LO a-sha-LAY-akh

³ They answered, "The God of the Hebrews has manifested Himself to us. Let us go, we pray, a distance of three days into the wilderness to sacrifice to *Hashem* our God, lest He strike us with pestilence or sword."

ג וַיֹּאמְרוּ אֱלֹהֵי הָעִבְרִים נִקְרָא עָלֵינוּ נֵלֲכָה נָּא דֶּרֶךְ שְׁלֹשֶׁת יָמִים בַּמִּדְבָּר וְנִזְבְּחָה לַיהוָה אֱלֹהֵינוּ פֶּן־יִפְגָּעֵנוּ בַּדֶּבֶר אוֹ בֶחָֽרֶב׃

⁴ But the king of Egypt said to them, "*Moshe* and *Aharon*, why do you distract the people from their tasks? Get to your labors!"

ד וַיֹּאמֶר אֲלֵהֶם מֶלֶךְ מִצְרַיִם לָמָּה מֹשֶׁה וְאַהֲרֹן תַּפְרִיעוּ אֶת־הָעָם מִמַּעֲשָׂיו לְכוּ לְסִבְלֹתֵיכֶֽם׃

⁵ And Pharaoh continued, "The people of the land are already so numerous, and you would have them cease from their labors!"

ה וַיֹּאמֶר פַּרְעֹה הֵן־רַבִּים עַתָּה עַם הָאָרֶץ וְהִשְׁבַּתֶּם אֹתָם מִסִּבְלֹתָֽם׃

⁶ That same day Pharaoh charged the taskmasters and foremen of the people, saying,

ו וַיְצַו פַּרְעֹה בַּיּוֹם הַהוּא אֶת־הַנֹּגְשִׂים בָּעָם וְאֶת־שֹׁטְרָיו לֵאמֹֽר׃

⁷ "You shall no longer provide the people with straw for making bricks as heretofore; let them go and gather straw for themselves.

ז לֹא תֹאסִפוּן לָתֵת תֶּבֶן לָעָם לִלְבֹּן הַלְּבֵנִים כִּתְמוֹל שִׁלְשֹׁם הֵם יֵלְכוּ וְקֹשְׁשׁוּ לָהֶם תֶּֽבֶן׃

⁸ But impose upon them the same quota of bricks as they have been making heretofore; do not reduce it, for they are shirkers; that is why they cry, 'Let us go and sacrifice to our God!'

ח וְאֶת־מַתְכֹּנֶת הַלְּבֵנִים אֲשֶׁר הֵם עֹשִׂים תְּמוֹל שִׁלְשֹׁם תָּשִׂימוּ עֲלֵיהֶם לֹא תִגְרְעוּ מִמֶּנּוּ כִּי־נִרְפִּים הֵם עַל־כֵּן הֵם צֹעֲקִים לֵאמֹר נֵלְכָה נִזְבְּחָה לֵאלֹהֵֽינוּ׃

⁹ Let heavier work be laid upon the men; let them keep at it and not pay attention to deceitful promises."

ט תִּכְבַּד הָעֲבֹדָה עַל־הָאֲנָשִׁים וְיַעֲשׂוּ־בָהּ וְאַל־יִשְׁעוּ בְּדִבְרֵי־שָֽׁקֶר׃

5:2 I do not know *Hashem* Only in complete absence of recognition of *Hashem* and His ways can one treat others the way Pharaoh treated the Israelites. Had he acknowledged the Lord, Pharaoh would not have been able to treat them that way. Therefore, God emphasizes (Exodus 7:5) that the purpose of the ten plagues is to prove to the Egyptians and the entire world that He is the one and only omnipotent God.

Sunset in the Negev desert

10 So the taskmasters and foremen of the people went out and said to the people, "Thus says Pharaoh: I will not give you any straw.

יַיֵּצְאוּ נֹגְשֵׂי הָעָם וְשֹׁטְרָיו וַיֹּאמְרוּ אֶל־הָעָם לֵאמֹר כֹּה אָמַר פַּרְעֹה אֵינֶנִּי נֹתֵן לָכֶם תֶּבֶן:

11 You must go and get the straw yourselves wherever you can find it; but there shall be no decrease whatever in your work."

יא אַתֶּם לְכוּ קְחוּ לָכֶם תֶּבֶן מֵאֲשֶׁר תִּמְצָאוּ כִּי אֵין נִגְרָע מֵעֲבֹדַתְכֶם דָּבָר:

12 Then the people scattered throughout the land of Egypt to gather stubble for straw.

יב וַיָּפֶץ הָעָם בְּכָל־אֶרֶץ מִצְרָיִם לְקֹשֵׁשׁ קַשׁ לַתֶּבֶן:

13 And the taskmasters pressed them, saying, "You must complete the same work assignment each day as when you had straw."

יג וְהַנֹּגְשִׂים אָצִים לֵאמֹר כַּלּוּ מַעֲשֵׂיכֶם דְּבַר־יוֹם בְּיוֹמוֹ כַּאֲשֶׁר בִּהְיוֹת הַתֶּבֶן:

14 And the foremen of the Israelites, whom Pharaoh's taskmasters had set over them, were beaten. "Why," they were asked, "did you not complete the prescribed amount of bricks, either yesterday or today, as you did before?"

יד וַיֻּכּוּ שֹׁטְרֵי בְּנֵי יִשְׂרָאֵל אֲשֶׁר־שָׂמוּ עֲלֵהֶם נֹגְשֵׂי פַרְעֹה לֵאמֹר מַדּוּעַ לֹא כִלִּיתֶם חָקְכֶם לִלְבֹּן כִּתְמוֹל שִׁלְשֹׁם גַּם־תְּמוֹל גַּם־הַיּוֹם:

15 Then the foremen of the Israelites came to Pharaoh and cried: "Why do you deal thus with your servants?

טו וַיָּבֹאוּ שֹׁטְרֵי בְּנֵי יִשְׂרָאֵל וַיִּצְעֲקוּ אֶל־פַּרְעֹה לֵאמֹר לָמָּה תַעֲשֶׂה כֹה לַעֲבָדֶיךָ:

16 No straw is issued to your servants, yet they demand of us: Make bricks! Thus your servants are being beaten, when the fault is with your own people."

טז תֶּבֶן אֵין נִתָּן לַעֲבָדֶיךָ וּלְבֵנִים אֹמְרִים לָנוּ עֲשׂוּ וְהִנֵּה עֲבָדֶיךָ מֻכִּים וְחָטָאת עַמֶּךָ:

17 He replied, "You are shirkers, shirkers! That is why you say, 'Let us go and sacrifice to *Hashem*.'

יז וַיֹּאמֶר נִרְפִּים אַתֶּם נִרְפִּים עַל־כֵּן אַתֶּם אֹמְרִים נֵלְכָה נִזְבְּחָה לַיהוָה:

18 Be off now to your work! No straw shall be issued to you, but you must produce your quota of bricks!"

יח וְעַתָּה לְכוּ עִבְדוּ וְתֶבֶן לֹא־יִנָּתֵן לָכֶם וְתֹכֶן לְבֵנִים תִּתֵּנּוּ:

19 Now the foremen of the Israelites found themselves in trouble because of the order, "You must not reduce your daily quantity of bricks."

יט וַיִּרְאוּ שֹׁטְרֵי בְנֵי־יִשְׂרָאֵל אֹתָם בְּרָע לֵאמֹר לֹא־תִגְרְעוּ מִלִּבְנֵיכֶם דְּבַר־יוֹם בְּיוֹמוֹ:

20 As they left Pharaoh's presence, they came upon *Moshe* and *Aharon* standing in their path,

כ וַיִּפְגְּעוּ אֶת־מֹשֶׁה וְאֶת־אַהֲרֹן נִצָּבִים לִקְרָאתָם בְּצֵאתָם מֵאֵת פַּרְעֹה:

21 and they said to them, "May *Hashem* look upon you and punish you for making us loathsome to Pharaoh and his courtiers – putting a sword in their hands to slay us."

כא וַיֹּאמְרוּ אֲלֵהֶם יֵרֶא יְהוָה עֲלֵיכֶם וְיִשְׁפֹּט אֲשֶׁר הִבְאַשְׁתֶּם אֶת־רֵיחֵנוּ בְּעֵינֵי פַרְעֹה וּבְעֵינֵי עֲבָדָיו לָתֶת־חֶרֶב בְּיָדָם לְהָרְגֵנוּ:

22 Then *Moshe* returned to *Hashem* and said, "O *Hashem*, why did You bring harm upon this people? Why did You send me?

כב וַיָּשָׁב מֹשֶׁה אֶל־יְהוָה וַיֹּאמַר אֲדֹנָי לָמָה הֲרֵעֹתָה לָעָם הַזֶּה לָמָּה זֶּה שְׁלַחְתָּנִי:

23 Ever since I came to Pharaoh to speak in Your name, he has dealt worse with this people; and still You have not delivered Your people."

כג וּמֵאָז בָּאתִי אֶל־פַּרְעֹה לְדַבֵּר בִּשְׁמֶךָ הֵרַע לָעָם הַזֶּה וְהַצֵּל לֹא־הִצַּלְתָּ אֶת־עַמֶּךָ:

6 ¹ Then *Hashem* said to *Moshe*, "You shall soon see what I will do to Pharaoh: he shall let them go because of a greater might; indeed, because of a greater might he shall drive them from his land."

א וַיֹּאמֶר יְהוָֹה אֶל־מֹשֶׁה עַתָּה תִרְאֶה אֲשֶׁר אֶעֱשֶׂה לְפַרְעֹה כִּי בְיָד חֲזָקָה יְשַׁלְּחֵם וּבְיָד חֲזָקָה יְגָרְשֵׁם מֵאַרְצוֹ:

² *Hashem* spoke to *Moshe* and said to him, "I am *Hashem*.

ב וַיְדַבֵּר אֱלֹהִים אֶל־מֹשֶׁה וַיֹּאמֶר אֵלָיו אֲנִי יְהוָֹה:

³ I appeared to *Avraham*, *Yitzchak*, and *Yaakov* as *El Shaddai*, but I did not make Myself known to them by My name *Hashem*

ג וָאֵרָא אֶל־אַבְרָהָם אֶל־יִצְחָק וְאֶל־יַעֲקֹב בְּאֵל שַׁדָּי וּשְׁמִי יְהוָֹה לֹא נוֹדַעְתִּי לָהֶם:

⁴ I also established My covenant with them, to give them the land of Canaan, the land in which they lived as sojourners.

ד וְגַם הֲקִמֹתִי אֶת־בְּרִיתִי אִתָּם לָתֵת לָהֶם אֶת־אֶרֶץ כְּנָעַן אֵת אֶרֶץ מְגֻרֵיהֶם אֲשֶׁר־גָּרוּ בָהּ:

v'-GAM ha-ki-MO-tee et b'-ree-TEE i-TAM la-TAYT la-HEM et E-retz k'-NA-an AYT E-retz m'-gu-ray-HEM a-sher GA-ru VAH

⁵ I have now heard the moaning of the Israelites because the Egyptians are holding them in bondage, and I have remembered My covenant.

ה וְגַם אֲנִי שָׁמַעְתִּי אֶת־נַאֲקַת בְּנֵי יִשְׂרָאֵל אֲשֶׁר מִצְרַיִם מַעֲבִדִים אֹתָם וָאֶזְכֹּר אֶת־בְּרִיתִי:

⁶ Say, therefore, to *B'nei Yisrael*: I am *Hashem*. I will free you from the labors of the Egyptians and deliver you from their bondage. I will redeem you with an outstretched arm and through extraordinary chastisements.

ו לָכֵן אֱמֹר לִבְנֵי־יִשְׂרָאֵל אֲנִי יְהוָֹה וְהוֹצֵאתִי אֶתְכֶם מִתַּחַת סִבְלֹת מִצְרַיִם וְהִצַּלְתִּי אֶתְכֶם מֵעֲבֹדָתָם וְגָאַלְתִּי אֶתְכֶם בִּזְרוֹעַ נְטוּיָה וּבִשְׁפָטִים גְּדֹלִים:

⁷ And I will take you to be My people, and I will be your God. And you shall know that I, *Hashem*, am your God who freed you from the labors of the Egyptians.

ז וְלָקַחְתִּי אֶתְכֶם לִי לְעָם וְהָיִיתִי לָכֶם לֵאלֹהִים וִידַעְתֶּם כִּי אֲנִי יְהוָֹה אֱלֹהֵיכֶם הַמּוֹצִיא אֶתְכֶם מִתַּחַת סִבְלוֹת מִצְרָיִם:

⁸ I will bring you into the land which I swore to give to *Avraham*, *Yitzchak*, and *Yaakov*, and I will give it to you for a possession, I *Hashem*."

ח וְהֵבֵאתִי אֶתְכֶם אֶל־הָאָרֶץ אֲשֶׁר נָשָׂאתִי אֶת־יָדִי לָתֵת אֹתָהּ לְאַבְרָהָם לְיִצְחָק וּלְיַעֲקֹב וְנָתַתִּי אֹתָהּ לָכֶם מוֹרָשָׁה אֲנִי יְהוָֹה:

v'-hay-vay-TEE et-KHEM el ha-A-retz a-SHER na-SA-tee et ya-DEE la-TAYT o-TAH l'-av-ra-HAM l'-yitz-KHAK ul-ya-a-KOV v'-na-ta-TEE o-TAH la-KHEM mo-ra-SHAH a-NEE a-do-NAI

6:8 I will bring you into the land Four cups of wine are drunk at the *Pesach* seder, corresponding to the four expressions of redemption used in this verse to describe the exodus from Egypt: "Free," "deliver," "redeem," and "take" (verses 6–8). A close reading of this chapter, however, uncovers that there is a fifth expression, "I will bring you," found in the following verse. Why, then, do we not have five cups of wine at the Seder? The Talmud (*Pesachim* 118) explain that while the

first four expressions of redemption from Egypt have in fact been realized, the fifth expression, "I will bring you into the land" has not yet been completely fulfilled. Only when all the Jews return to Israel and *Mashiach* comes to Jerusalem will we rejoice with a fifth cup.

Four cups of wine for the *Pesach* seder

6:8 I will give it to you for a possession Biblical Hebrew has two words relating to bequests: *Morasha* (מורשה), and *yerusha* (ירושה). *Morasha*,

12

Exodus

9 But when *Moshe* told this to the Israelites, they would not listen to *Moshe*, their spirits crushed by cruel bondage.

10 *Hashem* spoke to *Moshe*, saying,

11 "Go and tell Pharaoh king of Egypt to let the Israelites depart from his land."

12 But *Moshe* appealed to *Hashem*, saying, "The Israelites would not listen to me; how then should Pharaoh heed me, a man of impeded speech!"

13 So *Hashem* spoke to both *Moshe* and *Aharon* in regard to the Israelites and Pharaoh king of Egypt, instructing them to deliver the Israelites from the land of Egypt.

14 The following are the heads of their respective clans. The sons of *Reuven, Yisrael*'s first-born: Enoch and Pallu, *Chetzron* and Carmi; those are the families of *Reuven*.

15 The sons of *Shimon*: Jemuel, Jamin, Ohad, Jachin, Zohar, and *Shaul* the son of a Canaanite woman; those are the families of *Shimon*.

16 These are the names of *Levi*'s sons by their lineage: *Gershon, Kehat,* and *Merari*; and the span of *Levi*'s life was 137 years.

17 The sons of *Gershon*: Libni and *Shim'i*, by their families.

18 The sons of *Kehat: Amram*, Izhar, *Chevron*, and Uzziel; and the span of *Kehat*'s life was 133 years.

19 The sons of *Merari*: Mahli and Mushi. These are the families of the *Leviim* by their lineage.

ט וַיְדַבֵּר מֹשֶׁה כֵּן אֶל־בְּנֵי יִשְׂרָאֵל וְלֹא שָׁמְעוּ אֶל־מֹשֶׁה מִקֹּצֶר רוּחַ וּמֵעֲבֹדָה קָשָׁה:

י וַיְדַבֵּר יְהוָה אֶל־מֹשֶׁה לֵּאמֹר:

יא בֹּא דַבֵּר אֶל־פַּרְעֹה מֶלֶךְ מִצְרָיִם וִישַׁלַּח אֶת־בְּנֵי־יִשְׂרָאֵל מֵאַרְצוֹ:

יב וַיְדַבֵּר מֹשֶׁה לִפְנֵי יְהוָה לֵאמֹר הֵן בְּנֵי־יִשְׂרָאֵל לֹא־שָׁמְעוּ אֵלַי וְאֵיךְ יִשְׁמָעֵנִי פַרְעֹה וַאֲנִי עֲרַל שְׂפָתָיִם:

יג וַיְדַבֵּר יְהוָה אֶל־מֹשֶׁה וְאֶל־אַהֲרֹן וַיְצַוֵּם אֶל־בְּנֵי יִשְׂרָאֵל וְאֶל־פַּרְעֹה מֶלֶךְ מִצְרָיִם לְהוֹצִיא אֶת־בְּנֵי־יִשְׂרָאֵל מֵאֶרֶץ מִצְרָיִם:

יד אֵלֶּה רָאשֵׁי בֵית־אֲבֹתָם בְּנֵי רְאוּבֵן בְּכֹר יִשְׂרָאֵל חֲנוֹךְ וּפַלּוּא חֶצְרוֹן וְכַרְמִי אֵלֶּה מִשְׁפְּחֹת רְאוּבֵן:

טו וּבְנֵי שִׁמְעוֹן יְמוּאֵל וְיָמִין וְאֹהַד וְיָכִין וְצֹחַר וְשָׁאוּל בֶּן־הַכְּנַעֲנִית אֵלֶּה מִשְׁפְּחֹת שִׁמְעוֹן:

טז וְאֵלֶּה שְׁמוֹת בְּנֵי־לֵוִי לְתֹלְדֹתָם גֵּרְשׁוֹן וּקְהָת וּמְרָרִי וּשְׁנֵי חַיֵּי לֵוִי שֶׁבַע וּשְׁלֹשִׁים וּמְאַת שָׁנָה:

יז בְּנֵי גֵרְשׁוֹן לִבְנִי וְשִׁמְעִי לְמִשְׁפְּחֹתָם:

יח וּבְנֵי קְהָת עַמְרָם וְיִצְהָר וְחֶבְרוֹן וְעֻזִּיאֵל וּשְׁנֵי חַיֵּי קְהָת שָׁלֹשׁ וּשְׁלֹשִׁים וּמְאַת שָׁנָה:

יט וּבְנֵי מְרָרִי מַחְלִי וּמוּשִׁי אֵלֶּה מִשְׁפְּחֹת הַלֵּוִי לְתֹלְדֹתָם:

Israeli children in a field of buttercups

מורשה
ירושה

the Hebrew word for 'possession' in this verse, is generally translated as 'heritage,' while *yerusha* is translated as 'inheritance.' The use of different words suggests a difference in meaning. An inheritance is simply passed on from the previous generation, while a heritage requires the receiver's active involvement and participation, like a family business which the founder's children must work

hard to maintain. An inheritance may be squandered; a heritage must be preserved intact for the next generation. This certainly explains why the verse uses the word *morasha* with regard to *Eretz Yisrael*. The land requires our active involvement to maintain and preserve it, and it is not ours to squander.

20 *Amram* took to wife his father's sister *Yocheved*, and she bore him *Aharon* and *Moshe*; and the span of *Amram*'s life was 137 years.

כ וַיִּקַּח עַמְרָם אֶת־יוֹכֶבֶד דֹּדָתוֹ לוֹ לְאִשָּׁה וַתֵּלֶד לוֹ אֶת־אַהֲרֹן וְאֶת־מֹשֶׁה וּשְׁנֵי חַיֵּי עַמְרָם שֶׁבַע וּשְׁלֹשִׁים וּמְאַת שָׁנָה:

21 The sons of *Izhar*: *Korach*, Nepheg, and Zichri.

כא וּבְנֵי יִצְהָר קֹרַח וָנֶפֶג וְזִכְרִי:

22 The sons of *Uzziel*: *Mishael*, Elzaphan, and Sithri.

כב וּבְנֵי עֻזִּיאֵל מִישָׁאֵל וְאֶלְצָפָן וְסִתְרִי:

23 *Aharon* took to wife *Elisheva*, daughter of *Aminadav* and sister of *Nachshon*, and she bore him *Nadav* and *Avihu*, *Elazar* and *Itamar*.

כג וַיִּקַּח אַהֲרֹן אֶת־אֱלִישֶׁבַע בַּת־עַמִּינָדָב אֲחוֹת נַחְשׁוֹן לוֹ לְאִשָּׁה וַתֵּלֶד לוֹ אֶת־נָדָב וְאֶת־אֲבִיהוּא אֶת־אֶלְעָזָר וְאֶת־אִיתָמָר:

24 The sons of *Korach*: Assir, Elkana, and Abiasaph. Those are the families of the Korahites.

כד וּבְנֵי קֹרַח אַסִּיר וְאֶלְקָנָה וַאֲבִיאָסָף אֵלֶּה מִשְׁפְּחֹת הַקָּרְחִי:

25 And *Aharon*'s son *Elazar* took to wife one of Putiel's daughters, and she bore him *Pinchas*. Those are the heads of the fathers' houses of the *Leviim* by their families.

כה וְאֶלְעָזָר בֶּן־אַהֲרֹן לָקַח־לוֹ מִבְּנוֹת פּוּטִיאֵל לוֹ לְאִשָּׁה וַתֵּלֶד לוֹ אֶת־פִּינְחָס אֵלֶּה רָאשֵׁי אֲבוֹת הַלְוִיִּם לְמִשְׁפְּחֹתָם:

26 It is the same *Aharon* and *Moshe* to whom *Hashem* said, "Bring forth the Israelites from the land of Egypt, troop by troop."

כו הוּא אַהֲרֹן וּמֹשֶׁה אֲשֶׁר אָמַר יְהֹוָה לָהֶם הוֹצִיאוּ אֶת־בְּנֵי יִשְׂרָאֵל מֵאֶרֶץ מִצְרַיִם עַל־צִבְאֹתָם:

27 It was they who spoke to Pharaoh king of Egypt to free the Israelites from the Egyptians; these are the same *Moshe* and *Aharon*.

כז הֵם הַמְדַבְּרִים אֶל־פַּרְעֹה מֶלֶךְ־מִצְרַיִם לְהוֹצִיא אֶת־בְּנֵי־יִשְׂרָאֵל מִמִּצְרָיִם הוּא מֹשֶׁה וְאַהֲרֹן:

28 For when *Hashem* spoke to *Moshe* in the land of Egypt

כח וַיְהִי בְּיוֹם דִּבֶּר יְהֹוָה אֶל־מֹשֶׁה בְּאֶרֶץ מִצְרָיִם:

29 and *Hashem* said to *Moshe*, "I am *Hashem*; speak to Pharaoh king of Egypt all that I will tell you,"

כט וַיְדַבֵּר יְהֹוָה אֶל־מֹשֶׁה לֵּאמֹר אֲנִי יְהֹוָה דַּבֵּר אֶל־פַּרְעֹה מֶלֶךְ מִצְרַיִם אֵת כָּל־אֲשֶׁר אֲנִי דֹּבֵר אֵלֶיךָ:

30 *Moshe* appealed to *Hashem*, saying, "See, I am of impeded speech; how then should Pharaoh heed me!"

ל וַיֹּאמֶר מֹשֶׁה לִפְנֵי יְהֹוָה הֵן אֲנִי עֲרַל שְׂפָתַיִם וְאֵיךְ יִשְׁמַע אֵלַי פַּרְעֹה:

7 1 *Hashem* replied to *Moshe*, "See, I place you in the role of *Hashem* to Pharaoh, with your brother *Aharon* as your *navi*.

ז א וַיֹּאמֶר יְהֹוָה אֶל־מֹשֶׁה רְאֵה נְתַתִּיךָ אֱלֹהִים לְפַרְעֹה וְאַהֲרֹן אָחִיךָ יִהְיֶה נְבִיאֶךָ:

2 You shall repeat all that I command you, and your brother *Aharon* shall speak to Pharaoh to let the Israelites depart from his land.

ב אַתָּה תְדַבֵּר אֵת כָּל־אֲשֶׁר אֲצַוֶּךָּ וְאַהֲרֹן אָחִיךָ יְדַבֵּר אֶל־פַּרְעֹה וְשִׁלַּח אֶת־בְּנֵי־יִשְׂרָאֵל מֵאַרְצוֹ:

3 But I will harden Pharaoh's heart, that I may multiply My signs and marvels in the land of Egypt.

ג וַאֲנִי אַקְשֶׁה אֶת־לֵב פַּרְעֹה וְהִרְבֵּיתִי אֶת־אֹתֹתַי וְאֶת־מוֹפְתַי בְּאֶרֶץ מִצְרָיִם:

Exodus

4 When Pharaoh does not heed you, I will lay My hand upon Egypt and deliver My ranks, My people the Israelites, from the land of Egypt with extraordinary chastisements.

ד וְלֹא־יִשְׁמַע אֲלֵכֶם פַּרְעֹה וְנָתַתִּי אֶת־יָדִי בְּמִצְרָיִם וְהוֹצֵאתִי אֶת־צִבְאֹתַי אֶת־עַמִּי בְנֵי־יִשְׂרָאֵל מֵאֶרֶץ מִצְרַיִם בִּשְׁפָטִים גְּדֹלִים:

5 And the Egyptians shall know that I am *Hashem*, when I stretch out My hand over Egypt and bring out the Israelites from their midst."

ה וְיָדְעוּ מִצְרַיִם כִּי־אֲנִי יְהוָה בִּנְטֹתִי אֶת־יָדִי עַל־מִצְרָיִם וְהוֹצֵאתִי אֶת־בְּנֵי־יִשְׂרָאֵל מִתּוֹכָם:

6 This *Moshe* and *Aharon* did; as *Hashem* commanded them, so they did.

ו וַיַּעַשׂ מֹשֶׁה וְאַהֲרֹן כַּאֲשֶׁר צִוָּה יְהוָה אֹתָם כֵּן עָשׂוּ:

7 *Moshe* was eighty years old and *Aharon* eighty-three, when they made their demand on Pharaoh.

ז וּמֹשֶׁה בֶּן־שְׁמֹנִים שָׁנָה וְאַהֲרֹן בֶּן־שָׁלֹשׁ וּשְׁמֹנִים שָׁנָה בְּדַבְּרָם אֶל־פַּרְעֹה:

8 *Hashem* said to *Moshe* and *Aharon*,

ח וַיֹּאמֶר יְהוָה אֶל־מֹשֶׁה וְאֶל־אַהֲרֹן לֵאמֹר:

9 "When Pharaoh speaks to you and says, 'Produce your marvel,' you shall say to *Aharon*, 'Take your rod and cast it down before Pharaoh.' It shall turn into a serpent."

ט כִּי יְדַבֵּר אֲלֵכֶם פַּרְעֹה לֵאמֹר תְּנוּ לָכֶם מוֹפֵת וְאָמַרְתָּ אֶל־אַהֲרֹן קַח אֶת־מַטְּךָ וְהַשְׁלֵךְ לִפְנֵי־פַרְעֹה יְהִי לְתַנִּין:

10 So *Moshe* and *Aharon* came before Pharaoh and did just as *Hashem* had commanded: *Aharon* cast down his rod in the presence of Pharaoh and his courtiers, and it turned into a serpent.

י וַיָּבֹא מֹשֶׁה וְאַהֲרֹן אֶל־פַּרְעֹה וַיַּעֲשׂוּ כֵן כַּאֲשֶׁר צִוָּה יְהוָה וַיַּשְׁלֵךְ אַהֲרֹן אֶת־מַטֵּהוּ לִפְנֵי פַרְעֹה וְלִפְנֵי עֲבָדָיו וַיְהִי לְתַנִּין:

11 Then Pharaoh, for his part, summoned the wise men and the sorcerers; and the Egyptian magicians, in turn, did the same with their spells;

יא וַיִּקְרָא גַּם־פַּרְעֹה לַחֲכָמִים וְלַמְכַשְּׁפִים וַיַּעֲשׂוּ גַם־הֵם חַרְטֻמֵּי מִצְרַיִם בְּלַהֲטֵיהֶם כֵּן:

12 each cast down his rod, and they turned into serpents. But *Aharon*'s rod swallowed their rods.

יב וַיַּשְׁלִיכוּ אִישׁ מַטֵּהוּ וַיִּהְיוּ לְתַנִּינִם וַיִּבְלַע מַטֵּה־אַהֲרֹן אֶת־מַטֹּתָם:

13 Yet Pharaoh's heart stiffened and he did not heed them, as *Hashem* had said.

יג וַיֶּחֱזַק לֵב פַּרְעֹה וְלֹא שָׁמַע אֲלֵהֶם כַּאֲשֶׁר דִּבֶּר יְהוָה:

14 And *Hashem* said to *Moshe*, "Pharaoh is stubborn; he refuses to let the people go.

יד וַיֹּאמֶר יְהוָה אֶל־מֹשֶׁה כָּבֵד לֵב פַּרְעֹה מֵאֵן לְשַׁלַּח הָעָם:

15 Go to Pharaoh in the morning, as he is coming out to the water, and station yourself before him at the edge of the Nile, taking with you the rod that turned into a snake.

טו לֵךְ אֶל־פַּרְעֹה בַּבֹּקֶר הִנֵּה יֹצֵא הַמַּיְמָה וְנִצַּבְתָּ לִקְרָאתוֹ עַל־שְׂפַת הַיְאֹר וְהַמַּטֶּה אֲשֶׁר־נֶהְפַּךְ לְנָחָשׁ תִּקַּח בְּיָדֶךָ:

16 And say to him, '*Hashem*, the God of the Hebrews, sent me to you to say, "Let My people go that they may worship Me in the wilderness." But you have paid no heed until now.

טז וְאָמַרְתָּ אֵלָיו יְהוָה אֱלֹהֵי הָעִבְרִים שְׁלָחַנִי אֵלֶיךָ לֵאמֹר שַׁלַּח אֶת־עַמִּי וְיַעַבְדֻנִי בַּמִּדְבָּר וְהִנֵּה לֹא־שָׁמַעְתָּ עַד־כֹּה:

17 Thus says *Hashem*, "By this you shall know that
I am *Hashem*." See, I shall strike the water in the
Nile with the rod that is in my hand, and it will be
turned into blood;

כֹּה אָמַר יְהוָֹה בְּזֹאת תֵּדַע כִּי אֲנִי
יְהוָֹה הִנֵּה אָנֹכִי מַכֶּה בַּמַּטֶּה אֲשֶׁר־
בְּיָדִי עַל־הַמַּיִם אֲשֶׁר בַּיְאֹר וְנֶהֶפְכוּ
לְדָם:

יז

> KO a-MAR a-do-NAI b'-ZOT tay-DA KEE a-NEE a-do-NAI
> hi-NAY a-no-KHEE ma-KEH ba-ma-TEH a-sher b'-ya-DEE al
> ha-MA-yim a-SHER bai-OR v'-ne-hef-KHU l'-DAM

18 and the fish in the Nile will die. The Nile will stink
so that the Egyptians will find it impossible to drink
the water of the Nile.'"

וְהַדָּגָה אֲשֶׁר־בַּיְאֹר תָּמוּת וּבָאַשׁ הַיְאֹר
וְנִלְאוּ מִצְרַיִם לִשְׁתּוֹת מַיִם מִן־הַיְאֹר:

יח

19 And *Hashem* said to *Moshe*, "Say to *Aharon*: Take
your rod and hold out your arm over the waters of
Egypt – its rivers, its canals, its ponds, all its bodies
of water – that they may turn to blood; there shall
be blood throughout the land of Egypt, even in
vessels of wood and stone."

וַיֹּאמֶר יְהוָֹה אֶל־מֹשֶׁה אֱמֹר אֶל־אַהֲרֹן
קַח מַטְּךָ וּנְטֵה־יָדְךָ עַל־מֵימֵי מִצְרַיִם
עַל־נַהֲרֹתָם עַל־יְאֹרֵיהֶם וְעַל־אַגְמֵיהֶם
וְעַל כָּל־מִקְוֵה מֵימֵיהֶם וְיִהְיוּ־דָם
וְהָיָה דָם בְּכָל־אֶרֶץ מִצְרַיִם וּבָעֵצִים
וּבָאֲבָנִים:

יט

20 *Moshe* and *Aharon* did just as *Hashem* commanded:
he lifted up the rod and struck the water in the Nile
in the sight of Pharaoh and his courtiers, and all the
water in the Nile was turned into blood

וַיַּעֲשׂוּ־כֵן מֹשֶׁה וְאַהֲרֹן כַּאֲשֶׁר צִוָּה
יְהוָֹה וַיָּרֶם בַּמַּטֶּה וַיַּךְ אֶת־הַמַּיִם אֲשֶׁר
בַּיְאֹר לְעֵינֵי פַרְעֹה וּלְעֵינֵי עֲבָדָיו
וַיֵּהָפְכוּ כָּל־הַמַּיִם אֲשֶׁר־בַּיְאֹר לְדָם:

כ

21 and the fish in the Nile died. The Nile stank so that
the Egyptians could not drink water from the Nile;
and there was blood throughout the land of Egypt.

וְהַדָּגָה אֲשֶׁר־בַּיְאֹר מֵתָה וַיִּבְאַשׁ הַיְאֹר
וְלֹא־יָכְלוּ מִצְרַיִם לִשְׁתּוֹת מַיִם מִן־
הַיְאֹר וַיְהִי הַדָּם בְּכָל־אֶרֶץ מִצְרָיִם:

כא

22 But when the Egyptian magicians did the same
with their spells, Pharaoh's heart stiffened and he
did not heed them – as *Hashem* had spoken.

וַיַּעֲשׂוּ־כֵן חַרְטֻמֵּי מִצְרַיִם בְּלָטֵיהֶם
וַיֶּחֱזַק לֵב־פַּרְעֹה וְלֹא־שָׁמַע אֲלֵהֶם
כַּאֲשֶׁר דִּבֶּר יְהוָֹה:

כב

23 Pharaoh turned and went into his palace, paying no
regard even to this.

וַיִּפֶן פַּרְעֹה וַיָּבֹא אֶל־בֵּיתוֹ וְלֹא־שָׁת
לִבּוֹ גַּם־לָזֹאת:

כג

24 And all the Egyptians had to dig round about the
Nile for drinking water, because they could not
drink the water of the Nile.

וַיַּחְפְּרוּ כָל־מִצְרַיִם סְבִיבֹת הַיְאֹר מַיִם
לִשְׁתּוֹת כִּי לֹא יָכְלוּ לִשְׁתֹּת מִמֵּימֵי
הַיְאֹר:

כד

A rain storm by the Mediterranean sea

7:17 The water in the Nile The first two of the ten plagues that *Hashem* inflicts upon Egypt specifically affect the Nile. When describing the attack on the Nile, *Yechezkel* says: "Thus said *Hashem*: I am going to deal with you, O Pharaoh king of Egypt, mighty monster, sprawling in your channels, who said, 'My Nile is my own; I made it for myself'." (Ezekiel 29:3). Unlike *Eretz Yisrael* which is dependent upon rain water, Egypt has the Nile as a reliable water source, and that is the key to its economic success. Since the Egyptians did not require rain, they saw themselves as self-sufficient and not dependent on God for their sustenance. Consequently, *Hashem* struck the Nile first. By contrast, the Land of Israel has no such water source, and therefore, its inhabitants are aware of their dependence on God and forge a relationship with Him through their daily prayers for rain. This spiritual relationship is built into the very geography of the *Eretz Yisrael*, in contrast with its neighbors.

25 When seven days had passed after *Hashem* struck the Nile,

כה וַיִּמָּלֵא שִׁבְעַת יָמִים אַחֲרֵי הַכּוֹת־יְהוָֹה אֶת־הַיְאֹר:

26 *Hashem* said to *Moshe*, "Go to Pharaoh and say to him, 'Thus says *Hashem*: Let My people go that they may worship Me.

כו וַיֹּאמֶר יְהוָֹה אֶל־מֹשֶׁה בֹּא אֶל־פַּרְעֹה וְאָמַרְתָּ אֵלָיו כֹּה אָמַר יְהוָֹה שַׁלַּח אֶת־עַמִּי וְיַעַבְדֻנִי:

27 If you refuse to let them go, then I will plague your whole country with frogs.

כז וְאִם־מָאֵן אַתָּה לְשַׁלֵּחַ הִנֵּה אָנֹכִי נֹגֵף אֶת־כָּל־גְּבוּלְךָ בַּצְפַרְדְּעִים:

28 The Nile shall swarm with frogs, and they shall come up and enter your palace, your bedchamber and your bed, the houses of your courtiers and your people, and your ovens and your kneading bowls.

כח וְשָׁרַץ הַיְאֹר צְפַרְדְּעִים וְעָלוּ וּבָאוּ בְּבֵיתֶךָ וּבַחֲדַר מִשְׁכָּבְךָ וְעַל־מִטָּתֶךָ וּבְבֵית עֲבָדֶיךָ וּבְעַמֶּךָ וּבְתַנּוּרֶיךָ וּבְמִשְׁאֲרוֹתֶיךָ:

29 The frogs shall come up on you and on your people and on all your courtiers.'"

כט וּבְכָה וּבְעַמְּךָ וּבְכָל־עֲבָדֶיךָ יַעֲלוּ הַצְפַרְדְּעִים:

8 **1** And *Hashem* said to *Moshe*, "Say to *Aharon*: Hold out your arm with the rod over the rivers, the canals, and the ponds, and bring up the frogs on the land of Egypt."

ח א וַיֹּאמֶר יְהוָֹה אֶל־מֹשֶׁה אֱמֹר אֶל־אַהֲרֹן נְטֵה אֶת־יָדְךָ בְּמַטֶּךָ עַל־הַנְּהָרֹת עַל־הַיְאֹרִים וְעַל־הָאֲגַמִּים וְהַעַל אֶת־הַצְפַרְדְּעִים עַל־אֶרֶץ מִצְרָיִם:

2 *Aharon* held out his arm over the waters of Egypt, and the frogs came up and covered the land of Egypt.

ב וַיֵּט אַהֲרֹן אֶת־יָדוֹ עַל מֵימֵי מִצְרָיִם וַתַּעַל הַצְפַרְדֵּעַ וַתְּכַס אֶת־אֶרֶץ מִצְרָיִם:

3 But the magicians did the same with their spells, and brought frogs upon the land of Egypt.

ג וַיַּעֲשׂוּ־כֵן הַחַרְטֻמִּים בְּלָטֵיהֶם וַיַּעֲלוּ אֶת־הַצְפַרְדְּעִים עַל־אֶרֶץ מִצְרָיִם:

4 Then Pharaoh summoned *Moshe* and *Aharon* and said, "Plead with *Hashem* to remove the frogs from me and my people, and I will let the people go to sacrifice to *Hashem*."

ד וַיִּקְרָא פַרְעֹה לְמֹשֶׁה וּלְאַהֲרֹן וַיֹּאמֶר הַעְתִּירוּ אֶל־יְהוָֹה וְיָסֵר הַצְפַרְדְּעִים מִמֶּנִּי וּמֵעַמִּי וַאֲשַׁלְּחָה אֶת־הָעָם וְיִזְבְּחוּ לַיהוָֹה:

5 And *Moshe* said to Pharaoh, "You may have this triumph over me: for what time shall I plead in behalf of you and your courtiers and your people, that the frogs be cut off from you and your houses, to remain only in the Nile?"

ה וַיֹּאמֶר מֹשֶׁה לְפַרְעֹה הִתְפָּאֵר עָלַי לְמָתַי אַעְתִּיר לְךָ וְלַעֲבָדֶיךָ וּלְעַמְּךָ לְהַכְרִית הַצְפַרְדְּעִים מִמְּךָ וּמִבָּתֶּיךָ רַק בַּיְאֹר תִּשָּׁאַרְנָה:

6 "For tomorrow," he replied. And [*Moshe*] said, "As you say – that you may know that there is none like *Hashem* our God;

ו וַיֹּאמֶר לְמָחָר וַיֹּאמֶר כִּדְבָרְךָ לְמַעַן תֵּדַע כִּי־אֵין כַּיהוָֹה אֱלֹהֵינוּ:

7 the frogs shall retreat from you and your courtiers and your people; they shall remain only in the Nile."

ז וְסָרוּ הַצְפַרְדְּעִים מִמְּךָ וּמִבָּתֶּיךָ וּמֵעֲבָדֶיךָ וּמֵעַמֶּךָ רַק בַּיְאֹר תִּשָּׁאַרְנָה:

8 Then *Moshe* and *Aharon* left Pharaoh's presence, and *Moshe* cried out to *Hashem* in the matter of the frogs which He had inflicted upon Pharaoh.

ח וַיֵּצֵא מֹשֶׁה וְאַהֲרֹן מֵעִם פַּרְעֹה וַיִּצְעַק מֹשֶׁה אֶל־יְהוָֹה עַל־דְּבַר הַצְפַרְדְּעִים אֲשֶׁר־שָׂם לְפַרְעֹה:

9 And *Hashem* did as *Moshe* asked; the frogs died out in the houses, the courtyards, and the fields.

ט וַיַּ֥עַשׂ יְהֹוָ֖ה כִּדְבַ֣ר מֹשֶׁ֑ה וַיָּמֻ֙תוּ֙ הַֽצְפַרְדְּעִ֔ים מִן־הַבָּתִּ֥ים מִן־הַֽחֲצֵרֹ֖ת וּמִן־הַשָּׂדֹֽת:

10 And they piled them up in heaps, till the land stank.

י וַיִּצְבְּר֥וּ אֹתָ֖ם חֳמָרִ֣ם חֳמָרִ֑ם וַתִּבְאַ֖שׁ הָאָֽרֶץ:

11 But when Pharaoh saw that there was relief, he became stubborn and would not heed them, as *Hashem* had spoken.

יא וַיַּ֣רְא פַּרְעֹ֗ה כִּ֤י הָֽיְתָה֙ הָֽרְוָחָ֔ה וְהַכְבֵּד֙ אֶת־לִבּ֔וֹ וְלֹ֥א שָׁמַ֖ע אֲלֵהֶ֑ם כַּֽאֲשֶׁ֖ר דִּבֶּ֥ר יְהֹוָֽה:

12 Then *Hashem* said to *Moshe*, "Say to *Aharon*: Hold out your rod and strike the dust of the earth, and it shall turn to lice throughout the land of Egypt."

יב וַיֹּ֣אמֶר יְהֹוָה֮ אֶל־מֹשֶׁה֒ אֱמֹר֙ אֶל־אַֽהֲרֹ֔ן נְטֵ֣ה אֶת־מַטְּךָ֔ וְהַ֖ךְ אֶת־עֲפַ֣ר הָאָ֑רֶץ וְהָיָ֥ה לְכִנִּ֖ם בְּכָל־אֶ֥רֶץ מִצְרָֽיִם:

13 And they did so. *Aharon* held out his arm with the rod and struck the dust of the earth, and vermin came upon man and beast; all the dust of the earth turned to lice throughout the land of Egypt.

יג וַיַּֽעֲשׂוּ־כֵ֗ן וַיֵּט֩ אַֽהֲרֹ֨ן אֶת־יָד֤וֹ בְמַטֵּ֨הוּ֙ וַיַּ֙ךְ֙ אֶת־עֲפַ֣ר הָאָ֔רֶץ וַתְּהִי֙ הַכִּנָּ֔ם בָּֽאָדָ֖ם וּבַבְּהֵמָ֑ה כָּל־עֲפַ֥ר הָאָ֛רֶץ הָיָ֥ה כִנִּ֖ים בְּכָל־אֶ֥רֶץ מִצְרָֽיִם:

14 The magicians did the like with their spells to produce lice, but they could not. The vermin remained upon man and beast;

יד וַיַּֽעֲשׂוּ־כֵ֨ן הַֽחַרְטֻמִּ֧ים בְּלָֽטֵיהֶ֛ם לְהוֹצִ֥יא אֶת־הַכִּנִּ֖ים וְלֹ֣א יָכֹ֑לוּ וַתְּהִי֙ הַכִּנָּ֔ם בָּֽאָדָ֖ם וּבַבְּהֵמָֽה:

15 and the magicians said to Pharaoh, "This is the finger of *Hashem*!" But Pharaoh's heart stiffened and he would not heed them, as *Hashem* had spoken.

טו וַיֹּֽאמְר֤וּ הַֽחַרְטֻמִּם֙ אֶל־פַּרְעֹ֔ה אֶצְבַּ֥ע אֱלֹהִ֖ים הִ֑וא וַיֶּֽחֱזַ֤ק לֵב־פַּרְעֹה֙ וְלֹֽא־שָׁמַ֣ע אֲלֵהֶ֔ם כַּֽאֲשֶׁ֖ר דִּבֶּ֥ר יְהֹוָֽה:

va-yo-m'-RU ha-khar-tu-MEEM el par-OH ETZ-ba
e-lo-HEEM HEE va-ye-khe-ZAK layv par-OH v'-lo sha-MA
a-lay-HEM ka-a-SHER di-BER a-do-NAI

16 And *Hashem* said to *Moshe*, "Early in the morning present yourself to Pharaoh, as he is coming out to the water, and say to him, 'Thus says *Hashem*: Let My people go that they may worship Me.

טז וַיֹּ֨אמֶר יְהֹוָ֜ה אֶל־מֹשֶׁ֗ה הַשְׁכֵּ֤ם בַּבֹּ֨קֶר֙ וְהִתְיַצֵּב֙ לִפְנֵ֣י פַרְעֹ֔ה הִנֵּ֖ה יוֹצֵ֣א הַמָּ֑יְמָה וְאָֽמַרְתָּ֣ אֵלָ֗יו כֹּ֚ה אָמַ֣ר יְהֹוָ֔ה שַׁלַּ֥ח עַמִּ֖י וְיַֽעַבְדֻֽנִי:

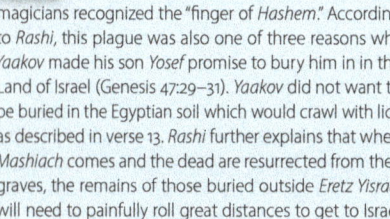

8:15 This is the finger of *Hashem* The plague of lice had theological implications for the Egyptians, as it was the first time that Pharaoh's magicians recognized the "finger of *Hashem*." According to *Rashi*, this plague was also one of three reasons why *Yaakov* made his son *Yosef* promise to bury him in the Land of Israel (Genesis 47:29–31). *Yaakov* did not want to be buried in the Egyptian soil which would crawl with lice, as described in verse 13. *Rashi* further explains that when *Mashiach* comes and the dead are resurrected from their graves, the remains of those buried outside *Eretz Yisrael* will need to painfully roll great distances to get to Israel. To avoid this, *Yosef* asks to be buried in the Holy Land.

Finally, *Rashi* writes that *Yaakov* did not want to be deified by the Egyptians after his death. Rabbi Samson Raphael Hirsch, however, suggests a fourth reason. Though he had lived in Egypt for seventeen years, he longed to be back in his homeland and wanted to impress upon his descendants that the Land of Israel is where they really belong. To this day, there are many who follow *Yaakov's* example. Appreciating the value and significance of the land, they ask their descendants to bury them in Israel even if they are unable to live there.

Yaakov's grave inside the Machpelah cave

17 For if you do not let My people go, I will let loose swarms of insects against you and your courtiers and your people and your houses; the houses of the Egyptians, and the very ground they stand on, shall be filled with swarms of insects.

יז כִּי אִם־אֵינְךָ מְשַׁלֵּחַ אֶת־עַמִּי הִנְנִי מַשְׁלִיחַ בְּךָ וּבַעֲבָדֶיךָ וּבְעַמְּךָ וּבְבָתֶּיךָ אֶת־הֶעָרֹב וּמָלְאוּ בָּתֵּי מִצְרַיִם אֶת־הֶעָרֹב וְגַם הָאֲדָמָה אֲשֶׁר־הֵם עָלֶיהָ:

18 But on that day I will set apart the region of Goshen, where My people dwell, so that no swarms of insects shall be there, that you may know that I *Hashem* am in the midst of the land.

יח וְהִפְלֵיתִי בַיּוֹם הַהוּא אֶת־אֶרֶץ גֹּשֶׁן אֲשֶׁר עַמִּי עֹמֵד עָלֶיהָ לְבִלְתִּי הֱיוֹת־שָׁם עָרֹב לְמַעַן תֵּדַע כִּי אֲנִי יְהֹוָה בְּקֶרֶב הָאָרֶץ:

19 And I will make a distinction between My people and your people. Tomorrow this sign shall come to pass.'"

יט וְשַׂמְתִּי פְדֻת בֵּין עַמִּי וּבֵין עַמֶּךָ לְמָחָר יִהְיֶה הָאֹת הַזֶּה:

20 And *Hashem* did so. Heavy swarms of insects invaded Pharaoh's palace and the houses of his courtiers; throughout the country of Egypt the land was ruined because of the swarms of insects.

כ וַיַּעַשׂ יְהֹוָה כֵּן וַיָּבֹא עָרֹב כָּבֵד בֵּיתָה פַרְעֹה וּבֵית עֲבָדָיו וּבְכָל־אֶרֶץ מִצְרַיִם תִּשָּׁחֵת הָאָרֶץ מִפְּנֵי הֶעָרֹב:

21 Then Pharaoh summoned *Moshe* and *Aharon* and said, "Go and sacrifice to your God within the land."

כא וַיִּקְרָא פַרְעֹה אֶל־מֹשֶׁה וּלְאַהֲרֹן וַיֹּאמֶר לְכוּ זִבְחוּ לֵאלֹהֵיכֶם בָּאָרֶץ:

22 But *Moshe* replied, "It would not be right to do this, for what we sacrifice to *Hashem* our God is untouchable to the Egyptians. If we sacrifice that which is untouchable to the Egyptians before their very eyes, will they not stone us!

כב וַיֹּאמֶר מֹשֶׁה לֹא נָכוֹן לַעֲשׂוֹת כֵּן כִּי תּוֹעֲבַת מִצְרַיִם נִזְבַּח לַיהֹוָה אֱלֹהֵינוּ הֵן נִזְבַּח אֶת־תּוֹעֲבַת מִצְרַיִם לְעֵינֵיהֶם וְלֹא יִסְקְלֻנוּ:

23 So we must go a distance of three days into the wilderness and sacrifice to *Hashem* our God as He may command us."

כג דֶּרֶךְ שְׁלֹשֶׁת יָמִים נֵלֵךְ בַּמִּדְבָּר וְזָבַחְנוּ לַיהֹוָה אֱלֹהֵינוּ כַּאֲשֶׁר יֹאמַר אֵלֵינוּ:

24 Pharaoh said, "I will let you go to sacrifice to *Hashem* your God in the wilderness; but do not go very far. Plead, then, for me."

כד וַיֹּאמֶר פַּרְעֹה אָנֹכִי אֲשַׁלַּח אֶתְכֶם וּזְבַחְתֶּם לַיהֹוָה אֱלֹהֵיכֶם בַּמִּדְבָּר רַק הַרְחֵק לֹא־תַרְחִיקוּ לָלֶכֶת הַעְתִּירוּ בַּעֲדִי:

25 And *Moshe* said, "When I leave your presence, I will plead with *Hashem* that the swarms of insects depart tomorrow from Pharaoh and his courtiers and his people; but let not Pharaoh again act deceitfully, not letting the people go to sacrifice to *Hashem*."

כה וַיֹּאמֶר מֹשֶׁה הִנֵּה אָנֹכִי יוֹצֵא מֵעִמָּךְ וְהַעְתַּרְתִּי אֶל־יְהֹוָה וְסָר הֶעָרֹב מִפַּרְעֹה מֵעֲבָדָיו וּמֵעַמּוֹ מָחָר רַק אַל־יֹסֵף פַּרְעֹה הָתֵל לְבִלְתִּי שַׁלַּח אֶת־הָעָם לִזְבֹּחַ לַיהֹוָה:

26 So *Moshe* left Pharaoh's presence and pleaded with *Hashem*.

כו וַיֵּצֵא מֹשֶׁה מֵעִם פַּרְעֹה וַיֶּעְתַּר אֶל־יְהֹוָה:

27 And *Hashem* did as *Moshe* asked: He removed the swarms of insects from Pharaoh, from his courtiers, and from his people; not one remained.

כז וַיַּעַשׂ יְהֹוָה כִּדְבַר מֹשֶׁה וַיָּסַר הֶעָרֹב מִפַּרְעֹה מֵעֲבָדָיו וּמֵעַמּוֹ לֹא נִשְׁאַר אֶחָד:

28 But Pharaoh became stubborn this time also, and would not let the people go.

כח וַיַּכְבֵּד פַּרְעֹה אֶת־לִבּוֹ גַּם בַּפַּעַם הַזֹּאת וְלֹא שִׁלַּח אֶת־הָעָם:

9 ¹ *Hashem* said to *Moshe*, "Go to Pharaoh and say to him, 'Thus says *Hashem*, the God of the Hebrews: Let My people go to worship Me.

ט א וַיֹּאמֶר יְהוָֹה אֶל־מֹשֶׁה בֹּא אֶל־פַּרְעֹה וְדִבַּרְתָּ אֵלָיו כֹּה־אָמַר יְהוָֹה אֱלֹהֵי הָעִבְרִים שַׁלַּח אֶת־עַמִּי וְיַעַבְדֻנִי:

va-YO-mer a-do-NAI el mo-SHEH BO el par-OH v'-di-bar-TA ay-LAV koh a-MAR a-do-NAI e-lo-HAY ha-iv-REEM sha-LAKH et a-MEE v'-ya-av-DU-nee

² For if you refuse to let them go, and continue to hold them,

ב כִּי אִם־מָאֵן אַתָּה לְשַׁלֵּחַ וְעוֹדְךָ מַחֲזִיק בָּם:

³ then the hand of *Hashem* will strike your livestock in the fields – the horses, the asses, the camels, the cattle, and the sheep – with a very severe pestilence.

ג הִנֵּה יַד־יְהוָֹה הוֹיָה בְּמִקְנְךָ אֲשֶׁר בַּשָּׂדֶה בַּסּוּסִים בַּחֲמֹרִים בַּגְּמַלִּים בַּבָּקָר וּבַצֹּאן דֶּבֶר כָּבֵד מְאֹד:

⁴ But *Hashem* will make a distinction between the livestock of *Yisrael* and the livestock of the Egyptians, so that nothing shall die of all that belongs to the Israelites.

ד וְהִפְלָה יְהוָֹה בֵּין מִקְנֵה יִשְׂרָאֵל וּבֵין מִקְנֵה מִצְרָיִם וְלֹא יָמוּת מִכָּל־לִבְנֵי יִשְׂרָאֵל דָּבָר:

⁵ *Hashem* has fixed the time: tomorrow *Hashem* will do this thing in the land.'"

ה וַיָּשֶׂם יְהוָֹה מוֹעֵד לֵאמֹר מָחָר יַעֲשֶׂה יְהוָֹה הַדָּבָר הַזֶּה בָּאָרֶץ:

⁶ And *Hashem* did so the next day: all the livestock of the Egyptians died, but of the livestock of the Israelites not a beast died.

ו וַיַּעַשׂ יְהוָֹה אֶת־הַדָּבָר הַזֶּה מִמָּחֳרָת וַיָּמָת כֹּל מִקְנֵה מִצְרָיִם וּמִמִּקְנֵה בְנֵי־יִשְׂרָאֵל לֹא־מֵת אֶחָד:

⁷ When Pharaoh inquired, he found that not a head of the livestock of *Yisrael* had died; yet Pharaoh remained stubborn, and he would not let the people go.

ז וַיִּשְׁלַח פַּרְעֹה וְהִנֵּה לֹא־מֵת מִמִּקְנֵה יִשְׂרָאֵל עַד־אֶחָד וַיִּכְבַּד לֵב פַּרְעֹה וְלֹא שִׁלַּח אֶת־הָעָם:

⁸ Then *Hashem* said to *Moshe* and *Aharon*, "Each of you take handfuls of soot from the kiln, and let *Moshe* throw it toward the sky in the sight of Pharaoh.

ח וַיֹּאמֶר יְהוָֹה אֶל־מֹשֶׁה וְאֶל־אַהֲרֹן קְחוּ לָכֶם מְלֹא חָפְנֵיכֶם פִּיחַ כִּבְשָׁן וּזְרָקוֹ מֹשֶׁה הַשָּׁמַיְמָה לְעֵינֵי פַרְעֹה:

⁹ It shall become a fine dust all over the land of Egypt, and cause an inflammation breaking out in boils on man and beast throughout the land of Egypt."

ט וְהָיָה לְאָבָק עַל כָּל־אֶרֶץ מִצְרָיִם וְהָיָה עַל־הָאָדָם וְעַל־הַבְּהֵמָה לִשְׁחִין פֹּרֵחַ אֲבַעְבֻּעֹת בְּכָל־אֶרֶץ מִצְרָיִם:

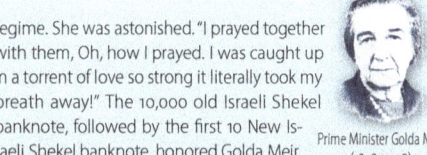

9:1 Let My people go Unfortunately, the bondage of Jews was not limited to the period of slavery in Egypt. There have been many other such incidents in history, even in the 20th and 21st centuries. Golda Meir (1898–1978), while serving as Israel's first ambassador to the Soviet Union, worked tirelessly to facilitate the immigration to Israel of Jews trapped behind the "Iron Curtain." Upon her arrival, some 50,000 Jews greeted Golda for the *Shabbat*, despite fear of the Soviet regime. She was astonished. "I prayed together with them, Oh, how I prayed. I was caught up in a torrent of love so strong it literally took my breath away!" The 10,000 old Israeli Shekel banknote, followed by the first 10 New Israeli Shekel banknote, honored Golda Meir with her image on one side and on the other, an illustration of the mass of Russian Jews and the expression, taken from this verse, "Let My people go."

Prime Minister Golda Meir (1898–1978)

20

10 So they took soot of the kiln and appeared before Pharaoh; *Moshe* threw it toward the sky, and it caused an inflammation breaking out in boils on man and beast.

יוַיִּקְחוּ אֶת־פִּיחַ הַכִּבְשָׁן וַיַּעַמְדוּ לִפְנֵי פַרְעֹה וַיִּזְרֹק אֹתוֹ מֹשֶׁה הַשָּׁמָיְמָה וַיְהִי שְׁחִין אֲבַעְבֻּעֹת פֹּרֵחַ בָּאָדָם וּבַבְּהֵמָה:

11 The magicians were unable to confront *Moshe* because of the inflammation, for the inflammation afflicted the magicians as well as all the other Egyptians.

יאוְלֹא־יָכְלוּ הַחַרְטֻמִּים לַעֲמֹד לִפְנֵי מֹשֶׁה מִפְּנֵי הַשְּׁחִין כִּי־הָיָה הַשְּׁחִין בַּחַרְטֻמִּם וּבְכָל־מִצְרָיִם:

12 But *Hashem* stiffened the heart of Pharaoh, and he would not heed them, just as *Hashem* had told *Moshe*.

יבוַיְחַזֵּק יְהֹוָה אֶת־לֵב פַּרְעֹה וְלֹא שָׁמַע אֲלֵהֶם כַּאֲשֶׁר דִּבֶּר יְהֹוָה אֶל־מֹשֶׁה:

13 *Hashem* said to *Moshe*, "Early in the morning present yourself to Pharaoh and say to him, 'Thus says *Hashem*, the God of the Hebrews: Let My people go to worship Me.

יגוַיֹּאמֶר יְהֹוָה אֶל־מֹשֶׁה הַשְׁכֵּם בַּבֹּקֶר וְהִתְיַצֵּב לִפְנֵי פַרְעֹה וְאָמַרְתָּ אֵלָיו כֹּה־אָמַר יְהֹוָה אֱלֹהֵי הָעִבְרִים שַׁלַּח אֶת־עַמִּי וְיַעַבְדֻנִי:

14 For this time I will send all My plagues upon your person, and your courtiers, and your people, in order that you may know that there is none like Me in all the world.

ידכִּי בַּפַּעַם הַזֹּאת אֲנִי שֹׁלֵחַ אֶת־כָּל־מַגֵּפֹתַי אֶל־לִבְּךָ וּבַעֲבָדֶיךָ וּבְעַמֶּךָ בַּעֲבוּר תֵּדַע כִּי אֵין כָּמֹנִי בְּכָל־הָאָרֶץ:

15 I could have stretched forth My hand and stricken you and your people with pestilence, and you would have been effaced from the earth.

טוכִּי עַתָּה שָׁלַחְתִּי אֶת־יָדִי וָאַךְ אוֹתְךָ וְאֶת־עַמְּךָ בַּדָּבֶר וַתִּכָּחֵד מִן־הָאָרֶץ:

16 Nevertheless I have spared you for this purpose: in order to show you My power, and in order that My fame may resound throughout the world.

טזוְאוּלָם בַּעֲבוּר זֹאת הֶעֱמַדְתִּיךָ בַּעֲבוּר הַרְאֹתְךָ אֶת־כֹּחִי וּלְמַעַן סַפֵּר שְׁמִי בְּכָל־הָאָרֶץ:

17 Yet you continue to thwart My people, and do not let them go!

יזעוֹדְךָ מִסְתּוֹלֵל בְּעַמִּי לְבִלְתִּי שַׁלְּחָם:

18 This time tomorrow I will rain down a very heavy hail, such as has not been in Egypt from the day it was founded until now.

יחהִנְנִי מַמְטִיר כָּעֵת מָחָר בָּרָד כָּבֵד מְאֹד אֲשֶׁר לֹא־הָיָה כָמֹהוּ בְּמִצְרַיִם לְמִן־הַיּוֹם הִוָּסְדָה וְעַד־עָתָּה:

19 Therefore, order your livestock and everything you have in the open brought under shelter; every man and beast that is found outside, not having been brought indoors, shall perish when the hail comes down upon them!'"

יטוְעַתָּה שְׁלַח הָעֵז אֶת־מִקְנְךָ וְאֵת כָּל־אֲשֶׁר לְךָ בַּשָּׂדֶה כָּל־הָאָדָם וְהַבְּהֵמָה אֲשֶׁר־יִמָּצֵא בַשָּׂדֶה וְלֹא יֵאָסֵף הַבַּיְתָה וְיָרַד עֲלֵהֶם הַבָּרָד וָמֵתוּ:

20 Those among Pharaoh's courtiers who feared *Hashem*'s word brought their slaves and livestock indoors to safety;

כהַיָּרֵא אֶת־דְּבַר יְהֹוָה מֵעַבְדֵי פַּרְעֹה הֵנִיס אֶת־עֲבָדָיו וְאֶת־מִקְנֵהוּ אֶל־הַבָּתִּים:

21 but those who paid no regard to the word of *Hashem* left their slaves and livestock in the open.

כאוַאֲשֶׁר לֹא־שָׂם לִבּוֹ אֶל־דְּבַר יְהֹוָה וַיַּעֲזֹב אֶת־עֲבָדָיו וְאֶת־מִקְנֵהוּ בַּשָּׂדֶה:

22 *Hashem* said to *Moshe*, "Hold out your arm toward the sky that hail may fall on all the land of Egypt, upon man and beast and all the grasses of the field in the land of Egypt."

כב וַיֹּ֨אמֶר יְהֹוָ֜ה אֶל־מֹשֶׁ֗ה נְטֵ֤ה אֶת־יָֽדְךָ֙ עַל־הַשָּׁמַ֔יִם וִיהִ֥י בָרָ֖ד בְּכָל־אֶ֣רֶץ מִצְרָ֑יִם עַל־הָֽאָדָ֣ם וְעַל־הַבְּהֵמָ֗ה וְעַ֛ל כָּל־עֵ֥שֶׂב הַשָּׂדֶ֖ה בְּאֶ֥רֶץ מִצְרָֽיִם:

23 So *Moshe* held out his rod toward the sky, and *Hashem* sent thunder and hail, and fire streamed down to the ground, as *Hashem* rained down hail upon the land of Egypt.

כג וַיֵּ֨ט מֹשֶׁ֣ה אֶת־מַטֵּהוּ֮ עַל־הַשָּׁמַיִם֒ וַֽיהֹוָ֗ה נָתַ֤ן קֹלֹת֙ וּבָרָ֔ד וַתִּ֥הֲלַךְ אֵ֖שׁ אָ֑רְצָה וַיַּמְטֵ֧ר יְהֹוָ֛ה בָּרָ֖ד עַל־אֶ֥רֶץ מִצְרָֽיִם:

24 The hail was very heavy – fire flashing in the midst of the hail – such as had not fallen on the land of Egypt since it had become a nation.

כד וַיְהִ֣י בָרָ֔ד וְאֵ֕שׁ מִתְלַקַּ֖חַת בְּת֣וֹךְ הַבָּרָ֑ד כָּבֵ֣ד מְאֹ֔ד אֲשֶׁ֨ר לֹֽא־הָיָ֤ה כָמֹ֨הוּ֙ בְּכָל־אֶ֣רֶץ מִצְרַ֔יִם מֵאָ֖ז הָיְתָ֥ה לְגֽוֹי:

vai-HEE va-RAD v'-AYSH mit-la-KA-khat b'-TOKH ha-ba-RAD
ka-VAYD m'-OD a-SHER lo ha-YAH kha-MO-hu b'-khol
E-retz mitz-RA-yim may-AZ ha-y'-TAH l'-GOY

25 Throughout the land of Egypt the hail struck down all that were in the open, both man and beast; the hail also struck down all the grasses of the field and shattered all the trees of the field.

כה וַיַּ֨ךְ הַבָּרָ֜ד בְּכָל־אֶ֣רֶץ מִצְרַ֗יִם אֵ֤ת כָּל־אֲשֶׁ֣ר בַּשָּׂדֶ֔ה מֵֽאָדָ֖ם וְעַד־בְּהֵמָ֑ה וְאֵ֨ת כָּל־עֵ֤שֶׂב הַשָּׂדֶה֙ הִכָּ֣ה הַבָּרָ֔ד וְאֶת־כָּל־עֵ֥ץ הַשָּׂדֶ֖ה שִׁבֵּֽר:

26 Only in the region of Goshen, where the Israelites were, there was no hail.

כו רַ֚ק בְּאֶ֣רֶץ גֹּ֔שֶׁן אֲשֶׁר־שָׁ֖ם בְּנֵ֣י יִשְׂרָאֵ֑ל לֹ֥א הָיָ֖ה בָּרָֽד:

27 Thereupon Pharaoh sent for *Moshe* and *Aharon* and said to them, "I stand guilty this time. *Hashem* is in the right, and I and my people are in the wrong.

כז וַיִּשְׁלַ֣ח פַּרְעֹ֗ה וַיִּקְרָא֙ לְמֹשֶׁ֣ה וּֽלְאַֽהֲרֹ֔ן וַיֹּ֤אמֶר אֲלֵהֶם֙ חָטָ֣אתִי הַפָּ֑עַם יְהֹוָה֙ הַצַּדִּ֔יק וַֽאֲנִ֥י וְעַמִּ֖י הָֽרְשָׁעִֽים:

28 Plead with *Hashem* that there may be an end of *Hashem*'s thunder and of hail. I will let you go; you need stay no longer."

כח הַעְתִּ֨ירוּ֙ אֶל־יְהֹוָ֔ה וְרַ֕ב מִֽהְיֹ֖ת קֹלֹ֣ת אֱלֹהִ֖ים וּבָרָ֑ד וַֽאֲשַׁלְּחָ֣ה אֶתְכֶ֔ם וְלֹ֥א תֹֽסִפ֖וּן לַֽעֲמֹֽד:

29 *Moshe* said to him, "As I go out of the city, I shall spread out my hands to *Hashem*; the thunder will cease and the hail will fall no more, so that you may know that the earth is *Hashem*'s.

כט וַיֹּ֤אמֶר אֵלָיו֙ מֹשֶׁ֔ה כְּצֵאתִי֙ אֶת־הָעִ֔יר אֶפְרֹ֥שׂ אֶת־כַּפַּ֖י אֶל־יְהֹוָ֑ה הַקֹּל֣וֹת יֶחְדָּל֗וּן וְהַבָּרָד֙ לֹ֣א יִֽהְיֶה־ע֔וֹד לְמַ֣עַן תֵּדַ֔ע כִּ֥י לַֽיהֹוָ֖ה הָאָֽרֶץ:

30 But I know that you and your courtiers do not yet fear *Hashem*."

ל וְאַתָּ֖ה וַֽעֲבָדֶ֑יךָ יָדַ֕עְתִּי כִּ֚י טֶ֣רֶם תִּֽירְא֔וּן מִפְּנֵ֖י יְהֹוָ֥ה אֱלֹהִֽים:

9:24 The hail was very heavy The hail contains both fire and ice coming down together to smite the Egyptians. Miraculously, the fire does not melt the ice and the ice does not extinguish the fire. The two ordinarily opposing forces work together harmoniously for the purpose of fulfilling God's will. Similarly, *Rashi* comments (Genesis 1:8) that the Hebrew word for 'heaven,' *shamayim* (שמים), comes from the Hebrew words *aish* (אש), 'fire,' and *mayim* (מים), 'water,' as the two came together in harmony to make up the heavens. This overruling of the laws of nature serves as a powerful lesson and is referenced in the daily Jewish prayer service. The following supplication appears multiple times in the liturgy: "He Who makes peace in His heights, may He make peace upon us and upon all Israel." With this request, humankind is reminded that the common goal of serving *Hashem* should override all differences between people and unite us in peace.

A heavenly sky at the Red Sea in Eilat

אש
שמים
מים

22

³¹ Now the flax and barley were ruined, for the barley was in the ear and the flax was in bud;

לא וְהַפִּשְׁתָּה וְהַשְּׂעֹרָה נֻכָּתָה כִּי הַשְּׂעֹרָה אָבִיב וְהַפִּשְׁתָּה גִּבְעֹל:

³² but the wheat and the emmer were not hurt, for they ripen late.

לב וְהַחִטָּה וְהַכֻּסֶּמֶת לֹא נֻכּוּ כִּי אֲפִילֹת הֵנָּה:

³³ Leaving Pharaoh, *Moshe* went outside the city and spread out his hands to *Hashem*: the thunder and the hail ceased, and no rain came pouring down upon the earth.

לג וַיֵּצֵא מֹשֶׁה מֵעִם פַּרְעֹה אֶת־הָעִיר וַיִּפְרֹשׂ כַּפָּיו אֶל־יְהֹוָה וַיַּחְדְּלוּ הַקֹּלוֹת וְהַבָּרָד וּמָטָר לֹא־נִתַּךְ אָרְצָה:

³⁴ But when Pharaoh saw that the rain and the hail and the thunder had ceased, he became stubborn and reverted to his guilty ways, as did his courtiers.

לד וַיַּרְא פַּרְעֹה כִּי־חָדַל הַמָּטָר וְהַבָּרָד וְהַקֹּלֹת וַיֹּסֶף לַחֲטֹא וַיַּכְבֵּד לִבּוֹ הוּא וַעֲבָדָיו:

³⁵ So Pharaoh's heart stiffened and he would not let the Israelites go, just as *Hashem* had foretold through *Moshe*.

לה וַיֶּחֱזַק לֵב פַּרְעֹה וְלֹא שִׁלַּח אֶת־בְּנֵי יִשְׂרָאֵל כַּאֲשֶׁר דִּבֶּר יְהֹוָה בְּיַד־מֹשֶׁה:

10 ¹ Then *Hashem* said to *Moshe*, "Go to Pharaoh. For I have hardened his heart and the hearts of his courtiers, in order that I may display these My signs among them,

י וַיֹּאמֶר יְהֹוָה אֶל־מֹשֶׁה בֹּא אֶל־פַּרְעֹה כִּי־אֲנִי הִכְבַּדְתִּי אֶת־לִבּוֹ וְאֶת־לֵב עֲבָדָיו לְמַעַן שִׁתִי אֹתֹתַי אֵלֶּה בְּקִרְבּוֹ:

² and that you may recount in the hearing of your sons and of your sons' sons how I made a mockery of the Egyptians and how I displayed My signs among them – in order that you may know that I am *Hashem*."

ב וּלְמַעַן תְּסַפֵּר בְּאָזְנֵי בִנְךָ וּבֶן־בִּנְךָ אֵת אֲשֶׁר הִתְעַלַּלְתִּי בְּמִצְרַיִם וְאֶת־אֹתֹתַי אֲשֶׁר־שַׂמְתִּי בָם וִידַעְתֶּם כִּי־אֲנִי יְהֹוָה:

ul-MA-an t'-sa-PAYR b'-oz-NAY vin-kha u-VEN bin-KHA AYT
a-SHER hit-a-LAL-tee b'-mitz-RA-yim v'-et o-to-TAI a-sher
SAM-tee VAM vee-da-TEM kee a-NEE a-do-NAI

³ So *Moshe* and *Aharon* went to Pharaoh and said to him, "Thus says *Hashem*, the God of the Hebrews, 'How long will you refuse to humble yourself before Me? Let My people go that they may worship Me.

ג וַיָּבֹא מֹשֶׁה וְאַהֲרֹן אֶל־פַּרְעֹה וַיֹּאמְרוּ אֵלָיו כֹּה־אָמַר יְהֹוָה אֱלֹהֵי הָעִבְרִים עַד־מָתַי מֵאַנְתָּ לֵעָנֹת מִפָּנָי שַׁלַּח עַמִּי וְיַעַבְדֻנִי:

⁴ For if you refuse to let My people go, tomorrow I will bring locusts on your territory.

ד כִּי אִם־מָאֵן אַתָּה לְשַׁלֵּחַ אֶת־עַמִּי הִנְנִי מֵבִיא מָחָר אַרְבֶּה בִּגְבֻלֶךָ:

A night storm over Kfar Saba

10:2 In order that you may know that I am *Hashem* Until now, *Hashem* has said that the ten plagues are meant to teach the Egyptians that He is the true God. At this point, He adds another dimension: The plagues are also intended to cause the Children of Israel to recognize God. Sometimes, even people of faith need a spiritual boost. After living in Egypt for generations, the Jewish people have been influenced by their idolatrous surroundings. The plagues serve to remind them that *Hashem* runs the world, as they demonstrate God's control over everything: Water, earth, the animal kingdom, health, flying insects, light and human life. This lesson is especially important as the Children of Israel are about to follow God into the wilderness on their journey to the Promised Land. Jews are commanded to remember the exodus every day of their lives. The memory of the miracles that took place then, helps strengthen our faith and ability to meet life's constant challenges.

5 The shall cover the surface of the land, so that no one will be able to see the land. The shall devour the surviving remnant that was left to you after the hail; and they shall eat away all your trees that grow in the field.

ה וְכִסָּה אֶת־עֵין הָאָרֶץ וְלֹא יוּכַל לִרְאֹת אֶת־הָאָרֶץ וְאָכַל אֶת־יֶתֶר הַפְּלֵטָה הַנִּשְׁאֶרֶת לָכֶם מִן־הַבָּרָד וְאָכַל אֶת־כָּל־הָעֵץ הַצֹּמֵחַ לָכֶם מִן־הַשָּׂדֶה:

6 Moreover, they shall fill your palaces and the houses of all your courtiers and of all the Egyptians – something that ne her your fathers nor fathers' fathers have seen from the day they appeared on earth to this day.'" With that he turned and left Pharaoh's presence.

ו וּמָלְאוּ בָתֶּיךָ וּבָתֵּי כָל־עֲבָדֶיךָ וּבָתֵּי כָל־מִצְרַיִם אֲשֶׁר לֹא־רָאוּ אֲבֹתֶיךָ וַאֲבוֹת אֲבֹתֶיךָ מִיּוֹם הֱיוֹתָם עַל־הָאֲדָמָה עַד הַיּוֹם הַזֶּה וַיִּפֶן וַיֵּצֵא מֵעִם פַּרְעֹה:

7 Pharaoh's courtiers said to him, "How long shall this one be a snare to us? Let the men go to worship *Hashem* their God! Are you not yet aware that Egypt is lost?"

ז וַיֹּאמְרוּ עַבְדֵי פַרְעֹה אֵלָיו עַד־מָתַי יִהְיֶה זֶה לָנוּ לְמוֹקֵשׁ שַׁלַּח אֶת־הָאֲנָשִׁים וְיַעַבְדוּ אֶת־יְהֹוָה אֱלֹהֵיהֶם הֲטֶרֶם תֵּדַע כִּי אָבְדָה מִצְרָיִם:

8 So *Moshe* and *Aharon* were brought back to Pharaoh and he said to them, "Go, worship *Hashem* your God! Who are the ones to go?"

ח וַיּוּשַׁב אֶת־מֹשֶׁה וְאֶת־אַהֲרֹן אֶל־פַּרְעֹה וַיֹּאמֶר אֲלֵהֶם לְכוּ עִבְדוּ אֶת־יְהֹוָה אֱלֹהֵיכֶם מִי וָמִי הַהֹלְכִים:

9 *Moshe* replied, "We will all go, young and old: we will go with our sons and daughters, our flocks and herds; for we must observe *Hashem*'s festival."

ט וַיֹּאמֶר מֹשֶׁה בִּנְעָרֵינוּ וּבִזְקֵנֵינוּ נֵלֵךְ בְּבָנֵינוּ וּבִבְנוֹתֵנוּ בְּצֹאנֵנוּ וּבִבְקָרֵנוּ נֵלֵךְ כִּי חַג־יְהֹוָה לָנוּ:

10 But he said to them, "*Hashem* be with you the same as I mean to let your children go with you! Clearly, you are bent on mischief.

י וַיֹּאמֶר אֲלֵהֶם יְהִי כֵן יְהֹוָה עִמָּכֶם כַּאֲשֶׁר אֲשַׁלַּח אֶתְכֶם וְאֶת־טַפְּכֶם רְאוּ כִּי רָעָה נֶגֶד פְּנֵיכֶם:

11 No! You menfolk go and worship *Hashem*, since that is what you want." And they were expelled from Pharaoh's presence.

יא לֹא כֵן לְכוּ־נָא הַגְּבָרִים וְעִבְדוּ אֶת־יְהֹוָה כִּי אֹתָהּ אַתֶּם מְבַקְשִׁים וַיְגָרֶשׁ אֹתָם מֵאֵת פְּנֵי פַרְעֹה:

12 Then *Hashem* said to *Moshe*, "Hold out your arm over the land of Egypt for the locusts, that they may come upon the land of Egypt and eat up all the grasses in the land, whatever the hail has left."

יב וַיֹּאמֶר יְהֹוָה אֶל־מֹשֶׁה נְטֵה יָדְךָ עַל־אֶרֶץ מִצְרַיִם בָּאַרְבֶּה וְיַעַל עַל־אֶרֶץ מִצְרָיִם וְיֹאכַל אֶת־כָּל־עֵשֶׂב הָאָרֶץ אֵת כָּל־אֲשֶׁר הִשְׁאִיר הַבָּרָד:

13 So *Moshe* held out his rod over the land of Egypt, and *Hashem* drove an east wind over the land all that day and all night; and when morning came, the east wind had brought the locusts.

יג וַיֵּט מֹשֶׁה אֶת־מַטֵּהוּ עַל־אֶרֶץ מִצְרַיִם וַיהֹוָה נִהַג רוּחַ קָדִים בָּאָרֶץ כָּל־הַיּוֹם הַהוּא וְכָל־הַלָּיְלָה הַבֹּקֶר הָיָה וְרוּחַ הַקָּדִים נָשָׂא אֶת־הָאַרְבֶּה:

14 Locusts invaded all the land of Egypt and settled within all the territory of Egypt in a thick mass; never before had there been so many, nor will there ever be so many again.

יד וַיַּעַל הָאַרְבֶּה עַל כָּל־אֶרֶץ מִצְרַיִם וַיָּנַח בְּכֹל גְּבוּל מִצְרָיִם כָּבֵד מְאֹד לְפָנָיו לֹא־הָיָה כֵן אַרְבֶּה כָּמֹהוּ וְאַחֲרָיו לֹא יִהְיֶה־כֵּן:

Exodus

¹⁵ The locust hid all the land from view, and the land was darkened; and they ate up all the grasses of the field and all the fruit of the trees which the hail had left, so that nothing green was left, of tree or grass of the field, in all the land of Egypt.

טו וַיְכַס אֶת־עֵין כָּל־הָאָרֶץ וַתֶּחְשַׁךְ הָאָרֶץ וַיֹּאכַל אֶת־כָּל־עֵשֶׂב הָאָרֶץ וְאֵת כָּל־פְּרִי הָעֵץ אֲשֶׁר הוֹתִיר הַבָּרָד וְלֹא־נוֹתַר כָּל־יֶרֶק בָּעֵץ וּבְעֵשֶׂב הַשָּׂדֶה בְּכָל־אֶרֶץ מִצְרָיִם:

¹⁶ Pharaoh hurriedly summoned *Moshe* and *Aharon* and said, "I stand guilty before *Hashem* your God and before you.

טז וַיְמַהֵר פַּרְעֹה לִקְרֹא לְמֹשֶׁה וּלְאַהֲרֹן וַיֹּאמֶר חָטָאתִי לַיהוָה אֱלֹהֵיכֶם וְלָכֶם:

¹⁷ Forgive my offense just this once, and plead with *Hashem* your God that He but remove this death from me."

יז וְעַתָּה שָׂא נָא חַטָּאתִי אַךְ הַפַּעַם וְהַעְתִּירוּ לַיהוָה אֱלֹהֵיכֶם וְיָסֵר מֵעָלַי רַק אֶת־הַמָּוֶת הַזֶּה:

¹⁸ So he left Pharaoh's presence and pleaded with *Hashem*.

יח וַיֵּצֵא מֵעִם פַּרְעֹה וַיֶּעְתַּר אֶל־יְהוָה:

¹⁹ *Hashem* caused a shift to a very strong west wind, which lifted the locusts and hurled them into the Sea of Reeds; not a single locust remained in all the territory of Egypt.

יט וַיַּהֲפֹךְ יְהוָה רוּחַ־יָם חָזָק מְאֹד וַיִּשָּׂא אֶת־הָאַרְבֶּה וַיִּתְקָעֵהוּ יָמָּה סּוּף לֹא נִשְׁאַר אַרְבֶּה אֶחָד בְּכֹל גְּבוּל מִצְרָיִם:

²⁰ But *Hashem* stiffened Pharaoh's heart, and he would not let the Israelites go.

כ וַיְחַזֵּק יְהוָה אֶת־לֵב פַּרְעֹה וְלֹא שִׁלַּח אֶת־בְּנֵי יִשְׂרָאֵל:

²¹ Then *Hashem* said to *Moshe*, "Hold out your arm toward the sky that there may be darkness upon the land of Egypt, a darkness that can be touched."

כא וַיֹּאמֶר יְהוָה אֶל־מֹשֶׁה נְטֵה יָדְךָ עַל־הַשָּׁמַיִם וִיהִי חֹשֶׁךְ עַל־אֶרֶץ מִצְרָיִם וְיָמֵשׁ חֹשֶׁךְ:

²² *Moshe* held out his arm toward the sky and thick darkness descended upon all the land of Egypt for three days.

כב וַיֵּט מֹשֶׁה אֶת־יָדוֹ עַל־הַשָּׁמָיִם וַיְהִי חֹשֶׁךְ־אֲפֵלָה בְּכָל־אֶרֶץ מִצְרַיִם שְׁלֹשֶׁת יָמִים:

²³ People could not see one another, and for three days no one could get up from where he was; but all the Israelites enjoyed light in their dwellings.

כג לֹא־רָאוּ אִישׁ אֶת־אָחִיו וְלֹא־קָמוּ אִישׁ מִתַּחְתָּיו שְׁלֹשֶׁת יָמִים וּלְכָל־בְּנֵי יִשְׂרָאֵל הָיָה אוֹר בְּמוֹשְׁבֹתָם:

²⁴ Pharaoh then summoned *Moshe* and said, "Go, worship *Hashem*! Only your flocks and your herds shall be left behind; even your children may go with you."

כד וַיִּקְרָא פַרְעֹה אֶל־מֹשֶׁה וַיֹּאמֶר לְכוּ עִבְדוּ אֶת־יְהוָה רַק צֹאנְכֶם וּבְקַרְכֶם יֻצָּג גַּם־טַפְּכֶם יֵלֵךְ עִמָּכֶם:

²⁵ But *Moshe* said, "You yourself must provide us with sacrifices and burnt offerings to offer up to *Hashem* our God;

כה וַיֹּאמֶר מֹשֶׁה גַּם־אַתָּה תִּתֵּן בְּיָדֵנוּ זְבָחִים וְעֹלוֹת וְעָשִׂינוּ לַיהוָה אֱלֹהֵינוּ:

²⁶ our own livestock, too, shall go along with us – not a hoof shall remain behind: for we must select from it for the worship of *Hashem* our God; and we shall not know with what we are to worship *Hashem* until we arrive there."

כו וְגַם־מִקְנֵנוּ יֵלֵךְ עִמָּנוּ לֹא תִשָּׁאֵר פַּרְסָה כִּי מִמֶּנּוּ נִקַּח לַעֲבֹד אֶת־יְהוָה אֱלֹהֵינוּ וַאֲנַחְנוּ לֹא־נֵדַע מַה־נַּעֲבֹד אֶת־יְהוָה עַד־בֹּאֵנוּ שָׁמָּה:

²⁷ But *Hashem* stiffened Pharaoh's heart and he would not agree to let them go.

כז וַיְחַזֵּק יְהוָה אֶת־לֵב פַּרְעֹה וְלֹא אָבָה לְשַׁלְּחָם:

²⁸ Pharaoh said to him, "Be gone from me! Take care not to see me again, for the moment you look upon my face you shall die."

²⁹ And *Moshe* replied, "You have spoken rightly. I shall not see your face again!"

כח וַיֹּאמֶר־לוֹ פַרְעֹה לֵךְ מֵעָלָי הִשָּׁמֶר לְךָ אַל־תֹּסֶף רְאוֹת פָּנַי כִּי בְּיוֹם רְאֹתְךָ פָנַי תָּמוּת:

כט וַיֹּאמֶר מֹשֶׁה כֵּן דִּבַּרְתָּ לֹא־אֹסִף עוֹד רְאוֹת פָּנֶיךָ:

11 ¹ And *Hashem* said to *Moshe*, "I will bring but one more plague upon Pharaoh and upon Egypt; after that he shall let you go from here; indeed, when he lets you go, he will drive you out of here one and all.

² Tell the people to borrow, each man from his neighbor and each woman from hers, objects of silver and gold."

³ *Hashem* disposed the Egyptians favorably toward the people. Moreover, *Moshe* himself was much esteemed in the land of Egypt, among Pharaoh's courtiers and among the people.

יא א וַיֹּאמֶר יְהוָֹה אֶל־מֹשֶׁה עוֹד נֶגַע אֶחָד אָבִיא עַל־פַּרְעֹה וְעַל־מִצְרַיִם אַחֲרֵי־כֵן יְשַׁלַּח אֶתְכֶם מִזֶּה כְּשַׁלְּחוֹ כָּלָה גָּרֵשׁ יְגָרֵשׁ אֶתְכֶם מִזֶּה:

ב דַּבֶּר־נָא בְּאָזְנֵי הָעָם וְיִשְׁאֲלוּ אִישׁ מֵאֵת רֵעֵהוּ וְאִשָּׁה מֵאֵת רְעוּתָהּ כְּלֵי־כֶסֶף וּכְלֵי זָהָב:

ג וַיִּתֵּן יְהוָֹה אֶת־חֵן הָעָם בְּעֵינֵי מִצְרַיִם גַּם הָאִישׁ מֹשֶׁה גָּדוֹל מְאֹד בְּאֶרֶץ מִצְרַיִם בְּעֵינֵי עַבְדֵי־פַרְעֹה וּבְעֵינֵי הָעָם:

va-yi-TAYN a-do-NAI et KHAYN ha-AM b'-ay-NAY mitz-RA-yim
GAM ha-EESH mo-SHEH ga-DOL m'-OD b'-E-retz mitz-RA-yim
b'-ay-NAY av-DAY far-OH uv-ay-NAY ha-AM

⁴ *Moshe* said, "Thus says *Hashem*: Toward midnight I will go forth among the Egyptians,

⁵ and every first-born in the land of Egypt shall die, from the first-born of Pharaoh who sits on his throne to the first-born of the slave girl who is behind the millstones; and all the first-born of the cattle.

⁶ And there shall be a loud cry in all the land of Egypt, such as has never been or will ever be again;

⁷ but not a dog shall snarl at any of the Israelites, at man or beast – in order that you may know that *Hashem* makes a distinction between Egypt and *Yisrael*.

ד וַיֹּאמֶר מֹשֶׁה כֹּה אָמַר יְהוָֹה כַּחֲצֹת הַלַּיְלָה אֲנִי יוֹצֵא בְּתוֹךְ מִצְרָיִם:

ה וּמֵת כָּל־בְּכוֹר בְּאֶרֶץ מִצְרַיִם מִבְּכוֹר פַּרְעֹה הַיֹּשֵׁב עַל־כִּסְאוֹ עַד בְּכוֹר הַשִּׁפְחָה אֲשֶׁר אַחַר הָרֵחָיִם וְכֹל בְּכוֹר בְּהֵמָה:

ו וְהָיְתָה צְעָקָה גְדֹלָה בְּכָל־אֶרֶץ מִצְרָיִם אֲשֶׁר כָּמֹהוּ לֹא נִהְיָתָה וְכָמֹהוּ לֹא תֹסִף:

ז וּלְכֹל בְּנֵי יִשְׂרָאֵל לֹא יֶחֱרַץ־כֶּלֶב לְשֹׁנוֹ לְמֵאִישׁ וְעַד־בְּהֵמָה לְמַעַן תֵּדְעוּן אֲשֶׁר יַפְלֶה יְהוָֹה בֵּין מִצְרַיִם וּבֵין יִשְׂרָאֵל:

11:3 *Hashem* **disposed the Egyptians favorably toward the people** What transpires at this time that causes the Egyptians to finally find value in the Jewish nation and *Moshe*? Rabbi Samson Raphael Hirsch posits that after the plague of darkness, when the Egyptians were able to see again, they finally acknowledge the morality of the people they have cruelly enslaved. For three days, Egypt was blind and immobilized; the Jews could have easily taken advantage of this situation. Yet, when the light returns at the conclusion of the plague, the Egyptians discover that nothing has been moved from its rightful place. At this juncture, the Egyptians stand in awe of the Jewish people and *Moshe*, their leader. The Jewish mission is to be a light unto the nations, an example of honesty, morality and closeness to *Hashem*. When the People of Israel live up to this mission, the world is in awe.

Ashalim solar power station in the Negev

Exodus

8 Then all these courtiers of yours shall come down to me and bow low to me, saying, 'Depart, you and all the people who follow you!' After that I will depart." And he left Pharaoh's presence in hot anger.

ח וְיָרְד֣וּ כָל־עֲבָדֶ֩יךָ֩ אֵ֨לֶּה אֵלַ֜י וְהִשְׁתַּֽחֲווּ־לִ֣י לֵאמֹ֗ר צֵ֤א אַתָּה֙ וְכָל־הָעָ֣ם אֲשֶׁר־בְּרַגְלֶ֔יךָ וְאַֽחֲרֵי־כֵ֖ן אֵצֵ֑א וַיֵּצֵ֥א מֵֽעִם־פַּרְעֹ֖ה בָּֽחֳרִי־אָֽף:

9 Now *Hashem* had said to *Moshe*, "Pharaoh will not heed you, in order that My marvels may be multiplied in the land of Egypt."

ט וַיֹּ֤אמֶר יְהֹוָה֙ אֶל־מֹשֶׁ֔ה לֹֽא־יִשְׁמַ֥ע אֲלֵיכֶ֖ם פַּרְעֹ֑ה לְמַ֛עַן רְב֥וֹת מֽוֹפְתַ֖י בְּאֶ֥רֶץ מִצְרָֽיִם:

10 *Moshe* and *Aharon* had performed all these marvels before Pharaoh, but *Hashem* had stiffened the heart of Pharaoh so that he would not let the Israelites go from his land.

י וּמֹשֶׁ֣ה וְאַֽהֲרֹ֗ן עָשׂ֛וּ אֶת־כָּל־הַמֹּֽפְתִ֥ים הָאֵ֖לֶּה לִפְנֵ֣י פַרְעֹ֑ה וַיְחַזֵּ֤ק יְהֹוָה֙ אֶת־לֵ֣ב פַּרְעֹ֔ה וְלֹֽא־שִׁלַּ֥ח אֶת־בְּנֵֽי־יִשְׂרָאֵ֖ל מֵֽאַרְצֽוֹ:

12 1 *Hashem* said to *Moshe* and *Aharon* in the land of Egypt:

יב א וַיֹּ֤אמֶר יְהֹוָה֙ אֶל־מֹשֶׁ֣ה וְאֶֽל־אַֽהֲרֹ֔ן בְּאֶ֥רֶץ מִצְרַ֖יִם לֵאמֹֽר:

2 This month shall mark for you the beginning of the months; it shall be the first of the months of the year for you.

ב הַחֹ֧דֶשׁ הַזֶּ֛ה לָכֶ֖ם רֹ֣אשׁ חֳדָשִׁ֑ים רִאשׁ֥וֹן הוּא֙ לָכֶ֔ם לְחָדְשֵׁ֖י הַשָּׁנָֽה:

*ha-KHO-desh ha-ZEH la-KHEM ROSH kho-da-SHEEM
ri-SHON HU la-KHEM l'-khod-SHAY ha-sha-NAH*

3 Speak to the whole community of *Yisrael* and say that on the tenth of this month each of them shall take a lamb to a family, a lamb to a household.

ג דַּבְּר֗וּ אֶל־כָּל־עֲדַ֤ת יִשְׂרָאֵל֙ לֵאמֹ֔ר בֶּֽעָשֹׂ֖ר לַחֹ֣דֶשׁ הַזֶּ֑ה וְיִקְח֣וּ לָהֶ֗ם אִ֛ישׁ שֶׂ֥ה לְבֵֽית־אָבֹ֖ת שֶׂ֥ה לַבָּֽיִת:

4 But if the household is too small for a lamb, let him share one with a neighbor who dwells nearby, in proportion to the number of persons: you shall contribute for the lamb according to what each household will eat.

ד וְאִם־יִמְעַ֣ט הַבַּ֘יִת֮ מִֽהְיֹ֣ת מִשֶּׂה֒ וְלָקַ֣ח ה֗וּא וּשְׁכֵנ֛וֹ הַקָּרֹ֥ב אֶל־בֵּית֖וֹ בְּמִכְסַ֣ת נְפָשֹׁ֑ת אִ֚ישׁ לְפִ֣י אָכְל֔וֹ תָּכֹ֖סּוּ עַל־הַשֶּֽׂה:

5 Your lamb shall be without blemish, a yearling male; you may take it from the sheep or from the goats.

ה שֶׂ֥ה תָמִ֛ים זָכָ֥ר בֶּן־שָׁנָ֖ה יִֽהְיֶ֣ה לָכֶ֑ם מִן־הַכְּבָשִׂ֥ים וּמִן־הָֽעִזִּ֖ים תִּקָּֽחוּ:

6 You shall keep watch over it until the fourteenth day of this month; and all the assembled congregation of the Israelites shall slaughter it at twilight.

ו וְהָיָ֤ה לָכֶם֙ לְמִשְׁמֶ֔רֶת עַ֣ד אַרְבָּעָ֥ה עָשָׂ֖ר י֣וֹם לַחֹ֣דֶשׁ הַזֶּ֑ה וְשָֽׁחֲט֣וּ אֹת֗וֹ כֹּ֛ל קְהַ֥ל עֲדַֽת־יִשְׂרָאֵ֖ל בֵּ֥ין הָֽעַרְבָּֽיִם:

New moon over *Be'er Sheva*

12:2 The beginning of the months *Rosh Chodesh* (ראש חודש), literally 'head of the month,' is celebrated when the first sliver of the new moon appears. In this verse, *Hashem* declares that the Hebrew month of *Nisan* is to be considered the first month in the Jewish calendar. It was in the month of *Nisan* that the Children of Israel were redeemed from Egypt and became a nation, and therefore God refers to this month as "the beginning of the months." Even though the Jewish year begins with the Hebrew month of *Tishrei* (when *Rosh Hashana* is celebrated), the months are numbered starting with the month of redemption. According to the Sages, just as Israel was originally redeemed during *Nisan*, so too, *Nisan* will also be the month in which our final redemption occurs.

7 They shall take some of the blood and put it on the two doorposts and the lintel of the houses in which they are to eat it.

וְלָקְחוּ מִן־הַדָּם וְנָתְנוּ עַל־שְׁתֵּי הַמְּזוּזֹת וְעַל־הַמַּשְׁקוֹף עַל הַבָּתִּים אֲשֶׁר־יֹאכְלוּ אֹתוֹ בָּהֶם:

8 They shall eat the flesh that same night; they shall eat it roasted over the fire, with unleavened bread and with bitter herbs.

וְאָכְלוּ אֶת־הַבָּשָׂר בַּלַּיְלָה הַזֶּה צְלִי־אֵשׁ וּמַצּוֹת עַל־מְרֹרִים יֹאכְלֻהוּ:

9 Do not eat any of it raw, or cooked in any way with water, but roasted – head, legs, and entrails – over the fire.

אַל־תֹּאכְלוּ מִמֶּנּוּ נָא וּבָשֵׁל מְבֻשָּׁל בַּמָּיִם כִּי אִם־צְלִי־אֵשׁ רֹאשׁוֹ עַל־כְּרָעָיו וְעַל־קִרְבּוֹ:

10 You shall not leave any of it over until morning; if any of it is left until morning, you shall burn it.

וְלֹא־תוֹתִירוּ מִמֶּנּוּ עַד־בֹּקֶר וְהַנֹּתָר מִמֶּנּוּ עַד־בֹּקֶר בָּאֵשׁ תִּשְׂרֹפוּ:

11 This is how you shall eat it: your loins girded, your sandals on your feet, and your staff in your hand; and you shall eat it hurriedly: it is a *Pesach* offering to *Hashem*.

וְכָכָה תֹּאכְלוּ אֹתוֹ מָתְנֵיכֶם חֲגֻרִים נַעֲלֵיכֶם בְּרַגְלֵיכֶם וּמַקֶּלְכֶם בְּיֶדְכֶם וַאֲכַלְתֶּם אֹתוֹ בְּחִפָּזוֹן פֶּסַח הוּא לַיהוָה:

12 For that night I will go through the land of Egypt and strike down every first-born in the land of Egypt, both man and beast; and I will mete out punishments to all the gods of Egypt, I *Hashem*.

וְעָבַרְתִּי בְאֶרֶץ־מִצְרַיִם בַּלַּיְלָה הַזֶּה וְהִכֵּיתִי כָל־בְּכוֹר בְּאֶרֶץ מִצְרַיִם מֵאָדָם וְעַד־בְּהֵמָה וּבְכָל־אֱלֹהֵי מִצְרַיִם אֶעֱשֶׂה שְׁפָטִים אֲנִי יְהוָה:

13 And the blood on the houses where you are staying shall be a sign for you: when I see the blood I will pass over you, so that no plague will destroy you when I strike the land of Egypt.

וְהָיָה הַדָּם לָכֶם לְאֹת עַל הַבָּתִּים אֲשֶׁר אַתֶּם שָׁם וְרָאִיתִי אֶת־הַדָּם וּפָסַחְתִּי עֲלֵכֶם וְלֹא־יִהְיֶה בָכֶם נֶגֶף לְמַשְׁחִית בְּהַכֹּתִי בְּאֶרֶץ מִצְרָיִם:

14 This day shall be to you one of remembrance: you shall celebrate it as a festival to *Hashem* throughout the ages; you shall celebrate it as an institution for all time.

וְהָיָה הַיּוֹם הַזֶּה לָכֶם לְזִכָּרוֹן וְחַגֹּתֶם אֹתוֹ חַג לַיהוָה לְדֹרֹתֵיכֶם חֻקַּת עוֹלָם תְּחָגֻּהוּ:

15 Seven days you shall eat unleavened bread; on the very first day you shall remove leaven from your houses, for whoever eats leavened bread from the first day to the seventh day, that person shall be cut off from *Yisrael*.

שִׁבְעַת יָמִים מַצּוֹת תֹּאכֵלוּ אַךְ בַּיּוֹם הָרִאשׁוֹן תַּשְׁבִּיתוּ שְּׂאֹר מִבָּתֵּיכֶם כִּי כָּל־אֹכֵל חָמֵץ וְנִכְרְתָה הַנֶּפֶשׁ הַהִוא מִיִּשְׂרָאֵל מִיּוֹם הָרִאשֹׁן עַד־יוֹם הַשְּׁבִעִי:

16 You shall celebrate a sacred occasion on the first day, and a sacred occasion on the seventh day; no work at all shall be done on them; only what every person is to eat, that alone may be prepared for you.

וּבַיּוֹם הָרִאשׁוֹן מִקְרָא־קֹדֶשׁ וּבַיּוֹם הַשְּׁבִיעִי מִקְרָא־קֹדֶשׁ יִהְיֶה לָכֶם כָּל־מְלָאכָה לֹא־יֵעָשֶׂה בָהֶם אַךְ אֲשֶׁר יֵאָכֵל לְכָל־נֶפֶשׁ הוּא לְבַדּוֹ יֵעָשֶׂה לָכֶם:

17 You shall observe the [Feast of] Unleavened Bread, for on this very day I brought your ranks out of the land of Egypt; you shall observe this day throughout the ages as an institution for all time.

וּשְׁמַרְתֶּם אֶת־הַמַּצּוֹת כִּי בְּעֶצֶם הַיּוֹם הַזֶּה הוֹצֵאתִי אֶת־צִבְאוֹתֵיכֶם מֵאֶרֶץ מִצְרָיִם וּשְׁמַרְתֶּם אֶת־הַיּוֹם הַזֶּה לְדֹרֹתֵיכֶם חֻקַּת עוֹלָם:

שמות יב

בא

18 In the first month, from the fourteenth day of the month at evening, you shall eat unleavened bread until the twenty-first day of the month at evening.

יח בָּרִאשֹׁן בְּאַרְבָּעָה עָשָׂר יוֹם לַחֹדֶשׁ בָּעֶרֶב תֹּאכְלוּ מַצֹּת עַד יוֹם הָאֶחָד וְעֶשְׂרִים לַחֹדֶשׁ בָּעָרֶב:

19 No leaven shall be found in your houses for seven days. For whoever eats what is leavened, that person shall be cut off from the community of *Yisrael,* whether he is a stranger or a citizen of the country.

יט שִׁבְעַת יָמִים שְׂאֹר לֹא יִמָּצֵא בְּבָתֵּיכֶם כִּי כָּל־אֹכֵל מַחְמֶצֶת וְנִכְרְתָה הַנֶּפֶשׁ הַהִוא מֵעֲדַת יִשְׂרָאֵל בַּגֵּר וּבְאֶזְרַח הָאָרֶץ:

20 You shall eat nothing leavened; in all your settlements you shall eat unleavened bread.

כ כָּל־מַחְמֶצֶת לֹא תֹאכֵלוּ בְּכֹל מוֹשְׁבֹתֵיכֶם תֹּאכְלוּ מַצּוֹת:

21 *Moshe* then summoned all the elders of *Yisrael* and said to them, "Go, pick out lambs for your families, and slaughter the *Pesach* offering.

כא וַיִּקְרָא מֹשֶׁה לְכָל־זִקְנֵי יִשְׂרָאֵל וַיֹּאמֶר אֲלֵהֶם מִשְׁכוּ וּקְחוּ לָכֶם צֹאן לְמִשְׁפְּחֹתֵיכֶם וְשַׁחֲטוּ הַפָּסַח:

22 Take a bunch of hyssop, dip it in the blood that is in the basin, and apply some of the blood that is in the basin to the lintel and to the two doorposts. None of you shall go outside the door of his house until morning.

כב וּלְקַחְתֶּם אֲגֻדַּת אֵזוֹב וּטְבַלְתֶּם בַּדָּם אֲשֶׁר־בַּסַּף וְהִגַּעְתֶּם אֶל־הַמַּשְׁקוֹף וְאֶל־שְׁתֵּי הַמְּזוּזֹת מִן־הַדָּם אֲשֶׁר בַּסָּף וְאַתֶּם לֹא תֵצְאוּ אִישׁ מִפֶּתַח־בֵּיתוֹ עַד־בֹּקֶר:

23 For when *Hashem* goes through to smite the Egyptians, He will see the blood on the lintel and the two doorposts, and *Hashem* will pass over the door and not let the Destroyer enter and smite your home.

כג וְעָבַר יְהֹוָה לִנְגֹּף אֶת־מִצְרַיִם וְרָאָה אֶת־הַדָּם עַל־הַמַּשְׁקוֹף וְעַל שְׁתֵּי הַמְּזוּזֹת וּפָסַח יְהֹוָה עַל־הַפֶּתַח וְלֹא יִתֵּן הַמַּשְׁחִית לָבֹא אֶל־בָּתֵּיכֶם לִנְגֹּף:

24 "You shall observe this as an institution for all time, for you and for your descendants.

כד וּשְׁמַרְתֶּם אֶת־הַדָּבָר הַזֶּה לְחָק־לְךָ וּלְבָנֶיךָ עַד־עוֹלָם:

25 And when you enter the land that *Hashem* will give you, as He has promised, you shall observe this rite.

כה וְהָיָה כִּי־תָבֹאוּ אֶל־הָאָרֶץ אֲשֶׁר יִתֵּן יְהֹוָה לָכֶם כַּאֲשֶׁר דִּבֵּר וּשְׁמַרְתֶּם אֶת־הָעֲבֹדָה הַזֹּאת:

26 And when your children ask you, 'What do you mean by this rite?'

כו וְהָיָה כִּי־יֹאמְרוּ אֲלֵיכֶם בְּנֵיכֶם מָה הָעֲבֹדָה הַזֹּאת לָכֶם:

27 you shall say, 'It is the *Pesach* sacrifice to *Hashem,* because He passed over the houses of the Israelites in Egypt when He smote the Egyptians, but saved our houses.'" The people then bowed low in homage.

כז וַאֲמַרְתֶּם זֶבַח־פֶּסַח הוּא לַיהֹוָה אֲשֶׁר פָּסַח עַל־בָּתֵּי בְנֵי־יִשְׂרָאֵל בְּמִצְרַיִם בְּנָגְפּוֹ אֶת־מִצְרַיִם וְאֶת־בָּתֵּינוּ הִצִּיל וַיִּקֹּד הָעָם וַיִּשְׁתַּחֲווּ:

28 And the Israelites went and did so; just as *Hashem* had commanded *Moshe* and *Aharon,* so they did.

כח וַיֵּלְכוּ וַיַּעֲשׂוּ בְּנֵי יִשְׂרָאֵל כַּאֲשֶׁר צִוָּה יְהֹוָה אֶת־מֹשֶׁה וְאַהֲרֹן כֵּן עָשׂוּ:

29 In the middle of the night *Hashem* struck down all the first-born in the land of Egypt, from the first-born of Pharaoh who sat on the throne to the first-born of the captive who was in the dungeon, and all the first-born of the cattle.

כט וַיְהִי בַּחֲצִי הַלַּיְלָה וַיהֹוָה הִכָּה כָל־בְּכוֹר בְּאֶרֶץ מִצְרַיִם מִבְּכֹר פַּרְעֹה הַיֹּשֵׁב עַל־כִּסְאוֹ עַד בְּכוֹר הַשְּׁבִי אֲשֶׁר בְּבֵית הַבּוֹר וְכֹל בְּכוֹר בְּהֵמָה:

30 And Pharaoh arose in the night, with all his courtiers and all the Egyptians – because there was a loud cry in Egypt; for there was no house where there was not someone dead.

לֹ וַיָּ֨קָם פַּרְעֹ֜ה לַ֗יְלָה ה֤וּא וְכָל־עֲבָדָיו֙ וְכָל־מִצְרַ֔יִם וַתְּהִ֛י צְעָקָ֥ה גְדֹלָ֖ה בְּמִצְרָ֑יִם כִּי־אֵ֣ין בַּ֔יִת אֲשֶׁ֥ר אֵֽין־שָׁ֖ם מֵֽת׃

31 He summoned *Moshe* and *Aharon* in the night and said, "Up, depart from among my people, you and the Israelites with you! Go, worship *Hashem* as you said!

לֹא וַיִּקְרָא֩ לְמֹשֶׁ֨ה וּֽלְאַהֲרֹ֜ן לַ֗יְלָה וַיֹּ֙אמֶר֙ ק֤וּמוּ צְּאוּ֙ מִתּ֣וֹךְ עַמִּ֔י גַּם־אַתֶּ֖ם גַּם־בְּנֵ֣י יִשְׂרָאֵ֑ל וּלְכ֛וּ עִבְד֥וּ אֶת־יְהֹוָ֖ה כְּדַבֶּרְכֶֽם׃

32 Take also your flocks and your herds, as you said, and begone! And may you bring a blessing upon me also!"

לֹב גַּם־צֹֽאנְכֶ֨ם גַּם־בְּקַרְכֶ֥ם קְח֛וּ כַּאֲשֶׁ֥ר דִּבַּרְתֶּ֖ם וָלֵ֑כוּ וּבֵֽרַכְתֶּ֖ם גַּם־אֹתִֽי׃

33 The Egyptians urged the people on, impatient to have them leave the country, for they said, "We shall all be dead."

לֹג וַתֶּחֱזַ֤ק מִצְרַ֙יִם֙ עַל־הָעָ֔ם לְמַהֵ֖ר לְשַׁלְּחָ֣ם מִן־הָאָ֑רֶץ כִּ֥י אָמְר֖וּ כֻּלָּ֥נוּ מֵתִֽים׃

34 So the people took their dough before it was leavened, their kneading bowls wrapped in their cloaks upon their shoulders.

לֹד וַיִּשָּׂ֥א הָעָ֛ם אֶת־בְּצֵק֖וֹ טֶ֣רֶם יֶחְמָ֑ץ מִשְׁאֲרֹתָ֛ם צְרֻרֹ֥ת בְּשִׂמְלֹתָ֖ם עַל־שִׁכְמָֽם׃

35 The Israelites had done *Moshe's* bidding and borrowed from the Egyptians objects of silver and gold, and clothing.

לֹה וּבְנֵֽי־יִשְׂרָאֵ֥ל עָשׂ֖וּ כִּדְבַ֣ר מֹשֶׁ֑ה וַֽיִּשְׁאֲלוּ֙ מִמִּצְרַ֔יִם כְּלֵי־כֶ֥סֶף וּכְלֵ֥י זָהָ֖ב וּשְׂמָלֹֽת׃

36 And *Hashem* had disposed the Egyptians favorably toward the people, and they let them have their request; thus they stripped the Egyptians.

לֹו וַֽיהֹוָ֞ה נָתַ֨ן אֶת־חֵ֥ן הָעָ֛ם בְּעֵינֵ֥י מִצְרַ֖יִם וַיַּשְׁאִל֑וּם וַֽיְנַצְּל֖וּ אֶת־מִצְרָֽיִם׃

37 The Israelites journeyed from Raamses to Succoth, about six hundred thousand men on foot, aside from children.

לֹז וַיִּסְע֧וּ בְנֵֽי־יִשְׂרָאֵ֛ל מֵֽרַעְמְסֵ֖ס סֻכֹּ֑תָה כְּשֵׁשׁ־מֵא֨וֹת אֶ֤לֶף רַגְלִי֙ הַגְּבָרִ֔ים לְבַ֖ד מִטָּֽף׃

38 Moreover, a mixed multitude went up with them, and very much livestock, both flocks and herds.

לֹח וְגַם־עֵ֥רֶב רַ֖ב עָלָ֣ה אִתָּ֑ם וְצֹ֣אן וּבָקָ֔ר מִקְנֶ֖ה כָּבֵ֥ד מְאֹֽד׃

39 And they baked unleavened cakes of the dough that they had taken out of Egypt, for it was not leavened, since they had been driven out of Egypt and could not delay; nor had they prepared any provisions for themselves.

לֹט וַיֹּאפ֨וּ אֶת־הַבָּצֵ֜ק אֲשֶׁ֨ר הוֹצִ֧יאוּ מִמִּצְרַ֛יִם עֻגֹ֥ת מַצּ֖וֹת כִּ֣י לֹ֣א חָמֵ֑ץ כִּֽי־גֹרְשׁ֣וּ מִמִּצְרַ֗יִם וְלֹ֤א יָֽכְלוּ֙ לְהִתְמַהְמֵ֔הַּ וְגַם־צֵדָ֖ה לֹא־עָשׂ֥וּ לָהֶֽם׃

40 The length of time that the Israelites lived in Egypt was four hundred and thirty years;

מ וּמוֹשַׁב֙ בְּנֵ֣י יִשְׂרָאֵ֔ל אֲשֶׁ֥ר יָשְׁב֖וּ בְּמִצְרָ֑יִם שְׁלֹשִׁ֣ים שָׁנָ֔ה וְאַרְבַּ֥ע מֵא֖וֹת שָׁנָֽה׃

41 at the end of the four hundred and thirtieth year, to the very day, all the ranks of *Hashem* departed from the land of Egypt.

מא וַיְהִ֗י מִקֵּץ֙ שְׁלֹשִׁ֣ים שָׁנָ֔ה וְאַרְבַּ֥ע מֵא֖וֹת שָׁנָ֑ה וַיְהִ֗י בְּעֶ֙צֶם֙ הַיּ֣וֹם הַזֶּ֔ה יָֽצְא֛וּ כָּל־צִבְא֥וֹת יְהֹוָ֖ה מֵאֶ֥רֶץ מִצְרָֽיִם׃

42 That was for *Hashem* a night of vigil to bring them out of the land of Egypt; that same night is *Hashem's*, one of vigil for all the children of *Yisrael* throughout the ages.

מב לֵ֣יל שִׁמֻּרִ֥ים הוּא֙ לַֽיהֹוָ֔ה לְהוֹצִיאָ֖ם מֵאֶ֣רֶץ מִצְרָ֑יִם הֽוּא־הַלַּ֤יְלָה הַזֶּה֙ לַֽיהֹוָ֔ה שִׁמֻּרִ֛ים לְכָל־בְּנֵ֥י יִשְׂרָאֵ֖ל לְדֹרֹתָֽם׃

43 *Hashem* said to *Moshe* and *Aharon*: This is the law of the *Pesach* offering: No foreigner shall eat of it.

מג וַיֹּאמֶר יְהוָה אֶל־מֹשֶׁה וְאַהֲרֹן זֹאת חֻקַּת הַפָּסַח כָּל־בֶּן־נֵכָר לֹא־יֹאכַל בּוֹ:

44 But any slave a man has bought may eat of it once he has been circumcised.

מד וְכָל־עֶבֶד אִישׁ מִקְנַת־כָּסֶף וּמַלְתָּה אֹתוֹ אָז יֹאכַל בּוֹ:

45 No bound or hired laborer shall eat of it.

מה תּוֹשָׁב וְשָׂכִיר לֹא־יֹאכַל־בּוֹ:

46 It shall be eaten in one house: you shall not take any of the flesh outside the house; nor shall you break a bone of it.

מו בְּבַיִת אֶחָד יֵאָכֵל לֹא־תוֹצִיא מִן־הַבַּיִת מִן־הַבָּשָׂר חוּצָה וְעֶצֶם לֹא תִשְׁבְּרוּ־בוֹ:

47 The whole community of *Yisrael* shall offer it.

מז כָּל־עֲדַת יִשְׂרָאֵל יַעֲשׂוּ אֹתוֹ:

48 If a stranger who dwells with you would offer the *Pesach* to *Hashem*, all his males must be circumcised; then he shall be admitted to offer it; he shall then be as a citizen of the country. But no uncircumcised person may eat of it.

מח וְכִי־יָגוּר אִתְּךָ גֵּר וְעָשָׂה פֶסַח לַיהוָה הִמּוֹל לוֹ כָל־זָכָר וְאָז יִקְרַב לַעֲשֹׂתוֹ וְהָיָה כְּאֶזְרַח הָאָרֶץ וְכָל־עָרֵל לֹא־יֹאכַל בּוֹ:

49 There shall be one law for the citizen and for the stranger who dwells among you.

מט תּוֹרָה אַחַת יִהְיֶה לָאֶזְרָח וְלַגֵּר הַגָּר בְּתוֹכְכֶם:

50 And all the Israelites did so; as *Hashem* had commanded *Moshe* and *Aharon*, so they did.

נ וַיַּעֲשׂוּ כָּל־בְּנֵי יִשְׂרָאֵל כַּאֲשֶׁר צִוָּה יְהוָה אֶת־מֹשֶׁה וְאֶת־אַהֲרֹן כֵּן עָשׂוּ:

51 That very day *Hashem* freed the Israelites from the land of Egypt, troop by troop.

נא וַיְהִי בְּעֶצֶם הַיּוֹם הַזֶּה הוֹצִיא יְהוָה אֶת־בְּנֵי יִשְׂרָאֵל מֵאֶרֶץ מִצְרַיִם עַל־צִבְאֹתָם:

13 **1** *Hashem* spoke further to *Moshe*, saying,

יג א וַיְדַבֵּר יְהוָה אֶל־מֹשֶׁה לֵּאמֹר:

2 "Consecrate to Me every first-born; man and beast, the first issue of every womb among the Israelites is Mine."

ב קַדֶּשׁ־לִי כָל־בְּכוֹר פֶּטֶר כָּל־רֶחֶם בִּבְנֵי יִשְׂרָאֵל בָּאָדָם וּבַבְּהֵמָה לִי הוּא:

3 And *Moshe* said to the people, "Remember this day, on which you went free from Egypt, the house of bondage, how *Hashem* freed you from it with a mighty hand: no leavened bread shall be eaten.

ג וַיֹּאמֶר מֹשֶׁה אֶל־הָעָם זָכוֹר אֶת־הַיּוֹם הַזֶּה אֲשֶׁר יְצָאתֶם מִמִּצְרַיִם מִבֵּית עֲבָדִים כִּי בְּחֹזֶק יָד הוֹצִיא יְהוָה אֶתְכֶם מִזֶּה וְלֹא יֵאָכֵל חָמֵץ:

4 You go free on this day, in the month of Abib.

ד הַיּוֹם אַתֶּם יֹצְאִים בְּחֹדֶשׁ הָאָבִיב:

ha-YOM a-TEM yo-tz'-EEM b'-KHO-desh ha-a-VEEV

אביב

13:4 In the month of Abib 'Abib' in Hebrew is *Aviv* (אביב), meaning 'springtime.' The *Torah* has already stated that the redemption from Egypt took place in the first month, the month of *Nisan*, which is in the springtime. Why is it necessary to state explicitly that in happened in the month of *Aviv*? Emphasizing that the redemption took place in the spring highlights *Hashem's* love and compassion for His children. He made sure to free the Israelites and set them on their journey through the desert when the weather was most pleasant; not too hot, too cold or too rainy. Furthermore, as springtime symbolizes the rebirth of the land, there was no better time to experience the rebirth of the nation than the spring.

Spring flowers in the Negev

⁵ So, when *Hashem* has brought you into the land of the Canaanites, the Hittites, the Amorites, the Hivites, and the Jebusites, which He swore to your fathers to give you, a land flowing with milk and honey, you shall observe in this month the following practice:

ה וְהָיָה כִי־יְבִיאֲךָ יְהֹוָה אֶל־אֶרֶץ הַכְּנַעֲנִי וְהַחִתִּי וְהָאֱמֹרִי וְהַחִוִּי וְהַיְבוּסִי אֲשֶׁר נִשְׁבַּע לַאֲבֹתֶיךָ לָתֶת לָךְ אֶרֶץ זָבַת חָלָב וּדְבָשׁ וְעָבַדְתָּ אֶת־הָעֲבֹדָה הַזֹּאת בַּחֹדֶשׁ הַזֶּה:

v'-ha-YA ki y'-vee-ah-KHA el eh-RETZ ha-k'-na-a'-nee v'-ha-khi-TEE v'-ha-eh-mo-REE v'-ha-khee-VEE v'-ha-y'-vu-SEE a-SHER nish-BA la-a-vo-te-KHA la-TAYT lakh eh-RETZ za-VAT kha-LAV u-d'-VASH v'-a-va-d'-TA et ha-a-vo-DA ha-ZOHT ba-kho-DESH ha-ZE

⁶ "Seven days you shall eat unleavened bread, and on the seventh day there shall be a festival of *Hashem*.

ו שִׁבְעַת יָמִים תֹּאכַל מַצֹּת וּבַיּוֹם הַשְּׁבִיעִי חַג לַיהֹוָה:

⁷ Throughout the seven days unleavened bread shall be eaten; no leavened bread shall be found with you, and no leaven shall be found in all your territory.

ז מַצּוֹת יֵאָכֵל אֵת שִׁבְעַת הַיָּמִים וְלֹא־יֵרָאֶה לְךָ חָמֵץ וְלֹא־יֵרָאֶה לְךָ שְׂאֹר בְּכָל־גְּבֻלֶךָ:

⁸ And you shall explain to your son on that day, 'It is because of what *Hashem* did for me when I went free from Egypt.'

ח וְהִגַּדְתָּ לְבִנְךָ בַּיּוֹם הַהוּא לֵאמֹר בַּעֲבוּר זֶה עָשָׂה יְהֹוָה לִי בְּצֵאתִי מִמִּצְרָיִם:

⁹ "And this shall serve you as a sign on your hand and as a reminder on your forehead – in order that the Teaching of *Hashem* may be in your mouth – that with a mighty hand *Hashem* freed you from Egypt.

ט וְהָיָה לְךָ לְאוֹת עַל־יָדְךָ וּלְזִכָּרוֹן בֵּין עֵינֶיךָ לְמַעַן תִּהְיֶה תּוֹרַת יְהֹוָה בְּפִיךָ כִּי בְּיָד חֲזָקָה הוֹצִאֲךָ יְהֹוָה מִמִּצְרָיִם:

¹⁰ You shall keep this institution at its set time from year to year.

י וְשָׁמַרְתָּ אֶת־הַחֻקָּה הַזֹּאת לְמוֹעֲדָהּ מִיָּמִים יָמִימָה:

¹¹ "And when *Hashem* has brought you into the land of the Canaanites, as He swore to you and to your fathers, and has given it to you,

יא וְהָיָה כִי־יְבִאֲךָ יְהֹוָה אֶל־אֶרֶץ הַכְּנַעֲנִי כַּאֲשֶׁר נִשְׁבַּע לְךָ וְלַאֲבֹתֶיךָ וּנְתָנָהּ לָךְ:

¹² you shall set apart for *Hashem* every first issue of the womb: every male firstling that your cattle drop shall be *Hashem*'s.

יב וְהַעֲבַרְתָּ כָל־פֶּטֶר־רֶחֶם לַיהֹוָה וְכָל־פֶּטֶר שֶׁגֶר בְּהֵמָה אֲשֶׁר יִהְיֶה לְךָ הַזְּכָרִים לַיהֹוָה:

¹³ But every firstling ass you shall redeem with a sheep; if you do not redeem it, you must break its neck. And you must redeem every first-born male among your children.

יג וְכָל־פֶּטֶר חֲמֹר תִּפְדֶּה בְשֶׂה וְאִם־לֹא תִפְדֶּה וַעֲרַפְתּוֹ וְכֹל בְּכוֹר אָדָם בְּבָנֶיךָ תִּפְדֶּה:

13:5 A land flowing with milk and honey *Eretz Yisrael* is described many times throughout the Bible as a land flowing with milk and honey. *Rashi* explains this expression quite literally: Milk flows from the goats, and honey comes from the dates and figs that Israel is known for. *Ramban* adds that the word "flowing" is used, which indicates exceptional fertility and abundance. On a metaphorical level, the *Midrash* explains that milk is a nutritional necessity whereas honey is a savory delicacy. *Hashem* promises that the Land of Israel will provide not only the essential things needed to survive, but also sweet luxuries.

Ripe dates in northern Israel

14 And when, in time to come, your son asks you, saying, 'What does this mean?' you shall say to him, 'It was with a mighty hand that *Hashem* brought us out from Egypt, the house of bondage.

15 When Pharaoh stubbornly refused to let us go, *Hashem* slew every first-born in the land of Egypt, the first-born of both man and beast. Therefore I sacrifice to *Hashem* every first male issue of the womb, but redeem every first-born among my sons.'

16 "And so it shall be as a sign upon your hand and as a symbol on your forehead that with a mighty hand *Hashem* freed us from Egypt."

17 Now when Pharaoh let the people go, *Hashem* did not lead them by way of the land of the Phillistines, although it was nearer; for *Hashem* said, "The people may have a change of heart when they see war, and return to Egypt."

18 So *Hashem* led the people roundabout, by way of the wilderness at the Sea of Reeds. Now the Israelites went up armed out of the land of Egypt.

19 And *Moshe* took with him the bones of *Yosef*, who had exacted an oath from the children of *Yisrael*, saying, "*Hashem* will be sure to take notice of you: then you shall carry up my bones from here with you."

20 They set out from Succoth, and encamped at Etham, at the edge of the wilderness.

21 *Hashem* went before them in a pillar of cloud by day, to guide them along the way, and in a pillar of fire by night, to give them light, that they might travel day and night.

22 The pillar of cloud by day and the pillar of fire by night did not depart from before the people.

14 1 *Hashem* said to *Moshe*:

2 Tell the Israelites to turn back and encamp before Pi-hahiroth, between Migdol and the sea, before Baal-zephon; you shall encamp facing it, by the sea.

3 Pharaoh will say of the Israelites, "They are astray in the land; the wilderness has closed in on them."

4 Then I will stiffen Pharaoh's heart and he will pursue them, that I may gain glory through Pharaoh and all his host; and the Egyptians shall know that I am *Hashem*. And they did so.

יד וְהָיָה כִּי־יִשְׁאָלְךָ בִנְךָ מָחָר לֵאמֹר מַה־זֹּאת וְאָמַרְתָּ אֵלָיו בְּחֹזֶק יָד הוֹצִיאָנוּ יְהוָֹה מִמִּצְרַיִם מִבֵּית עֲבָדִים:

טו וַיְהִי כִּי־הִקְשָׁה פַרְעֹה לְשַׁלְּחֵנוּ וַיַּהֲרֹג יְהוָֹה כָּל־בְּכוֹר בְּאֶרֶץ מִצְרַיִם מִבְּכֹר אָדָם וְעַד־בְּכוֹר בְּהֵמָה עַל־כֵּן אֲנִי זֹבֵחַ לַיהוָֹה כָּל־פֶּטֶר רֶחֶם הַזְּכָרִים וְכָל־בְּכוֹר בָּנַי אֶפְדֶּה:

טז וְהָיָה לְאוֹת עַל־יָדְכָה וּלְטוֹטָפֹת בֵּין עֵינֶיךָ כִּי בְּחֹזֶק יָד הוֹצִיאָנוּ יְהוָֹה מִמִּצְרָיִם:

יז וַיְהִי בְּשַׁלַּח פַּרְעֹה אֶת־הָעָם וְלֹא־נָחָם אֱלֹהִים דֶּרֶךְ אֶרֶץ פְּלִשְׁתִּים כִּי קָרוֹב הוּא כִּי אָמַר אֱלֹהִים פֶּן־יִנָּחֵם הָעָם בִּרְאֹתָם מִלְחָמָה וְשָׁבוּ מִצְרָיְמָה:

יח וַיַּסֵּב אֱלֹהִים אֶת־הָעָם דֶּרֶךְ הַמִּדְבָּר יַם־סוּף וַחֲמֻשִׁים עָלוּ בְנֵי־יִשְׂרָאֵל מֵאֶרֶץ מִצְרָיִם:

יט וַיִּקַּח מֹשֶׁה אֶת־עַצְמוֹת יוֹסֵף עִמּוֹ כִּי הַשְׁבֵּעַ הִשְׁבִּיעַ אֶת־בְּנֵי יִשְׂרָאֵל לֵאמֹר פָּקֹד יִפְקֹד אֱלֹהִים אֶתְכֶם וְהַעֲלִיתֶם אֶת־עַצְמֹתַי מִזֶּה אִתְּכֶם:

כ וַיִּסְעוּ מִסֻּכֹּת וַיַּחֲנוּ בְאֵתָם בִּקְצֵה הַמִּדְבָּר:

כא וַיהוָֹה הֹלֵךְ לִפְנֵיהֶם יוֹמָם בְּעַמּוּד עָנָן לַנְחֹתָם הַדֶּרֶךְ וְלַיְלָה בְּעַמּוּד אֵשׁ לְהָאִיר לָהֶם לָלֶכֶת יוֹמָם וָלָיְלָה:

כב לֹא־יָמִישׁ עַמּוּד הֶעָנָן יוֹמָם וְעַמּוּד הָאֵשׁ לָיְלָה לִפְנֵי הָעָם:

יד א וַיְדַבֵּר יְהוָֹה אֶל־מֹשֶׁה לֵּאמֹר:

ב דַּבֵּר אֶל־בְּנֵי יִשְׂרָאֵל וְיָשֻׁבוּ וְיַחֲנוּ לִפְנֵי פִּי הַחִירֹת בֵּין מִגְדֹּל וּבֵין הַיָּם לִפְנֵי בַּעַל צְפֹן נִכְחוֹ תַחֲנוּ עַל־הַיָּם:

ג וְאָמַר פַּרְעֹה לִבְנֵי יִשְׂרָאֵל נְבֻכִים הֵם בָּאָרֶץ סָגַר עֲלֵיהֶם הַמִּדְבָּר:

ד וְחִזַּקְתִּי אֶת־לֵב־פַּרְעֹה וְרָדַף אַחֲרֵיהֶם וְאִכָּבְדָה בְּפַרְעֹה וּבְכָל־חֵילוֹ וְיָדְעוּ מִצְרַיִם כִּי־אֲנִי יְהוָֹה וַיַּעֲשׂוּ־כֵן:

5 When the king of Egypt was told that the people had fled, Pharaoh and his courtiers had a change of heart about the people and said, "What is this we have done, releasing *Yisrael* from our service?"

ה וַיֻּגַּד לְמֶלֶךְ מִצְרַיִם כִּי בָרַח הָעָם וַיֵּהָפֵךְ לְבַב פַּרְעֹה וַעֲבָדָיו אֶל־הָעָם וַיֹּאמְרוּ מַה־זֹּאת עָשִׂינוּ כִּי־שִׁלַּחְנוּ אֶת־יִשְׂרָאֵל מֵעָבְדֵנוּ:

6 He ordered his chariot and took his men with him;

ו וַיֶּאְסֹר אֶת־רִכְבּוֹ וְאֶת־עַמּוֹ לָקַח עִמּוֹ:

7 he took six hundred of his picked chariots, and the rest of the chariots of Egypt, with officers in all of them.

ז וַיִּקַּח שֵׁשׁ־מֵאוֹת רֶכֶב בָּחוּר וְכֹל רֶכֶב מִצְרָיִם וְשָׁלִשִׁם עַל־כֻּלּוֹ:

8 *Hashem* stiffened the heart of Pharaoh king of Egypt, and he gave chase to the Israelites. As the Israelites were departing defiantly,

ח וַיְחַזֵּק יְהֹוָה אֶת־לֵב פַּרְעֹה מֶלֶךְ מִצְרַיִם וַיִּרְדֹּף אַחֲרֵי בְּנֵי יִשְׂרָאֵל וּבְנֵי יִשְׂרָאֵל יֹצְאִים בְּיָד רָמָה:

9 the Egyptians gave chase to them, and all the chariot horses of Pharaoh, his horsemen, and his warriors overtook them encamped by the sea, near Pi-hahiroth, before Baal-zephon.

ט וַיִּרְדְּפוּ מִצְרַיִם אַחֲרֵיהֶם וַיַּשִּׂיגוּ אוֹתָם חֹנִים עַל־הַיָּם כָּל־סוּס רֶכֶב פַּרְעֹה וּפָרָשָׁיו וְחֵילוֹ עַל־פִּי הַחִירֹת לִפְנֵי בַּעַל צְפֹן:

10 As Pharaoh drew near, the Israelites caught sight of the Egyptians advancing upon them. Greatly frightened, the Israelites cried out to *Hashem*.

י וּפַרְעֹה הִקְרִיב וַיִּשְׂאוּ בְנֵי־יִשְׂרָאֵל אֶת־עֵינֵיהֶם וְהִנֵּה מִצְרַיִם נֹסֵעַ אַחֲרֵיהֶם וַיִּירְאוּ מְאֹד וַיִּצְעֲקוּ בְנֵי־יִשְׂרָאֵל אֶל־יְהֹוָה:

11 And they said to *Moshe*, "Was it for want of graves in Egypt that you brought us to die in the wilderness? What have you done to us, taking us out of Egypt?

יא וַיֹּאמְרוּ אֶל־מֹשֶׁה הֲמִבְּלִי אֵין־קְבָרִים בְּמִצְרַיִם לְקַחְתָּנוּ לָמוּת בַּמִּדְבָּר מַה־זֹּאת עָשִׂיתָ לָּנוּ לְהוֹצִיאָנוּ מִמִּצְרָיִם:

12 Is this not the very thing we told you in Egypt, saying, 'Let us be, and we will serve the Egyptians, for it is better for us to serve the Egyptians than to die in the wilderness'?"

יב הֲלֹא־זֶה הַדָּבָר אֲשֶׁר דִּבַּרְנוּ אֵלֶיךָ בְמִצְרַיִם לֵאמֹר חֲדַל מִמֶּנּוּ וְנַעַבְדָה אֶת־מִצְרָיִם כִּי טוֹב לָנוּ עֲבֹד אֶת־מִצְרַיִם מִמֻּתֵנוּ בַּמִּדְבָּר:

13 But *Moshe* said to the people, "Have no fear! Stand by, and witness the deliverance which *Hashem* will work for you today; for the Egyptians whom you see today you will never see again.

יג וַיֹּאמֶר מֹשֶׁה אֶל־הָעָם אַל־תִּירָאוּ הִתְיַצְּבוּ וּרְאוּ אֶת־יְשׁוּעַת יְהֹוָה אֲשֶׁר־יַעֲשֶׂה לָכֶם הַיּוֹם כִּי אֲשֶׁר רְאִיתֶם אֶת־מִצְרַיִם הַיּוֹם לֹא תֹסִפוּ לִרְאֹתָם עוֹד עַד־עוֹלָם:

14 *Hashem* will battle for you; you hold your peace!"

יד יְהֹוָה יִלָּחֵם לָכֶם וְאַתֶּם תַּחֲרִשׁוּן:

15 Then *Hashem* said to *Moshe*, "Why do you cry out to Me? Tell the Israelites to go forward.

טו וַיֹּאמֶר יְהֹוָה אֶל־מֹשֶׁה מַה־תִּצְעַק אֵלָי דַּבֵּר אֶל־בְּנֵי־יִשְׂרָאֵל וְיִסָּעוּ:

16 And you lift up your rod and hold out your arm over the sea and split it, so that the Israelites may march into the sea on dry ground.

טז וְאַתָּה הָרֵם אֶת־מַטְּךָ וּנְטֵה אֶת־יָדְךָ עַל־הַיָּם וּבְקָעֵהוּ וְיָבֹאוּ בְנֵי־יִשְׂרָאֵל בְּתוֹךְ הַיָּם בַּיַּבָּשָׁה:

17 And I will stiffen the hearts of the Egyptians so that they go in after them; and I will gain glory through Pharaoh and all his warriors, his chariots and his horsemen.

יז וַאֲנִי הִנְנִי מְחַזֵּק אֶת־לֵב מִצְרַיִם וְיָבֹאוּ אַחֲרֵיהֶם וְאִכָּבְדָה בְּפַרְעֹה וּבְכָל־חֵילוֹ בְּרִכְבּוֹ וּבְפָרָשָׁיו:

Exodus

18 Let the Egyptians know that I am *Hashem*, when I gain glory through Pharaoh, his chariots, and his horsemen."

יח וְיָדְעוּ מִצְרַיִם כִּי־אֲנִי יְהֹוָה בְּהִכָּבְדִי בְּפַרְעֹה בְּרִכְבּוֹ וּבְפָרָשָׁיו:

19 The angel of *Hashem*, who had been going ahead of the Israelite army, now moved and followed behind them; and the pillar of cloud shifted from in front of them and took up a place behind them,

יט וַיִּסַּע מַלְאַךְ הָאֱלֹהִים הַהֹלֵךְ לִפְנֵי מַחֲנֵה יִשְׂרָאֵל וַיֵּלֶךְ מֵאַחֲרֵיהֶם וַיִּסַּע עַמּוּד הֶעָנָן מִפְּנֵיהֶם וַיַּעֲמֹד מֵאַחֲרֵיהֶם:

va-yi-SA mal-AKH ha-e-lo-HEEM ha-ho-LAYKH lif-NAY ma-kha-NAY yis-ra-AYL va-YAY-lekh may-a-kha-ray-HEM va-yi-SA a-MUD he-a-NAN mi-p'-nay-HEM va-ya-a-MOD may-a-kha-ray-HEM

20 and it came between the army of the Egyptians and the army of *Yisrael*. Thus there was the cloud with the darkness, and it cast a spell upon the night, so that the one could not come near the other all through the night.

כ וַיָּבֹא בֵּין מַחֲנֵה מִצְרַיִם וּבֵין מַחֲנֵה יִשְׂרָאֵל וַיְהִי הֶעָנָן וְהַחֹשֶׁךְ וַיָּאֶר אֶת־הַלָּיְלָה וְלֹא־קָרַב זֶה אֶל־זֶה כָּל־הַלָּיְלָה:

21 Then *Moshe* held out his arm over the sea and *Hashem* drove back the sea with a strong east wind all that night, and turned the sea into dry ground. The waters were split,

כא וַיֵּט מֹשֶׁה אֶת־יָדוֹ עַל־הַיָּם וַיּוֹלֶךְ יְהֹוָה אֶת־הַיָּם בְּרוּחַ קָדִים עַזָּה כָּל־הַלַּיְלָה וַיָּשֶׂם אֶת־הַיָּם לֶחָרָבָה וַיִּבָּקְעוּ הַמָּיִם:

22 and the Israelites went into the sea on dry ground, the waters forming a wall for them on their right and on their left.

כב וַיָּבֹאוּ בְנֵי־יִשְׂרָאֵל בְּתוֹךְ הַיָּם בַּיַּבָּשָׁה וְהַמַּיִם לָהֶם חֹמָה מִימִינָם וּמִשְּׂמֹאלָם:

23 The Egyptians came in pursuit after them into the sea, all of Pharaoh's horses, chariots, and horsemen.

כג וַיִּרְדְּפוּ מִצְרַיִם וַיָּבֹאוּ אַחֲרֵיהֶם כֹּל סוּס פַּרְעֹה רִכְבּוֹ וּפָרָשָׁיו אֶל־תּוֹךְ הַיָּם:

24 At the morning watch, *Hashem* looked down upon the Egyptian army from a pillar of fire and cloud, and threw the Egyptian army into panic.

כד וַיְהִי בְּאַשְׁמֹרֶת הַבֹּקֶר וַיַּשְׁקֵף יְהֹוָה אֶל־מַחֲנֵה מִצְרַיִם בְּעַמּוּד אֵשׁ וְעָנָן וַיָּהָם אֵת מַחֲנֵה מִצְרָיִם:

25 He locked the wheels of their chariots so that they moved forward with difficulty. And the Egyptians said, "Let us flee from the Israelites, for *Hashem* is fighting for them against Egypt."

כה וַיָּסַר אֵת אֹפַן מַרְכְּבֹתָיו וַיְנַהֲגֵהוּ בִּכְבֵדֻת וַיֹּאמֶר מִצְרַיִם אָנוּסָה מִפְּנֵי יִשְׂרָאֵל כִּי יְהֹוָה נִלְחָם לָהֶם בְּמִצְרָיִם

26 Then *Hashem* said to *Moshe*, "Hold out your arm over the sea, that the waters may come back upon the Egyptians and upon their chariots and upon their horsemen."

כו וַיֹּאמֶר יְהֹוָה אֶל־מֹשֶׁה נְטֵה אֶת־יָדְךָ עַל־הַיָּם וְיָשֻׁבוּ הַמַּיִם עַל־מִצְרַיִם עַל־רִכְבּוֹ וְעַל־פָּרָשָׁיו:

14:19 And the pillar of cloud shifted from in front of them According to *Rashi*, the pillar of cloud that led the Jewish people in the desert during the day moved behind the camp, and obscured the Egyptians' vision as they progressed in their bloodthirsty pursuit of the Jewish people. The cloud protected Israel as they fled and absorbed the arrows shot by the Egyptians at the fleeing nation. Today, the soldiers of the Israeli Defense Forces are a pillar of defense, shielding Israel from her enemies. May the God of Israel continue to protect His people through His modern-day pillar of defense, just as He did long ago.

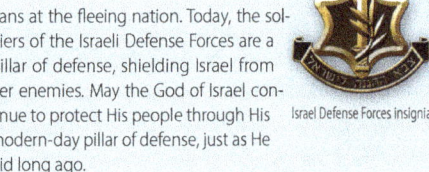

Israel Defense Forces insignia

27 *Moshe* held out his arm over the sea, and at daybreak the sea returned to its normal state, and the Egyptians fled at its approach. But *Hashem* hurled the Egyptians into the sea.

כז וַיֵּט מֹשֶׁה אֶת־יָדוֹ עַל־הַיָּם וַיָּשָׁב הַיָּם לִפְנוֹת בֹּקֶר לְאֵיתָנוֹ וּמִצְרַיִם נָסִים לִקְרָאתוֹ וַיְנַעֵר יְהֹוָה אֶת־מִצְרַיִם בְּתוֹךְ הַיָּם:

28 The waters turned back and covered the chariots and the horsemen – Pharaoh's entire army that followed them into the sea; not one of them remained.

כח וַיָּשֻׁבוּ הַמַּיִם וַיְכַסּוּ אֶת־הָרֶכֶב וְאֶת־הַפָּרָשִׁים לְכֹל חֵיל פַּרְעֹה הַבָּאִים אַחֲרֵיהֶם בַּיָּם לֹא־נִשְׁאַר בָּהֶם עַד־אֶחָד:

29 But the Israelites had marched through the sea on dry ground, the waters forming a wall for them on their right and on their left.

כט וּבְנֵי יִשְׂרָאֵל הָלְכוּ בַיַּבָּשָׁה בְּתוֹךְ הַיָּם וְהַמַּיִם לָהֶם חֹמָה מִימִינָם וּמִשְּׂמֹאלָם:

30 Thus *Hashem* delivered *Yisrael* that day from the Egyptians. *Yisrael* saw the Egyptians dead on the shore of the sea.

ל וַיּוֹשַׁע יְהֹוָה בַּיּוֹם הַהוּא אֶת־יִשְׂרָאֵל מִיַּד מִצְרָיִם וַיַּרְא יִשְׂרָאֵל אֶת־מִצְרַיִם מֵת עַל־שְׂפַת הַיָּם:

31 And when *Yisrael* saw the wondrous power which *Hashem* had wielded against the Egyptians, the people feared *Hashem*; they had faith in *Hashem* and His servant *Moshe*.

לא וַיַּרְא יִשְׂרָאֵל אֶת־הַיָּד הַגְּדֹלָה אֲשֶׁר עָשָׂה יְהֹוָה בְּמִצְרַיִם וַיִּירְאוּ הָעָם אֶת־יְהֹוָה וַיַּאֲמִינוּ בַּיהֹוָה וּבְמֹשֶׁה עַבְדּוֹ:

15 ¹ Then *Moshe* and the Israelites sang this song to *Hashem*. They said: I will sing to *Hashem*, for He has triumphed gloriously; Horse and driver He has hurled into the sea.

טו א אָז יָשִׁיר־מֹשֶׁה וּבְנֵי יִשְׂרָאֵל אֶת־הַשִּׁירָה הַזֹּאת לַיהֹוָה וַיֹּאמְרוּ לֵאמֹר אָשִׁירָה לַיהֹוָה כִּי־גָאֹה גָּאָה סוּס וְרֹכְבוֹ רָמָה בַיָּם:

² *Hashem* is my strength and might; He is become my deliverance. This is my God and I will enshrine Him; The God of my father, and I will exalt Him.

ב עָזִּי וְזִמְרָת יָהּ וַיְהִי־לִי לִישׁוּעָה זֶה אֵלִי וְאַנְוֵהוּ אֱלֹהֵי אָבִי וַאֲרֹמְמֶנְהוּ:

³ *Hashem*, the Warrior – *Hashem* is His name!

ג יְהֹוָה אִישׁ מִלְחָמָה יְהֹוָה שְׁמוֹ:

⁴ Pharaoh's chariots and his army He has cast into the sea; And the pick of his officers Are drowned in the Sea of Reeds.

ד מַרְכְּבֹת פַּרְעֹה וְחֵילוֹ יָרָה בַיָּם וּמִבְחַר שָׁלִשָׁיו טֻבְּעוּ בְיַם־סוּף:

⁵ The deeps covered them; They went down into the depths like a stone.

ה תְּהֹמֹת יְכַסְיֻמוּ יָרְדוּ בִמְצוֹלֹת כְּמוֹ־אָבֶן:

⁶ Your right hand, *Hashem*, glorious in power, Your right hand, *Hashem*, shatters the foe!

ו יְמִינְךָ יְהֹוָה נֶאְדָּרִי בַּכֹּחַ יְמִינְךָ יְהֹוָה תִּרְעַץ אוֹיֵב:

⁷ In Your great triumph You break Your opponents; You send forth Your fury, it consumes them like straw.

ז וּבְרֹב גְּאוֹנְךָ תַּהֲרֹס קָמֶיךָ תְּשַׁלַּח חֲרֹנְךָ יֹאכְלֵמוֹ כַּקַּשׁ:

⁸ At the blast of Your nostrils the waters piled up, The floods stood straight like a wall; The deeps froze in the heart of the sea.

ח וּבְרוּחַ אַפֶּיךָ נֶעֶרְמוּ מַיִם נִצְּבוּ כְמוֹ־נֵד נֹזְלִים קָפְאוּ תְהֹמֹת בְּלֶב־יָם:

⁹ The foe said, "I will pursue, I will overtake, I will divide the spoil; My desire shall have its fill of them. I will bare my sword – My hand shall subdue them."

ט אָמַר אוֹיֵב אֶרְדֹּף אַשִּׂיג אֲחַלֵּק שָׁלָל תִּמְלָאֵמוֹ נַפְשִׁי אָרִיק חַרְבִּי תּוֹרִישֵׁמוֹ יָדִי:

Exodus

10 You made Your wind blow, the sea covered them;
They sank like lead in the majestic waters.

נָשַׁפְתָּ בְרוּחֲךָ כִּסָּמוֹ יָם צָלֲלוּ כַּעוֹפֶרֶת
בְּמַיִם אַדִּירִים:

11 Who is like You, *Hashem*, among the celestials;
Who is like You, majestic in holiness, Awesome in
splendor, working wonders!

מִי־כָמֹכָה בָּאֵלִם יְהוָה מִי כָּמֹכָה נֶאְדָּר
בַּקֹּדֶשׁ נוֹרָא תְהִלֹּת עֹשֵׂה פֶלֶא:

mee kha-MO-khah ba-ay-LEEM a-do-NAI MEE ka-MO-khah
ne-DAR ba-KO-desh no-RA t'-hi-LOT O-say FE-le

12 You put out Your right hand, The earth swallowed
them.

נָטִיתָ יְמִינְךָ תִּבְלָעֵמוֹ אָרֶץ:

13 In Your love You lead the people You redeemed; In
Your strength You guide them to Your holy abode.

נָחִיתָ בְחַסְדְּךָ עַם־זוּ גָּאָלְתָּ נֵהַלְתָּ בְעָזְּךָ
אֶל־נְוֵה קָדְשֶׁךָ:

14 The peoples hear, they tremble; Agony grips the
dwellers in Philistia.

שָׁמְעוּ עַמִּים יִרְגָּזוּן חִיל אָחַז יֹשְׁבֵי
פְּלָשֶׁת:

15 Now are the clans of Edom dismayed; The tribes of
Moab – trembling grips them; All the dwellers in
Canaan are aghast.

אָז נִבְהֲלוּ אַלּוּפֵי אֱדוֹם אֵילֵי מוֹאָב
יֹאחֲזֵמוֹ רָעַד נָמֹגוּ כֹּל יֹשְׁבֵי כְנָעַן:

16 Terror and dread descend upon them; Through the
might of Your arm they are still as stone – Till Your
people cross over, *Hashem*, Till Your people cross
whom You have ransomed.

תִּפֹּל עֲלֵיהֶם אֵימָתָה וָפַחַד בִּגְדֹל
זְרוֹעֲךָ יִדְּמוּ כָּאָבֶן עַד־יַעֲבֹר עַמְּךָ יְהוָה
עַד־יַעֲבֹר עַם־זוּ קָנִיתָ:

17 You will bring them and plant them in Your
own mountain, The place You made to dwell in,
Hashem, The sanctuary, *Hashem*, which Your hands
established.

תְּבִאֵמוֹ וְתִטָּעֵמוֹ בְּהַר נַחֲלָתְךָ מָכוֹן
לְשִׁבְתְּךָ פָּעַלְתָּ יְהוָה מִקְּדָשׁ אֲדֹנָי
כּוֹנְנוּ יָדֶיךָ:

t'-vi-AY-mo v'-ti-ta-AY-mo b'-HAR na-kha-la-t'-KHA ma-KHON l'-shiv'-t'-KHA
pa-al-TA ah-do-NAI mik'-DASH ah-do-NAI ko-n'-NU ya-de-KHA

18 *Hashem* will reign for ever and ever!

יְהוָה יִמְלֹךְ לְעֹלָם וָעֶד:

19 For the horses of Pharaoh, with his chariots and
horsemen, went into the sea; and *Hashem* turned
back on them the waters of the sea; but the
Israelites marched on dry ground in the midst of
the sea.

כִּי בָא סוּס פַּרְעֹה בְּרִכְבּוֹ וּבְפָרָשָׁיו בַּיָּם
וַיָּשֶׁב יְהוָה עֲלֵהֶם אֶת־מֵי הַיָּם וּבְנֵי
יִשְׂרָאֵל הָלְכוּ בַיַּבָּשָׁה בְּתוֹךְ הַיָּם:

20 Then *Miriam* the *Neviah*, *Aharon*'s sister, took a
timbrel in her hand, and all the women went out
after her in dance with timbrels.

וַתִּקַּח מִרְיָם הַנְּבִיאָה אֲחוֹת אַהֲרֹן אֶת־
הַתֹּף בְּיָדָהּ וַתֵּצֶאןָ כָל־הַנָּשִׁים אַחֲרֶיהָ
בְּתֻפִּים וּבִמְחֹלֹת:

15:17 And plant them in Your own mountain "And plant them in Your own mountain" is understood as a reference either to *Har Habayit* or to the entire Land of Israel. When *Hashem* says that the Jewish people will be planted in *Eretz Yisrael*, He means that they will establish roots there and flourish. The *Midrash* ex-

City of Karmiel on the Shagor mountain range

plains that this is a reference to the time of *Mashiach*, when the Children of Israel will be brought back to the Land of Israel, never to be uprooted again. For two thousand years, Jews have been asking for the fulfillment of this verse each week as part of the *Shabbat* prayers, "bring us with happiness to our land and plant us in our borders."

²¹ And *Miriam* chanted for them: Sing to *Hashem*, for He has triumphed gloriously; Horse and driver He has hurled into the sea.

כא וַתַּעַן לָהֶם מִרְיָם שִׁירוּ לַיהֹוָה כִּי־גָאֹה גָּאָה סוּס וְרֹכְבוֹ רָמָה בַיָּם:

²² Then *Moshe* caused *Yisrael* to set out from the Sea of Reeds. They went on into the wilderness of Shur; they traveled three days in the wilderness and found no water.

כב וַיַּסַּע מֹשֶׁה אֶת־יִשְׂרָאֵל מִיַּם־סוּף וַיֵּצְאוּ אֶל־מִדְבַּר־שׁוּר וַיֵּלְכוּ שְׁלֹשֶׁת־יָמִים בַּמִּדְבָּר וְלֹא־מָצְאוּ מָיִם:

²³ They came to Marah, but they could not drink the water of Marah because it was bitter; that is why it was named Marah.

כג וַיָּבֹאוּ מָרָתָה וְלֹא יָכְלוּ לִשְׁתֹּת מַיִם מִמָּרָה כִּי מָרִים הֵם עַל־כֵּן קָרָא־שְׁמָהּ מָרָה:

²⁴ And the people grumbled against *Moshe*, saying, "What shall we drink?"

כד וַיִּלֹּנוּ הָעָם עַל־מֹשֶׁה לֵּאמֹר מַה־נִּשְׁתֶּה:

²⁵ So he cried out to *Hashem*, and *Hashem* showed him a piece of wood; he threw it into the water and the water became sweet. There He made for them a fixed rule, and there He put them to the test.

כה וַיִּצְעַק אֶל־יְהֹוָה וַיּוֹרֵהוּ יְהֹוָה עֵץ וַיַּשְׁלֵךְ אֶל־הַמַּיִם וַיִּמְתְּקוּ הַמָּיִם שָׁם שָׂם לוֹ חֹק וּמִשְׁפָּט וְשָׁם נִסָּהוּ:

²⁶ He said, "If you will heed *Hashem* your God diligently, doing what is upright in His sight, giving ear to His commandments and keeping all His laws, then I will not bring upon you any of the diseases that I brought upon the Egyptians, for I *Hashem* am your healer."

כו וַיֹּאמֶר אִם־שָׁמוֹעַ תִּשְׁמַע לְקוֹל יְהֹוָה אֱלֹהֶיךָ וְהַיָּשָׁר בְּעֵינָיו תַּעֲשֶׂה וְהַאֲזַנְתָּ לְמִצְוֹתָיו וְשָׁמַרְתָּ כָּל־חֻקָּיו כָּל־הַמַּחֲלָה אֲשֶׁר־שַׂמְתִּי בְמִצְרַיִם לֹא־אָשִׂים עָלֶיךָ כִּי אֲנִי יְהֹוָה רֹפְאֶךָ:

*va-YO-mer im sha-MO-a tish-MA l'-KOL a-do-NAI e-lo-HE-kha
v'-ha-ya-SHAR b'-ay-NAV ta-a-SEH v'-ha-a-zan-TA l'-mitz-vo-TAV
v'-sha-mar-TA kol khu-KAV kol ha-ma-kha-LAH a-sher SAM-tee
v'-mitz-RA-yim lo a-SEEM a-LE-kha kee a-NEE a-do-NAI ro-f'-E-kha*

²⁷ And they came to Elim, where there were twelve springs of water and seventy palm trees; and they encamped there beside the water.

כז וַיָּבֹאוּ אֵילִמָה וְשָׁם שְׁתֵּים עֶשְׂרֵה עֵינֹת מַיִם וְשִׁבְעִים תְּמָרִים וַיַּחֲנוּ־שָׁם עַל־הַמָּיִם:

16 ¹ Setting out from Elim, the whole Israelite community came to the wilderness of Sin, which is between Elim and Sinai, on the fifteenth day of the second month after their departure from the land of Egypt.

טז א וַיִּסְעוּ מֵאֵילִם וַיָּבֹאוּ כָּל־עֲדַת בְּנֵי־יִשְׂרָאֵל אֶל־מִדְבַּר־סִין אֲשֶׁר בֵּין־אֵילִם וּבֵין סִינָי בַּחֲמִשָּׁה עָשָׂר יוֹם לַחֹדֶשׁ הַשֵּׁנִי לְצֵאתָם מֵאֶרֶץ מִצְרָיִם:

² In the wilderness, the whole Israelite community grumbled against *Moshe* and *Aharon*.

ב וַיִּלּוֹנוּ [וַיִּלֹּנוּ] כָּל־עֲדַת בְּנֵי־יִשְׂרָאֵל עַל־מֹשֶׁה וְעַל־אַהֲרֹן בַּמִּדְבָּר:

³ The Israelites said to them, "If only we had died by the hand of *Hashem* in the land of Egypt, when we sat by the fleshpots, when we ate our fill of bread! For you have brought us out into this wilderness to starve this whole congregation to death."

ג וַיֹּאמְרוּ אֲלֵהֶם בְּנֵי יִשְׂרָאֵל מִי־יִתֵּן מוּתֵנוּ בְיַד־יְהֹוָה בְּאֶרֶץ מִצְרַיִם בְּשִׁבְתֵּנוּ עַל־סִיר הַבָּשָׂר בְּאָכְלֵנוּ לֶחֶם לָשֹׂבַע כִּי־הוֹצֵאתֶם אֹתָנוּ אֶל־הַמִּדְבָּר הַזֶּה לְהָמִית אֶת־כָּל־הַקָּהָל הַזֶּה בָּרָעָב:

4 And *Hashem* said to *Moshe*, "I will rain down bread for you from the sky, and the people shall go out and gather each day that day's portion – that I may thus test them, to see whether they will follow My instructions or not.

5 But on the sixth day, when they apportion what they have brought in, it shall prove to be double the amount they gather each day."

6 So *Moshe* and *Aharon* said to all the Israelites, "By evening you shall know it was *Hashem* who brought you out from the land of Egypt;

7 and in the morning you shall behold the Presence of *Hashem*, because He has heard your grumblings against *Hashem*. For who are we that you should grumble against us?

8 Since it is *Hashem*," *Moshe* continued, "who will give you flesh to eat in the evening and bread in the morning to the full, because *Hashem* has heard the grumblings you utter against Him, what is our part? Your grumbling is not against us, but against *Hashem*!"

9 Then *Moshe* said to *Aharon*, "Say to the whole Israelite community: Advance toward *Hashem*, for He has heard your grumbling."

10 And as *Aharon* spoke to the whole Israelite community, they turned toward the wilderness, and there, in a cloud, appeared the Presence of *Hashem*.

11 *Hashem* spoke to *Moshe*:

12 "I have heard the grumbling of the Israelites. Speak to them and say: By evening you shall eat flesh, and in the morning you shall have your fill of bread; and you shall know that I *Hashem* am your God."

13 In the evening quail appeared and covered the camp; in the morning there was a fall of dew about the camp.

14 When the fall of dew lifted, there, over the surface of the wilderness, lay a fine and flaky substance, as fine as frost on the ground.

15 When the Israelites saw it, they said to one another, "What is it?" – for they did not know what it was. And *Moshe* said to them, "That is the bread which *Hashem* has given you to eat.

ד וַיֹּ֤אמֶר יְהוָה֙ אֶל־מֹשֶׁ֔ה הִנְנִ֨י מַמְטִ֥יר לָכֶ֛ם לֶ֖חֶם מִן־הַשָּׁמָ֑יִם וְיָצָ֨א הָעָ֤ם וְלָֽקְטוּ֙ דְּבַר־י֣וֹם בְּיוֹמ֔וֹ לְמַ֣עַן אֲנַסֶּ֔נּוּ הֲיֵלֵ֥ךְ בְּתֽוֹרָתִ֖י אִם־לֹֽא:

ה וְהָיָה֙ בַּיּ֣וֹם הַשִּׁשִּׁ֔י וְהֵכִ֖ינוּ אֵ֣ת אֲשֶׁר־יָבִ֑יאוּ וְהָיָ֣ה מִשְׁנֶ֔ה עַ֥ל אֲשֶׁר־יִלְקְט֖וּ י֥וֹם יֽוֹם:

ו וַיֹּ֤אמֶר מֹשֶׁה֙ וְאַֽהֲרֹ֔ן אֶֽל־כָּל־בְּנֵ֖י יִשְׂרָאֵ֑ל עֶ֕רֶב וִֽידַעְתֶּ֕ם כִּ֧י יְהוָ֛ה הוֹצִ֥יא אֶתְכֶ֖ם מֵאֶ֥רֶץ מִצְרָֽיִם:

ז וּבֹ֗קֶר וּרְאִיתֶם֙ אֶת־כְּב֣וֹד יְהוָ֔ה בְּשָׁמְע֥וֹ אֶת־תְּלֻנֹּֽתֵיכֶ֖ם עַל־יְהוָ֑ה וְנַ֣חְנוּ מָ֔ה כִּ֥י תלונו [תַלִּ֖ינוּ] עָלֵֽינוּ:

ח וַיֹּ֣אמֶר מֹשֶׁ֗ה בְּתֵ֣ת יְהוָה֩ לָכֶ֨ם בָּעֶ֜רֶב בָּשָׂ֣ר לֶֽאֱכֹ֗ל וְלֶ֤חֶם בַּבֹּ֨קֶר֙ לִשְׂבֹּ֔עַ בִּשְׁמֹ֤עַ יְהוָה֙ אֶת־תְּלֻנֹּ֣תֵיכֶ֔ם אֲשֶׁר־אַתֶּ֥ם מַלִּינִ֖ם עָלָ֑יו וְנַ֣חְנוּ מָ֔ה לֹֽא־עָלֵ֥ינוּ תְלֻנֹּֽתֵיכֶ֖ם כִּ֥י עַל־יְהוָֽה:

ט וַיֹּ֤אמֶר מֹשֶׁה֙ אֶֽל־אַֽהֲרֹ֔ן אֱמֹ֗ר אֶֽל־כָּל־עֲדַת֙ בְּנֵ֣י יִשְׂרָאֵ֔ל קִרְב֖וּ לִפְנֵ֣י יְהוָ֑ה כִּ֣י שָׁמַ֔ע אֵ֖ת תְּלֻנֹּֽתֵיכֶֽם:

י וַיְהִ֗י כְּדַבֵּ֤ר אַֽהֲרֹן֙ אֶל־כָּל־עֲדַ֣ת בְּנֵֽי־יִשְׂרָאֵ֔ל וַיִּפְנ֖וּ אֶל־הַמִּדְבָּ֑ר וְהִנֵּה֙ כְּב֣וֹד יְהוָ֔ה נִרְאָ֖ה בֶּֽעָנָֽן:

יא וַיְדַבֵּ֥ר יְהוָ֖ה אֶל־מֹשֶׁ֥ה לֵּאמֹֽר:

יב שָׁמַ֗עְתִּי אֶת־תְּלוּנֹּת֮ בְּנֵ֣י יִשְׂרָאֵל֒ דַּבֵּ֨ר אֲלֵהֶ֜ם לֵאמֹ֗ר בֵּ֤ין הָֽעַרְבַּ֨יִם֙ תֹּֽאכְל֣וּ בָשָׂ֔ר וּבַבֹּ֖קֶר תִּשְׂבְּעוּ־לָ֑חֶם וִֽידַעְתֶּ֕ם כִּ֛י אֲנִ֥י יְהוָ֖ה אֱלֹֽהֵיכֶֽם:

יג וַיְהִ֣י בָעֶ֔רֶב וַתַּ֣עַל הַשְּׂלָ֔ו וַתְּכַ֖ס אֶת־הַֽמַּֽחֲנֶ֑ה וּבַבֹּ֗קֶר הָֽיְתָה֙ שִׁכְבַ֣ת הַטַּ֔ל סָבִ֖יב לַֽמַּֽחֲנֶֽה:

יד וַתַּ֖עַל שִׁכְבַ֣ת הַטָּ֑ל וְהִנֵּ֞ה עַל־פְּנֵ֤י הַמִּדְבָּר֙ דַּ֣ק מְחֻסְפָּ֔ס דַּ֥ק כַּכְּפֹ֖ר עַל־הָאָֽרֶץ:

טו וַיִּרְא֣וּ בְנֵֽי־יִשְׂרָאֵ֗ל וַיֹּ֨אמְר֜וּ אִ֤ישׁ אֶל־אָחִיו֙ מָ֣ן ה֔וּא כִּ֛י לֹ֥א יָֽדְע֖וּ מַה־ה֑וּא וַיֹּ֤אמֶר מֹשֶׁה֙ אֲלֵהֶ֔ם ה֣וּא הַלֶּ֔חֶם אֲשֶׁ֨ר נָתַ֧ן יְהוָ֛ה לָכֶ֖ם לְאָכְלָֽה:

16 This is what *Hashem* has commanded: Gather as much of it as each of you requires to eat, an *omer* to a person for as many of you as there are; each of you shall fetch for those in his tent."

טו זֶה הַדָּבָר אֲשֶׁר צִוָּה יְהוָֹה לִקְטוּ מִמֶּנּוּ אִישׁ לְפִי אָכְלוֹ עֹמֶר לַגֻּלְגֹּלֶת מִסְפַּר נַפְשֹׁתֵיכֶם אִישׁ לַאֲשֶׁר בְּאָהֳלוֹ תִּקָּחוּ:

17 The Israelites did so, some gathering much, some little.

יז וַיַּעֲשׂוּ־כֵן בְּנֵי יִשְׂרָאֵל וַיִּלְקְטוּ הַמַּרְבֶּה וְהַמַּמְעִיט:

18 But when they measured it by the *omer*, he who had gathered much had no excess, and he who had gathered little had no deficiency: they had gathered as much as they needed to eat.

יח וַיָּמֹדּוּ בָעֹמֶר וְלֹא הֶעְדִּיף הַמַּרְבֶּה וְהַמַּמְעִיט לֹא הֶחְסִיר אִישׁ לְפִי־אָכְלוֹ לָקָטוּ:

19 And *Moshe* said to them, "Let no one leave any of it over until morning."

יט וַיֹּאמֶר מֹשֶׁה אֲלֵהֶם אִישׁ אַל־יוֹתֵר מִמֶּנּוּ עַד־בֹּקֶר:

20 But they paid no attention to *Moshe*; some of them left of it until morning, and it became infested with maggots and stank. And *Moshe* was angry with them.

כ וְלֹא־שָׁמְעוּ אֶל־מֹשֶׁה וַיּוֹתִרוּ אֲנָשִׁים מִמֶּנּוּ עַד־בֹּקֶר וַיָּרֻם תּוֹלָעִים וַיִּבְאַשׁ וַיִּקְצֹף עֲלֵהֶם מֹשֶׁה:

21 So they gathered it every morning, each as much as he needed to eat; for when the sun grew hot, it would melt.

כא וַיִּלְקְטוּ אֹתוֹ בַּבֹּקֶר בַּבֹּקֶר אִישׁ כְּפִי אָכְלוֹ וְחַם הַשֶּׁמֶשׁ וְנָמָס:

22 On the sixth day they gathered double the amount of food, two *omer*s for each; and when all the chieftains of the community came and told *Moshe*,

כב וַיְהִי בַּיּוֹם הַשִּׁשִּׁי לָקְטוּ לֶחֶם מִשְׁנֶה שְׁנֵי הָעֹמֶר לָאֶחָד וַיָּבֹאוּ כָּל־נְשִׂיאֵי הָעֵדָה וַיַּגִּידוּ לְמֹשֶׁה:

23 he said to them, "This is what *Hashem* meant: Tomorrow is a day of rest, a holy *Shabbat* of *Hashem*. Bake what you would bake and boil what you would boil; and all that is left put aside to be kept until morning."

כג וַיֹּאמֶר אֲלֵהֶם הוּא אֲשֶׁר דִּבֶּר יְהוָֹה שַׁבָּתוֹן שַׁבַּת־קֹדֶשׁ לַיהוָֹה מָחָר אֵת אֲשֶׁר־תֹּאפוּ אֵפוּ וְאֵת אֲשֶׁר־תְּבַשְּׁלוּ בַּשֵּׁלוּ וְאֵת כָּל־הָעֹדֵף הַנִּיחוּ לָכֶם לְמִשְׁמֶרֶת עַד־הַבֹּקֶר:

24 So they put it aside until morning, as *Moshe* had ordered; and it did not turn foul, and there were no maggots in it.

כד וַיַּנִּיחוּ אֹתוֹ עַד־הַבֹּקֶר כַּאֲשֶׁר צִוָּה מֹשֶׁה וְלֹא הִבְאִישׁ וְרִמָּה לֹא־הָיְתָה בּוֹ:

25 Then *Moshe* said, "Eat it today, for today is a *Shabbat* of *Hashem*; you will not find it today on the plain.

כה וַיֹּאמֶר מֹשֶׁה אִכְלֻהוּ הַיּוֹם כִּי־שַׁבָּת הַיּוֹם לַיהוָֹה הַיּוֹם לֹא תִמְצָאֻהוּ בַּשָּׂדֶה:

26 Six days you shall gather it; on the seventh day, the *Shabbat*, there will be none."

כו שֵׁשֶׁת יָמִים תִּלְקְטֻהוּ וּבַיּוֹם הַשְּׁבִיעִי שַׁבָּת לֹא יִהְיֶה־בּוֹ:

27 Yet some of the people went out on the seventh day to gather, but they found nothing.

כז וַיְהִי בַּיּוֹם הַשְּׁבִיעִי יָצְאוּ מִן־הָעָם לִלְקֹט וְלֹא מָצָאוּ:

28 And *Hashem* said to *Moshe*, "How long will you men refuse to obey My commandments and My teachings?

כח וַיֹּאמֶר יְהוָֹה אֶל־מֹשֶׁה עַד־אָנָה מֵאַנְתֶּם לִשְׁמֹר מִצְוֹתַי וְתוֹרֹתָי:

שמות יז
בשלח

29 Mark that *Hashem* has given you the *Shabbat*; therefore He gives you two days' food on the sixth day. Let everyone remain where he is: let no one leave his place on the seventh day."

רְאוּ כִּי־יְהֹוָה נָתַן לָכֶם הַשַּׁבָּת עַל־ כֵּן הוּא נֹתֵן לָכֶם בַּיּוֹם הַשִּׁשִּׁי לֶחֶם יוֹמָיִם שְׁבוּ אִישׁ תַּחְתָּיו אַל־יֵצֵא אִישׁ מִמְּקֹמוֹ בַּיּוֹם הַשְּׁבִיעִי:

30 So the people remained inactive on the seventh day.

וַיִּשְׁבְּתוּ הָעָם בַּיּוֹם הַשְּׁבִעִי:

31 The house of *Yisrael* named it manna; it was like coriander seed, white, and it tasted like wafers in honey.

וַיִּקְרְאוּ בֵית־יִשְׂרָאֵל אֶת־שְׁמוֹ מָן וְהוּא כְּזֶרַע גַּד לָבָן וְטַעְמוֹ כְּצַפִּיחִת בִּדְבָשׁ:

32 *Moshe* said, "This is what *Hashem* has commanded: Let one *omer* of it be kept throughout the ages, in order that they may see the bread that I fed you in the wilderness when I brought you out from the land of Egypt."

וַיֹּאמֶר מֹשֶׁה זֶה הַדָּבָר אֲשֶׁר צִוָּה יְהֹוָה מְלֹא הָעֹמֶר מִמֶּנּוּ לְמִשְׁמֶרֶת לְדֹרֹתֵיכֶם לְמַעַן יִרְאוּ אֶת־הַלֶּחֶם אֲשֶׁר הֶאֱכַלְתִּי אֶתְכֶם בַּמִּדְבָּר בְּהוֹצִיאִי אֶתְכֶם מֵאֶרֶץ מִצְרָיִם:

33 And *Moshe* said to *Aharon*, "Take a jar, put one *omer* of manna in it, and place it before *Hashem*, to be kept throughout the ages."

וַיֹּאמֶר מֹשֶׁה אֶל־אַהֲרֹן קַח צִנְצֶנֶת אַחַת וְתֶן־שָׁמָּה מְלֹא־הָעֹמֶר מָן וְהַנַּח אֹתוֹ לִפְנֵי יְהֹוָה לְמִשְׁמֶרֶת לְדֹרֹתֵיכֶם:

34 As *Hashem* had commanded *Moshe*, *Aharon* placed it before the Pact, to be kept.

כַּאֲשֶׁר צִוָּה יְהֹוָה אֶל־מֹשֶׁה וַיַּנִּיחֵהוּ אַהֲרֹן לִפְנֵי הָעֵדֻת לְמִשְׁמָרֶת:

35 And the Israelites ate manna forty years, until they came to a settled land; they ate the manna until they came to the border of the land of Canaan.

וּבְנֵי יִשְׂרָאֵל אָכְלוּ אֶת־הַמָּן אַרְבָּעִים שָׁנָה עַד־בֹּאָם אֶל־אֶרֶץ נוֹשָׁבֶת אֶת־ הַמָּן אָכְלוּ עַד־בֹּאָם אֶל־קְצֵה אֶרֶץ כְּנָעַן:

uv-NAY yis-ra-AYL a-kh'-LU et ha-MAN ar-ba-EEM sha-NAH ad bo-AM el E-retz no-SHA-vet et ha-MAN a-kh'-LU ad bo-AM el k'-TZAY E-retz k'-NA-an

36 The *omer* is a tenth of an *efah*.

וְהָעֹמֶר עֲשִׂרִית הָאֵיפָה הוּא:

17 1 From the wilderness of Sin the whole Israelite community continued by stages as *Hashem* would command. They encamped at Rephidim, and there was no water for the people to drink.

יז וַיִּסְעוּ כָּל־עֲדַת בְּנֵי־יִשְׂרָאֵל מִמִּדְבַּר־ סִין לְמַסְעֵיהֶם עַל־פִּי יְהֹוָה וַיַּחֲנוּ בִּרְפִידִים וְאֵין מַיִם לִשְׁתֹּת הָעָם:

2 The people quarreled with *Moshe*. "Give us water to drink," they said; and *Moshe* replied to them, "Why do you quarrel with me? Why do you try *Hashem*?"

וַיָּרֶב הָעָם עִם־מֹשֶׁה וַיֹּאמְרוּ תְּנוּ־לָנוּ מַיִם וְנִשְׁתֶּה וַיֹּאמֶר לָהֶם מֹשֶׁה מַה־ תְּרִיבוּן עִמָּדִי מַה־תְּנַסּוּן אֶת־יְהֹוָה:

16:35 Until they came to a settled land The Children of Israel were fed manna from heaven during the entire period of forty years of wandering in the desert, until they were within sight of the Promised Land. At that point, they went from being directly sustained by the manna to being nourished by the bountiful produce of *Eretz Yisrael*. Rabbi Samson Raphael Hirsch notes that *Hashem* intended for the produce of the land to be enjoyed as though it, too, is like the miraculous manna, provided directly by God.

"Produce of the land" — Wheat field near *Tiveria*

3 But the people thirsted there for water; and the people grumbled against *Moshe* and said, "Why did you bring us up from Egypt, to kill us and our children and livestock with thirst?"

ג וַיִּצְמָא שָׁם הָעָם לַמַּיִם וַיָּלֶן הָעָם עַל־מֹשֶׁה וַיֹּאמֶר לָמָּה זֶּה הֶעֱלִיתָנוּ מִמִּצְרַיִם לְהָמִית אֹתִי וְאֶת־בָּנַי וְאֶת־מִקְנַי בַּצָּמָא:

4 *Moshe* cried out to *Hashem*, saying, "What shall I do with this people? Before long they will be stoning me!"

ד וַיִּצְעַק מֹשֶׁה אֶל־יְהוָה לֵאמֹר מָה אֶעֱשֶׂה לָעָם הַזֶּה עוֹד מְעַט וּסְקָלֻנִי:

5 Then *Hashem* said to *Moshe*, "Pass before the people; take with you some of the elders of *Yisrael*, and take along the rod with which you struck the Nile, and set out.

ה וַיֹּאמֶר יְהוָה אֶל־מֹשֶׁה עֲבֹר לִפְנֵי הָעָם וְקַח אִתְּךָ מִזִּקְנֵי יִשְׂרָאֵל וּמַטְּךָ אֲשֶׁר הִכִּיתָ בּוֹ אֶת־הַיְאֹר קַח בְּיָדְךָ וְהָלָכְתָּ:

6 I will be standing there before you on the rock at Horeb. Strike the rock and water will issue from it, and the people will drink." And *Moshe* did so in the sight of the elders of *Yisrael*.

ו הִנְנִי עֹמֵד לְפָנֶיךָ שָּׁם עַל־הַצּוּר בְּחֹרֵב וְהִכִּיתָ בַצּוּר וְיָצְאוּ מִמֶּנּוּ מַיִם וְשָׁתָה הָעָם וַיַּעַשׂ כֵּן מֹשֶׁה לְעֵינֵי זִקְנֵי יִשְׂרָאֵל:

7 The place was named Massah and Meribah, because the Israelites quarreled and because they tried *Hashem*, saying, "Is *Hashem* present among us or not?"

ז וַיִּקְרָא שֵׁם הַמָּקוֹם מַסָּה וּמְרִיבָה עַל־רִיב בְּנֵי יִשְׂרָאֵל וְעַל נַסֹּתָם אֶת־יְהוָה לֵאמֹר הֲיֵשׁ יְהוָה בְּקִרְבֵּנוּ אִם־אָיִן:

va-yik-RA SHAYM ha-ma-KOM ma-SAH um-ree-VAH al REEV b'-NAY yis-ra-AYL v'-AL na-so-TAM et a-do-NAI lay-MOR ha-YAYSH a-do-NAI b'-kir-BAY-nu im A-yin

8 Amalek came and fought with *Yisrael* at Rephidim.

ח וַיָּבֹא עֲמָלֵק וַיִּלָּחֶם עִם־יִשְׂרָאֵל בִּרְפִידִם:

9 *Moshe* said to *Yehoshua*, "Pick some men for us, and go out and do battle with Amalek. Tomorrow I will station myself on the top of the hill, with the rod of *Hashem* in my hand."

ט וַיֹּאמֶר מֹשֶׁה אֶל־יְהוֹשֻׁעַ בְּחַר־לָנוּ אֲנָשִׁים וְצֵא הִלָּחֵם בַּעֲמָלֵק מָחָר אָנֹכִי נִצָּב עַל־רֹאשׁ הַגִּבְעָה וּמַטֵּה הָאֱלֹהִים בְּיָדִי:

10 *Yehoshua* did as *Moshe* told him and fought with Amalek, while *Moshe*, *Aharon*, and *Chur* went up to the top of the hill.

י וַיַּעַשׂ יְהוֹשֻׁעַ כַּאֲשֶׁר אָמַר־לוֹ מֹשֶׁה לְהִלָּחֵם בַּעֲמָלֵק וּמֹשֶׁה אַהֲרֹן וְחוּר עָלוּ רֹאשׁ הַגִּבְעָה:

11 Then, whenever *Moshe* held up his hand, *Yisrael* prevailed; but whenever he let down his hand, Amalek prevailed.

יא וְהָיָה כַּאֲשֶׁר יָרִים מֹשֶׁה יָדוֹ וְגָבַר יִשְׂרָאֵל וְכַאֲשֶׁר יָנִיחַ יָדוֹ וְגָבַר עֲמָלֵק:

17:7 Is *Hashem* present among us or not? The People of Israel are not questioning their faith in *Hashem*. Rather, they are wondering to what extent He is involved in their everyday lives. In Egypt, and in other civilizations at that time, God was understood as a static force, and nature as governed by unchanging rules. The newly freed Children of Israel are therefore questioning God's involvement in their day-to-day affairs. In turn, *Hashem* is educating the nation about His supremacy and control over nature and all the workings of the world. Not only did *Hashem* create water, but He also controls its supply, providing it or withholding it as He sees fit. This message becomes embedded in the psyche of the Chosen Nation and its practical application bears fruit in the Chosen Land where the Jews pray daily to God for water and see His active involvement in everyday life.

Waterfall at Nahal HaShofet

¹² But *Moshe*'s hands grew heavy; so they took a stone and put it under him and he sat on it, while *Aharon* and *Chur*, one on each side, supported his hands; thus his hands remained steady until the sun set.

יב וִידֵי מֹשֶׁה כְּבֵדִים וַיִּקְחוּ־אֶבֶן וַיָּשִׂימוּ תַחְתָּיו וַיֵּשֶׁב עָלֶיהָ וְאַהֲרֹן וְחוּר תָּמְכוּ בְיָדָיו מִזֶּה אֶחָד וּמִזֶּה אֶחָד וַיְהִי יָדָיו אֱמוּנָה עַד־בֹּא הַשָּׁמֶשׁ:

¹³ And *Yehoshua* overwhelmed the people of Amalek with the sword.

יג וַיַּחֲלֹשׁ יְהוֹשֻׁעַ אֶת־עֲמָלֵק וְאֶת־עַמּוֹ לְפִי־חָרֶב:

¹⁴ Then *Hashem* said to *Moshe*, "Inscribe this in a document as a reminder, and read it aloud to *Yehoshua*: I will utterly blot out the memory of Amalek from under heaven!"

יד וַיֹּאמֶר יְהוָה אֶל־מֹשֶׁה כְּתֹב זֹאת זִכָּרוֹן בַּסֵּפֶר וְשִׂים בְּאָזְנֵי יְהוֹשֻׁעַ כִּי־מָחֹה אֶמְחֶה אֶת־זֵכֶר עֲמָלֵק מִתַּחַת הַשָּׁמָיִם:

¹⁵ And *Moshe* built a *Mizbayach* and named it Adonai-nissi.

טו וַיִּבֶן מֹשֶׁה מִזְבֵּחַ וַיִּקְרָא שְׁמוֹ יְהוָה נִסִּי:

¹⁶ He said, "It means, 'Hand upon the throne of *Hashem*!' *Hashem* will be at war with Amalek throughout the ages."

טז וַיֹּאמֶר כִּי־יָד עַל־כֵּס יָהּ מִלְחָמָה לַיהוָה בַּעֲמָלֵק מִדֹּר דֹּר:

18 ¹ Jethro priest of Midian, *Moshe*'s father-in-law, heard all that *Hashem* had done for *Moshe* and for *Yisrael* His people, how *Hashem* had brought *Yisrael* out from Egypt.

יח א וַיִּשְׁמַע יִתְרוֹ כֹהֵן מִדְיָן חֹתֵן מֹשֶׁה אֵת כָּל־אֲשֶׁר עָשָׂה אֱלֹהִים לְמֹשֶׁה וּלְיִשְׂרָאֵל עַמּוֹ כִּי־הוֹצִיא יְהוָה אֶת־יִשְׂרָאֵל מִמִּצְרָיִם:

² So Jethro, *Moshe*'s father-in-law, took *Tzipora*, *Moshe*'s wife, after she had been sent home,

ב וַיִּקַּח יִתְרוֹ חֹתֵן מֹשֶׁה אֶת־צִפֹּרָה אֵשֶׁת מֹשֶׁה אַחַר שִׁלּוּחֶיהָ:

³ and her two sons – of whom one was named *Gershom*, that is to say, "I have been a stranger in a foreign land";

ג וְאֵת שְׁנֵי בָנֶיהָ אֲשֶׁר שֵׁם הָאֶחָד גֵּרְשֹׁם כִּי אָמַר גֵּר הָיִיתִי בְּאֶרֶץ נָכְרִיָּה:

⁴ and the other was named *Eliezer*, meaning, "The God of my father was my help, and He delivered me from the sword of Pharaoh."

ד וְשֵׁם הָאֶחָד אֱלִיעֶזֶר כִּי־אֱלֹהֵי אָבִי בְּעֶזְרִי וַיַּצִּלֵנִי מֵחֶרֶב פַּרְעֹה:

⁵ Jethro, *Moshe*'s father-in-law, brought *Moshe*'s sons and wife to him in the wilderness, where he was encamped at the mountain of *Hashem*.

ה וַיָּבֹא יִתְרוֹ חֹתֵן מֹשֶׁה וּבָנָיו וְאִשְׁתּוֹ אֶל־מֹשֶׁה אֶל־הַמִּדְבָּר אֲשֶׁר־הוּא חֹנֶה שָׁם הַר הָאֱלֹהִים:

⁶ He sent word to *Moshe*, "I, your father-in-law Jethro, am coming to you, with your wife and her two sons."

ו וַיֹּאמֶר אֶל־מֹשֶׁה אֲנִי חֹתֶנְךָ יִתְרוֹ בָּא אֵלֶיךָ וְאִשְׁתְּךָ וּשְׁנֵי בָנֶיהָ עִמָּהּ:

⁷ *Moshe* went out to meet his father-in-law; he bowed low and kissed him; each asked after the other's welfare, and they went into the tent.

ז וַיֵּצֵא מֹשֶׁה לִקְרַאת חֹתְנוֹ וַיִּשְׁתַּחוּ וַיִּשַּׁק־לוֹ וַיִּשְׁאֲלוּ אִישׁ־לְרֵעֵהוּ לְשָׁלוֹם וַיָּבֹאוּ הָאֹהֱלָה:

⁸ *Moshe* then recounted to his father-in-law everything that *Hashem* had done to Pharaoh and to the Egyptians for *Yisrael*'s sake, all the hardships that had befallen them on the way, and how *Hashem* had delivered them.

ח וַיְסַפֵּר מֹשֶׁה לְחֹתְנוֹ אֵת כָּל־אֲשֶׁר עָשָׂה יְהוָה לְפַרְעֹה וּלְמִצְרַיִם עַל אוֹדֹת יִשְׂרָאֵל אֵת כָּל־הַתְּלָאָה אֲשֶׁר מְצָאָתַם בַּדֶּרֶךְ וַיַּצִּלֵם יְהוָה:

9 And Jethro rejoiced over all the kindness that *Hashem* had shown *Yisrael* when He delivered them from the Egyptians.

ט וַיִּחַדְּ יִתְרֹו עַל כָּל־הַטּוֹבָה אֲשֶׁר־עָשָׂה יְהוָה לְיִשְׂרָאֵל אֲשֶׁר הִצִּילוֹ מִיַּד מִצְרָיִם:

10 "Blessed be *Hashem*," Jethro said, "who delivered you from the Egyptians and from Pharaoh, and who delivered the people from under the hand of the Egyptians.

י וַיֹּאמֶר יִתְרוֹ בָּרוּךְ יְהוָה אֲשֶׁר הִצִּיל אֶתְכֶם מִיַּד מִצְרַיִם וּמִיַּד פַּרְעֹה אֲשֶׁר הִצִּיל אֶת־הָעָם מִתַּחַת יַד־מִצְרָיִם:

11 Now I know that *Hashem* is greater than all gods, yes, by the result of their very schemes against [the people]."

יא עַתָּה יָדַעְתִּי כִּי־גָדוֹל יְהוָה מִכָּל־הָאֱלֹהִים כִּי בַדָּבָר אֲשֶׁר זָדוּ עֲלֵיהֶם:

12 And Jethro, *Moshe*'s father-in-law, brought a burnt offering and sacrifices for *Hashem*; and *Aharon* came with all the elders of *Yisrael* to partake of the meal before *Hashem* with *Moshe*'s father-in-law.

יב וַיִּקַּח יִתְרוֹ חֹתֵן מֹשֶׁה עֹלָה וּזְבָחִים לֵאלֹהִים וַיָּבֹא אַהֲרֹן וְכֹל זִקְנֵי יִשְׂרָאֵל לֶאֱכָל־לֶחֶם עִם־חֹתֵן מֹשֶׁה לִפְנֵי הָאֱלֹהִים:

13 Next day, *Moshe* sat as magistrate among the people, while the people stood about *Moshe* from morning until evening.

יג וַיְהִי מִמָּחֳרָת וַיֵּשֶׁב מֹשֶׁה לִשְׁפֹּט אֶת־הָעָם וַיַּעֲמֹד הָעָם עַל־מֹשֶׁה מִן־הַבֹּקֶר עַד־הָעָרֶב:

14 But when *Moshe*'s father-in-law saw how much he had to do for the people, he said, "What is this thing that you are doing to the people? Why do you act alone, while all the people stand about you from morning until evening?"

יד וַיַּרְא חֹתֵן מֹשֶׁה אֵת כָּל־אֲשֶׁר־הוּא עֹשֶׂה לָעָם וַיֹּאמֶר מָה־הַדָּבָר הַזֶּה אֲשֶׁר אַתָּה עֹשֶׂה לָעָם מַדּוּעַ אַתָּה יוֹשֵׁב לְבַדֶּךָ וְכָל־הָעָם נִצָּב עָלֶיךָ מִן־בֹּקֶר עַד־עָרֶב:

15 *Moshe* replied to his father-in-law, "It is because the people come to me to inquire of *Hashem*.

טו וַיֹּאמֶר מֹשֶׁה לְחֹתְנוֹ כִּי־יָבֹא אֵלַי הָעָם לִדְרֹשׁ אֱלֹהִים:

16 When they have a dispute, it comes before me, and I decide between one person and another, and I make known the laws and teachings of *Hashem*."

טז כִּי־יִהְיֶה לָהֶם דָּבָר בָּא אֵלַי וְשָׁפַטְתִּי בֵּין אִישׁ וּבֵין רֵעֵהוּ וְהוֹדַעְתִּי אֶת־חֻקֵּי הָאֱלֹהִים וְאֶת־תּוֹרֹתָיו:

17 But *Moshe*'s father-in-law said to him, "The thing you are doing is not right;

יז וַיֹּאמֶר חֹתֵן מֹשֶׁה אֵלָיו לֹא־טוֹב הַדָּבָר אֲשֶׁר אַתָּה עֹשֶׂה:

18 you will surely wear yourself out, and these people as well. For the task is too heavy for you; you cannot do it alone.

יח נָבֹל תִּבֹּל גַּם־אַתָּה גַּם־הָעָם הַזֶּה אֲשֶׁר עִמָּךְ כִּי־כָבֵד מִמְּךָ הַדָּבָר לֹא־תוּכַל עֲשֹׂהוּ לְבַדֶּךָ:

19 Now listen to me. I will give you counsel, and *Hashem* be with you! You represent the people before *Hashem*: you bring the disputes before *Hashem*,

יט עַתָּה שְׁמַע בְּקֹלִי אִיעָצְךָ וִיהִי אֱלֹהִים עִמָּךְ הֱיֵה אַתָּה לָעָם מוּל הָאֱלֹהִים וְהֵבֵאתָ אַתָּה אֶת־הַדְּבָרִים אֶל־הָאֱלֹהִים:

20 and enjoin upon them the laws and the teachings, and make known to them the way they are to go and the practices they are to follow.

כ וְהִזְהַרְתָּה אֶתְהֶם אֶת־הַחֻקִּים וְאֶת־הַתּוֹרֹת וְהוֹדַעְתָּ לָהֶם אֶת־הַדֶּרֶךְ יֵלְכוּ בָהּ וְאֶת־הַמַּעֲשֶׂה אֲשֶׁר יַעֲשׂוּן:

21 You shall also seek out from among all the people capable men who fear *Hashem*, trustworthy men who spurn ill-gotten gain. Set these over them as chiefs of thousands, hundreds, fifties, and tens, and

כא וְאַתָּה תֶחֱזֶה מִכָּל־הָעָם אַנְשֵׁי־חַיִל יִרְאֵי אֱלֹהִים אַנְשֵׁי אֱמֶת שֹׂנְאֵי בָצַע וְשַׂמְתָּ עֲלֵהֶם שָׂרֵי אֲלָפִים שָׂרֵי מֵאוֹת שָׂרֵי חֲמִשִּׁים וְשָׂרֵי עֲשָׂרֹת:

22 let them judge the people at all times. Have them bring every major dispute to you, but let them decide every minor dispute themselves. Make it easier for yourself by letting them share the burden with you.

כב וְשָׁפְטוּ אֶת־הָעָם בְּכָל־עֵת וְהָיָה כָּל־הַדָּבָר הַגָּדֹל יָבִיאוּ אֵלֶיךָ וְכָל־הַדָּבָר הַקָּטֹן יִשְׁפְּטוּ־הֵם וְהָקֵל מֵעָלֶיךָ וְנָשְׂאוּ אִתָּךְ:

23 If you do this – and *Hashem* so commands you – you will be able to bear up; and all these people too will go home unwearied."

כג אִם אֶת־הַדָּבָר הַזֶּה תַּעֲשֶׂה וְצִוְּךָ אֱלֹהִים וְיָכָלְתָּ עֲמֹד וְגַם כָּל־הָעָם הַזֶּה עַל־מְקֹמוֹ יָבֹא בְשָׁלוֹם:

IM et ha-da-VAR ha-ZEH ta-a-SEH v'-tzi-v'-KHA e-lo-HEEM v'-ya-khol-TA a-MOD v'-GAM kol ha-AM ha-ZEH al m'-ko-MO ya-VO v'-sha-LOM

24 *Moshe* heeded his father-in-law and did just as he had said.

כד וַיִּשְׁמַע מֹשֶׁה לְקוֹל חֹתְנוֹ וַיַּעַשׂ כֹּל אֲשֶׁר אָמָר:

25 *Moshe* chose capable men out of all *Yisrael*, and appointed them heads over the people – chiefs of thousands, hundreds, fifties, and tens;

כה וַיִּבְחַר מֹשֶׁה אַנְשֵׁי־חַיִל מִכָּל־יִשְׂרָאֵל וַיִּתֵּן אֹתָם רָאשִׁים עַל־הָעָם שָׂרֵי אֲלָפִים שָׂרֵי מֵאוֹת שָׂרֵי חֲמִשִּׁים וְשָׂרֵי עֲשָׂרֹת:

26 and they judged the people at all times: the difficult matters they would bring to *Moshe*, and all the minor matters they would decide themselves.

כו וְשָׁפְטוּ אֶת־הָעָם בְּכָל־עֵת אֶת־הַדָּבָר הַקָּשֶׁה יְבִיאוּן אֶל־מֹשֶׁה וְכָל־הַדָּבָר הַקָּטֹן יִשְׁפּוּטוּ הֵם:

27 Then *Moshe* bade his father-in-law farewell, and he went his way to his own land.

כז וַיְשַׁלַּח מֹשֶׁה אֶת־חֹתְנוֹ וַיֵּלֶךְ לוֹ אֶל־אַרְצוֹ:

19 1 On the third new moon after the Israelites had gone forth from the land of Egypt, on that very day, they entered the wilderness of Sinai.

יט א בַּחֹדֶשׁ הַשְּׁלִישִׁי לְצֵאת בְּנֵי־יִשְׂרָאֵל מֵאֶרֶץ מִצְרָיִם בַּיּוֹם הַזֶּה בָּאוּ מִדְבַּר סִינָי:

2 Having journeyed from Rephidim, they entered the wilderness of Sinai and encamped in the wilderness. *Yisrael* encamped there in front of the mountain,

ב וַיִּסְעוּ מֵרְפִידִים וַיָּבֹאוּ מִדְבַּר סִינַי וַיַּחֲנוּ בַּמִּדְבָּר וַיִּחַן־שָׁם יִשְׂרָאֵל נֶגֶד הָהָר:

The Supreme Court of Israel

18:23 All these people too will go home unwearied A simple reading of this verse implies that after the implementation of Jethro's suggestion for expediting the judicial process, every individual would be able to return to their homes much sooner. Based on a careful reading of the Hebrew words, however, the *Kli Yakar* explains that the verse does not refer to individuals returning to their private homes, but rather, to the Nation of Israel arriving in their national home, *Eretz Yisrael*. Improving their system of justice was a vital step towards entering the land. Similarly, a renewed commitment to justice will ultimately lead to the final return of the People of Israel to the Land of Israel, as it says (Isaiah 1:27), "*Tzion* shall be saved in the judgement."

3 and *Moshe* went up to *Hashem*. *Hashem* called to
him from the mountain, saying, "Thus shall you say
to the house of *Yaakov* and declare to the children
of *Yisrael*:

ג וּמֹשֶׁה עָלָה אֶל־הָאֱלֹהִים וַיִּקְרָא אֵלָיו
יְהוָה מִן־הָהָר לֵאמֹר כֹּה תֹאמַר לְבֵית
יַעֲקֹב וְתַגֵּיד לִבְנֵי יִשְׂרָאֵל:

4 'You have seen what I did to the Egyptians, how I
bore you on eagles' wings and brought you to Me.

ד אַתֶּם רְאִיתֶם אֲשֶׁר עָשִׂיתִי לְמִצְרָיִם
וָאֶשָּׂא אֶתְכֶם עַל־כַּנְפֵי נְשָׁרִים וָאָבִא
אֶתְכֶם אֵלָי:

*a-TEM r'-ee-TEM a-SHER a-SEE-tee l'-mitz-RA-yim va-e-SA
et-KHEM al kan-FAY n'-sha-REEM va-a-VEE et-KHEM ay-LAI*

5 Now then, if you will obey Me faithfully and keep
My covenant, you shall be My treasured possession
among all the peoples. Indeed, all the earth is Mine,

ה וְעַתָּה אִם־שָׁמוֹעַ תִּשְׁמְעוּ בְּקֹלִי
וּשְׁמַרְתֶּם אֶת־בְּרִיתִי וִהְיִיתֶם לִי סְגֻלָּה
מִכָּל־הָעַמִּים כִּי־לִי כָּל־הָאָרֶץ:

6 but you shall be to Me a kingdom of priests and
a holy nation.' These are the words that you shall
speak to the children of *Yisrael*."

ו וְאַתֶּם תִּהְיוּ־לִי מַמְלֶכֶת כֹּהֲנִים וְגוֹי
קָדוֹשׁ אֵלֶּה הַדְּבָרִים אֲשֶׁר תְּדַבֵּר אֶל־
בְּנֵי יִשְׂרָאֵל:

*v'-a-TEM tih-yu LEE mam-LE-khet ko-ha-NEEM v'-GOY ka-DOSH
AY-leh ha-d'-va-REEM a-SHER t'-da-BAYR el b'-NAY yis-ra-AYL*

7 *Moshe* came and summoned the elders of the
people and put before them all that *Hashem* had
commanded him.

ז וַיָּבֹא מֹשֶׁה וַיִּקְרָא לְזִקְנֵי הָעָם וַיָּשֶׂם
לִפְנֵיהֶם אֵת כָּל־הַדְּבָרִים הָאֵלֶּה אֲשֶׁר
צִוָּהוּ יְהוָה:

8 All the people answered as one, saying, "All that
Hashem has spoken we will do!" And *Moshe*
brought back the people's words to *Hashem*.

ח וַיַּעֲנוּ כָל־הָעָם יַחְדָּו וַיֹּאמְרוּ כֹּל אֲשֶׁר־
דִּבֶּר יְהוָה נַעֲשֶׂה וַיָּשֶׁב מֹשֶׁה אֶת־דִּבְרֵי
הָעָם אֶל־יְהוָה:

9 And *Hashem* said to *Moshe*, "I will come to you in a
thick cloud, in order that the people may hear when
I speak with you and so trust you ever after." Then
Moshe reported the people's words to *Hashem*,

ט וַיֹּאמֶר יְהוָה אֶל־מֹשֶׁה הִנֵּה אָנֹכִי בָּא
אֵלֶיךָ בְּעַב הֶעָנָן בַּעֲבוּר יִשְׁמַע הָעָם
בְּדַבְּרִי עִמָּךְ וְגַם־בְּךָ יַאֲמִינוּ לְעוֹלָם
וַיַּגֵּד מֹשֶׁה אֶת־דִּבְרֵי הָעָם אֶל־יְהוָה:

10 and *Hashem* said to *Moshe*, "Go to the people and
warn them to stay pure today and tomorrow. Let
them wash their clothes.

י וַיֹּאמֶר יְהוָה אֶל־מֹשֶׁה לֵךְ אֶל־הָעָם
וְקִדַּשְׁתָּם הַיּוֹם וּמָחָר וְכִבְּסוּ שִׂמְלֹתָם:

11 Let them be ready for the third day; for on the third
day *Hashem* will come down, in the sight of all the
people, on *Har Sinai*.

יא וְהָיוּ נְכֹנִים לַיּוֹם הַשְּׁלִישִׁי כִּי בַּיּוֹם
הַשְּׁלִישִׁי יֵרֵד יְהוָה לְעֵינֵי כָל־הָעָם עַל־
הַר סִינָי:

19:4 How I bore you on eagles' wings "Operation
Magic Carpet", also called "Operation On Wings
of Eagles" based on this verse, secretly airlifted
almost fifty thousand Yemenite Jews to Israel between
June 1949 and September 1950. Many of the Yemenite
Jews had never seen an airplane before, and they likened
the ride from Yemen to Israel as a fulfillment of this verse,
"I bore you on eagles' wings." This Operation was just one
example of the fulfillment of the State of Israel's responsibility toward all Jews worldwide,
summarized by Prime Minister Yitzhak
Rabin in a speech he delivered to the
Zionist Congress in 1992: "Our responsibility also extends to all Jews
throughout the world…World Jewry
should know that we are responsible
for them and will do all we can to
assist them when they are in need."

Operation On Wings of Eagles, 1949

46

12 You shall set bounds for the people round about, saying, 'Beware of going up the mountain or touching the border of it. Whoever touches the mountain shall be put to death:

וְהִגְבַּלְתָּ אֶת־הָעָם סָבִיב לֵאמֹר הִשָּׁמְרוּ לָכֶם עֲלוֹת בָּהָר וּנְגֹעַ בְּקָצֵהוּ כָּל־הַנֹּגֵעַ בָּהָר מוֹת יוּמָת:

13 no hand shall touch him, but he shall be either stoned or shot; beast or man, he shall not live.' When the ram's horn sounds a long blast, they may go up on the mountain."

לֹא־תִגַּע בּוֹ יָד כִּי־סָקוֹל יִסָּקֵל אוֹ־יָרֹה יִיָּרֶה אִם־בְּהֵמָה אִם־אִישׁ לֹא יִחְיֶה בִּמְשֹׁךְ הַיֹּבֵל הֵמָּה יַעֲלוּ בָהָר:

14 *Moshe* came down from the mountain to the people and warned the people to stay pure, and they washed their clothes.

וַיֵּרֶד מֹשֶׁה מִן־הָהָר אֶל־הָעָם וַיְקַדֵּשׁ אֶת־הָעָם וַיְכַבְּסוּ שִׂמְלֹתָם:

15 And he said to the people, "Be ready for the third day: do not go near a woman."

וַיֹּאמֶר אֶל־הָעָם הֱיוּ נְכֹנִים לִשְׁלֹשֶׁת יָמִים אַל־תִּגְּשׁוּ אֶל־אִשָּׁה:

16 On the third day, as morning dawned, there was thunder, and lightning, and a dense cloud upon the mountain, and a very loud blast of the *shofar*; and all the people who were in the camp trembled.

וַיְהִי בַיּוֹם הַשְּׁלִישִׁי בִּהְיֹת הַבֹּקֶר וַיְהִי קֹלֹת וּבְרָקִים וְעָנָן כָּבֵד עַל־הָהָר וְקֹל שֹׁפָר חָזָק מְאֹד וַיֶּחֱרַד כָּל־הָעָם אֲשֶׁר בַּמַּחֲנֶה:

17 *Moshe* led the people out of the camp toward *Hashem*, and they took their places at the foot of the mountain.

וַיּוֹצֵא מֹשֶׁה אֶת־הָעָם לִקְרַאת הָאֱלֹהִים מִן־הַמַּחֲנֶה וַיִּתְיַצְּבוּ בְּתַחְתִּית הָהָר:

18 Now *Har Sinai* was all in smoke, for *Hashem* had come down upon it in fire; the smoke rose like the smoke of a kiln, and the whole mountain trembled violently.

וְהַר סִינַי עָשַׁן כֻּלּוֹ מִפְּנֵי אֲשֶׁר יָרַד עָלָיו יְהוָה בָּאֵשׁ וַיַּעַל עֲשָׁנוֹ כְּעֶשֶׁן הַכִּבְשָׁן וַיֶּחֱרַד כָּל־הָהָר מְאֹד:

19 The blare of the *shofar* grew louder and louder. As *Moshe* spoke, *Hashem* answered him in thunder.

וַיְהִי קוֹל הַשּׁוֹפָר הוֹלֵךְ וְחָזֵק מְאֹד מֹשֶׁה יְדַבֵּר וְהָאֱלֹהִים יַעֲנֶנּוּ בְקוֹל:

20 *Hashem* came down upon *Har Sinai*, on the top of the mountain, and *Hashem* called *Moshe* to the top of the mountain and *Moshe* went up.

וַיֵּרֶד יְהוָה עַל־הַר סִינַי אֶל־רֹאשׁ הָהָר וַיִּקְרָא יְהוָה לְמֹשֶׁה אֶל־רֹאשׁ הָהָר וַיַּעַל מֹשֶׁה:

21 *Hashem* said to *Moshe*, "Go down, warn the people not to break through to *Hashem* to gaze, lest many of them perish.

וַיֹּאמֶר יְהוָה אֶל־מֹשֶׁה רֵד הָעֵד בָּעָם פֶּן־יֶהֶרְסוּ אֶל־יְהוָה לִרְאוֹת וְנָפַל מִמֶּנּוּ רָב:

22 The *Kohanim* also, who come near *Hashem*, must stay pure, lest *Hashem* break out against them."

וְגַם הַכֹּהֲנִים הַנִּגָּשִׁים אֶל־יְהוָה יִתְקַדָּשׁוּ פֶּן־יִפְרֹץ בָּהֶם יְהוָה:

23 But *Moshe* said to *Hashem*, "The people cannot come up to *Har Sinai*, for You warned us saying, 'Set bounds about the mountain and sanctify it.'"

וַיֹּאמֶר מֹשֶׁה אֶל־יְהוָה לֹא־יוּכַל הָעָם לַעֲלֹת אֶל־הַר סִינָי כִּי־אַתָּה הַעֵדֹתָה בָּנוּ לֵאמֹר הַגְבֵּל אֶת־הָהָר וְקִדַּשְׁתּוֹ:

24 So *Hashem* said to him, "Go down, and come back together with *Aharon*; but let not the *Kohanim* or the people break through to come up to *Hashem*, lest He break out against them."

וַיֹּאמֶר אֵלָיו יְהוָה לֶךְ־רֵד וְעָלִיתָ אַתָּה וְאַהֲרֹן עִמָּךְ וְהַכֹּהֲנִים וְהָעָם אַל־יֶהֶרְסוּ לַעֲלֹת אֶל־יְהוָה פֶּן־יִפְרָץ־בָּם:

25 And *Moshe* went down to the people and spoke to them.

וַיֵּרֶד מֹשֶׁה אֶל־הָעָם וַיֹּאמֶר אֲלֵהֶם:

20 ¹ *Hashem* spoke all these words, saying:

כ א וַיְדַבֵּר אֱלֹהִים אֵת כָּל־הַדְּבָרִים הָאֵלֶּה לֵאמֹר:

² I *Hashem* am your God who brought you out of the land of Egypt, the house of bondage:

ב אָנֹכִי יְהֹוָה אֱלֹהֶיךָ אֲשֶׁר הוֹצֵאתִיךָ מֵאֶרֶץ מִצְרַיִם מִבֵּית עֲבָדִים:

³ You shall have no other gods besides Me.

ג לֹא יִהְיֶה־לְךָ אֱלֹהִים אֲחֵרִים עַל־פָּנָי:

⁴ You shall not make for yourself a sculptured image, or any likeness of what is in the heavens above, or on the earth below, or in the waters under the earth.

ד לֹא תַעֲשֶׂה־לְךָ פֶסֶל וְכָל־תְּמוּנָה אֲשֶׁר בַּשָּׁמַיִם מִמַּעַל וַאֲשֶׁר בָּאָרֶץ מִתַּחַת וַאֲשֶׁר בַּמַּיִם מִתַּחַת לָאָרֶץ:

⁵ You shall not bow down to them or serve them. For I *Hashem* your God am an impassioned God, visiting the guilt of the parents upon the children, upon the third and upon the fourth generations of those who reject Me,

ה לֹא־תִשְׁתַּחֲוֶה לָהֶם וְלֹא תָעָבְדֵם כִּי אָנֹכִי יְהֹוָה אֱלֹהֶיךָ אֵל קַנָּא פֹּקֵד עֲוֹן אָבֹת עַל־בָּנִים עַל־שִׁלֵּשִׁים וְעַל־רִבֵּעִים לְשֹׂנְאָי:

⁶ but showing kindness to the thousandth generation of those who love Me and keep My commandments.

ו וְעֹשֶׂה חֶסֶד לַאֲלָפִים לְאֹהֲבַי וּלְשֹׁמְרֵי מִצְוֹתָי:

⁷ You shall not swear falsely by the name of *Hashem* your God; for *Hashem* will not clear one who swears falsely by His name.

ז לֹא תִשָּׂא אֶת־שֵׁם־יְהֹוָה אֱלֹהֶיךָ לַשָּׁוְא כִּי לֹא יְנַקֶּה יְהֹוָה אֵת אֲשֶׁר־יִשָּׂא אֶת־שְׁמוֹ לַשָּׁוְא:

⁸ Remember the *Shabbat* day and keep it holy.

ח זָכוֹר אֶת־יוֹם הַשַּׁבָּת לְקַדְּשׁוֹ:

⁹ Six days you shall labor and do all your work,

ט שֵׁשֶׁת יָמִים תַּעֲבֹד וְעָשִׂיתָ כָּל־מְלַאכְתֶּךָ:

¹⁰ but the seventh day is a *Shabbat* of *Hashem* your God: you shall not do any work – you, your son or daughter, your male or female slave, or your cattle, or the stranger who is within your settlements.

י וְיוֹם הַשְּׁבִיעִי שַׁבָּת לַיהֹוָה אֱלֹהֶיךָ לֹא־תַעֲשֶׂה כָל־מְלָאכָה אַתָּה וּבִנְךָ־וּבִתֶּךָ עַבְדְּךָ וַאֲמָתְךָ וּבְהֶמְתֶּךָ וְגֵרְךָ אֲשֶׁר בִּשְׁעָרֶיךָ:

¹¹ For in six days *Hashem* made heaven and earth and sea, and all that is in them, and He rested on the seventh day; therefore *Hashem* blessed the *Shabbat* day and hallowed it.

יא כִּי שֵׁשֶׁת־יָמִים עָשָׂה יְהֹוָה אֶת־הַשָּׁמַיִם וְאֶת־הָאָרֶץ אֶת־הַיָּם וְאֶת־כָּל־אֲשֶׁר־בָּם וַיָּנַח בַּיּוֹם הַשְּׁבִיעִי עַל־כֵּן בֵּרַךְ יְהֹוָה אֶת־יוֹם הַשַּׁבָּת וַיְקַדְּשֵׁהוּ:

¹² Honor your father and your mother, that you may long endure on the land that *Hashem* your God is assigning to you.

יב כַּבֵּד אֶת־אָבִיךָ וְאֶת־אִמֶּךָ לְמַעַן יַאֲרִכוּן יָמֶיךָ עַל הָאֲדָמָה אֲשֶׁר־יְהֹוָה אֱלֹהֶיךָ נֹתֵן לָךְ:

¹³ You shall not murder. You shall not commit adultery. You shall not steal. You shall not bear false witness against your neighbor.

יג לֹא תִרְצָח: לֹא תִנְאָף: לֹא תִגְנֹב: לֹא־תַעֲנֶה בְרֵעֲךָ עֵד שָׁקֶר:

¹⁴ You shall not covet your neighbor's house: you shall not covet your neighbor's wife, or his male or female slave, or his ox or his ass, or anything that is your neighbor's.

יד לֹא תַחְמֹד בֵּית רֵעֶךָ לֹא־תַחְמֹד אֵשֶׁת רֵעֶךָ וְעַבְדּוֹ וַאֲמָתוֹ וְשׁוֹרוֹ וַחֲמֹרוֹ וְכֹל אֲשֶׁר לְרֵעֶךָ:

¹⁵ All the people witnessed the thunder and lightning, the blare of the *shofar* and the mountain smoking; and when the people saw it, they fell back and stood at a distance.

טו וְכָל־הָעָם רֹאִים אֶת־הַקּוֹלֹת וְאֶת־הַלַּפִּידִם וְאֵת קוֹל הַשֹּׁפָר וְאֶת־הָהָר עָשֵׁן וַיַּרְא הָעָם וַיָּנֻעוּ וַיַּעַמְדוּ מֵרָחֹק:

¹⁶ "You speak to us," they said to *Moshe*, "and we will obey; but let not *Hashem* speak to us, lest we die."

טז וַיֹּאמְרוּ אֶל־מֹשֶׁה דַּבֵּר־אַתָּה עִמָּנוּ וְנִשְׁמָעָה וְאַל־יְדַבֵּר עִמָּנוּ אֱלֹהִים פֶּן־נָמוּת:

¹⁷ *Moshe* answered the people, "Be not afraid; for *Hashem* has come only in order to test you, and in order that the fear of Him may be ever with you, so that you do not go astray."

יז וַיֹּאמֶר מֹשֶׁה אֶל־הָעָם אַל־תִּירָאוּ כִּי לְבַעֲבוּר נַסּוֹת אֶתְכֶם בָּא הָאֱלֹהִים וּבַעֲבוּר תִּהְיֶה יִרְאָתוֹ עַל־פְּנֵיכֶם לְבִלְתִּי תֶחֱטָאוּ:

¹⁸ So the people remained at a distance, while *Moshe* approached the thick cloud where *Hashem* was.

יח וַיַּעֲמֹד הָעָם מֵרָחֹק וּמֹשֶׁה נִגַּשׁ אֶל־הָעֲרָפֶל אֲשֶׁר־שָׁם הָאֱלֹהִים:

¹⁹ *Hashem* said to *Moshe*: Thus shall you say to the Israelites: You yourselves saw that I spoke to you from the very heavens:

יט וַיֹּאמֶר יְהֹוָה אֶל־מֹשֶׁה כֹּה תֹאמַר אֶל־בְּנֵי יִשְׂרָאֵל אַתֶּם רְאִיתֶם כִּי מִן־הַשָּׁמַיִם דִּבַּרְתִּי עִמָּכֶם:

²⁰ With Me, therefore, you shall not make any gods of silver, nor shall you make for yourselves any gods of gold.

כ לֹא תַעֲשׂוּן אִתִּי אֱלֹהֵי כֶסֶף וֵאלֹהֵי זָהָב לֹא תַעֲשׂוּ לָכֶם:

miz-BAKH a-da-MAH ta-a-seh LEE v'-za-vakh-TA a-LAV et o-lo-TE-kha
v'-et sh'-la-ME-kha et tzo-n'-KHA v'-et b'-ka-RE-kha b'-khol ha-ma-KOM
a-SHER az-KEER et sh'-MEE a-VO ay-LE-kha u-vay-rakh-TEE-kha

²¹ Make for Me a *Mizbayach* of earth and sacrifice on it your burnt offerings and your sacrifices of well-being, your sheep and your oxen; in every place where I cause My name to be mentioned I will come to you and bless you.

כא מִזְבַּח אֲדָמָה תַּעֲשֶׂה־לִּי וְזָבַחְתָּ עָלָיו אֶת־עֹלֹתֶיךָ וְאֶת־שְׁלָמֶיךָ אֶת־צֹאנְךָ וְאֶת־בְּקָרֶךָ בְּכָל־הַמָּקוֹם אֲשֶׁר אַזְכִּיר אֶת־שְׁמִי אָבוֹא אֵלֶיךָ וּבֵרַכְתִּיךָ:

miz-BAKH a-da-MAH ta-a-SEH lee v'-za-vakh-TA a-LAV et o-lo-TE-kha
v'-ET sh'-la-ME-kha et tzo-n'-KHA v'-ET b'-ka-RE-kha b'-KHOL ha-ma-KOM
a-SHER az-KEER et sh'-MEE a-VO ay-LE-kha u-vay-rakh-TEE-kha

²² And if you make for Me a *Mizbayach* of stones, do not build it of hewn stones; for by wielding your tool upon them you have profaned them.

כב וְאִם־מִזְבַּח אֲבָנִים תַּעֲשֶׂה־לִּי לֹא־תִבְנֶה אֶתְהֶן גָּזִית כִּי חַרְבְּךָ הֵנַפְתָּ עָלֶיהָ וַתְּחַלְלֶהָ:

20:21 In every place where I cause My name to be mentioned Based on this verse, *Rashi* explains that God's forty-two letter name can only be uttered where the Divine Presence resides. The *Beit Hamikdash* in *Yerushalayim* was, therefore, the only place where the *Kohanim* could use this special name when giving the priestly blessing to the people. The description of the blessing, found in *Sefer Bamidbar* (6:23–27), ends with the following verse: "Thus they shall link My name with the People of Israel, and I will bless them." Even though the *Kohanim* were the ones standing in front of the people and invoking *Hashem*'s name to bless them, the blessing itself comes from *Hashem*. To this day, the priestly blessing is recited daily throughout Israel. In

The Priestly Blessing at the Western Wall

the rest of the world, this blessing is only recited a few times a year, on holidays. The recitation of the Priestly Blessing is a constant reminder that all blessing in our lives ultimately comes from *Hashem*.

Exodus

23 Do not ascend My *Mizbayach* by steps, that your nakedness may not be exposed upon it.

כג וְלֹא־תַעֲלֶה בְמַעֲלֹת עַל־מִזְבְּחִי אֲשֶׁר לֹא־תִגָּלֶה עֶרְוָתְךָ עָלָיו:

21 1 These are the rules that you shall set before them:

כא א וְאֵלֶּה הַמִּשְׁפָּטִים אֲשֶׁר תָּשִׂים לִפְנֵיהֶם:

v'-AY-leh ha-mish-pa-TEEM a-SHER ta-SEEM lif-nay-HEM

2 When you acquire a Hebrew slave, he shall serve six years; in the seventh year he shall go free, without payment.

ב כִּי תִקְנֶה עֶבֶד עִבְרִי שֵׁשׁ שָׁנִים יַעֲבֹד וּבַשְּׁבִעִת יֵצֵא לַחָפְשִׁי חִנָּם:

3 If he came single, he shall leave single; if he had a wife, his wife shall leave with him.

ג אִם־בְּגַפּוֹ יָבֹא בְּגַפּוֹ יֵצֵא אִם־בַּעַל אִשָּׁה הוּא וְיָצְאָה אִשְׁתּוֹ עִמּוֹ:

4 If his master gave him a wife, and she has borne him children, the wife and her children shall belong to the master, and he shall leave alone.

ד אִם־אֲדֹנָיו יִתֶּן־לוֹ אִשָּׁה וְיָלְדָה־לוֹ בָנִים אוֹ בָנוֹת הָאִשָּׁה וִילָדֶיהָ תִּהְיֶה לַאדֹנֶיהָ וְהוּא יֵצֵא בְגַפּוֹ:

5 But if the slave declares, "I love my master, and my wife and children: I do not wish to go free,"

ה וְאִם־אָמֹר יֹאמַר הָעֶבֶד אָהַבְתִּי אֶת־אֲדֹנִי אֶת־אִשְׁתִּי וְאֶת־בָּנָי לֹא אֵצֵא חָפְשִׁי:

6 his master shall take him before *Hashem*. He shall be brought to the door or the doorpost, and his master shall pierce his ear with an awl; and he shall then remain his slave for life.

ו וְהִגִּישׁוֹ אֲדֹנָיו אֶל־הָאֱלֹהִים וְהִגִּישׁוֹ אֶל־הַדֶּלֶת אוֹ אֶל־הַמְּזוּזָה וְרָצַע אֲדֹנָיו אֶת־אָזְנוֹ בַּמַּרְצֵעַ וַעֲבָדוֹ לְעֹלָם:

7 When a man sells his daughter as a slave, she shall not be freed as male slaves are.

ז וְכִי־יִמְכֹּר אִישׁ אֶת־בִּתּוֹ לְאָמָה לֹא תֵצֵא כְּצֵאת הָעֲבָדִים:

8 If she proves to be displeasing to her master, who designated her for himself, he must let her be redeemed; he shall not have the right to sell her to outsiders, since he broke faith with her.

ח אִם־רָעָה בְּעֵינֵי אֲדֹנֶיהָ אֲשֶׁר־לֹא [לוֹ] יְעָדָהּ וְהֶפְדָּהּ לְעַם נָכְרִי לֹא־יִמְשֹׁל לְמָכְרָהּ בְּבִגְדוֹ־בָהּ:

9 And if he designated her for his son, he shall deal with her as is the practice with free maidens.

ט וְאִם־לִבְנוֹ יִיעָדֶנָּה כְּמִשְׁפַּט הַבָּנוֹת יַעֲשֶׂה־לָּהּ:

10 If he marries another, he must not withhold from this one her food, her clothing, or her conjugal rights.

י אִם־אַחֶרֶת יִקַּח־לוֹ שְׁאֵרָהּ כְּסוּתָהּ וְעֹנָתָהּ לֹא יִגְרָע:

11 If he fails her in these three ways, she shall go free, without payment.

יא וְאִם־שְׁלָשׁ־אֵלֶּה לֹא יַעֲשֶׂה לָהּ וְיָצְאָה חִנָּם אֵין כָּסֶף:

12 He who fatally strikes a man shall be put to death.

יב מַכֵּה אִישׁ וָמֵת מוֹת יוּמָת:

21:1 These are the rules Following the giving of the Ten Commandments, the *Torah* discusses numerous civil laws dealing with honest and ethical business practices and interpersonal relationships. These laws precede the dictates regulating our relationship with *Hashem*, teaching us that religion demands not just belief, but ethical conduct as well. In fact, there is an oft-quoted adage, "*derech eretz kadma laTorah*" (דרך ארץ קדמה לתורה), which means that 'ethics precedes *Torah*.' Decency and common courtesy serve as the foundation for keeping the rest of the *Torah's* commandments.

Tel Aviv and Ramat Gan financial district

Exodus

13   If he did not do it by design, but it came about by
     an act of *Hashem*, I will assign you a place to which
     he can flee.

יג   וַאֲשֶׁר֙ לֹ֣א צָדָ֔ה וְהָאֱלֹהִ֖ים אִנָּ֣ה לְיָד֑וֹ
     וְשַׂמְתִּ֤י לְךָ֙ מָק֔וֹם אֲשֶׁ֥ר יָנ֖וּס שָֽׁמָּה׃

14   When a man schemes against another and kills him
     treacherously, you shall take him from My very
     Mizbayach to be put to death.

יד   וְכִֽי־יָזִ֥ד אִ֛ישׁ עַל־רֵעֵ֖הוּ לְהׇרְג֣וֹ בְעׇרְמָ֑ה
     מֵעִ֣ם מִזְבְּחִ֔י תִּקָּחֶ֖נּוּ לָמֽוּת׃

15   He who strikes his father or his mother shall be put
     to death.

טו   וּמַכֵּ֥ה אָבִ֛יו וְאִמּ֖וֹ מ֥וֹת יוּמָֽת׃

16   He who kidnaps a man – whether he has sold him
     or is still holding him – shall be put to death.

טז   וְגֹנֵ֨ב אִ֧ישׁ וּמְכָר֛וֹ וְנִמְצָ֥א בְיָד֖וֹ מ֥וֹת
     יוּמָֽת׃

17   He who insults his father or his mother shall be put
     to death.

יז   וּמְקַלֵּ֥ל אָבִ֛יו וְאִמּ֖וֹ מ֥וֹת יוּמָֽת׃

18   When men quarrel and one strikes the other with
     stone or fist, and he does not die but has to take to
     his bed

יח   וְכִֽי־יְרִיבֻ֣ן אֲנָשִׁ֗ים וְהִכָּה־אִישׁ֙ אֶת־
     רֵעֵ֔הוּ בְּאֶ֖בֶן א֣וֹ בְאֶגְרֹ֑ף וְלֹ֥א יָמ֖וּת וְנָפַ֥ל
     לְמִשְׁכָּֽב׃

19   if he then gets up and walks outdoors upon his staff,
     the assailant shall go unpunished, except that he
     must pay for his idleness and his cure.

יט   אִם־יָק֞וּם וְהִתְהַלֵּ֥ךְ בַּח֛וּץ עַל־מִשְׁעַנְתּ֖וֹ
     וְנִקָּ֣ה הַמַּכֶּ֑ה רַ֥ק שִׁבְתּ֛וֹ יִתֵּ֖ן וְרַפֹּ֥א
     יְרַפֵּֽא׃

20   When a man strikes his slave, male or female,
     with a rod, and he dies there and then, he must be
     avenged.

כ   וְכִֽי־יַכֶּה֩ אִ֨ישׁ אֶת־עַבְדּ֜וֹ א֤וֹ אֶת־אֲמָתוֹ֙
     בַּשֵּׁ֔בֶט וּמֵ֖ת תַּ֣חַת יָד֑וֹ נָקֹ֖ם יִנָּקֵֽם׃

21   But if he survives a day or two, he is not to be
     avenged, since he is the other's property.

כא   אַ֥ךְ אִם־י֛וֹם א֥וֹ יוֹמַ֖יִם יַעֲמֹ֑ד לֹ֣א יֻקַּ֔ם כִּ֥י
     כַסְפּ֖וֹ הֽוּא׃

22   When men fight, and one of them pushes a
     pregnant woman and a miscarriage results, but no
     other damage ensues, the one responsible shall be
     fined according as the woman's husband may exact
     from him, the payment to be based on reckoning.

כב   וְכִֽי־יִנָּצ֣וּ אֲנָשִׁ֗ים וְנָ֨גְפ֜וּ אִשָּׁ֤ה הָרָה֙
     וְיָצְא֣וּ יְלָדֶ֔יהָ וְלֹ֥א יִהְיֶ֖ה אָס֑וֹן עָנ֣וֹשׁ
     יֵעָנֵ֗שׁ כַּאֲשֶׁ֨ר יָשִׁ֤ית עָלָיו֙ בַּ֣עַל הָֽאִשָּׁ֔ה
     וְנָתַ֖ן בִּפְלִלִֽים׃

23   But if other damage ensues, the penalty shall be life
     for life,

כג   וְאִם־אָס֖וֹן יִהְיֶ֑ה וְנָתַתָּ֥ה נֶ֖פֶשׁ תַּ֥חַת
     נָֽפֶשׁ׃

24   eye for eye, tooth for tooth, hand for hand, foot for
     foot,

כד   עַ֤יִן תַּ֣חַת עַ֙יִן֙ שֵׁ֣ן תַּ֣חַת שֵׁ֔ן יָ֖ד תַּ֣חַת יָ֑ד
     רֶ֖גֶל תַּ֥חַת רָֽגֶל׃

25   burn for burn, wound for wound, bruise for bruise.

כה   כְּוִיָּה֙ תַּ֣חַת כְּוִיָּ֔ה פֶּ֖צַע תַּ֣חַת פָּ֑צַע
     חַבּוּרָ֕ה תַּ֖חַת חַבּוּרָֽה׃

26   When a man strikes the eye of his slave, male or
     female, and destroys it, he shall let him go free on
     account of his eye.

כו   וְכִֽי־יַכֶּ֨ה אִ֜ישׁ אֶת־עֵ֥ין עַבְדּ֛וֹ אֽוֹ־אֶת־עֵ֥ין
     אֲמָת֖וֹ וְשִֽׁחֲתָ֑הּ לַֽחׇפְשִׁ֥י יְשַׁלְּחֶ֖נּוּ תַּ֥חַת
     עֵינֽוֹ׃

27   If he knocks out the tooth of his slave, male or
     female, he shall let him go free on account of his
     tooth.

כז   וְאִם־שֵׁ֥ן עַבְדּ֛וֹ אֽוֹ־שֵׁ֥ן אֲמָת֖וֹ יַפִּ֑יל
     לַֽחׇפְשִׁ֥י יְשַׁלְּחֶ֖נּוּ תַּ֥חַת שִׁנּֽוֹ׃

28 When an ox gores a man or a woman to death, the ox shall be stoned and its flesh shall not be eaten, but the owner of the ox is not to be punished.

כח וְכִי־יִגַּח שׁוֹר אֶת־אִישׁ אוֹ אֶת־אִשָּׁה וָמֵת סָקוֹל יִסָּקֵל הַשּׁוֹר וְלֹא יֵאָכֵל אֶת־בְּשָׂרוֹ וּבַעַל הַשּׁוֹר נָקִי:

29 If, however, that ox has been in the habit of goring, and its owner, though warned, has failed to guard it, and it kills a man or a woman – the ox shall be stoned and its owner, too, shall be put to death.

כט וְאִם שׁוֹר נַגָּח הוּא מִתְּמֹל שִׁלְשֹׁם וְהוּעַד בִּבְעָלָיו וְלֹא יִשְׁמְרֶנּוּ וְהֵמִית אִישׁ אוֹ אִשָּׁה הַשּׁוֹר יִסָּקֵל וְגַם־בְּעָלָיו יוּמָת:

30 If ransom is laid upon him, he must pay whatever is laid upon him to redeem his life.

ל אִם־כֹּפֶר יוּשַׁת עָלָיו וְנָתַן פִּדְיֹן נַפְשׁוֹ כְּכֹל אֲשֶׁר־יוּשַׁת עָלָיו:

31 So, too, if it gores a minor, male or female, [the owner] shall be dealt with according to the same rule.

לא אוֹ־בֵן יִגָּח אוֹ־בַת יִגָּח כַּמִּשְׁפָּט הַזֶּה יֵעָשֶׂה לּוֹ:

32 But if the ox gores a slave, male or female, he shall pay thirty *shekalim* of silver to the master, and the ox shall be stoned.

לב אִם־עֶבֶד יִגַּח הַשּׁוֹר אוֹ אָמָה כֶּסֶף שְׁלֹשִׁים שְׁקָלִים יִתֵּן לַאדֹנָיו וְהַשּׁוֹר יִסָּקֵל:

33 When a man opens a pit, or digs a pit and does not cover it, and an ox or an ass falls into it,

לג וְכִי־יִפְתַּח אִישׁ בּוֹר אוֹ כִּי־יִכְרֶה אִישׁ בֹּר וְלֹא יְכַסֶּנּוּ וְנָפַל־שָׁמָּה שׁוֹר אוֹ חֲמוֹר:

34 the one responsible for the pit must make restitution; he shall pay the price to the owner, but shall keep the dead animal.

לד בַּעַל הַבּוֹר יְשַׁלֵּם כֶּסֶף יָשִׁיב לִבְעָלָיו וְהַמֵּת יִהְיֶה־לּוֹ:

35 When a man's ox injures his neighbor's ox and it dies, they shall sell the live ox and divide its price; they shall also divide the dead animal.

לה וְכִי־יִגֹּף שׁוֹר־אִישׁ אֶת־שׁוֹר רֵעֵהוּ וָמֵת וּמָכְרוּ אֶת־הַשּׁוֹר הַחַי וְחָצוּ אֶת־כַּסְפּוֹ וְגַם אֶת־הַמֵּת יֶחֱצוּן:

36 If, however, it is known that the ox was in the habit of goring, and its owner has failed to guard it, he must restore ox for ox, but shall keep the dead animal.

לו אוֹ נוֹדַע כִּי שׁוֹר נַגָּח הוּא מִתְּמוֹל שִׁלְשֹׁם וְלֹא יִשְׁמְרֶנּוּ בְּעָלָיו שַׁלֵּם יְשַׁלֵּם שׁוֹר תַּחַת הַשּׁוֹר וְהַמֵּת יִהְיֶה־לּוֹ:

37 When a man steals an ox or a sheep, and slaughters it or sells it, he shall pay five oxen for the ox, and four sheep for the sheep

לז כִּי יִגְנֹב־אִישׁ שׁוֹר אוֹ־שֶׂה וּטְבָחוֹ אוֹ מְכָרוֹ חֲמִשָּׁה בָקָר יְשַׁלֵּם תַּחַת הַשּׁוֹר וְאַרְבַּע־צֹאן תַּחַת הַשֶּׂה:

22 1 If the thief is seized while tunneling, and he is beaten to death, there is no bloodguilt in his case.

כב א אִם־בַּמַּחְתֶּרֶת יִמָּצֵא הַגַּנָּב וְהֻכָּה וָמֵת אֵין לוֹ דָּמִים:

2 If the sun has risen on him, there is bloodguilt in that case. – He must make restitution; if he lacks the means, he shall be sold for his theft.

ב אִם־זָרְחָה הַשֶּׁמֶשׁ עָלָיו דָּמִים לוֹ שַׁלֵּם יְשַׁלֵּם אִם־אֵין לוֹ וְנִמְכַּר בִּגְנֵבָתוֹ:

Exodus

3 But if what he stole – whether ox or ass or sheep –
is found alive in his possession, he shall pay double.

ג אִם־הִמָּצֵא תִמָּצֵא בְיָדוֹ הַגְּנֵבָה מִשּׁוֹר
עַד־חֲמוֹר עַד־שֶׂה חַיִּים שְׁנַיִם יְשַׁלֵּם׃

*im hi-ma-TZAY ti-ma-TZAY v'-ya-DO ha-g'-nay-VAH mi-SHOR ad
kha-MOR ad SEH kha-YEEM sh'-NA-yim y'-sha-LAYM*

4 When a man lets his livestock loose to graze in
another's land, and so allows a field or a vineyard
to be grazed bare, he must make restitution for the
impairment of that field or vineyard.

ד כִּי יַבְעֶר־אִישׁ שָׂדֶה אוֹ־כֶרֶם וְשִׁלַּח
אֶת־בְּעִירֹה [בְּעִירוֹ] וּבִעֵר בִּשְׂדֵה אַחֵר
מֵיטַב שָׂדֵהוּ וּמֵיטַב כַּרְמוֹ יְשַׁלֵּם׃

5 When a fire is started and spreads to thorns, so that
stacked, standing, or growing grain is consumed, he
who started the fire must make restitution.

ה כִּי־תֵצֵא אֵשׁ וּמָצְאָה קֹצִים וְנֶאֱכַל
גָּדִישׁ אוֹ הַקָּמָה אוֹ הַשָּׂדֶה שַׁלֵּם יְשַׁלֵּם
הַמַּבְעִר אֶת־הַבְּעֵרָה׃

6 When a man gives money or goods to another for
safekeeping, and they are stolen from the man's
house – if the thief is caught, he shall pay double;

ו כִּי־יִתֵּן אִישׁ אֶל־רֵעֵהוּ כֶּסֶף אוֹ־כֵלִים
לִשְׁמֹר וְגֻנַּב מִבֵּית הָאִישׁ אִם־יִמָּצֵא
הַגַּנָּב יְשַׁלֵּם שְׁנָיִם׃

7 if the thief is not caught, the owner of the house
shall depose before *Hashem* that he has not laid
hands on the other's property.

ז אִם־לֹא יִמָּצֵא הַגַּנָּב וְנִקְרַב בַּעַל־
הַבַּיִת אֶל־הָאֱלֹהִים אִם־לֹא שָׁלַח יָדוֹ
בִּמְלֶאכֶת רֵעֵהוּ׃

8 In all charges of misappropriation – pertaining to
an ox, an ass, a sheep, a garment, or any other loss,
whereof one party alleges, "This is it" – the case of
both parties shall come before *Hashem*: he whom
Hashem declares guilty shall pay double to the other.

ח עַל־כָּל־דְּבַר־פֶּשַׁע עַל־שׁוֹר עַל־חֲמוֹר
עַל־שֶׂה עַל־שַׂלְמָה עַל־כָּל־אֲבֵדָה
אֲשֶׁר יֹאמַר כִּי־הוּא זֶה עַד הָאֱלֹהִים
יָבֹא דְּבַר־שְׁנֵיהֶם אֲשֶׁר יַרְשִׁיעֻן אֱלֹהִים
יְשַׁלֵּם שְׁנַיִם לְרֵעֵהוּ׃

9 When a man gives to another an ass, an ox, a sheep
or any other animal to guard, and it dies or is
injured or is carried off, with no witness about,

ט כִּי־יִתֵּן אִישׁ אֶל־רֵעֵהוּ חֲמוֹר אוֹ־שׁוֹר
אוֹ־שֶׂה וְכָל־בְּהֵמָה לִשְׁמֹר וּמֵת אוֹ־
נִשְׁבַּר אוֹ־נִשְׁבָּה אֵין רֹאֶה׃

10 an oath before *Hashem* shall decide between the
two of them that the one has not laid hands on the
property of the other; the owner must acquiesce,
and no restitution shall be made.

י שְׁבֻעַת יְהוָה תִּהְיֶה בֵּין שְׁנֵיהֶם אִם־לֹא
שָׁלַח יָדוֹ בִּמְלֶאכֶת רֵעֵהוּ וְלָקַח בְּעָלָיו
וְלֹא יְשַׁלֵּם׃

11 But if [the animal] was stolen from him, he shall
make restitution to its owner.

יא וְאִם־גָּנֹב יִגָּנֵב מֵעִמּוֹ יְשַׁלֵּם לִבְעָלָיו׃

12 If it was torn by beasts, he shall bring it as evidence;
he need not replace what has been torn by beasts.

יב אִם־טָרֹף יִטָּרֵף יְבִאֵהוּ עֵד הַטְּרֵפָה לֹא
יְשַׁלֵּם׃

22:3 He shall pay double The double payment
for damages commanded in this verse is considered a penalty. Rabbi Moshe Lichtman, in his
book *Eretz Yisrael* in the *Parsha*, reflects that according to
Jewish Law, the authority for implementation of this
penalty, and many others, rests only upon judges who
have been ordained with a special authorization that was
passed down from teacher to student beginning with
Moshe. This chain of ordination was unfortunately broken
at the time of the Bar Kochba revolt in the second century CE. However, Mai-
monides, a medieval
scholar, philosopher
and physician known
by his Hebrew acro-
nym *Rambam*, rules
that once the masses
of Jews reside in *Eretz
Yisrael* and the rabbinic authorities there agree, this special ordination can be reinstated.

Archeological excavations at Tzipori, home of the
High Court (*Sanhedrin*) in the 3rd century CE

13 When a man borrows [an animal] from another and it dies or is injured, its owner not being with it, he must make restitution.

יג וְכִי־יִשְׁאַל אִישׁ מֵעִם רֵעֵהוּ וְנִשְׁבַּר אוֹ־מֵת בְּעָלָיו אֵין־עִמּוֹ שַׁלֵּם יְשַׁלֵּם:

14 If its owner was with it, no restitution need be made; but if it was hired, he is entitled to the hire.

יד אִם־בְּעָלָיו עִמּוֹ לֹא יְשַׁלֵּם אִם־שָׂכִיר הוּא בָּא בִּשְׂכָרוֹ:

15 If a man seduces a virgin for whom the bride-price has not been paid, and lies with her, he must make her his wife by payment of a bride-price.

טו וְכִי־יְפַתֶּה אִישׁ בְּתוּלָה אֲשֶׁר לֹא־אֹרָשָׂה וְשָׁכַב עִמָּהּ מָהֹר יִמְהָרֶנָּה לּוֹ לְאִשָּׁה:

16 If her father refuses to give her to him, he must still weigh out silver in accordance with the bride-price for virgins.

טז אִם־מָאֵן יְמָאֵן אָבִיהָ לְתִתָּהּ לוֹ כֶּסֶף יִשְׁקֹל כְּמֹהַר הַבְּתוּלֹת:

17 You shall not tolerate a sorceress.

יז מְכַשֵּׁפָה לֹא תְחַיֶּה:

18 Whoever lies with a beast shall be put to death.

יח כָּל־שֹׁכֵב עִם־בְּהֵמָה מוֹת יוּמָת:

19 Whoever sacrifices to a god other than *Hashem* alone shall be proscribed.

יט זֹבֵחַ לָאֱלֹהִים יָחֳרָם בִּלְתִּי לַיהוָה לְבַדּוֹ:

20 You shall not wrong a stranger or oppress him, for you were strangers in the land of Egypt.

כ וְגֵר לֹא־תוֹנֶה וְלֹא תִלְחָצֶנּוּ כִּי־גֵרִים הֱיִיתֶם בְּאֶרֶץ מִצְרָיִם:

21 You shall not ill-treat any widow or orphan.

כא כָּל־אַלְמָנָה וְיָתוֹם לֹא תְעַנּוּן:

22 If you do mistreat them, I will heed their outcry as soon as they cry out to Me,

כב אִם־עַנֵּה תְעַנֶּה אֹתוֹ כִּי אִם־צָעֹק יִצְעַק אֵלַי שָׁמֹעַ אֶשְׁמַע צַעֲקָתוֹ:

23 and My anger shall blaze forth and I will put you to the sword, and your own wives shall become widows and your children orphans.

כג וְחָרָה אַפִּי וְהָרַגְתִּי אֶתְכֶם בֶּחָרֶב וְהָיוּ נְשֵׁיכֶם אַלְמָנוֹת וּבְנֵיכֶם יְתֹמִים:

24 If you lend money to My people, to the poor among you, do not act toward them as a creditor; exact no interest from them.

כד אִם־כֶּסֶף תַּלְוֶה אֶת־עַמִּי אֶת־הֶעָנִי עִמָּךְ לֹא־תִהְיֶה לוֹ כְּנֹשֶׁה לֹא־תְשִׂימוּן עָלָיו נֶשֶׁךְ:

25 If you take your neighbor's garment in pledge, you must return it to him before the sun sets;

כה אִם־חָבֹל תַּחְבֹּל שַׂלְמַת רֵעֶךָ עַד־בֹּא הַשֶּׁמֶשׁ תְּשִׁיבֶנּוּ לוֹ:

26 it is his only clothing, the sole covering for his skin. In what else shall he sleep? Therefore, if he cries out to Me, I will pay heed, for I am compassionate.

כו כִּי הִוא כְסוּתֹה [כְסוּתוֹ] לְבַדָּהּ הִוא שִׂמְלָתוֹ לְעֹרוֹ בַּמֶּה יִשְׁכָּב וְהָיָה כִּי־יִצְעַק אֵלַי וְשָׁמַעְתִּי כִּי־חַנּוּן אָנִי:

27 You shall not revile *Hashem*, nor put a curse upon a chieftain among your people.

כז אֱלֹהִים לֹא תְקַלֵּל וְנָשִׂיא בְעַמְּךָ לֹא תָאֹר:

28 You shall not put off the skimming of the first yield of your vats. You shall give Me the first-born among your sons.

כח מְלֵאָתְךָ וְדִמְעֲךָ לֹא תְאַחֵר בְּכוֹר בָּנֶיךָ תִּתֶּן־לִי:

29 You shall do the same with your cattle and your flocks: seven days it shall remain with its mother; on the eighth day you shall give it to Me.

כט כֵּן־תַּעֲשֶׂה לְשֹׁרְךָ לְצֹאנֶךָ שִׁבְעַת יָמִים יִהְיֶה עִם־אִמּוֹ בַּיּוֹם הַשְּׁמִינִי תִּתְּנוֹ־לִי:

30 You shall be holy people to Me: you must not eat flesh torn by beasts in the field; you shall cast it to the dogs.

ל וְאַנְשֵׁי־קֹדֶשׁ תִּהְיוּן לִי וּבָשָׂר בַּשָּׂדֶה טְרֵפָה לֹא תֹאכֵלוּ לַכֶּלֶב תַּשְׁלִכוּן אֹתוֹ:

23 1 You must not carry false rumors; you shall not join hands with the guilty to act as a malicious witness:

כג א לֹא תִשָּׂא שֵׁמַע שָׁוְא אַל־תָּשֶׁת יָדְךָ עִם־רָשָׁע לִהְיֹת עֵד חָמָס:

2 You shall neither side with the mighty to do wrong – you shall not give perverse testimony in a dispute so as to pervert it in favor of the mighty

ב לֹא־תִהְיֶה אַחֲרֵי־רַבִּים לְרָעֹת וְלֹא־תַעֲנֶה עַל־רִב לִנְטֹת אַחֲרֵי רַבִּים לְהַטֹּת:

3 nor shall you show deference to a poor man in his dispute.

ג וְדָל לֹא תֶהְדַּר בְּרִיבוֹ:

4 When you encounter your enemy's ox or ass wandering, you must take it back to him.

ד כִּי תִפְגַּע שׁוֹר אֹיִבְךָ אוֹ חֲמֹרוֹ תֹּעֶה הָשֵׁב תְּשִׁיבֶנּוּ לוֹ:

5 When you see the ass of your enemy lying under its burden and would refrain from raising it, you must nevertheless raise it with him.

ה כִּי־תִרְאֶה חֲמוֹר שֹׂנַאֲךָ רֹבֵץ תַּחַת מַשָּׂאוֹ וְחָדַלְתָּ מֵעֲזֹב לוֹ עָזֹב תַּעֲזֹב עִמּוֹ:

6 You shall not subvert the rights of your needy in their disputes.

ו לֹא תַטֶּה מִשְׁפַּט אֶבְיֹנְךָ בְּרִיבוֹ:

7 Keep far from a false charge; do not bring death on those who are innocent and in the right, for I will not acquit the wrongdoer.

ז מִדְּבַר־שֶׁקֶר תִּרְחָק וְנָקִי וְצַדִּיק אַל־תַּהֲרֹג כִּי לֹא־אַצְדִּיק רָשָׁע:

8 Do not take bribes, for bribes blind the clear-sighted and upset the pleas of those who are in the right.

ח וְשֹׁחַד לֹא תִקָּח כִּי הַשֹּׁחַד יְעַוֵּר פִּקְחִים וִיסַלֵּף דִּבְרֵי צַדִּיקִים:

9 You shall not oppress a stranger, for you know the feelings of the stranger, having yourselves been strangers in the land of Egypt.

ט וְגֵר לֹא תִלְחָץ וְאַתֶּם יְדַעְתֶּם אֶת־נֶפֶשׁ הַגֵּר כִּי־גֵרִים הֱיִיתֶם בְּאֶרֶץ מִצְרָיִם:

10 Six years you shall sow your land and gather in its yield;

י וְשֵׁשׁ שָׁנִים תִּזְרַע אֶת־אַרְצֶךָ וְאָסַפְתָּ אֶת־תְּבוּאָתָהּ:

11 but in the seventh you shall let it rest and lie fallow. Let the needy among your people eat of it, and what they leave let the wild beasts eat. You shall do the same with your vineyards and your olive groves.

יא וְהַשְּׁבִיעִת תִּשְׁמְטֶנָּה וּנְטַשְׁתָּהּ וְאָכְלוּ אֶבְיֹנֵי עַמֶּךָ וְיִתְרָם תֹּאכַל חַיַּת הַשָּׂדֶה כֵּן־תַּעֲשֶׂה לְכַרְמְךָ לְזֵיתֶךָ:

v'-ha-sh'-vee-IT tish-m'-TE-nah un-tash-TAH v'-a-kh'-LU ev-yo-NAY a-ME-kha v'-yit-RAM to-KHAL kha-YAT ha-sa-DEH kayn ta-a-SEH l'-khar-m'-KHA l'-zay-TE-kha

23:11 In the seventh you shall let it rest and lie fallow Every seventh year, all farms, fields, orchards and vineyards in *Eretz Yisrael* are left untended and unharvested. To this very day, the Sabbatical year is kept in Israel. The message of this unique commandment is similar to that of *Shabbat*. Just as we are commanded to keep *Shabbat* and cease our daily activities every seventh day, we are similarly to rest from working the fields every seventh year. Just as *Shabbat* reminds us that *Hashem* created the world (Exodus 20:10) and everything in it belongs to Him, the Sabbatical year reminds us that our economic success and all that we produce is in the hands of our Creator.

Grape vines in the Ayalon Valley

12 Six days you shall do your work, but on the seventh day you shall cease from labor, in order that your ox and your ass may rest, and that your bondman and the stranger may be refreshed.

יב שֵׁשֶׁת יָמִים תַּעֲשֶׂה מַעֲשֶׂיךָ וּבַיּוֹם הַשְּׁבִיעִי תִּשְׁבֹּת לְמַעַן יָנוּחַ שׁוֹרְךָ וַחֲמֹרֶךָ וְיִנָּפֵשׁ בֶּן־אֲמָתְךָ וְהַגֵּר:

13 Be on guard concerning all that I have told you. Make no mention of the names of other gods; they shall not be heard on your lips.

יג וּבְכֹל אֲשֶׁר־אָמַרְתִּי אֲלֵיכֶם תִּשָּׁמֵרוּ וְשֵׁם אֱלֹהִים אֲחֵרִים לֹא תַזְכִּירוּ לֹא יִשָּׁמַע עַל־פִּיךָ:

14 Three times a year you shall hold a festival for Me:

יד שָׁלֹשׁ רְגָלִים תָּחֹג לִי בַּשָּׁנָה:

15 You shall observe the Feast of Unleavened Bread – eating unleavened bread for seven days as I have commanded you – at the set time in the month of Abib, for in it you went forth from Egypt; and none shall appear before Me empty-handed;

טו אֶת־חַג הַמַּצּוֹת תִּשְׁמֹר שִׁבְעַת יָמִים תֹּאכַל מַצּוֹת כַּאֲשֶׁר צִוִּיתִךָ לְמוֹעֵד חֹדֶשׁ הָאָבִיב כִּי־בוֹ יָצָאתָ מִמִּצְרָיִם וְלֹא־יֵרָאוּ פָנַי רֵיקָם:

16 and the Feast of the Harvest, of the first fruits of your work, of what you sow in the field; and the Feast of Ingathering at the end of the year, when you gather in the results of your work from the field.

טז וְחַג הַקָּצִיר בִּכּוּרֵי מַעֲשֶׂיךָ אֲשֶׁר תִּזְרַע בַּשָּׂדֶה וְחַג הָאָסִף בְּצֵאת הַשָּׁנָה בְּאָסְפְּךָ אֶת־מַעֲשֶׂיךָ מִן־הַשָּׂדֶה:

17 Three times a year all your males shall appear before the Sovereign, *Hashem*.

יז שָׁלֹשׁ פְּעָמִים בַּשָּׁנָה יֵרָאֶה כָּל־זְכוּרְךָ אֶל־פְּנֵי הָאָדֹן יְהוָה:

18 You shall not offer the blood of My sacrifice with anything leavened; and the fat of My festal offering shall not be left lying until morning.

יח לֹא־תִזְבַּח עַל־חָמֵץ דַּם־זִבְחִי וְלֹא־יָלִין חֵלֶב־חַגִּי עַד־בֹּקֶר:

19 The choice first fruits of your soil you shall bring to the house of *Hashem* your God. You shall not boil a kid in its mother's milk.

יט רֵאשִׁית בִּכּוּרֵי אַדְמָתְךָ תָּבִיא בֵּית יְהוָה אֱלֹהֶיךָ לֹא־תְבַשֵּׁל גְּדִי בַּחֲלֵב אִמּוֹ:

20 I am sending an angel before you to guard you on the way and to bring you to the place that I have made ready.

כ הִנֵּה אָנֹכִי שֹׁלֵחַ מַלְאָךְ לְפָנֶיךָ לִשְׁמָרְךָ בַּדָּרֶךְ וְלַהֲבִיאֲךָ אֶל־הַמָּקוֹם אֲשֶׁר הֲכִנֹתִי:

*hi-NAY a-no-KHEE sho-LAY-akh mal-AKH l'-fa-NE-kha lish-mor-KHA
ba-DA-rekh v'-la-ha-VEE-a-KHA el ha-ma-KOM a-SHER ha-khi-NO-tee*

21 Pay heed to him and obey him. Do not defy him, for he will not pardon your offenses, since My Name is in him;

כא הִשָּׁמֶר מִפָּנָיו וּשְׁמַע בְּקֹלוֹ אַל־תַּמֵּר בּוֹ כִּי לֹא יִשָּׂא לְפִשְׁעֲכֶם כִּי שְׁמִי בְּקִרְבּוֹ:

22 but if you obey him and do all that I say, I will be an enemy to your enemies and a foe to your foes.

כב כִּי אִם־שָׁמֹעַ תִּשְׁמַע בְּקֹלוֹ וְעָשִׂיתָ כֹּל אֲשֶׁר אֲדַבֵּר וְאָיַבְתִּי אֶת־אֹיְבֶיךָ וְצַרְתִּי אֶת־צֹרְרֶיךָ:

23 When My angel goes before you and brings you to the Amorites, the Hittites, the Perizzites, the Canaanites, the Hivites, and the Jebusites, and I annihilate them,

כג כִּי־יֵלֵךְ מַלְאָכִי לְפָנֶיךָ וֶהֱבִיאֲךָ אֶל־הָאֱמֹרִי וְהַחִתִּי וְהַפְּרִזִּי וְהַכְּנַעֲנִי הַחִוִּי וְהַיְבוּסִי וְהִכְחַדְתִּיו:

24 you shall not bow down to their gods in worship or follow their practices, but shall tear them down and smash their pillars to bits.

כד לֹא־תִשְׁתַּחֲוֶה לֵאלֹהֵיהֶם וְלֹא תָעָבְדֵם וְלֹא תַעֲשֶׂה כְּמַעֲשֵׂיהֶם כִּי הָרֵס תְּהָרְסֵם וְשַׁבֵּר תְּשַׁבֵּר מַצֵּבֹתֵיהֶם:

Exodus

²⁵ You shall serve *Hashem* your God, and He will bless your bread and your water. And I will remove sickness from your midst.

כה וַעֲבַדְתֶּם אֵת יְהֹוָה אֱלֹהֵיכֶם וּבֵרַךְ אֶת־לַחְמְךָ וְאֶת־מֵימֶיךָ וַהֲסִרֹתִי מַחֲלָה מִקִּרְבֶּךָ:

²⁶ No woman in your land shall miscarry or be barren. I will let you enjoy the full count of your days.

כו לֹא תִהְיֶה מְשַׁכֵּלָה וַעֲקָרָה בְּאַרְצֶךָ אֶת־מִסְפַּר יָמֶיךָ אֲמַלֵּא:

²⁷ I will send forth My terror before you, and I will throw into panic all the people among whom you come, and I will make all your enemies turn tail before you.

כז אֶת־אֵימָתִי אֲשַׁלַּח לְפָנֶיךָ וְהַמֹּתִי אֶת־כָּל־הָעָם אֲשֶׁר תָּבֹא בָּהֶם וְנָתַתִּי אֶת־כָּל־אֹיְבֶיךָ אֵלֶיךָ עֹרֶף:

²⁸ I will send a plague ahead of you, and it shall drive out before you the Hivites, the Canaanites, and the Hittites.

כח וְשָׁלַחְתִּי אֶת־הַצִּרְעָה לְפָנֶיךָ וְגֵרְשָׁה אֶת־הַחִוִּי אֶת־הַכְּנַעֲנִי וְאֶת־הַחִתִּי מִלְּפָנֶיךָ:

²⁹ I will not drive them out before you in a single year, lest the land become desolate and the wild beasts multiply to your hurt.

כט לֹא אֲגָרְשֶׁנּוּ מִפָּנֶיךָ בְּשָׁנָה אֶחָת פֶּן־תִּהְיֶה הָאָרֶץ שְׁמָמָה וְרַבָּה עָלֶיךָ חַיַּת הַשָּׂדֶה:

³⁰ I will drive them out before you little by little, until you have increased and possess the land.

ל מְעַט מְעַט אֲגָרְשֶׁנּוּ מִפָּנֶיךָ עַד אֲשֶׁר תִּפְרֶה וְנָחַלְתָּ אֶת־הָאָרֶץ:

*m'-AT m'-AT a-ga-r'-SHE-nu mi-pa-NE-kha AD
a-SHER tif-REH v'-na-khal-TA et ha-A-retz*

³¹ I will set your borders from the Sea of Reeds to the Sea of Philistia, and from the wilderness to the Euphrates; for I will deliver the inhabitants of the land into your hands, and you will drive them out before you.

לא וְשַׁתִּי אֶת־גְּבֻלְךָ מִיַּם־סוּף וְעַד־יָם פְּלִשְׁתִּים וּמִמִּדְבָּר עַד־הַנָּהָר כִּי אֶתֵּן בְּיֶדְכֶם אֵת יֹשְׁבֵי הָאָרֶץ וְגֵרַשְׁתָּמוֹ מִפָּנֶיךָ:

³² You shall make no covenant with them and their gods.

לב לֹא־תִכְרֹת לָהֶם וְלֵאלֹהֵיהֶם בְּרִית:

³³ They shall not remain in your land, lest they cause you to sin against Me; for you will serve their gods – and it will prove a snare to you.

לג לֹא יֵשְׁבוּ בְּאַרְצְךָ פֶּן־יַחֲטִיאוּ אֹתְךָ לִי כִּי תַעֲבֹד אֶת־אֱלֹהֵיהֶם כִּי־יִהְיֶה לְךָ לְמוֹקֵשׁ:

24 ¹ Then He said to *Moshe*, "Come up to *Hashem*, with *Aharon*, *Nadav* and *Avihu*, and seventy elders of *Yisrael*, and bow low from afar.

כד א וְאֶל־מֹשֶׁה אָמַר עֲלֵה אֶל־יְהֹוָה אַתָּה וְאַהֲרֹן נָדָב וַאֲבִיהוּא וְשִׁבְעִים מִזִּקְנֵי יִשְׂרָאֵל וְהִשְׁתַּחֲוִיתֶם מֵרָחֹק:

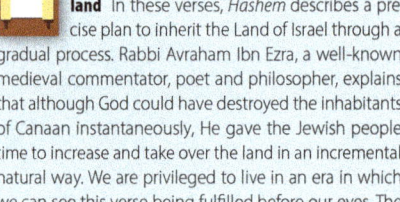

23:30 until you have increased and possess the land In these verses, *Hashem* describes a precise plan to inherit the Land of Israel through a gradual process. Rabbi Avraham Ibn Ezra, a well-known medieval commentator, poet and philosopher, explains that although God could have destroyed the inhabitants of Canaan instantaneously, He gave the Jewish people time to increase and take over the land in an incremental, natural way. We are privileged to live in an era in which we can see this verse being fulfilled before our eyes. The once desolate land has warmly embraced the gradual return of the Jewish people and has become a source of spiritual blessing and economic success. Israel is known around the world for its scientific, medical, economic, technological and agricultural research and innovation.

A water desalination plant in Hadera

2 *Moshe* alone shall come near *Hashem*; but the others shall not come near, nor shall the people come up with him."

ב וְנִגַּשׁ מֹשֶׁה לְבַדּוֹ אֶל־יְהֹוָה וְהֵם לֹא יִגָּשׁוּ וְהָעָם לֹא יַעֲלוּ עִמּוֹ:

3 *Moshe* went and repeated to the people all the commands of *Hashem* and all the rules; and all the people answered with one voice, saying, "All the things that *Hashem* has commanded we will do!"

ג וַיָּבֹא מֹשֶׁה וַיְסַפֵּר לָעָם אֵת כָּל־דִּבְרֵי יְהֹוָה וְאֵת כָּל־הַמִּשְׁפָּטִים וַיַּעַן כָּל־הָעָם קוֹל אֶחָד וַיֹּאמְרוּ כָּל־הַדְּבָרִים אֲשֶׁר־דִּבֶּר יְהֹוָה נַעֲשֶׂה:

4 *Moshe* then wrote down all the commands of *Hashem*. Early in the morning, he set up a *Mizbayach* at the foot of the mountain, with twelve pillars for the twelve tribes of *Yisrael*.

ד וַיִּכְתֹּב מֹשֶׁה אֵת כָּל־דִּבְרֵי יְהֹוָה וַיַּשְׁכֵּם בַּבֹּקֶר וַיִּבֶן מִזְבֵּחַ תַּחַת הָהָר וּשְׁתֵּים עֶשְׂרֵה מַצֵּבָה לִשְׁנֵים עָשָׂר שִׁבְטֵי יִשְׂרָאֵל:

*va-yikh-TOV mo-SHEH AYT kol div-RAY a-do-NAI va-yash-KAYM
ba-BO-ker va-YI-ven miz-BAY-akh TA-khat ha-HAR u-sh'-TAYM
es-RAY ma-tzay-VAH lish-NAYM a-SAR shiv-TAY yis-ra-AYL*

5 He designated some young men among the Israelites, and they offered burnt offerings and sacrificed bulls as offerings of well-being to *Hashem*.

ה וַיִּשְׁלַח אֶת־נַעֲרֵי בְּנֵי יִשְׂרָאֵל וַיַּעֲלוּ עֹלֹת וַיִּזְבְּחוּ זְבָחִים שְׁלָמִים לַיהֹוָה פָּרִים:

6 *Moshe* took one part of the blood and put it in basins, and the other part of the blood he dashed against the *Mizbayach*.

ו וַיִּקַּח מֹשֶׁה חֲצִי הַדָּם וַיָּשֶׂם בָּאַגָּנֹת וַחֲצִי הַדָּם זָרַק עַל־הַמִּזְבֵּחַ:

7 Then he took the record of the covenant and read it aloud to the people. And they said, "All that *Hashem* has spoken we will faithfully do!"

ז וַיִּקַּח סֵפֶר הַבְּרִית וַיִּקְרָא בְּאָזְנֵי הָעָם וַיֹּאמְרוּ כֹּל אֲשֶׁר־דִּבֶּר יְהֹוָה נַעֲשֶׂה וְנִשְׁמָע:

8 *Moshe* took the blood and dashed it on the people and said, "This is the blood of the covenant that *Hashem* now makes with you concerning all these commands."

ח וַיִּקַּח מֹשֶׁה אֶת־הַדָּם וַיִּזְרֹק עַל־הָעָם וַיֹּאמֶר הִנֵּה דַם־הַבְּרִית אֲשֶׁר כָּרַת יְהֹוָה עִמָּכֶם עַל כָּל־הַדְּבָרִים הָאֵלֶּה:

9 Then *Moshe* and *Aharon, Nadav* and *Avihu,* and seventy elders of *Yisrael* ascended;

ט וַיַּעַל מֹשֶׁה וְאַהֲרֹן נָדָב וַאֲבִיהוּא וְשִׁבְעִים מִזִּקְנֵי יִשְׂרָאֵל:

10 and they saw the God of *Yisrael*: under His feet there was the likeness of a pavement of sapphire, like the very sky for purity.

י וַיִּרְאוּ אֵת אֱלֹהֵי יִשְׂרָאֵל וְתַחַת רַגְלָיו כְּמַעֲשֵׂה לִבְנַת הַסַּפִּיר וּכְעֶצֶם הַשָּׁמַיִם לָטֹהַר:

24:4 With twelve pillars If the Twelve Tribes are physically present at the foot of the mountain, what is the meaning behind the symbolic representation of the tribes through the twelve pillars erected by *Moshe*? Commentators reflect that these pillars are meant to represent all future descendants of the nation alongside the generation that exited Egypt. Based on this verse, the Sages of the *Midrash* teach that, in a sense, all the future souls of the Jewish nation were present at Sinai; they too witnessed the revelation of God and personally accepted the *Torah* and its laws upon themselves.

Mosaic of the Twelve Tribes of Israel in the Cardo in *Yerushalayim*

11 Yet He did not raise His hand against the leaders of the Israelites; they beheld *Hashem*, and they ate and drank.

יא וְאֶל־אֲצִילֵי בְּנֵי יִשְׂרָאֵל לֹא שָׁלַח יָדוֹ וַיֶּחֱזוּ אֶת־הָאֱלֹהִים וַיֹּאכְלוּ וַיִּשְׁתּוּ:

12 *Hashem* said to *Moshe*, "Come up to Me on the mountain and wait there, and I will give you the stone tablets with the teachings and commandments which I have inscribed to instruct them."

יב וַיֹּאמֶר יְהוָה אֶל־מֹשֶׁה עֲלֵה אֵלַי הָהָרָה וֶהְיֵה־שָׁם וְאֶתְּנָה לְךָ אֶת־לֻחֹת הָאֶבֶן וְהַתּוֹרָה וְהַמִּצְוָה אֲשֶׁר כָּתַבְתִּי לְהוֹרֹתָם:

13 So *Moshe* and his attendant *Yehoshua* arose, and *Moshe* ascended the mountain of *Hashem*.

יג וַיָּקָם מֹשֶׁה וִיהוֹשֻׁעַ מְשָׁרְתוֹ וַיַּעַל מֹשֶׁה אֶל־הַר הָאֱלֹהִים:

14 To the elders he had said, "Wait here for us until we return to you. You have *Aharon* and *Chur* with you; let anyone who has a legal matter approach them."

יד וְאֶל־הַזְּקֵנִים אָמַר שְׁבוּ־לָנוּ בָזֶה עַד אֲשֶׁר־נָשׁוּב אֲלֵיכֶם וְהִנֵּה אַהֲרֹן וְחוּר עִמָּכֶם מִי־בַעַל דְּבָרִים יִגַּשׁ אֲלֵהֶם:

15 When *Moshe* had ascended the mountain, the cloud covered the mountain.

טו וַיַּעַל מֹשֶׁה אֶל־הָהָר וַיְכַס הֶעָנָן אֶת־הָהָר:

16 The Presence of *Hashem* abode on *Har Sinai*, and the cloud hid it for six days. On the seventh day He called to *Moshe* from the midst of the cloud.

טז וַיִּשְׁכֹּן כְּבוֹד־יְהוָה עַל־הַר סִינַי וַיְכַסֵּהוּ הֶעָנָן שֵׁשֶׁת יָמִים וַיִּקְרָא אֶל־מֹשֶׁה בַּיּוֹם הַשְּׁבִיעִי מִתּוֹךְ הֶעָנָן:

17 Now the Presence of *Hashem* appeared in the sight of the Israelites as a consuming fire on the top of the mountain.

יז וּמַרְאֵה כְּבוֹד יְהוָה כְּאֵשׁ אֹכֶלֶת בְּרֹאשׁ הָהָר לְעֵינֵי בְּנֵי יִשְׂרָאֵל:

18 *Moshe* went inside the cloud and ascended the mountain; and *Moshe* remained on the mountain forty days and forty nights.

יח וַיָּבֹא מֹשֶׁה בְּתוֹךְ הֶעָנָן וַיַּעַל אֶל־הָהָר וַיְהִי מֹשֶׁה בָּהָר אַרְבָּעִים יוֹם וְאַרְבָּעִים לָיְלָה:

25 ¹ *Hashem* spoke to *Moshe*, saying:

ה א וַיְדַבֵּר יְהוָה אֶל־מֹשֶׁה לֵּאמֹר:

2 Tell *B'nei Yisrael* to bring Me gifts; you shall accept gifts for Me from every person whose heart so moves him.

ב דַּבֵּר אֶל־בְּנֵי יִשְׂרָאֵל וְיִקְחוּ־לִי תְּרוּמָה מֵאֵת כָּל־אִישׁ אֲשֶׁר יִדְּבֶנּוּ לִבּוֹ תִּקְחוּ אֶת־תְּרוּמָתִי:

3 And these are the gifts that you shall accept from them: gold, silver, and copper;

ג וְזֹאת הַתְּרוּמָה אֲשֶׁר תִּקְחוּ מֵאִתָּם זָהָב וָכֶסֶף וּנְחֹשֶׁת:

4 blue, purple, and crimson yarns, fine linen, goats' hair;

ד וּתְכֵלֶת וְאַרְגָּמָן וְתוֹלַעַת שָׁנִי וְשֵׁשׁ וְעִזִּים:

5 tanned ram skins, dolphin skins, and acacia wood;

ה וְעֹרֹת אֵילִם מְאָדָּמִים וְעֹרֹת תְּחָשִׁים וַעֲצֵי שִׁטִּים:

6 oil for lighting, spices for the anointing oil and for the aromatic incense;

ו שֶׁמֶן לַמָּאֹר בְּשָׂמִים לְשֶׁמֶן הַמִּשְׁחָה וְלִקְטֹרֶת הַסַּמִּים:

7 lapis lazuli and other stones for setting, for the ephod and for the breastpiece.

ז אַבְנֵי־שֹׁהַם וְאַבְנֵי מִלֻּאִים לָאֵפֹד וְלַחֹשֶׁן:

8 And let them make Me a sanctuary that I may dwell among them.

וְעָשׂוּ לִי מִקְדָּשׁ וְשָׁכַנְתִּי בְּתוֹכָם: ח

v'-a-SU LEE mik-DASH v'-sha-khan-TEE b'-to-KHAM

9 Exactly as I show you – the pattern of the *Mishkan* and the pattern of all its furnishings – so shall you make it.

כְּכֹל אֲשֶׁר אֲנִי מַרְאֶה אוֹתְךָ אֵת תַּבְנִית הַמִּשְׁכָּן וְאֵת תַּבְנִית כָּל־כֵּלָיו וְכֵן תַּעֲשׂוּ: ט

10 They shall make an ark of acacia wood, two and a half *amot* long, an *amah* and a half wide, and an *amah* and a half high.

וְעָשׂוּ אֲרוֹן עֲצֵי שִׁטִּים אַמָּתַיִם וָחֵצִי אָרְכּוֹ וְאַמָּה וָחֵצִי רָחְבּוֹ וְאַמָּה וָחֵצִי קֹמָתוֹ: י

11 Overlay it with pure gold – overlay it inside and out – and make upon it a gold molding round about.

וְצִפִּיתָ אֹתוֹ זָהָב טָהוֹר מִבַּיִת וּמִחוּץ תְּצַפֶּנּוּ וְעָשִׂיתָ עָלָיו זֵר זָהָב סָבִיב: יא

12 Cast four gold rings for it, to be attached to its four feet, two rings on one of its side walls and two on the other.

וְיָצַקְתָּ לּוֹ אַרְבַּע טַבְּעֹת זָהָב וְנָתַתָּה עַל אַרְבַּע פַּעֲמֹתָיו וּשְׁתֵּי טַבָּעֹת עַל־צַלְעוֹ הָאֶחָת וּשְׁתֵּי טַבָּעֹת עַל־צַלְעוֹ הַשֵּׁנִית: יב

13 Make poles of acacia wood and overlay them with gold;

וְעָשִׂיתָ בַדֵּי עֲצֵי שִׁטִּים וְצִפִּיתָ אֹתָם זָהָב: יג

14 then insert the poles into the rings on the side walls of the ark, for carrying the ark.

וְהֵבֵאתָ אֶת־הַבַּדִּים בַּטַּבָּעֹת עַל צַלְעֹת הָאָרֹן לָשֵׂאת אֶת־הָאָרֹן בָּהֶם: יד

15 The poles shall remain in the rings of the ark: they shall not be removed from it.

בְּטַבְּעֹת הָאָרֹן יִהְיוּ הַבַּדִּים לֹא יָסֻרוּ מִמֶּנּוּ: טו

16 And deposit in the *Aron* [the tablets of] the Pact which I will give you.

וְנָתַתָּ אֶל־הָאָרֹן אֵת הָעֵדֻת אֲשֶׁר אֶתֵּן אֵלֶיךָ: טז

17 You shall make a cover of pure gold, two and a half *amot* long and an *amah* and a half wide.

וְעָשִׂיתָ כַפֹּרֶת זָהָב טָהוֹר אַמָּתַיִם וָחֵצִי אָרְכָּהּ וְאַמָּה וָחֵצִי רָחְבָּהּ: יז

18 Make two cherubim of gold – make them of hammered work – at the two ends of the cover.

וְעָשִׂיתָ שְׁנַיִם כְּרֻבִים זָהָב מִקְשָׁה תַּעֲשֶׂה אֹתָם מִשְּׁנֵי קְצוֹת הַכַּפֹּרֶת: יח

19 Make one cherub at one end and the other cherub at the other end; of one piece with the cover shall you make the cherubim at its two ends.

וַעֲשֵׂה כְּרוּב אֶחָד מִקָּצָה מִזֶּה וּכְרוּב־אֶחָד מִקָּצָה מִזֶּה מִן־הַכַּפֹּרֶת תַּעֲשׂוּ אֶת־הַכְּרֻבִים עַל־שְׁנֵי קְצוֹתָיו: יט

25:8 That I may dwell among them Significantly, the verse does not say "that I may dwell within it." The *Mishkan* is not intended to physically contain *Hashem* within its walls. Rather, the *Seforno* explains, it is a place which enables *Hashem* to dwell "among them," meaning in the midst of the Children of Israel. Unlike pagan places of worship, the *Mishkan* is not meant to provide a home on earth for a god. Rather, the *Mishkan*, and ultimately the *Beit Hamikdash* in *Yerushalayim*, are designed to facilitate the relationship between *Hashem* and His children, where every person can go to elevate himself or herself spiritually.

Model of the *Mishkan* at Timna Park

20 The cherubim shall have their wings spread out above, shielding the cover with their wings. They shall confront each other, the faces of the cherubim being turned toward the cover.

כ וְהָיוּ הַכְּרֻבִים פֹּרְשֵׂי כְנָפַיִם לְמַעְלָה סֹכְכִים בְּכַנְפֵיהֶם עַל־הַכַּפֹּרֶת וּפְנֵיהֶם אִישׁ אֶל־אָחִיו אֶל־הַכַּפֹּרֶת יִהְיוּ פְּנֵי הַכְּרֻבִים:

21 Place the cover on top of the *Aron*, after depositing inside the *Aron* the Pact that I will give you.

כא וְנָתַתָּ אֶת־הַכַּפֹּרֶת עַל־הָאָרֹן מִלְמָעְלָה וְאֶל־הָאָרֹן תִּתֵּן אֶת־הָעֵדֻת אֲשֶׁר אֶתֵּן אֵלֶיךָ:

22 There I will meet with you, and I will impart to you – from above the cover, from between the two cherubim that are on top of the *Aron HaBrit* – all that I will command you concerning *B'nei Yisrael.*

כב וְנוֹעַדְתִּי לְךָ שָׁם וְדִבַּרְתִּי אִתְּךָ מֵעַל הַכַּפֹּרֶת מִבֵּין שְׁנֵי הַכְּרֻבִים אֲשֶׁר עַל־אֲרֹן הָעֵדֻת אֵת כָּל־אֲשֶׁר אֲצַוֶּה אוֹתְךָ אֶל־בְּנֵי יִשְׂרָאֵל:

23 You shall make a table of acacia wood, two *amot* long, one *amah* wide, and an *amah* and a half high.

כג וְעָשִׂיתָ שֻׁלְחָן עֲצֵי שִׁטִּים אַמָּתַיִם אָרְכּוֹ וְאַמָּה רָחְבּוֹ וְאַמָּה וָחֵצִי קֹמָתוֹ:

24 Overlay it with pure gold, and make a gold molding around it.

כד וְצִפִּיתָ אֹתוֹ זָהָב טָהוֹר וְעָשִׂיתָ לּוֹ זֵר זָהָב סָבִיב:

25 Make a rim of a hand's breadth around it, and make a gold molding for its rim round about.

כה וְעָשִׂיתָ לּוֹ מִסְגֶּרֶת טֹפַח סָבִיב וְעָשִׂיתָ זֵר־זָהָב לְמִסְגַּרְתּוֹ סָבִיב:

26 Make four gold rings for it, and attach the rings to the four corners at its four legs.

כו וְעָשִׂיתָ לּוֹ אַרְבַּע טַבְּעֹת זָהָב וְנָתַתָּ אֶת־הַטַּבָּעֹת עַל אַרְבַּע הַפֵּאֹת אֲשֶׁר לְאַרְבַּע רַגְלָיו:

27 The rings shall be next to the rim, as holders for poles to carry the table.

כז לְעֻמַּת הַמִּסְגֶּרֶת תִּהְיֶיןָ הַטַּבָּעֹת לְבָתִּים לְבַדִּים לָשֵׂאת אֶת־הַשֻּׁלְחָן:

28 Make the poles of acacia wood, and overlay them with gold; by these the table shall be carried.

כח וְעָשִׂיתָ אֶת־הַבַּדִּים עֲצֵי שִׁטִּים וְצִפִּיתָ אֹתָם זָהָב וְנִשָּׂא־בָם אֶת־הַשֻּׁלְחָן:

29 Make its bowls, ladles, jars and jugs with which to offer libations; make them of pure gold.

כט וְעָשִׂיתָ קְּעָרֹתָיו וְכַפֹּתָיו וּקְשׂוֹתָיו וּמְנַקִּיֹּתָיו אֲשֶׁר יֻסַּךְ בָּהֵן זָהָב טָהוֹר תַּעֲשֶׂה אֹתָם:

30 And on the table you shall set the bread of display, to be before Me always.

ל וְנָתַתָּ עַל־הַשֻּׁלְחָן לֶחֶם פָּנִים לְפָנַי תָּמִיד:

31 You shall make a *menorah* of pure gold; the *menorah* shall be made of hammered work; its base and its shaft, its cups, calyxes, and petals shall be of one piece.

לא וְעָשִׂיתָ מְנֹרַת זָהָב טָהוֹר מִקְשָׁה תֵּעָשֶׂה הַמְּנוֹרָה יְרֵכָהּ וְקָנָהּ גְּבִיעֶיהָ כַּפְתֹּרֶיהָ וּפְרָחֶיהָ מִמֶּנָּה יִהְיוּ:

32 Six branches shall issue from its sides; three branches from one side of the *menorah* and three branches from the other side of the *menorah*.

לב וְשִׁשָּׁה קָנִים יֹצְאִים מִצִּדֶּיהָ שְׁלֹשָׁה קְנֵי מְנֹרָה מִצִּדָּהּ הָאֶחָד וּשְׁלֹשָׁה קְנֵי מְנֹרָה מִצִּדָּהּ הַשֵּׁנִי:

33 On one branch there shall be three cups shaped like almond-blossoms, each with calyx and petals, and on the next branch there shall be three cups shaped like almond-blossoms, each with calyx and petals; so for all six branches issuing from the *menorah*.

לג שְׁלֹשָׁה גְבִעִים מְשֻׁקָּדִים בַּקָּנֶה הָאֶחָד כַּפְתֹּר וָפֶרַח וּשְׁלֹשָׁה גְבִעִים מְשֻׁקָּדִים בַּקָּנֶה הָאֶחָד כַּפְתֹּר וָפָרַח כֵּן לְשֵׁשֶׁת הַקָּנִים הַיֹּצְאִים מִן־הַמְּנֹרָה:

³⁴ And on the *menorah* itself there shall be four cups shaped like almond-blossoms, each with calyx and petals:

³⁵ a calyx, of one piece with it, under a pair of branches; and a calyx, of one piece with it, under the second pair of branches, and a calyx, of one piece with it, under the last pair of branches; so for all six branches issuing from the *menorah*.

³⁶ Their calyxes and their stems shall be of one piece with it, the whole of it a single hammered piece of pure gold.

³⁷ Make its seven lamps – the lamps shall be so mounted as to give the light on its front side

³⁸ and its tongs and fire pans of pure gold.

³⁹ It shall be made, with all these furnishings, out of a *kikar* of pure gold.

⁴⁰ Note well, and follow the patterns for them that are being shown you on the mountain.

26 ¹ As for the *Mishkan*, make it of ten strips of cloth; make these of fine twisted linen, of blue, purple, and crimson yarns, with a design of cherubim worked into them.

² The length of each cloth shall be twenty-eight *amot*, and the width of each cloth shall be four *amot*, all the cloths to have the same measurements.

³ Five of the cloths shall be joined to one another, and the other five cloths shall be joined to one another.

⁴ Make loops of blue wool on the edge of the outermost cloth of the one set; and do likewise on the edge of the outermost cloth of the other set:

⁵ make fifty loops on the one cloth, and fifty loops on the edge of the end cloth of the other set, the loops to be opposite one another.

⁶ And make fifty gold clasps, and couple the cloths to one another with the clasps, so that the *Mishkan* becomes one whole.

⁷ You shall then make cloths of goats' hair for a tent over the *Mishkan*; make the cloths eleven in number.

לד וּבַמְּנֹרָה אַרְבָּעָה גְבִעִים מְשֻׁקָּדִים כַּפְתֹּרֶיהָ וּפְרָחֶיהָ:

לה וְכַפְתֹּר תַּחַת שְׁנֵי הַקָּנִים מִמֶּנָּה וְכַפְתֹּר תַּחַת שְׁנֵי הַקָּנִים מִמֶּנָּה וְכַפְתֹּר תַּחַת־שְׁנֵי הַקָּנִים מִמֶּנָּה לְשֵׁשֶׁת הַקָּנִים הַיֹּצְאִים מִן־הַמְּנֹרָה:

לו כַּפְתֹּרֵיהֶם וּקְנֹתָם מִמֶּנָּה יִהְיוּ כֻּלָּהּ מִקְשָׁה אַחַת זָהָב טָהוֹר:

לז וְעָשִׂיתָ אֶת־נֵרֹתֶיהָ שִׁבְעָה וְהֶעֱלָה אֶת־נֵרֹתֶיהָ וְהֵאִיר עַל־עֵבֶר פָּנֶיהָ:

לח וּמַלְקָחֶיהָ וּמַחְתֹּתֶיהָ זָהָב טָהוֹר:

לט כִּכָּר זָהָב טָהוֹר יַעֲשֶׂה אֹתָהּ אֵת כָּל־הַכֵּלִים הָאֵלֶּה:

מ וּרְאֵה וַעֲשֵׂה בְּתַבְנִיתָם אֲשֶׁר־אַתָּה מָרְאֶה בָּהָר:

כו א וְאֶת־הַמִּשְׁכָּן תַּעֲשֶׂה עֶשֶׂר יְרִיעֹת שֵׁשׁ מָשְׁזָר וּתְכֵלֶת וְאַרְגָּמָן וְתֹלַעַת שָׁנִי כְּרֻבִים מַעֲשֵׂה חֹשֵׁב תַּעֲשֶׂה אֹתָם:

ב אֹרֶךְ הַיְרִיעָה הָאַחַת שְׁמֹנֶה וְעֶשְׂרִים בָּאַמָּה וְרֹחַב אַרְבַּע בָּאַמָּה הַיְרִיעָה הָאֶחָת מִדָּה אַחַת לְכָל־הַיְרִיעֹת:

ג חֲמֵשׁ הַיְרִיעֹת תִּהְיֶיןָ חֹבְרֹת אִשָּׁה אֶל־אֲחֹתָהּ וְחָמֵשׁ יְרִיעֹת חֹבְרֹת אִשָּׁה אֶל־אֲחֹתָהּ:

ד וְעָשִׂיתָ לֻלְאֹת תְּכֵלֶת עַל שְׂפַת הַיְרִיעָה הָאֶחָת מִקָּצָה בַּחֹבָרֶת וְכֵן תַּעֲשֶׂה בִּשְׂפַת הַיְרִיעָה הַקִּיצוֹנָה בַּמַּחְבֶּרֶת הַשֵּׁנִית:

ה חֲמִשִּׁים לֻלָאֹת תַּעֲשֶׂה בַּיְרִיעָה הָאֶחָת וַחֲמִשִּׁים לֻלָאֹת תַּעֲשֶׂה בִּקְצֵה הַיְרִיעָה אֲשֶׁר בַּמַּחְבֶּרֶת הַשֵּׁנִית מַקְבִּילֹת הַלֻּלָאֹת אִשָּׁה אֶל־אֲחֹתָהּ:

ו וְעָשִׂיתָ חֲמִשִּׁים קַרְסֵי זָהָב וְחִבַּרְתָּ אֶת־הַיְרִיעֹת אִשָּׁה אֶל־אֲחֹתָהּ בַּקְּרָסִים וְהָיָה הַמִּשְׁכָּן אֶחָד:

ז וְעָשִׂיתָ יְרִיעֹת עִזִּים לְאֹהֶל עַל־הַמִּשְׁכָּן עַשְׁתֵּי־עֶשְׂרֵה יְרִיעֹת תַּעֲשֶׂה אֹתָם:

8 The length of each cloth shall be thirty *amot*, and the width of each cloth shall be four *amot*, the eleven cloths to have the same measurements.

ח אֹרֶךְ הַיְרִיעָה הָאַחַת שְׁלֹשִׁים בָּאַמָּה וְרֹחַב אַרְבַּע בָּאַמָּה הַיְרִיעָה הָאֶחָת מִדָּה אַחַת לְעַשְׁתֵּי עֶשְׂרֵה יְרִיעֹת:

9 Join five of the cloths by themselves, and the other six cloths by themselves; and fold over the sixth cloth at the front of the tent.

ט וְחִבַּרְתָּ אֶת־חֲמֵשׁ הַיְרִיעֹת לְבָד וְאֶת־שֵׁשׁ הַיְרִיעֹת לְבָד וְכָפַלְתָּ אֶת־הַיְרִיעָה הַשִּׁשִּׁית אֶל־מוּל פְּנֵי הָאֹהֶל:

10 Make fifty loops on the edge of the outermost cloth of the one set, and fifty loops on the edge of the cloth of the other set.

י וְעָשִׂיתָ חֲמִשִּׁים לֻלָאֹת עַל שְׂפַת הַיְרִיעָה הָאֶחָת הַקִּיצֹנָה בַּחֹבָרֶת וַחֲמִשִּׁים לֻלָאֹת עַל שְׂפַת הַיְרִיעָה הַחֹבֶרֶת הַשֵּׁנִית:

11 Make fifty copper clasps, and fit the clasps into the loops, and couple the tent together so that it becomes one whole.

יא וְעָשִׂיתָ קַרְסֵי נְחֹשֶׁת חֲמִשִּׁים וְהֵבֵאתָ אֶת־הַקְּרָסִים בַּלֻּלָאֹת וְחִבַּרְתָּ אֶת־הָאֹהֶל וְהָיָה אֶחָד:

12 As for the overlapping excess of the cloths of the tent, the extra half-cloth shall overlap the back of the *Mishkan*,

יב וְסֶרַח הָעֹדֵף בִּירִיעֹת הָאֹהֶל חֲצִי הַיְרִיעָה הָעֹדֶפֶת תִּסְרַח עַל אֲחֹרֵי הַמִּשְׁכָּן:

13 while the extra *amah* at either end of each length of tent cloth shall hang down to the bottom of the two sides of the *Mishkan* and cover it.

יג וְהָאַמָּה מִזֶּה וְהָאַמָּה מִזֶּה בָּעֹדֵף בְּאֹרֶךְ יְרִיעֹת הָאֹהֶל יִהְיֶה סָרוּחַ עַל־צִדֵּי הַמִּשְׁכָּן מִזֶּה וּמִזֶּה לְכַסֹּתוֹ:

14 And make for the tent a covering of tanned ram skins, and a covering of dolphin skins above.

יד וְעָשִׂיתָ מִכְסֶה לָאֹהֶל עֹרֹת אֵילִם מְאָדָּמִים וּמִכְסֵה עֹרֹת תְּחָשִׁים מִלְמָעְלָה:

15 You shall make the planks for the *Mishkan* of acacia wood, upright.

טו וְעָשִׂיתָ אֶת־הַקְּרָשִׁים לַמִּשְׁכָּן עֲצֵי שִׁטִּים עֹמְדִים:

v'-a-SEE-ta et ha-k'-ra-SHEEM la-mish-KAN a-TZAY shi-TEEM o-m'-DEEM

16 The length of each plank shall be ten *amot* and the width of each plank an *amah* and a half.

טז עֶשֶׂר אַמּוֹת אֹרֶךְ הַקָּרֶשׁ וְאַמָּה וַחֲצִי הָאַמָּה רֹחַב הַקֶּרֶשׁ הָאֶחָד:

17 Each plank shall have two tenons, parallel to each other; do the same with all the planks of the *Mishkan*.

יז שְׁתֵּי יָדוֹת לַקֶּרֶשׁ הָאֶחָד מְשֻׁלָּבֹת אִשָּׁה אֶל־אֲחֹתָהּ כֵּן תַּעֲשֶׂה לְכֹל קַרְשֵׁי הַמִּשְׁכָּן:

26:15 You shall make the planks Why is the definite article 'the' used in reference to the planks used in the construction of the *Mishkan*? *Rashi* answers that this refers to specific planks with great significance. He cites the tradition that *Yaakov* planted acacia trees in Egypt in preparation for the redemption, and commanded his sons to take these trees with them upon exiting Egypt hundreds of years in the future. In this way, *Yaakov* was not only preparing the materials for the future building of the *Mishkan*, but also imparting a message, teaching the coming generations of his descendants that their exile is temporary. Later in history, throughout the bitter exile, the children of *Yaakov* have similarly longed continuously and prepared for their redemption and return to their homeland. How fortunate are we to witness the beginning of this final redemption.

Acacia tree growing in the Negev

18 Of the planks of the *Mishkan*, make twenty planks on the south side:

יח וְעָשִׂ֥יתָ אֶת־הַקְּרָשִׁ֖ים לַמִּשְׁכָּ֑ן עֶשְׂרִ֣ים קֶ֔רֶשׁ לִפְאַ֖ת נֶ֥גְבָּה תֵימָֽנָה׃

19 making forty silver sockets under the twenty planks, two sockets under the one plank for its two tenons and two sockets under each following plank for its two tenons;

יט וְאַרְבָּעִ֞ים אַדְנֵי־כֶ֗סֶף תַּעֲשֶׂ֘ה תַּ֣חַת עֶשְׂרִ֣ים הַקֶּ֒רֶשׁ֒ שְׁנֵ֣י אֲדָנִ֗ים תַּֽחַת־הַקֶּ֤רֶשׁ הָֽאֶחָד֙ לִשְׁתֵּ֣י יְדֹתָ֔יו וּשְׁנֵ֣י אֲדָנִ֗ים תַּֽחַת־הַקֶּ֥רֶשׁ הָֽאֶחָ֖ד לִשְׁתֵּ֥י יְדֹתָֽיו׃

20 and for the other side wall of the *Mishkan,* on the north side, twenty planks.

כ וּלְצֶ֧לַע הַמִּשְׁכָּ֛ן הַשֵּׁנִ֖ית לִפְאַ֣ת צָפ֑וֹן עֶשְׂרִ֖ים קָֽרֶשׁ׃

21 with forty silver sockets, two sockets under the one plank and two sockets under each following plank.

כא וְאַרְבָּעִ֥ים אַדְנֵיהֶ֖ם כָּ֑סֶף שְׁנֵ֣י אֲדָנִ֗ים תַּ֚חַת הַקֶּ֣רֶשׁ הָֽאֶחָ֔ד וּשְׁנֵ֣י אֲדָנִ֔ים תַּ֖חַת הַקֶּ֥רֶשׁ הָֽאֶחָֽד׃

22 And for the rear of the *Mishkan*, to the west, make six planks;

כב וּֽלְיַרְכְּתֵ֥י הַמִּשְׁכָּ֖ן יָ֑מָּה תַּעֲשֶׂ֖ה שִׁשָּׁ֥ה קְרָשִֽׁים׃

23 and make two planks for the corners of the *Mishkan* at the rear.

כג וּשְׁנֵ֤י קְרָשִׁים֙ תַּעֲשֶׂ֔ה לִמְקֻצְעֹ֖ת הַמִּשְׁכָּ֑ן בַּיַּרְכָתָֽיִם׃

24 They shall match at the bottom, and terminate alike at the top inside one ring; thus shall it be with both of them: they shall form the two corners.

כד וְיִֽהְי֣וּ תֹֽאֲמִם֮ מִלְּמַטָּה֒ וְיַחְדָּ֗ו יִֽהְי֤וּ תַמִּים֙ עַל־רֹאשׁ֔וֹ אֶל־הַטַּבַּ֖עַת הָֽאֶחָ֑ת כֵּ֚ן יִֽהְיֶ֣ה לִשְׁנֵיהֶ֔ם לִשְׁנֵ֥י הַמִּקְצֹעֹ֖ת יִֽהְיֽוּ׃

25 Thus there shall be eight planks with their sockets of silver: sixteen sockets, two sockets under the first plank, and two sockets under each of the other planks.

כה וְהָיוּ֙ שְׁמֹנָ֣ה קְרָשִׁ֔ים וְאַדְנֵיהֶ֣ם כֶּ֔סֶף שִׁשָּׁ֥ה עָשָׂ֖ר אֲדָנִ֑ים שְׁנֵ֣י אֲדָנִ֗ים תַּ֚חַת הַקֶּ֣רֶשׁ הָֽאֶחָ֔ד וּשְׁנֵ֣י אֲדָנִ֔ים תַּ֖חַת הַקֶּ֥רֶשׁ הָֽאֶחָֽד׃

26 You shall make bars of acacia wood: five for the planks of the one side wall of the *Mishkan,*

כו וְעָשִׂ֥יתָ בְרִיחִ֖ם עֲצֵ֣י שִׁטִּ֑ים חֲמִשָּׁ֕ה לְקַרְשֵׁ֥י צֶֽלַע־הַמִּשְׁכָּ֖ן הָֽאֶחָֽד׃

27 five bars for the planks of the other side wall of the *Mishkan*, and five bars for the planks of the wall of the *Mishkan* at the rear to the west.

כז וַחֲמִשָּׁ֣ה בְרִיחִ֔ם לְקַרְשֵׁ֥י צֶֽלַע־הַמִּשְׁכָּ֖ן הַשֵּׁנִ֑ית וַחֲמִשָּׁ֣ה בְרִיחִ֗ם לְקַרְשֵׁ֙י צֶ֤לַע הַמִּשְׁכָּן֙ לַיַּרְכָתַ֖יִם יָֽמָּה׃

28 The center bar halfway up the planks shall run from end to end.

כח וְהַבְּרִ֥יחַ הַתִּיכֹ֖ן בְּת֣וֹךְ הַקְּרָשִׁ֑ים מַבְרִ֕חַ מִן־הַקָּצֶ֖ה אֶל־הַקָּצֶֽה׃

29 Overlay the planks with gold, and make their rings of gold, as holders for the bars; and overlay the bars with gold.

כט וְֽאֶת־הַקְּרָשִׁ֞ים תְּצַפֶּ֣ה זָהָ֗ב וְאֶת־ טַבְּעֹֽתֵיהֶם֙ תַּעֲשֶׂ֣ה זָהָ֔ב בָּתִּ֖ים לַבְּרִיחִ֑ם וְצִפִּיתָ֥ אֶת־הַבְּרִיחִ֖ם זָהָֽב׃

30 Then set up the *Mishkan* according to the manner of it that you were shown on the mountain.

ל וַהֲקֵמֹתָ֖ אֶת־הַמִּשְׁכָּ֑ן כְּמִ֨שְׁפָּט֔וֹ אֲשֶׁ֥ר הׇרְאֵ֖יתָ בָּהָֽר׃

31 You shall make a curtain of blue, purple, and crimson yarns, and fine twisted linen; it shall have a design of cherubim worked into it.

לא וְעָשִׂ֣יתָ פָרֹ֗כֶת תְּכֵ֧לֶת וְאַרְגָּמָ֛ן וְתוֹלַ֥עַת שָׁנִ֖י וְשֵׁ֣שׁ מׇשְׁזָ֑ר מַעֲשֵׂ֥ה חֹשֵׁ֛ב יַעֲשֶׂ֥ה אֹתָ֖הּ כְּרֻבִֽים׃

32 Hang it upon four posts of acacia wood overlaid with gold and having hooks of gold, [set] in four sockets of silver.

לב וְנָתַתָּה אֹתָהּ עַל־אַרְבָּעָה עַמּוּדֵי שִׁטִּים מְצֻפִּים זָהָב וָוֵיהֶם זָהָב עַל־אַרְבָּעָה אַדְנֵי־כָסֶף:

33 Hang the curtain under the clasps, and carry the *Aron HaBrit* there, behind the curtain, so that the curtain shall serve you as a partition between the Holy and the Holy of Holies.

לג וְנָתַתָּה אֶת־הַפָּרֹכֶת תַּחַת הַקְּרָסִים וְהֵבֵאתָ שָׁמָּה מִבֵּית לַפָּרֹכֶת אֵת אֲרוֹן הָעֵדוּת וְהִבְדִּילָה הַפָּרֹכֶת לָכֶם בֵּין הַקֹּדֶשׁ וּבֵין קֹדֶשׁ הַקֳּדָשִׁים:

34 Place the cover upon the *Aron HaBrit* in the Holy of Holies.

לד וְנָתַתָּ אֶת־הַכַּפֹּרֶת עַל אֲרוֹן הָעֵדֻת בְּקֹדֶשׁ הַקֳּדָשִׁים:

35 Place the table outside the curtain, and the *menorah* by the south wall of the *Mishkan* opposite the table, which is to be placed by the north wall.

לה וְשַׂמְתָּ אֶת־הַשֻּׁלְחָן מִחוּץ לַפָּרֹכֶת וְאֶת־הַמְּנֹרָה נֹכַח הַשֻּׁלְחָן עַל צֶלַע הַמִּשְׁכָּן תֵּימָנָה וְהַשֻּׁלְחָן תִּתֵּן עַל־צֶלַע צָפוֹן:

36 You shall make a screen for the entrance of the Tent, of blue, purple, and crimson yarns, and fine twisted linen, done in embroidery.

לו וְעָשִׂיתָ מָסָךְ לְפֶתַח הָאֹהֶל תְּכֵלֶת וְאַרְגָּמָן וְתוֹלַעַת שָׁנִי וְשֵׁשׁ מָשְׁזָר מַעֲשֵׂה רֹקֵם:

37 Make five posts of acacia wood for the screen and overlay them with gold – their hooks being of gold – and cast for them five sockets of copper.

לז וְעָשִׂיתָ לַמָּסָךְ חֲמִשָּׁה עַמּוּדֵי שִׁטִּים וְצִפִּיתָ אֹתָם זָהָב וָוֵיהֶם זָהָב וְיָצַקְתָּ לָהֶם חֲמִשָּׁה אַדְנֵי נְחֹשֶׁת:

27 1 You shall make the *Mizbayach* of acacia wood, five *amot* long and five *amot* wide – the *Mizbayach* is to be square – and three *amot* high.

כז א וְעָשִׂיתָ אֶת־הַמִּזְבֵּחַ עֲצֵי שִׁטִּים חָמֵשׁ אַמּוֹת אֹרֶךְ וְחָמֵשׁ אַמּוֹת רֹחַב רָבוּעַ יִהְיֶה הַמִּזְבֵּחַ וְשָׁלֹשׁ אַמּוֹת קֹמָתוֹ:

2 Make its horns on the four corners, the horns to be of one piece with it; and overlay it with copper.

ב וְעָשִׂיתָ קַרְנֹתָיו עַל אַרְבַּע פִּנֹּתָיו מִמֶּנּוּ תִּהְיֶיןָ קַרְנֹתָיו וְצִפִּיתָ אֹתוֹ נְחֹשֶׁת:

3 Make the pails for removing its ashes, as well as its scrapers, basins, flesh hooks, and fire pans – make all its utensils of copper.

ג וְעָשִׂיתָ סִּירֹתָיו לְדַשְּׁנוֹ וְיָעָיו וּמִזְרְקֹתָיו וּמִזְלְגֹתָיו וּמַחְתֹּתָיו לְכָל־כֵּלָיו תַּעֲשֶׂה נְחֹשֶׁת:

4 Make for it a grating of meshwork in copper; and on the mesh make four copper rings at its four corners.

ד וְעָשִׂיתָ לּוֹ מִכְבָּר מַעֲשֵׂה רֶשֶׁת נְחֹשֶׁת וְעָשִׂיתָ עַל־הָרֶשֶׁת אַרְבַּע טַבְּעֹת נְחֹשֶׁת עַל אַרְבַּע קְצוֹתָיו:

5 Set the mesh below, under the ledge of the *Mizbayach*, so that it extends to the middle of the *Mizbayach*.

ה וְנָתַתָּה אֹתָהּ תַּחַת כַּרְכֹּב הַמִּזְבֵּחַ מִלְּמָטָּה וְהָיְתָה הָרֶשֶׁת עַד חֲצִי הַמִּזְבֵּחַ:

6 And make poles for the *Mizbayach*, poles of acacia wood, and overlay them with copper.

ו וְעָשִׂיתָ בַדִּים לַמִּזְבֵּחַ בַּדֵּי עֲצֵי שִׁטִּים וְצִפִּיתָ אֹתָם נְחֹשֶׁת:

7 The poles shall be inserted into the rings, so that the poles remain on the two sides of the *Mizbayach* when it is carried.

ז וְהוּבָא אֶת־בַּדָּיו בַּטַּבָּעֹת וְהָיוּ הַבַּדִּים עַל־שְׁתֵּי צַלְעֹת הַמִּזְבֵּחַ בִּשְׂאֵת אֹתוֹ:

8 Make it hollow, of boards. As you were shown on the mountain, so shall they be made.

ח נְבוּב לֻחֹת תַּעֲשֶׂה אֹתוֹ כַּאֲשֶׁר הֶרְאָה אֹתְךָ בָּהָר כֵּן יַעֲשׂוּ:

n'-VUV lu-KHOT ta-a-SEH o-TO ka-a-SHER her-AH
o-t'-KHA ba-HAR KAYN ya-a-SU

9 You shall make the enclosure of the *Mishkan*: On the south side, a hundred *amot* of hangings of fine twisted linen for the length of the enclosure on that side

ט וְעָשִׂיתָ אֵת חֲצַר הַמִּשְׁכָּן לִפְאַת נֶגֶב־תֵּימָנָה קְלָעִים לֶחָצֵר שֵׁשׁ מָשְׁזָר מֵאָה בָאַמָּה אֹרֶךְ לַפֵּאָה הָאֶחָת:

10 with its twenty posts and their twenty sockets of copper, the hooks and bands of the posts to be of silver.

י וְעַמֻּדָיו עֶשְׂרִים וְאַדְנֵיהֶם עֶשְׂרִים נְחֹשֶׁת וָוֵי הָעַמֻּדִים וַחֲשֻׁקֵיהֶם כָּסֶף:

11 Again a hundred *amot* of hangings for its length along the north side – with its twenty posts and their twenty sockets of copper, the hooks and bands of the posts to be of silver.

יא וְכֵן לִפְאַת צָפוֹן בָּאֹרֶךְ קְלָעִים מֵאָה אֹרֶךְ וְעַמּוּדָו [וְעַמּוּדָיו] עֶשְׂרִים וְאַדְנֵיהֶם עֶשְׂרִים נְחֹשֶׁת וָוֵי הָעַמֻּדִים וַחֲשֻׁקֵיהֶם כָּסֶף:

12 For the width of the enclosure, on the west side, fifty *amot* of hangings, with their ten posts and their ten sockets.

יב וְרֹחַב הֶחָצֵר לִפְאַת־יָם קְלָעִים חֲמִשִּׁים אַמָּה עַמֻּדֵיהֶם עֲשָׂרָה וְאַדְנֵיהֶם עֲשָׂרָה:

13 For the width of the enclosure on the front, or east side, fifty *amot*:

יג וְרֹחַב הֶחָצֵר לִפְאַת קֵדְמָה מִזְרָחָה חֲמִשִּׁים אַמָּה:

14 fifteen *amot* of hangings on the one flank, with their three posts and their three sockets;

יד וַחֲמֵשׁ עֶשְׂרֵה אַמָּה קְלָעִים לַכָּתֵף עַמֻּדֵיהֶם שְׁלֹשָׁה וְאַדְנֵיהֶם שְׁלֹשָׁה:

15 fifteen *amot* of hangings on the other flank, with their three posts and their three sockets;

טו וְלַכָּתֵף הַשֵּׁנִית חֲמֵשׁ עֶשְׂרֵה קְלָעִים עַמֻּדֵיהֶם שְׁלֹשָׁה וְאַדְנֵיהֶם שְׁלֹשָׁה:

16 and for the gate of the enclosure, a screen of twenty *amot*, of blue, purple, and crimson yarns, and fine twisted linen, done in embroidery, with their four posts and their four sockets.

טז וּלְשַׁעַר הֶחָצֵר מָסָךְ עֶשְׂרִים אַמָּה תְּכֵלֶת וְאַרְגָּמָן וְתוֹלַעַת שָׁנִי וְשֵׁשׁ מָשְׁזָר מַעֲשֵׂה רֹקֵם עַמֻּדֵיהֶם אַרְבָּעָה וְאַדְנֵיהֶם אַרְבָּעָה:

17 All the posts round the enclosure shall be banded with silver and their hooks shall be of silver; their sockets shall be of copper.

יז כָּל־עַמּוּדֵי הֶחָצֵר סָבִיב מְחֻשָּׁקִים כֶּסֶף וָוֵיהֶם כָּסֶף וְאַדְנֵיהֶם נְחֹשֶׁת:

18 The length of the enclosure shall be a hundred *amot*, and the width fifty throughout; and the height five *amot* – [with hangings] of fine twisted linen. The sockets shall be of copper:

יח אֹרֶךְ הֶחָצֵר מֵאָה בָאַמָּה וְרֹחַב חֲמִשִּׁים בַּחֲמִשִּׁים וְקֹמָה חָמֵשׁ אַמּוֹת שֵׁשׁ מָשְׁזָר וְאַדְנֵיהֶם נְחֹשֶׁת:

27:8 Hollow, of boards The altar is constructed from hollow boards that are filled with earth whenever the Israelites camp and reassemble the *Mishkan* in the desert. Only once the nation reaches *Eretz Yisrael* is a permanent, solid altar of stone constructed. These hollow planks reflect the transitory life of the Israelites in the desert. Only once they reach the Land of Israel can they finally settle into their permanent home. This is a timeless message to Jews in exile: Life outside of Israel should be seen as temporary, and homes and businesses should be built accordingly. The Land of Israel is the only truly permanent home for the People of Israel.

Stone altar found at Tel Be'er Sheva

Exodus

19 all the utensils of the *Mishkan*, for all its service, as well as all its pegs and all the pegs of the court, shall be of copper.

לְכֹל כְּלֵי הַמִּשְׁכָּן בְּכֹל עֲבֹדָתוֹ וְכָל־יְתֵדֹתָיו וְכָל־יִתְדֹת הֶחָצֵר נְחֹשֶׁת:

20 You shall further instruct the Israelites to bring you clear oil of beaten olives for lighting, for kindling lamps regularly.

כ וְאַתָּה **תְּצַוֶּה** אֶת־בְּנֵי יִשְׂרָאֵל וְיִקְחוּ אֵלֶיךָ שֶׁמֶן זַיִת זָךְ כָּתִית לַמָּאוֹר לְהַעֲלֹת נֵר תָּמִיד:

21 *Aharon* and his sons shall set them up in the Tent of Meeting, outside the curtain which is over [the *Aron* of] the Pact, [to burn] from evening to morning before *Hashem*. It shall be a due from the Israelites for all time, throughout the ages.

כא בְּאֹהֶל מוֹעֵד מִחוּץ לַפָּרֹכֶת אֲשֶׁר עַל־הָעֵדֻת יַעֲרֹךְ אֹתוֹ אַהֲרֹן וּבָנָיו מֵעֶרֶב עַד־בֹּקֶר לִפְנֵי יְהוָה חֻקַּת עוֹלָם לְדֹרֹתָם מֵאֵת בְּנֵי יִשְׂרָאֵל:

28 1 You shall bring forward your brother *Aharon*, with his sons, from among the Israelites, to serve Me as *Kohanim*: *Aharon, Nadav* and *Avihu, Elazar* and *Itamar*, the sons of *Aharon*.

כח א וְאַתָּה הַקְרֵב אֵלֶיךָ אֶת־אַהֲרֹן אָחִיךָ וְאֶת־בָּנָיו אִתּוֹ מִתּוֹךְ בְּנֵי יִשְׂרָאֵל לְכַהֲנוֹ־לִי אַהֲרֹן נָדָב וַאֲבִיהוּא אֶלְעָזָר וְאִיתָמָר בְּנֵי אַהֲרֹן:

2 Make sacral vestments for your brother *Aharon*, for dignity and adornment.

ב וְעָשִׂיתָ בִגְדֵי־קֹדֶשׁ לְאַהֲרֹן אָחִיךָ לְכָבוֹד וּלְתִפְאָרֶת:

v'-a-SEE-ta vig-day KO-desh l'-a-ha-RON a-KHEE-kha l'-kha-VOD ul-tif-A-ret

3 Next you shall instruct all who are skillful, whom I have endowed with the gift of skill, to make *Aharon*'s vestments, for consecrating him to serve Me as *Kohen*.

ג וְאַתָּה תְּדַבֵּר אֶל־כָּל־חַכְמֵי־לֵב אֲשֶׁר מִלֵּאתִיו רוּחַ חָכְמָה וְעָשׂוּ אֶת־בִּגְדֵי אַהֲרֹן לְקַדְּשׁוֹ לְכַהֲנוֹ־לִי:

4 These are the vestments they are to make: a breastpiece, an ephod, a robe, a fringed tunic, a headdress, and a sash. They shall make those sacral vestments for your brother *Aharon* and his sons, for priestly service to Me;

ד וְאֵלֶּה הַבְּגָדִים אֲשֶׁר יַעֲשׂוּ חֹשֶׁן וְאֵפוֹד וּמְעִיל וּכְתֹנֶת תַּשְׁבֵּץ מִצְנֶפֶת וְאַבְנֵט וְעָשׂוּ בִגְדֵי־קֹדֶשׁ לְאַהֲרֹן אָחִיךָ וּלְבָנָיו לְכַהֲנוֹ־לִי:

5 they, therefore, shall receive the gold, the blue, purple, and crimson yarns, and the fine linen.

ה וְהֵם יִקְחוּ אֶת־הַזָּהָב וְאֶת־הַתְּכֵלֶת וְאֶת־הָאַרְגָּמָן וְאֶת־תּוֹלַעַת הַשָּׁנִי וְאֶת־הַשֵּׁשׁ:

6 They shall make the ephod of gold, of blue, purple, and crimson yarns, and of fine twisted linen, worked into designs.

ו וְעָשׂוּ אֶת־הָאֵפֹד זָהָב תְּכֵלֶת וְאַרְגָּמָן תּוֹלַעַת שָׁנִי וְשֵׁשׁ מָשְׁזָר מַעֲשֵׂה חֹשֵׁב:

7 It shall have two shoulder-pieces attached; they shall be attached at its two ends.

ז שְׁתֵּי כְתֵפֹת חֹבְרֹת יִהְיֶה־לּוֹ אֶל־שְׁנֵי קְצוֹתָיו וְחֻבָּר:

Watercolor drawing of the High Priest

כבוד
תפארת

28:2 For dignity and adornment The verse says that the purpose of the priestly garments is for *kavod* (כבוד), 'dignity,' and *tiferet* (תפארת), 'adornment.' What is the difference between these two words? The *Malbim* explains that *kavod* is the honor a person gets for the things that are part of his inherent nature.

Tiferet, on the other hand, is the glory one receives as a result of his own efforts and accomplishments. The special priestly garments signify both the dignity of their God-given position as well as the "adornment" of the accomplishments the priests would achieve by investing effort and energy in their elevated spiritual position.

8   And the decorated band that is upon it shall be
made like it, of one piece with it: of gold, of blue,
purple, and crimson yarns, and of fine twisted linen.

ח   וְחֵשֶׁב אֲפֻדָּתוֹ אֲשֶׁר עָלָיו כְּמַעֲשֵׂהוּ
מִמֶּנּוּ יִהְיֶה זָהָב תְּכֵלֶת וְאַרְגָּמָן
וְתוֹלַעַת שָׁנִי וְשֵׁשׁ מָשְׁזָר:

9   Then take two lazuli stones and engrave on them
the names of the sons of *Yisrael*:

ט   וְלָקַחְתָּ אֶת־שְׁתֵּי אַבְנֵי־שֹׁהַם וּפִתַּחְתָּ
עֲלֵיהֶם שְׁמוֹת בְּנֵי יִשְׂרָאֵל:

10   six of their names on the one stone, and the names
of the remaining six on the other stone, in the order
of their birth.

י   שִׁשָּׁה מִשְּׁמֹתָם עַל הָאֶבֶן הָאֶחָת וְאֶת־
שְׁמוֹת הַשִּׁשָּׁה הַנּוֹתָרִים עַל־הָאֶבֶן
הַשֵּׁנִית כְּתוֹלְדֹתָם:

11   On the two stones you shall make seal engravings –
the work of a lapidary – of the names of the sons of
Yisrael. Having bordered them with frames of gold,

יא   מַעֲשֵׂה חָרַשׁ אֶבֶן פִּתּוּחֵי חֹתָם תְּפַתַּח
אֶת־שְׁתֵּי הָאֲבָנִים עַל־שְׁמֹת בְּנֵי
יִשְׂרָאֵל מֻסַבֹּת מִשְׁבְּצוֹת זָהָב תַּעֲשֶׂה
אֹתָם:

12   attach the two stones to the shoulder-pieces of the
ephod, as stones for remembrance of *B'nei Yisrael*,
whose names *Aharon* shall carry upon his two
shoulder-pieces for remembrance before *Hashem*.

יב   וְשַׂמְתָּ אֶת־שְׁתֵּי הָאֲבָנִים עַל כִּתְפֹת
הָאֵפֹד אַבְנֵי זִכָּרֹן לִבְנֵי יִשְׂרָאֵל וְנָשָׂא
אַהֲרֹן אֶת־שְׁמוֹתָם לִפְנֵי יְהֹוָה עַל־שְׁתֵּי
כְתֵפָיו לְזִכָּרֹן:

13   Then make frames of gold

יג   וְעָשִׂיתָ מִשְׁבְּצֹת זָהָב:

14   and two chains of pure gold; braid these like corded
work, and fasten the corded chains to the frames.

יד   וּשְׁתֵּי שַׁרְשְׁרֹת זָהָב טָהוֹר מִגְבָּלֹת
תַּעֲשֶׂה אֹתָם מַעֲשֵׂה עֲבֹת וְנָתַתָּה אֶת־
שַׁרְשְׁרֹת הָעֲבֹתֹת עַל־הַמִּשְׁבְּצֹת:

15   You shall make a breastpiece of decision, worked
into a design; make it in the style of the ephod:
make it of gold, of blue, purple, and crimson yarns,
and of fine twisted linen.

טו   וְעָשִׂיתָ חֹשֶׁן מִשְׁפָּט מַעֲשֵׂה חֹשֵׁב
כְּמַעֲשֵׂה אֵפֹד תַּעֲשֶׂנּוּ זָהָב תְּכֵלֶת
וְאַרְגָּמָן וְתוֹלַעַת שָׁנִי וְשֵׁשׁ מָשְׁזָר
תַּעֲשֶׂה אֹתוֹ:

16   It shall be square and doubled, a *zeret* in length and
a *zeret* in width.

טז   רָבוּעַ יִהְיֶה כָּפוּל זֶרֶת אָרְכּוֹ וְזֶרֶת
רָחְבּוֹ:

17   Set in it mounted stones, in four rows of stones. The
first row shall be a row of carnelian, chrysolite, and
emerald;

יז   וּמִלֵּאתָ בוֹ מִלֻּאַת אֶבֶן אַרְבָּעָה טוּרִים
אָבֶן טוּר אֹדֶם פִּטְדָה וּבָרֶקֶת הַטּוּר
הָאֶחָד:

18   the second row: a turquoise, a sapphire, and an
amethyst;

יח   וְהַטּוּר הַשֵּׁנִי נֹפֶךְ סַפִּיר וְיָהֲלֹם:

19   the third row: a jacinth, an agate, and a crystal;

יט   וְהַטּוּר הַשְּׁלִישִׁי לֶשֶׁם שְׁבוֹ וְאַחְלָמָה:

20   and the fourth row: a beryl, a lapis lazuli, and a
jasper. They shall be framed with gold in their
mountings.

כ   וְהַטּוּר הָרְבִיעִי תַּרְשִׁישׁ וְשֹׁהַם וְיָשְׁפֵה
מְשֻׁבָּצִים זָהָב יִהְיוּ בְּמִלּוּאֹתָם:

21   The stones shall correspond [in number] to the
names of the sons of *Yisrael*: twelve, corresponding
to their names. They shall be engraved like seals,
each with its name, for the twelve tribes.

כא   וְהָאֲבָנִים תִּהְיֶיןָ עַל־שְׁמֹת בְּנֵי־יִשְׂרָאֵל
שְׁתֵּים עֶשְׂרֵה עַל־שְׁמֹתָם פִּתּוּחֵי
חוֹתָם אִישׁ עַל־שְׁמוֹ תִּהְיֶיןָ לִשְׁנֵי עָשָׂר
שָׁבֶט:

22   On the breastpiece make braided chains of corded
work in pure gold.

כב   וְעָשִׂיתָ עַל־הַחֹשֶׁן שַׁרְשֹׁת גַּבְלֻת
מַעֲשֵׂה עֲבֹת זָהָב טָהוֹר:

23 Make two rings of gold on the breastpiece,
and fasten the two rings at the two ends of the
breastpiece,

כג וְעָשִׂיתָ עַל־הַחֹשֶׁן שְׁתֵּי טַבְּעוֹת זָהָב
וְנָתַתָּ אֶת־שְׁתֵּי הַטַּבָּעוֹת עַל־שְׁנֵי
קְצוֹת הַחֹשֶׁן:

24 attaching the two golden cords to the two rings at
the ends of the breastpiece.

כד וְנָתַתָּה אֶת־שְׁתֵּי עֲבֹתֹת הַזָּהָב עַל־
שְׁתֵּי הַטַּבָּעֹת אֶל־קְצוֹת הַחֹשֶׁן:

25 Then fasten the two ends of the cords to the two
frames, which you shall attach to the shoulder-
pieces of the ephod, at the front.

כה וְאֵת שְׁתֵּי קְצוֹת שְׁתֵּי הָעֲבֹתֹת תִּתֵּן
עַל־שְׁתֵּי הַמִּשְׁבְּצוֹת וְנָתַתָּה עַל־
כִּתְפוֹת הָאֵפֹד אֶל־מוּל פָּנָיו:

26 Make two rings of gold and attach them to the two
ends of the breastpiece, at its inner edge, which
faces the ephod.

כו וְעָשִׂיתָ שְׁתֵּי טַבְּעוֹת זָהָב וְשַׂמְתָּ אֹתָם
עַל־שְׁנֵי קְצוֹת הַחֹשֶׁן עַל־שְׂפָתוֹ אֲשֶׁר
אֶל־עֵבֶר הָאֵפֹד בָּיְתָה:

27 And make two other rings of gold and fasten them
on the front of the ephod, low on the two shoulder-
pieces, close to its seam above the decorated band.

כז וְעָשִׂיתָ שְׁתֵּי טַבְּעוֹת זָהָב וְנָתַתָּה אֹתָם
עַל־שְׁתֵּי כִתְפוֹת הָאֵפוֹד מִלְּמַטָּה
מִמּוּל פָּנָיו לְעֻמַּת מֶחְבַּרְתּוֹ מִמַּעַל
לְחֵשֶׁב הָאֵפוֹד:

28 The breastpiece shall be held in place by a cord of
blue from its rings to the rings of the ephod, so that
the breastpiece rests on the decorated band and
does not come loose from the ephod.

כח וְיִרְכְּסוּ אֶת־הַחֹשֶׁן מטבעתו
[מִטַּבְּעֹתָיו] אֶל־טַבְּעֹת הָאֵפֹד בִּפְתִיל
תְּכֵלֶת לִהְיוֹת עַל־חֵשֶׁב הָאֵפוֹד וְלֹא־
יִזַּח הַחֹשֶׁן מֵעַל הָאֵפוֹד:

29 *Aharon* shall carry the names of the sons of *Yisrael*
on the breastpiece of decision over his heart, when
he enters the sanctuary, for remembrance before
Hashem at all times.

כט וְנָשָׂא אַהֲרֹן אֶת־שְׁמוֹת בְּנֵי־יִשְׂרָאֵל
בְּחֹשֶׁן הַמִּשְׁפָּט עַל־לִבּוֹ בְּבֹאוֹ אֶל־
הַקֹּדֶשׁ לְזִכָּרֹן לִפְנֵי־יהוה תָּמִיד:

30 Inside the breastpiece of decision you shall place
the Urim and Thummim, so that they are over
Aharon's heart when he comes before *Hashem*. Thus
Aharon shall carry the instrument of decision for
the Israelites over his heart before *Hashem* at all
times.

ל וְנָתַתָּ אֶל־חֹשֶׁן הַמִּשְׁפָּט אֶת־הָאוּרִים
וְאֶת־הַתֻּמִּים וְהָיוּ עַל־לֵב אַהֲרֹן בְּבֹאוֹ
לִפְנֵי יהוה וְנָשָׂא אַהֲרֹן אֶת־מִשְׁפַּט
בְּנֵי־יִשְׂרָאֵל עַל־לִבּוֹ לִפְנֵי יהוה תָּמִיד:

31 You shall make the robe of the ephod of pure blue.

לא וְעָשִׂיתָ אֶת־מְעִיל הָאֵפוֹד כְּלִיל תְּכֵלֶת:

32 The opening for the head shall be in the middle of
it; the opening shall have a binding of woven work
round about – it shall be like the opening of a coat
of mail – so that it does not tear.

לב וְהָיָה פִי־רֹאשׁוֹ בְּתוֹכוֹ שָׂפָה יִהְיֶה לְפִיו
סָבִיב מַעֲשֵׂה אֹרֵג כְּפִי תַחְרָא יִהְיֶה־לּוֹ
לֹא יִקָּרֵעַ:

33 On its hem make pomegranates of blue, purple,
and crimson yarns, all around the hem, with bells of
gold between them all around:

לג וְעָשִׂיתָ עַל־שׁוּלָיו רִמֹּנֵי תְּכֵלֶת וְאַרְגָּמָן
וְתוֹלַעַת שָׁנִי עַל־שׁוּלָיו סָבִיב וּפַעֲמֹנֵי
זָהָב בְּתוֹכָם סָבִיב:

34 a golden bell and a pomegranate, a golden bell and a
pomegranate, all around the hem of the robe.

לד פַּעֲמֹן זָהָב וְרִמּוֹן פַּעֲמֹן זָהָב וְרִמּוֹן עַל־
שׁוּלֵי הַמְּעִיל סָבִיב:

35 *Aharon* shall wear it while officiating, so that
the sound of it is heard when he comes into the
sanctuary before *Hashem* and when he goes out –
that he may not die.

לה וְהָיָה עַל־אַהֲרֹן לְשָׁרֵת וְנִשְׁמַע קוֹלוֹ
בְּבֹאוֹ אֶל־הַקֹּדֶשׁ לִפְנֵי יהוה וּבְצֵאתוֹ
וְלֹא יָמוּת:

36 You shall make a frontlet of pure gold and engrave on it the seal inscription: "Holy to *Hashem*."

לו וְעָשִׂיתָ צִּיץ זָהָב טָהֹור וּפִתַּחְתָּ עָלָיו פִּתּוּחֵי חֹתָם קֹדֶשׁ לַיהֹוָה:

37 Suspend it on a cord of blue, so that it may remain on the headdress; it shall remain on the front of the headdress.

לז וְשַׂמְתָּ אֹתֹו עַל־פְּתִיל תְּכֵלֶת וְהָיָה עַל־הַמִּצְנָפֶת אֶל־מוּל פְּנֵי־הַמִּצְנֶפֶת יִהְיֶה:

38 It shall be on *Aharon*'s forehead, that *Aharon* may take away any sin arising from the holy things that the Israelites consecrate, from any of their sacred donations; it shall be on his forehead at all times, to win acceptance for them before *Hashem*.

לח וְהָיָה עַל־מֵצַח אַהֲרֹן וְנָשָׂא אַהֲרֹן אֶת־עֲוֹן הַקֳּדָשִׁים אֲשֶׁר יַקְדִּישׁוּ בְּנֵי יִשְׂרָאֵל לְכָל־מַתְּנֹת קָדְשֵׁיהֶם וְהָיָה עַל־מִצְחֹו תָּמִיד לְרָצֹון לָהֶם לִפְנֵי יְהֹוָה:

39 You shall make the fringed tunic of fine linen. You shall make the headdress of fine linen. You shall make the sash of embroidered work.

לט וְשִׁבַּצְתָּ הַכְּתֹנֶת שֵׁשׁ וְעָשִׂיתָ מִצְנֶפֶת שֵׁשׁ וְאַבְנֵט תַּעֲשֶׂה מַעֲשֵׂה רֹקֵם:

40 And for *Aharon*'s sons also you shall make tunics, and make sashes for them, and make turbans for them, for dignity and adornment.

מ וְלִבְנֵי אַהֲרֹן תַּעֲשֶׂה כֻתֳּנֹת וְעָשִׂיתָ לָהֶם אַבְנֵטִים וּמִגְבָּעֹות תַּעֲשֶׂה לָהֶם לְכָבֹוד וּלְתִפְאָרֶת:

41 Put these on your brother *Aharon* and on his sons as well; anoint them, and ordain them and consecrate them to serve Me as *Kohanim*.

מא וְהִלְבַּשְׁתָּ אֹתָם אֶת־אַהֲרֹן אָחִיךָ וְאֶת־בָּנָיו אִתֹּו וּמָשַׁחְתָּ אֹתָם וּמִלֵּאתָ אֶת־יָדָם וְקִדַּשְׁתָּ אֹתָם וְכִהֲנוּ לִי:

42 You shall also make for them linen breeches to cover their nakedness; they shall extend from the hips to the thighs.

מב וַעֲשֵׂה לָהֶם מִכְנְסֵי־בָד לְכַסֹּות בְּשַׂר עֶרְוָה מִמָּתְנַיִם וְעַד־יְרֵכַיִם יִהְיוּ:

43 They shall be worn by *Aharon* and his sons when they enter the Tent of Meeting or when they approach the *Mizbayach* to officiate in the sanctuary, so that they do not incur punishment and die. It shall be a law for all time for him and for his offspring to come.

מג וְהָיוּ עַל־אַהֲרֹן וְעַל־בָּנָיו בְּבֹאָם אֶל־אֹהֶל מֹועֵד אֹו בְגִשְׁתָּם אֶל־הַמִּזְבֵּחַ לְשָׁרֵת בַּקֹּדֶשׁ וְלֹא־יִשְׂאוּ עָוֹן וָמֵתוּ חֻקַּת עֹולָם לֹו וּלְזַרְעֹו אַחֲרָיו:

29 1 This is what you shall do to them in consecrating them to serve Me as *Kohanim*: Take a young bull of the herd and two rams without blemish;

כט א וְזֶה הַדָּבָר אֲשֶׁר־תַּעֲשֶׂה לָהֶם לְקַדֵּשׁ אֹתָם לְכַהֵן לִי לְקַח פַּר אֶחָד בֶּן־בָּקָר וְאֵילִם שְׁנַיִם תְּמִימִם:

v'-ZEH ha-da-VAR a-SHER ta-a-SEH la-HEM l'-ka-DAYSH o-TAM l'-kha-HAYN LEE l'-KAKH PAR e-KHAD ben ba-KAR v'-ay-LEEM sh'-NA-yim t'-mee-MIM

הדבר

א

29:1 This is what you shall do to them This verse starts with the words *v'zeh hadavar asher ta'aseh lahem* (וזה הדבר אשר תעשה להם), 'this is what you shall do to them.' In the context of this verse, the Hebrew word *hadavar* (הדבר) means 'the thing.' However, *hadavar* can also mean 'the word.' According to the Sages, the use of this term in the chapter describing the inaugu-

ration ritual of the *Mishkan* alludes to an important lesson. *Hashem* is not found exclusively in the *Mishkan*, nor is the *Mishkan* service the only way to access Him. Even when there is no longer a Holy Temple and sacrifices are not brought, *Hashem* is still accessible through words, the words of our prayers.

Praying at the Western Wall

Tetzaveh

2 also unleavened bread, unleavened cakes with oil mixed in, and unleavened wafers spread with oil – make these of choice wheat flour.

ב וְלֶ֣חֶם מַצּ֗וֹת וְחַלֹּ֤ת מַצֹּת֙ בְּלוּלֹ֣ת בַּשֶּׁ֔מֶן וּרְקִיקֵ֥י מַצּ֖וֹת מְשֻׁחִ֣ים בַּשָּׁ֑מֶן סֹ֥לֶת חִטִּ֖ים תַּעֲשֶׂ֥ה אֹתָֽם׃

3 Place these in one basket and present them in the basket, along with the bull and the two rams.

ג וְנָתַתָּ֤ אוֹתָם֙ עַל־סַ֣ל אֶחָ֔ד וְהִקְרַבְתָּ֥ אֹתָ֖ם בַּסָּ֑ל וְאֶ֨ת־הַפָּ֔ר וְאֵ֖ת שְׁנֵ֥י הָאֵילִֽם׃

4 Lead *Aharon* and his sons up to the entrance of the Tent of Meeting, and wash them with water.

ד וְאֶת־אַהֲרֹ֤ן וְאֶת־בָּנָיו֙ תַּקְרִ֔יב אֶל־פֶּ֖תַח אֹ֣הֶל מוֹעֵ֑ד וְרָחַצְתָּ֥ אֹתָ֖ם בַּמָּֽיִם׃

5 Then take the vestments, and clothe *Aharon* with the tunic, the robe of the ephod, the ephod, and the breastpiece, and gird him with the decorated band of the ephod.

ה וְלָקַחְתָּ֣ אֶת־הַבְּגָדִ֗ים וְהִלְבַּשְׁתָּ֤ אֶת־אַהֲרֹן֙ אֶת־הַכֻּתֹּ֔נֶת וְאֵת֙ מְעִ֣יל הָאֵפֹ֔ד וְאֶת־הָ֣אֵפֹ֔ד וְאֶת־הַחֹ֑שֶׁן וְאָפַדְתָּ֣ ל֔וֹ בְּחֵ֖שֶׁב הָאֵפֹֽד׃

6 Put the headdress on his head, and place the holy diadem upon the headdress.

ו וְשַׂמְתָּ֥ הַמִּצְנֶ֖פֶת עַל־רֹאשׁ֑וֹ וְנָתַתָּ֛ אֶת־נֵ֥זֶר הַקֹּ֖דֶשׁ עַל־הַמִּצְנָֽפֶת׃

7 Take the anointing oil and pour it on his head and anoint him.

ז וְלָקַחְתָּ֙ אֶת־שֶׁ֣מֶן הַמִּשְׁחָ֔ה וְיָצַקְתָּ֖ עַל־רֹאשׁ֑וֹ וּמָשַׁחְתָּ֖ אֹתֽוֹ׃

8 Then bring his sons forward; clothe them with tunics

ח וְאֶת־בָּנָ֖יו תַּקְרִ֑יב וְהִלְבַּשְׁתָּ֖ם כֻּתֳּנֹֽת׃

9 and wind turbans upon them. And gird both *Aharon* and his sons with sashes. And so they shall have priesthood as their right for all time. You shall then ordain *Aharon* and his sons.

ט וְחָגַרְתָּ֩ אֹתָ֨ם אַבְנֵ֜ט אַהֲרֹ֣ן וּבָנָ֗יו וְחָבַשְׁתָּ֤ לָהֶם֙ מִגְבָּעֹ֔ת וְהָיְתָ֥ה לָהֶ֛ם כְּהֻנָּ֖ה לְחֻקַּ֣ת עוֹלָ֑ם וּמִלֵּאתָ֥ יַד־אַהֲרֹ֖ן וְיַד־בָּנָֽיו׃

10 Lead the bull up to the front of the Tent of Meeting, and let *Aharon* and his sons lay their hands upon the head of the bull.

י וְהִקְרַבְתָּ֙ אֶת־הַפָּ֔ר לִפְנֵ֖י אֹ֣הֶל מוֹעֵ֑ד וְסָמַ֨ךְ אַהֲרֹ֤ן וּבָנָיו֙ אֶת־יְדֵיהֶ֔ם עַל־רֹ֥אשׁ הַפָּֽר׃

11 Slaughter the bull before *Hashem*, at the entrance of the Tent of Meeting,

יא וְשָׁחַטְתָּ֥ אֶת־הַפָּ֖ר לִפְנֵ֣י יְהֹוָ֑ה פֶּ֖תַח אֹ֥הֶל מוֹעֵֽד׃

12 and take some of the bull's blood and put it on the horns of the *Mizbayach* with your finger; then pour out the rest of the blood at the base of the *Mizbayach*.

יב וְלָקַחְתָּ֙ מִדַּ֣ם הַפָּ֔ר וְנָתַתָּ֛ה עַל־קַרְנֹ֥ת הַמִּזְבֵּ֖חַ בְּאֶצְבָּעֶ֑ךָ וְאֶת־כׇּל־הַדָּ֣ם תִּשְׁפֹּ֔ךְ אֶל־יְס֖וֹד הַמִּזְבֵּֽחַ׃

13 Take all the fat that covers the entrails, the protuberance on the liver, and the two kidneys with the fat on them, and turn them into smoke upon the *Mizbayach*.

יג וְלָקַחְתָּ֗ אֶֽת־כׇּל־הַחֵלֶב֮ הַֽמְכַסֶּ֣ה אֶת־הַקֶּרֶב֒ וְאֵ֗ת הַיֹּתֶ֙רֶת֙ עַל־הַכָּבֵ֔ד וְאֵת֙ שְׁתֵּ֣י הַכְּלָיֹ֔ת וְאֶת־הַחֵ֖לֶב אֲשֶׁ֣ר עֲלֵיהֶ֑ן וְהִקְטַרְתָּ֖ הַמִּזְבֵּֽחָה׃

14 The rest of the flesh of the bull, its hide, and its dung shall be put to the fire outside the camp; it is a sin offering.

יד וְאֶת־בְּשַׂ֤ר הַפָּר֙ וְאֶת־עֹר֣וֹ וְאֶת־פִּרְשׁ֔וֹ תִּשְׂרֹ֣ף בָּאֵ֔שׁ מִח֖וּץ לַֽמַּחֲנֶ֑ה חַטָּ֖את הֽוּא׃

15 Next take the one ram, and let *Aharon* and his sons lay their hands upon the ram's head.

טו וְאֶת־הָאַ֥יִל הָאֶחָ֖ד תִּקָּ֑ח וְסָ֨מְכ֜וּ אַהֲרֹ֧ן וּבָנָ֛יו אֶת־יְדֵיהֶ֖ם עַל־רֹ֥אשׁ הָאָֽיִל׃

16 Slaughter the ram, and take its blood and dash it against all sides of the *Mizbayach*.

טז וְשָׁחַטְתָּ֖ אֶת־הָאָ֑יִל וְלָקַחְתָּ֙ אֶת־דָּמ֔וֹ וְזָרַקְתָּ֥ עַל־הַמִּזְבֵּ֖חַ סָבִֽיב׃

17 Cut up the ram into sections, wash its entrails and legs, and put them with its quarters and its head.

יז וְאֶת־הָאַיִל תְּנַתֵּחַ לִנְתָחָיו וְרָחַצְתָּ קִרְבּוֹ וּכְרָעָיו וְנָתַתָּ עַל־נְתָחָיו וְעַל־רֹאשֽׁוֹ:

18 Turn all of the ram into smoke upon the *Mizbayach*. It is a burnt offering to *Hashem*, a pleasing odor, an offering by fire to *Hashem*.

יח וְהִקְטַרְתָּ אֶת־כָּל־הָאַיִל הַמִּזְבֵּחָה עֹלָה הוּא לַֽיהֹוָה רֵיחַ נִיחוֹחַ אִשֶּׁה לַיהֹוָה הֽוּא:

19 Then take the other ram, and let *Aharon* and his sons lay their hands upon the ram's head.

יט וְלָקַחְתָּ אֵת הָאַיִל הַשֵּׁנִי וְסָמַךְ אַהֲרֹן וּבָנָיו אֶת־יְדֵיהֶם עַל־רֹאשׁ הָאָֽיִל:

20 Slaughter the ram, and take some of its blood and put it on the ridge of *Aharon*'s right ear and on the ridges of his sons' right ears, and on the thumbs of their right hands, and on the big toes of their right feet; and dash the rest of the blood against every side of the *Mizbayach* round about.

כ וְשָׁחַטְתָּ אֶת־הָאַיִל וְלָקַחְתָּ מִדָּמוֹ וְנָתַתָּה עַל־תְּנוּךְ אֹזֶן אַהֲרֹן וְעַל־תְּנוּךְ אֹזֶן בָּנָיו הַיְמָנִית וְעַל־בֹּהֶן יָדָם הַיְמָנִית וְעַל־בֹּהֶן רַגְלָם הַיְמָנִית וְזָרַקְתָּ אֶת־הַדָּם עַל־הַמִּזְבֵּחַ סָבִֽיב:

21 Take some of the blood that is on the *Mizbayach* and some of the anointing oil and sprinkle upon *Aharon* and his vestments, and also upon his sons and his sons' vestments. Thus shall he and his vestments be holy, as well as his sons and his sons' vestments.

כא וְלָקַחְתָּ מִן־הַדָּם אֲשֶׁר עַל־הַמִּזְבֵּחַ וּמִשֶּׁמֶן הַמִּשְׁחָה וְהִזֵּיתָ עַל־אַהֲרֹן וְעַל־בְּגָדָיו וְעַל־בָּנָיו וְעַל־בִּגְדֵי בָנָיו אִתּוֹ וְקָדַשׁ הוּא וּבְגָדָיו וּבָנָיו וּבִגְדֵי בָנָיו אִתּֽוֹ:

22 You shall take from the ram the fat parts – the broad tail, the fat that covers the entrails, the protuberance on the liver, the two kidneys with the fat on them – and the right thigh; for this is a ram of ordination.

כב וְלָקַחְתָּ מִן־הָאַיִל הַחֵלֶב וְהָאַלְיָה וְאֶת־הַחֵלֶב הַֽמְכַסֶּה אֶת־הַקֶּרֶב וְאֵת יֹתֶרֶת הַכָּבֵד וְאֵת שְׁתֵּי הַכְּלָיֹת וְאֶת־הַחֵלֶב אֲשֶׁר עֲלֵיהֶן וְאֵת שׁוֹק הַיָּמִין כִּי אֵיל מִלֻּאִים הֽוּא:

23 Add one flat loaf of bread, one cake of oil bread, and one wafer, from the basket of unleavened bread that is before *Hashem*.

כג וְכִכַּר לֶחֶם אַחַת וַחַלַּת לֶחֶם שֶׁמֶן אַחַת וְרָקִיק אֶחָד מִסַּל הַמַּצּוֹת אֲשֶׁר לִפְנֵי יְהֹוָֽה:

24 Place all these on the palms of *Aharon* and his sons, and offer them as an elevation offering before *Hashem*.

כד וְשַׂמְתָּ הַכֹּל עַל כַּפֵּי אַהֲרֹן וְעַל כַּפֵּי בָנָיו וְהֵנַפְתָּ אֹתָם תְּנוּפָה לִפְנֵי יְהֹוָֽה:

25 Take them from their hands and turn them into smoke upon the *Mizbayach* with the burnt offering, as a pleasing odor before *Hashem*; it is an offering by fire to *Hashem*.

כה וְלָקַחְתָּ אֹתָם מִיָּדָם וְהִקְטַרְתָּ הַמִּזְבֵּחָה עַל־הָעֹלָה לְרֵיחַ נִיחוֹחַ לִפְנֵי יְהֹוָה אִשֶּׁה הוּא לַיהֹוָֽה:

26 Then take the breast of *Aharon*'s ram of ordination and offer it as an elevation offering before *Hashem*; it shall be your portion.

כו וְלָקַחְתָּ אֶת־הֶחָזֶה מֵאֵיל הַמִּלֻּאִים אֲשֶׁר לְאַהֲרֹן וְהֵנַפְתָּ אֹתוֹ תְּנוּפָה לִפְנֵי יְהֹוָה וְהָיָה לְךָ לְמָנָֽה:

27 You shall consecrate the breast that was offered as an elevation offering and the thigh that was offered as a gift offering from the ram of ordination – from that which was *Aharon*'s and from that which was his sons'

כז וְקִדַּשְׁתָּ אֵת חֲזֵה הַתְּנוּפָה וְאֵת שׁוֹק הַתְּרוּמָה אֲשֶׁר הוּנַף וַאֲשֶׁר הוּרָם מֵאֵיל הַמִּלֻּאִים מֵאֲשֶׁר לְאַהֲרֹן וּמֵאֲשֶׁר לְבָנָֽיו:

28 and those parts shall be a due for all time from the Israelites to *Aharon* and his descendants. For they are a gift; and so shall they be a gift from the Israelites, their gift to *Hashem* out of their sacrifices of well-being.

כח וְהָיָה לְאַהֲרֹן וּלְבָנָיו לְחָק־עוֹלָם מֵאֵת בְּנֵי יִשְׂרָאֵל כִּי תְרוּמָה הוּא וּתְרוּמָה יִהְיֶה מֵאֵת בְּנֵי־יִשְׂרָאֵל מִזִּבְחֵי שַׁלְמֵיהֶם תְּרוּמָתָם לַיהוָה:

29 The sacral vestments of *Aharon* shall pass on to his sons after him, for them to be anointed and ordained in.

כט וּבִגְדֵי הַקֹּדֶשׁ אֲשֶׁר לְאַהֲרֹן יִהְיוּ לְבָנָיו אַחֲרָיו לְמָשְׁחָה בָהֶם וּלְמַלֵּא־בָם אֶת־יָדָם:

30 He among his sons who becomes *Kohen* in his stead, who enters the Tent of Meeting to officiate within the sanctuary, shall wear them seven days.

ל שִׁבְעַת יָמִים יִלְבָּשָׁם הַכֹּהֵן תַּחְתָּיו מִבָּנָיו אֲשֶׁר יָבֹא אֶל־אֹהֶל מוֹעֵד לְשָׁרֵת בַּקֹּדֶשׁ:

31 You shall take the ram of ordination and boil its flesh in the sacred precinct;

לא וְאֵת אֵיל הַמִּלֻּאִים תִּקָּח וּבִשַּׁלְתָּ אֶת־בְּשָׂרוֹ בְּמָקֹם קָדֹשׁ:

32 and *Aharon* and his sons shall eat the flesh of the ram, and the bread that is in the basket, at the entrance of the Tent of Meeting.

לב וְאָכַל אַהֲרֹן וּבָנָיו אֶת־בְּשַׂר הָאַיִל וְאֶת־הַלֶּחֶם אֲשֶׁר בַּסָּל פֶּתַח אֹהֶל מוֹעֵד:

33 These things shall be eaten only by those for whom expiation was made with them when they were ordained and consecrated; they may not be eaten by a layman, for they are holy.

לג וְאָכְלוּ אֹתָם אֲשֶׁר כֻּפַּר בָּהֶם לְמַלֵּא אֶת־יָדָם לְקַדֵּשׁ אֹתָם וְזָר לֹא־יֹאכַל כִּי־קֹדֶשׁ הֵם:

34 And if any of the flesh of ordination, or any of the bread, is left until morning, you shall put what is left to the fire; it shall not be eaten, for it is holy.

לד וְאִם־יִוָּתֵר מִבְּשַׂר הַמִּלֻּאִים וּמִן־הַלֶּחֶם עַד־הַבֹּקֶר וְשָׂרַפְתָּ אֶת־הַנּוֹתָר בָּאֵשׁ לֹא יֵאָכֵל כִּי־קֹדֶשׁ הוּא:

35 Thus you shall do to *Aharon* and his sons, just as I have commanded you. You shall ordain them through seven days,

לה וְעָשִׂיתָ לְאַהֲרֹן וּלְבָנָיו כָּכָה כְּכֹל אֲשֶׁר־צִוִּיתִי אֹתָכָה שִׁבְעַת יָמִים תְּמַלֵּא יָדָם:

36 and each day you shall prepare a bull as a sin offering for expiation; you shall purge the *Mizbayach* by performing purification upon it, and you shall anoint it to consecrate it.

לו וּפַר חַטָּאת תַּעֲשֶׂה לַיּוֹם עַל־הַכִּפֻּרִים וְחִטֵּאתָ עַל־הַמִּזְבֵּחַ בְּכַפֶּרְךָ עָלָיו וּמָשַׁחְתָּ אֹתוֹ לְקַדְּשׁוֹ:

37 Seven days you shall perform purification for the *Mizbayach* to consecrate it, and the *Mizbayach* shall become most holy; whatever touches the *Mizbayach* shall become consecrated.

לז שִׁבְעַת יָמִים תְּכַפֵּר עַל־הַמִּזְבֵּחַ וְקִדַּשְׁתָּ אֹתוֹ וְהָיָה הַמִּזְבֵּחַ קֹדֶשׁ קָדָשִׁים כָּל־הַנֹּגֵעַ בַּמִּזְבֵּחַ יִקְדָּשׁ:

38 Now this is what you shall offer upon the *Mizbayach*: two yearling lambs each day, regularly.

לח וְזֶה אֲשֶׁר תַּעֲשֶׂה עַל־הַמִּזְבֵּחַ כְּבָשִׂים בְּנֵי־שָׁנָה שְׁנַיִם לַיּוֹם תָּמִיד:

39 You shall offer the one lamb in the morning, and you shall offer the other lamb at twilight.

לט אֶת־הַכֶּבֶשׂ הָאֶחָד תַּעֲשֶׂה בַבֹּקֶר וְאֵת הַכֶּבֶשׂ הַשֵּׁנִי תַּעֲשֶׂה בֵּין הָעַרְבָּיִם:

40 There shall be a tenth of a measure of choice flour with a quarter of a *hin* of beaten oil mixed in, and a libation of a quarter *hin* of wine for one lamb;

מ וְעִשָּׂרֹן סֹלֶת בָּלוּל בְּשֶׁמֶן כָּתִית רֶבַע הַהִין וְנֵסֶךְ רְבִיעִת הַהִין יַיִן לַכֶּבֶשׂ הָאֶחָד:

41 and you shall offer the other lamb at twilight, repeating with it the meal offering of the morning with its libation – an offering by fire for a pleasing odor to *Hashem*,

מא וְאֵת הַכֶּבֶשׂ הַשֵּׁנִי תַּעֲשֶׂה בֵּין הָעַרְבָּיִם כְּמִנְחַת הַבֹּקֶר וּכְנִסְכָּהּ תַּעֲשֶׂה לָּהּ לְרֵיחַ נִיחֹחַ אִשֶּׁה לַיהוָה:

42 a regular burnt offering throughout the generations, at the entrance of the Tent of Meeting before *Hashem*. For there I will meet with you, and there I will speak with you,

מב עֹלַת תָּמִיד לְדֹרֹתֵיכֶם פֶּתַח אֹהֶל־מוֹעֵד לִפְנֵי יְהוָה אֲשֶׁר אִוָּעֵד לָכֶם שָׁמָּה לְדַבֵּר אֵלֶיךָ שָׁם:

43 and there I will meet with the Israelites, and it shall be sanctified by My Presence.

מג וְנֹעַדְתִּי שָׁמָּה לִבְנֵי יִשְׂרָאֵל וְנִקְדַּשׁ בִּכְבֹדִי:

44 I will sanctify the Tent of Meeting and the *Mizbayach*, and I will consecrate *Aharon* and his sons to serve Me as *Kohanim*.

מד וְקִדַּשְׁתִּי אֶת־אֹהֶל מוֹעֵד וְאֶת־הַמִּזְבֵּחַ וְאֶת־אַהֲרֹן וְאֶת־בָּנָיו אֲקַדֵּשׁ לְכַהֵן לִי:

45 I will abide among the Israelites, and I will be their God.

מה וְשָׁכַנְתִּי בְּתוֹךְ בְּנֵי יִשְׂרָאֵל וְהָיִיתִי לָהֶם לֵאלֹהִים:

46 And they shall know that I *Hashem* am their God, who brought them out from the land of Egypt that I might abide among them, I *Hashem* their God.

מו וְיָדְעוּ כִּי אֲנִי יְהוָה אֱלֹהֵיהֶם אֲשֶׁר הוֹצֵאתִי אֹתָם מֵאֶרֶץ מִצְרַיִם לְשָׁכְנִי בְתוֹכָם אֲנִי יְהוָה אֱלֹהֵיהֶם:

30 1 You shall make a *Mizbayach* for burning incense; make it of acacia wood.

ל א וְעָשִׂיתָ מִזְבֵּחַ מִקְטַר קְטֹרֶת עֲצֵי שִׁטִּים תַּעֲשֶׂה אֹתוֹ:

2 It shall be an *amah* long and an *amah* wide – it shall be square – and two *amot* high, its horns of one piece with it.

ב אַמָּה אָרְכּוֹ וְאַמָּה רָחְבּוֹ רָבוּעַ יִהְיֶה וְאַמָּתַיִם קֹמָתוֹ מִמֶּנּוּ קַרְנֹתָיו:

3 Overlay it with pure gold: its top, its sides round about, and its horns; and make a gold molding for it round about.

ג וְצִפִּיתָ אֹתוֹ זָהָב טָהוֹר אֶת־גַּגּוֹ וְאֶת־קִירֹתָיו סָבִיב וְאֶת־קַרְנֹתָיו וְעָשִׂיתָ לּוֹ זֵר זָהָב סָבִיב:

4 And make two gold rings for it under its molding; make them on its two side walls, on opposite sides. They shall serve as holders for poles with which to carry it.

ד וּשְׁתֵּי טַבְּעֹת זָהָב תַּעֲשֶׂה־לּוֹ מִתַּחַת לְזֵרוֹ עַל שְׁתֵּי צַלְעֹתָיו תַּעֲשֶׂה עַל־שְׁנֵי צִדָּיו וְהָיָה לְבָתִּים לְבַדִּים לָשֵׂאת אֹתוֹ בָּהֵמָּה:

5 Make the poles of acacia wood, and overlay them with gold.

ה וְעָשִׂיתָ אֶת־הַבַּדִּים עֲצֵי שִׁטִּים וְצִפִּיתָ אֹתָם זָהָב:

6 Place it in front of the curtain that is over the *Aron HaBrit* – in front of the cover that is over the Pact – where I will meet with you.

ו וְנָתַתָּה אֹתוֹ לִפְנֵי הַפָּרֹכֶת אֲשֶׁר עַל־אֲרֹן הָעֵדֻת לִפְנֵי הַכַּפֹּרֶת אֲשֶׁר עַל־הָעֵדֻת אֲשֶׁר אִוָּעֵד לְךָ שָׁמָּה:

7 On it *Aharon* shall burn aromatic incense: he shall burn it every morning when he tends the lamps,

ז וְהִקְטִיר עָלָיו אַהֲרֹן קְטֹרֶת סַמִּים בַּבֹּקֶר בַּבֹּקֶר בְּהֵיטִיבוֹ אֶת־הַנֵּרֹת יַקְטִירֶנָּה:

8 and *Aharon* shall burn it at twilight when he lights the lamps – a regular incense offering before *Hashem* throughout the ages.

ח וּבְהַעֲלֹת אַהֲרֹן אֶת־הַנֵּרֹת בֵּין הָעַרְבַּיִם יַקְטִירֶנָּה קְטֹרֶת תָּמִיד לִפְנֵי יְהוָה לְדֹרֹתֵיכֶם:

9 You shall not offer alien incense on it, or a burnt offering or a meal offering; neither shall you pour a libation on it.

ט לֹא־תַעֲלוּ עָלָיו קְטֹרֶת זָרָה וְעֹלָה וּמִנְחָה וְנֵסֶךְ לֹא תִסְּכוּ עָלָיו:

10 Once a year *Aharon* shall perform purification upon its horns with blood of the sin offering of purification; purification shall be performed upon it once a year throughout the ages. It is most holy to *Hashem*.

י וְכִפֶּר אַהֲרֹן עַל־קַרְנֹתָיו אַחַת בַּשָּׁנָה מִדַּם חַטַּאת הַכִּפֻּרִים אַחַת בַּשָּׁנָה יְכַפֵּר עָלָיו לְדֹרֹתֵיכֶם קֹדֶשׁ־קָדָשִׁים הוּא לַיהֹוָה:

11 *Hashem* spoke to *Moshe*, saying:

יא וַיְדַבֵּר יְהֹוָה אֶל־מֹשֶׁה לֵּאמֹר:

12 When you take a census of *B'nei Yisrael* according to their enrollment, each shall pay *Hashem* a ransom for himself on being enrolled, that no plague may come upon them through their being enrolled.

יב כִּי תִשָּׂא אֶת־רֹאשׁ בְּנֵי־יִשְׂרָאֵל לִפְקֻדֵיהֶם וְנָתְנוּ אִישׁ כֹּפֶר נַפְשׁוֹ לַיהֹוָה בִּפְקֹד אֹתָם וְלֹא־יִהְיֶה בָהֶם נֶגֶף בִּפְקֹד אֹתָם:

> *kee ti-SA et ROSH b'-nay yis-ra-AYL lif-ku-day-HEM*
> *v'-na-t'-NU EESH KO-fer naf-SHO la-do-NAI bif-KOD o-TAM*
> *v'-lo yih-YEH va-HEM NE-gef bif-KOD o-TAM*

13 This is what everyone who is entered in the records shall pay: a half-*shekel* by the sanctuary weight – twenty *giera* to the *shekel* – a half-*shekel* as an offering to *Hashem*.

יג זֶה יִתְּנוּ כָּל־הָעֹבֵר עַל־הַפְּקֻדִים מַחֲצִית הַשֶּׁקֶל בְּשֶׁקֶל הַקֹּדֶשׁ עֶשְׂרִים גֵּרָה הַשֶּׁקֶל מַחֲצִית הַשֶּׁקֶל תְּרוּמָה לַיהֹוָה:

14 Everyone who is entered in the records, from the age of twenty years up, shall give *Hashem*'s offering:

יד כֹּל הָעֹבֵר עַל־הַפְּקֻדִים מִבֶּן עֶשְׂרִים שָׁנָה וָמָעְלָה יִתֵּן תְּרוּמַת יְהֹוָה:

15 the rich shall not pay more and the poor shall not pay less than half a *shekel* when giving *Hashem*'s offering as expiation for your persons.

טו הֶעָשִׁיר לֹא־יַרְבֶּה וְהַדַּל לֹא יַמְעִיט מִמַּחֲצִית הַשָּׁקֶל לָתֵת אֶת־תְּרוּמַת יְהֹוָה לְכַפֵּר עַל־נַפְשֹׁתֵיכֶם:

16 You shall take the expiation money from the Israelites and assign it to the service of the Tent of Meeting; it shall serve the Israelites as a reminder before *Hashem*, as expiation for your persons.

טז וְלָקַחְתָּ אֶת־כֶּסֶף הַכִּפֻּרִים מֵאֵת בְּנֵי יִשְׂרָאֵל וְנָתַתָּ אֹתוֹ עַל־עֲבֹדַת אֹהֶל מוֹעֵד וְהָיָה לִבְנֵי יִשְׂרָאֵל לְזִכָּרוֹן לִפְנֵי יְהֹוָה לְכַפֵּר עַל־נַפְשֹׁתֵיכֶם:

17 *Hashem* spoke to *Moshe*, saying:

יז וַיְדַבֵּר יְהֹוָה אֶל־מֹשֶׁה לֵּאמֹר:

18 Make a laver of copper and a stand of copper for it, for washing; and place it between the Tent of Meeting and the *Mizbayach*. Put water in it,

יח וְעָשִׂיתָ כִּיּוֹר נְחֹשֶׁת וְכַנּוֹ נְחֹשֶׁת לְרָחְצָה וְנָתַתָּ אֹתוֹ בֵּין־אֹהֶל מוֹעֵד וּבֵין הַמִּזְבֵּחַ וְנָתַתָּ שָׁמָּה מָיִם:

30:12 When you take a census of the *B'nei Yisrael* *Moshe* is commanded to count the Nation of Israel. However, he is not to count individuals. Instead, each person being counted is to make a donation of half a *shekel* to the *Mishkan*, and the half *shekel* coins are to then be counted. Rabbi Samson Raphael Hirsch explains the symbolism of this method: Merely existing among others does not make one an integral part of a society. In order to be counted as part of the nation, each member has to give of themselves and contribute to the community.

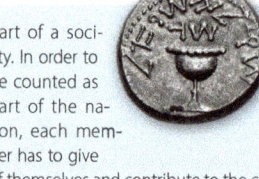

Ancient half-shekel coin

19 and let *Aharon* and his sons wash their hands and feet [in water drawn] from it.

יט וְרָחֲצוּ אַהֲרֹן וּבָנָיו מִמֶּנּוּ אֶת־יְדֵיהֶם וְאֶת־רַגְלֵיהֶם:

20 When they enter the Tent of Meeting they shall wash with water, that they may not die; or when they approach the *Mizbayach* to serve, to turn into smoke an offering by fire to *Hashem*,

כ בְּבֹאָם אֶל־אֹהֶל מוֹעֵד יִרְחֲצוּ־מַיִם וְלֹא יָמֻתוּ אוֹ בְגִשְׁתָּם אֶל־הַמִּזְבֵּחַ לְשָׁרֵת לְהַקְטִיר אִשֶּׁה לַיהוָה:

21 they shall wash their hands and feet, that they may not die. It shall be a law for all time for them – for him and his offspring – throughout the ages.

כא וְרָחֲצוּ יְדֵיהֶם וְרַגְלֵיהֶם וְלֹא יָמֻתוּ וְהָיְתָה לָהֶם חָק־עוֹלָם לוֹ וּלְזַרְעוֹ לְדֹרֹתָם:

22 *Hashem* spoke to *Moshe*, saying:

כב וַיְדַבֵּר יְהוָה אֶל־מֹשֶׁה לֵּאמֹר:

23 Next take choice spices: five hundred weight of solidified myrrh, half as much – two hundred and fifty – of fragrant cinnamon, two hundred and fifty of aromatic cane,

כג וְאַתָּה קַח־לְךָ בְּשָׂמִים רֹאשׁ מָר־דְּרוֹר חֲמֵשׁ מֵאוֹת וְקִנְּמָן־בֶּשֶׂם מַחֲצִיתוֹ חֲמִשִּׁים וּמָאתָיִם וּקְנֵה־בֹשֶׂם חֲמִשִּׁים וּמָאתָיִם:

24 five hundred – by the sanctuary weight – of cassia, and a *hin* of olive oil.

כד וְקִדָּה חֲמֵשׁ מֵאוֹת בְּשֶׁקֶל הַקֹּדֶשׁ וְשֶׁמֶן זַיִת הִין:

25 Make of this a sacred anointing oil, a compound of ingredients expertly blended, to serve as sacred anointing oil.

כה וְעָשִׂיתָ אֹתוֹ שֶׁמֶן מִשְׁחַת־קֹדֶשׁ רֹקַח מִרְקַחַת מַעֲשֵׂה רֹקֵחַ שֶׁמֶן מִשְׁחַת־קֹדֶשׁ יִהְיֶה:

26 With it anoint the Tent of Meeting, the *Aron HaBrit*,

כו וּמָשַׁחְתָּ בוֹ אֶת־אֹהֶל מוֹעֵד וְאֵת אֲרוֹן הָעֵדֻת:

27 the table and all its utensils, the *menorah* and all its fittings, the *Mizbayach* of incense,

כז וְאֶת־הַשֻּׁלְחָן וְאֶת־כָּל־כֵּלָיו וְאֶת־הַמְּנֹרָה וְאֶת־כֵּלֶיהָ וְאֵת מִזְבַּח הַקְּטֹרֶת:

28 the *Mizbayach* of burnt offering and all its utensils, and the laver and its stand.

כח וְאֶת־מִזְבַּח הָעֹלָה וְאֶת־כָּל־כֵּלָיו וְאֶת־הַכִּיֹּר וְאֶת־כַּנּוֹ:

29 Thus you shall consecrate them so that they may be most holy; whatever touches them shall be consecrated.

כט וְקִדַּשְׁתָּ אֹתָם וְהָיוּ קֹדֶשׁ קָדָשִׁים כָּל־הַנֹּגֵעַ בָּהֶם יִקְדָּשׁ:

30 You shall also anoint *Aharon* and his sons, consecrating them to serve Me as *Kohanim*.

ל וְאֶת־אַהֲרֹן וְאֶת־בָּנָיו תִּמְשָׁח וְקִדַּשְׁתָּ אֹתָם לְכַהֵן לִי:

31 And speak to *B'nei Yisrael*, as follows: This shall be an anointing oil sacred to Me throughout the ages.

לא וְאֶל־בְּנֵי יִשְׂרָאֵל תְּדַבֵּר לֵאמֹר שֶׁמֶן מִשְׁחַת־קֹדֶשׁ יִהְיֶה זֶה לִי לְדֹרֹתֵיכֶם:

32 It must not be rubbed on any person's body, and you must not make anything like it in the same proportions; it is sacred, to be held sacred by you.

לב עַל־בְּשַׂר אָדָם לֹא יִיסָךְ וּבְמַתְכֻּנְתּוֹ לֹא תַעֲשׂוּ כָּמֹהוּ קֹדֶשׁ הוּא קֹדֶשׁ יִהְיֶה לָכֶם:

33 Whoever compounds its like, or puts any of it on a layman, shall be cut off from his kin.

לג אִישׁ אֲשֶׁר יִרְקַח כָּמֹהוּ וַאֲשֶׁר יִתֵּן מִמֶּנּוּ עַל־זָר וְנִכְרַת מֵעַמָּיו:

34 And *Hashem* said to *Moshe*: Take the herbs stacte, onycha, and galbanum – these herbs together with pure frankincense; let there be an equal part of each.

לד וַיֹּאמֶר יְהוָה אֶל־מֹשֶׁה קַח־לְךָ סַמִּים נָטָף וּשְׁחֵלֶת וְחֶלְבְּנָה סַמִּים וּלְבֹנָה זַכָּה בַּד בְּבַד יִהְיֶה:

Exodus

35 Make them into incense, a compound expertly blended, refined, pure, sacred.

לה וְעָשִׂיתָ אֹתָהּ קְטֹרֶת רֹקַח מַעֲשֵׂה רוֹקֵחַ מְמֻלָּח טָהוֹר קֹדֶשׁ:

36 Beat some of it into powder, and put some before the Pact in the Tent of Meeting, where I will meet with you; it shall be most holy to you.

לו וְשָׁחַקְתָּ מִמֶּנָּה הָדֵק וְנָתַתָּה מִמֶּנָּה לִפְנֵי הָעֵדֻת בְּאֹהֶל מוֹעֵד אֲשֶׁר אִוָּעֵד לְךָ שָׁמָּה קֹדֶשׁ קָדָשִׁים תִּהְיֶה לָכֶם:

37 But when you make this incense, you must not make any in the same proportions for yourselves; it shall be held by you sacred to *Hashem*.

לז וְהַקְּטֹרֶת אֲשֶׁר תַּעֲשֶׂה בְּמַתְכֻּנְתָּהּ לֹא תַעֲשׂוּ לָכֶם קֹדֶשׁ תִּהְיֶה לְךָ לַיהוָה:

38 Whoever makes any like it, to smell of it, shall be cut off from his kin.

לח אִישׁ אֲשֶׁר־יַעֲשֶׂה כָמוֹהָ לְהָרִיחַ בָּהּ וְנִכְרַת מֵעַמָּיו:

31 1 *Hashem* spoke to *Moshe*:

א א וַיְדַבֵּר יְהוָה אֶל־מֹשֶׁה לֵּאמֹר:

2 See, I have singled out by name *Betzalel* son of *Uri* son of *Chur*, of the tribe of *Yehuda*.

ב רְאֵה קָרָאתִי בְשֵׁם בְּצַלְאֵל בֶּן־אוּרִי בֶן־חוּר לְמַטֵּה יְהוּדָה:

3 I have endowed him with a divine spirit of skill, ability, and knowledge in every kind of craft;

ג וָאֲמַלֵּא אֹתוֹ רוּחַ אֱלֹהִים בְּחָכְמָה וּבִתְבוּנָה וּבְדַעַת וּבְכָל־מְלָאכָה:

4 to make designs for work in gold, silver, and copper,

ד לַחְשֹׁב מַחֲשָׁבֹת לַעֲשׂוֹת בַּזָּהָב וּבַכֶּסֶף וּבַנְּחֹשֶׁת:

5 to cut stones for setting and to carve wood – to work in every kind of craft.

ה וּבַחֲרֹשֶׁת אֶבֶן לְמַלֹּאת וּבַחֲרֹשֶׁת עֵץ לַעֲשׂוֹת בְּכָל־מְלָאכָה:

6 Moreover, I have assigned to him *Oholiav* son of *Achisamach*, of the tribe of *Dan*; and I have also granted skill to all who are skillful, that they may make everything that I have commanded you:

ו וַאֲנִי הִנֵּה נָתַתִּי אִתּוֹ אֵת אָהֳלִיאָב בֶּן־אֲחִיסָמָךְ לְמַטֵּה־דָן וּבְלֵב כָּל־חֲכַם־לֵב נָתַתִּי חָכְמָה וְעָשׂוּ אֵת כָּל־אֲשֶׁר צִוִּיתִךָ:

7 the Tent of Meeting, the *Aron HaBrit* and the cover upon it, and all the furnishings of the Tent;

ז אֵת אֹהֶל מוֹעֵד וְאֶת־הָאָרֹן לָעֵדֻת וְאֶת־הַכַּפֹּרֶת אֲשֶׁר עָלָיו וְאֵת כָּל־כְּלֵי הָאֹהֶל:

8 the table and its utensils, the pure *menorah* and all its fittings, and the *Mizbayach* of incense;

ח וְאֶת־הַשֻּׁלְחָן וְאֶת־כֵּלָיו וְאֶת־הַמְּנֹרָה הַטְּהֹרָה וְאֶת־כָּל־כֵּלֶיהָ וְאֵת מִזְבַּח הַקְּטֹרֶת:

9 the *Mizbayach* of burnt offering and all its utensils, and the laver and its stand;

ט וְאֶת־מִזְבַּח הָעֹלָה וְאֶת־כָּל־כֵּלָיו וְאֶת־הַכִּיּוֹר וְאֶת־כַּנּוֹ:

10 the service vestments, the sacral vestments of *Aharon* the *Kohen* and the vestments of his sons, for their service as *Kohanim*;

י וְאֵת בִּגְדֵי הַשְּׂרָד וְאֶת־בִּגְדֵי הַקֹּדֶשׁ לְאַהֲרֹן הַכֹּהֵן וְאֶת־בִּגְדֵי בָנָיו לְכַהֵן:

11 as well as the anointing oil and the aromatic incense for the sanctuary. Just as I have commanded you, they shall do.

יא וְאֵת שֶׁמֶן הַמִּשְׁחָה וְאֶת־קְטֹרֶת הַסַּמִּים לַקֹּדֶשׁ כְּכֹל אֲשֶׁר־צִוִּיתִךָ יַעֲשׂוּ:

12 And *Hashem* said to *Moshe*:

יב וַיֹּאמֶר יְהֹוָה אֶל־מֹשֶׁה לֵּאמֹר:

13 Speak to *B'nei Yisrael* and say: Nevertheless, you must keep My *Shabbatot*, for this is a sign between Me and you throughout the ages, that you may know that I *Hashem* have consecrated you.

יג וְאַתָּה דַּבֵּר אֶל־בְּנֵי יִשְׂרָאֵל לֵאמֹר אַךְ אֶת־שַׁבְּתֹתַי תִּשְׁמֹרוּ כִּי אוֹת הִוא בֵּינִי וּבֵינֵיכֶם לְדֹרֹתֵיכֶם לָדַעַת כִּי אֲנִי יְהֹוָה מְקַדִּשְׁכֶם:

14 You shall keep the *Shabbat*, for it is holy for you. He who profanes it shall be put to death: whoever does work on it, that person shall be cut off from among his kin.

יד וּשְׁמַרְתֶּם אֶת־הַשַּׁבָּת כִּי קֹדֶשׁ הִוא לָכֶם מְחַלְלֶיהָ מוֹת יוּמָת כִּי כָּל־הָעֹשֶׂה בָהּ מְלָאכָה וְנִכְרְתָה הַנֶּפֶשׁ הַהִוא מִקֶּרֶב עַמֶּיהָ:

15 Six days may work be done, but on the seventh day there shall be a *Shabbat* of complete rest, holy to *Hashem*; whoever does work on the *Shabbat* day shall be put to death.

טו שֵׁשֶׁת יָמִים יֵעָשֶׂה מְלָאכָה וּבַיּוֹם הַשְּׁבִיעִי שַׁבַּת שַׁבָּתוֹן קֹדֶשׁ לַיהֹוָה כָּל־הָעֹשֶׂה מְלָאכָה בְּיוֹם הַשַּׁבָּת מוֹת יוּמָת:

16 *B'nei Yisrael* shall keep the *Shabbat*, observing the *Shabbat* throughout the ages as a covenant for all time:

טז וְשָׁמְרוּ בְנֵי־יִשְׂרָאֵל אֶת־הַשַּׁבָּת לַעֲשׂוֹת אֶת־הַשַּׁבָּת לְדֹרֹתָם בְּרִית עוֹלָם:

17 it shall be a sign for all time between Me and the people of *Yisrael*. For in six days *Hashem* made heaven and earth, and on the seventh day He ceased from work and was refreshed.

יז בֵּינִי וּבֵין בְּנֵי יִשְׂרָאֵל אוֹת הִוא לְעֹלָם כִּי־שֵׁשֶׁת יָמִים עָשָׂה יְהֹוָה אֶת־הַשָּׁמַיִם וְאֶת־הָאָרֶץ וּבַיּוֹם הַשְּׁבִיעִי שָׁבַת וַיִּנָּפַשׁ:

bay-NEE u-VAYN b'-NAY yis-ra-AYL OT HEE l'-o-LAM kee SHAY-shet ya-MEEM a-SAH a-do-NAI et ha-sha-MA-yim v'-ET ha-A-retz u-va-YOM ha-sh'-vee-EE sha-VAT va-yi-na-FASH

18 When He finished speaking with him on *Har Sinai*, He gave *Moshe* the two tablets of the Pact, stone tablets inscribed with the finger of *Hashem*.

יח וַיִּתֵּן אֶל־מֹשֶׁה כְּכַלֹּתוֹ לְדַבֵּר אִתּוֹ בְּהַר סִינַי שְׁנֵי לֻחֹת הָעֵדֻת לֻחֹת אֶבֶן כְּתֻבִים בְּאֶצְבַּע אֱלֹהִים:

לב 1 When the people saw that *Moshe* was so long in coming down from the mountain, the people gathered against *Aharon* and said to him, "Come, make us a god who shall go before us, for that man *Moshe*, who brought us from the land of Egypt – we do not know what has happened to him."

א וַיַּרְא הָעָם כִּי־בֹשֵׁשׁ מֹשֶׁה לָרֶדֶת מִן־הָהָר וַיִּקָּהֵל הָעָם עַל־אַהֲרֹן וַיֹּאמְרוּ אֵלָיו קוּם עֲשֵׂה־לָנוּ אֱלֹהִים אֲשֶׁר יֵלְכוּ לְפָנֵינוּ כִּי־זֶה מֹשֶׁה הָאִישׁ אֲשֶׁר הֶעֱלָנוּ מֵאֶרֶץ מִצְרַיִם לֹא יָדַעְנוּ מֶה־הָיָה לוֹ:

Shabbat table, 1947

31:17 It shall be a sign for all time between Me and the people of *Yisrael* The *Shabbat* (שבת), 'Sabbath,' is designated as a sign between *Hashem* and the Children of Israel that *Hashem* created the world, and resting from work on *Shabbat* is the sign that the Jewish Nation recognizes God as the Creator. Each week, Jews reaffirm their submission to *Hashem* by sanctifying the *Shabbat*, and they recite this verse during the *Shabbat* prayers. Though the observance of *Shabbat* was commanded to the Children of Israel, the message of *Shabbat*, that God created the universe and everything in it, is a universal one.

78

2 *Aharon* said to them, "Take off the gold rings that are on the ears of your wives, your sons, and your daughters, and bring them to me."

ב וַיֹּאמֶר אֲלֵהֶם אַהֲרֹן פָּרְקוּ נִזְמֵי הַזָּהָב אֲשֶׁר בְּאׇזְנֵי נְשֵׁיכֶם בְּנֵיכֶם וּבְנֹתֵיכֶם וְהָבִיאוּ אֵלָי:

3 And all the people took off the gold rings that were in their ears and brought them to *Aharon.*

ג וַיִּתְפָּרְקוּ כָּל־הָעָם אֶת־נִזְמֵי הַזָּהָב אֲשֶׁר בְּאׇזְנֵיהֶם וַיָּבִיאוּ אֶל־אַהֲרֹן:

4 This he took from them and cast in a mold, and made it into a molten calf. And they exclaimed, "This is your god, O *Yisrael,* who brought you out of the land of Egypt!"

ד וַיִּקַּח מִיָּדָם וַיָּצַר אֹתוֹ בַּחֶרֶט וַיַּעֲשֵׂהוּ עֵגֶל מַסֵּכָה וַיֹּאמְרוּ אֵלֶּה אֱלֹהֶיךָ יִשְׂרָאֵל אֲשֶׁר הֶעֱלוּךָ מֵאֶרֶץ מִצְרָיִם:

5 When *Aharon* saw this, he built a *Mizbayach* before it; and *Aharon* announced: "Tomorrow shall be a festival of *Hashem!*"

ה וַיַּרְא אַהֲרֹן וַיִּבֶן מִזְבֵּחַ לְפָנָיו וַיִּקְרָא אַהֲרֹן וַיֹּאמַר חַג לַיהוָה מָחָר:

6 Early next day, the people offered up burnt offerings and brought sacrifices of well-being; they sat down to eat and drink, and then rose to dance.

ו וַיַּשְׁכִּימוּ מִמׇּחֳרָת וַיַּעֲלוּ עֹלֹת וַיַּגִּשׁוּ שְׁלָמִים וַיֵּשֶׁב הָעָם לֶאֱכֹל וְשָׁתוֹ וַיָּקֻמוּ לְצַחֵק:

7 *Hashem* spoke to *Moshe,* "Hurry down, for your people, whom you brought out of the land of Egypt, have acted basely.

ז וַיְדַבֵּר יְהוָה אֶל־מֹשֶׁה לֶךְ־רֵד כִּי שִׁחֵת עַמְּךָ אֲשֶׁר הֶעֱלֵיתָ מֵאֶרֶץ מִצְרָיִם:

8 They have been quick to turn aside from the way that I enjoined upon them. They have made themselves a molten calf and bowed low to it and sacrificed to it, saying: 'This is your god, O *Yisrael,* who brought you out of the land of Egypt!'"

ח סָרוּ מַהֵר מִן־הַדֶּרֶךְ אֲשֶׁר צִוִּיתִם עָשׂוּ לָהֶם עֵגֶל מַסֵּכָה וַיִּשְׁתַּחֲווּ־לוֹ וַיִּזְבְּחוּ־לוֹ וַיֹּאמְרוּ אֵלֶּה אֱלֹהֶיךָ יִשְׂרָאֵל אֲשֶׁר הֶעֱלוּךָ מֵאֶרֶץ מִצְרָיִם:

9 *Hashem* further said to *Moshe,* "I see that this is a stiffnecked people.

ט וַיֹּאמֶר יְהוָה אֶל־מֹשֶׁה רָאִיתִי אֶת־הָעָם הַזֶּה וְהִנֵּה עַם־קְשֵׁה־עֹרֶף הוּא:

10 Now, let Me be, that My anger may blaze forth against them and that I may destroy them, and make of you a great nation."

י וְעַתָּה הַנִּיחָה לִּי וְיִחַר־אַפִּי בָהֶם וַאֲכַלֵּם וְאֶעֱשֶׂה אוֹתְךָ לְגוֹי גָּדוֹל:

11 But *Moshe* implored *Hashem* his God, saying, "Let not Your anger, O *Hashem,* blaze forth against Your people, whom You delivered from the land of Egypt with great power and with a mighty hand.

יא וַיְחַל מֹשֶׁה אֶת־פְּנֵי יְהוָה אֱלֹהָיו וַיֹּאמֶר לָמָה יְהוָה יֶחֱרֶה אַפְּךָ בְּעַמֶּךָ אֲשֶׁר הוֹצֵאתָ מֵאֶרֶץ מִצְרַיִם בְּכֹחַ גָּדוֹל וּבְיָד חֲזָקָה:

12 Let not the Egyptians say, 'It was with evil intent that He delivered them, only to kill them off in the mountains and annihilate them from the face of the earth.' Turn from Your blazing anger, and renounce the plan to punish Your people.

יב לָמָּה יֹאמְרוּ מִצְרַיִם לֵאמֹר בְּרָעָה הוֹצִיאָם לַהֲרֹג אֹתָם בֶּהָרִים וּלְכַלֹּתָם מֵעַל פְּנֵי הָאֲדָמָה שׁוּב מֵחֲרוֹן אַפֶּךָ וְהִנָּחֵם עַל־הָרָעָה לְעַמֶּךָ:

13 Remember Your servants, *Avraham*, *Yitzchak*, and *Yisrael*, how You swore to them by Your Self and said to them: I will make your offspring as numerous as the stars of heaven, and I will give to your offspring this whole land of which I spoke, to possess forever."

יג זְכֹר לְאַבְרָהָם לְיִצְחָק וּלְיִשְׂרָאֵל עֲבָדֶיךָ אֲשֶׁר נִשְׁבַּעְתָּ לָהֶם בָּךְ וַתְּדַבֵּר אֲלֵהֶם אַרְבֶּה אֶת־זַרְעֲכֶם כְּכוֹכְבֵי הַשָּׁמָיִם וְכָל־הָאָרֶץ הַזֹּאת אֲשֶׁר אָמַרְתִּי אֶתֵּן לְזַרְעֲכֶם וְנָחֲלוּ לְעֹלָם:

> z'-KHOR l'-av-ra-HAM l'-yitz-KHAK ul-yis-ra-AYL a-va-DE-kha
> a-SHER nish-BA-ta la-HEM BAKH va-t'-da-BAYR a-lay-HEM ar-BEH
> et zar-a-KHEM k'-kho-kh'-VAY ha-sha-MA-yim v'-khol ha-A-retz ha-ZOT
> a-SHER a-MAR-tee e-TAYN l'-zar-a-KHEM v'-na-kha-LU l'-o-LAM

14 And *Hashem* renounced the punishment He had planned to bring upon His people.

יד וַיִּנָּחֶם יְהוָה עַל־הָרָעָה אֲשֶׁר דִּבֶּר לַעֲשׂוֹת לְעַמּוֹ:

15 Thereupon *Moshe* turned and went down from the mountain bearing the two tablets of the Pact, tablets inscribed on both their surfaces: they were inscribed on the one side and on the other.

טו וַיִּפֶן וַיֵּרֶד מֹשֶׁה מִן־הָהָר וּשְׁנֵי לֻחֹת הָעֵדֻת בְּיָדוֹ לֻחֹת כְּתֻבִים מִשְּׁנֵי עֶבְרֵיהֶם מִזֶּה וּמִזֶּה הֵם כְּתֻבִים:

16 The tablets were *Hashem*'s work, and the writing was *Hashem*'s writing, incised upon the tablets.

טז וְהַלֻּחֹת מַעֲשֵׂה אֱלֹהִים הֵמָּה וְהַמִּכְתָּב מִכְתַּב אֱלֹהִים הוּא חָרוּת עַל־הַלֻּחֹת:

17 When *Yehoshua* heard the sound of the people in its boisterousness, he said to *Moshe*, There is a cry of war in the camp."

יז וַיִּשְׁמַע יְהוֹשֻׁעַ אֶת־קוֹל הָעָם בְּרֵעֹה וַיֹּאמֶר אֶל־מֹשֶׁה קוֹל מִלְחָמָה בַּמַּחֲנֶה:

18 But he answered, "It is not the sound of the tune of triumph, Or the sound of the tune of defeat; It is the sound of song that I hear!"

יח וַיֹּאמֶר אֵין קוֹל עֲנוֹת גְּבוּרָה וְאֵין קוֹל עֲנוֹת חֲלוּשָׁה קוֹל עַנּוֹת אָנֹכִי שֹׁמֵעַ:

19 As soon as *Moshe* came near the camp and saw the calf and the dancing, he became enraged; and he hurled the tablets from his hands and shattered them at the foot of the mountain.

יט וַיְהִי כַּאֲשֶׁר קָרַב אֶל־הַמַּחֲנֶה וַיַּרְא אֶת־הָעֵגֶל וּמְחֹלֹת וַיִּחַר־אַף מֹשֶׁה וַיַּשְׁלֵךְ מִיָּדוֹ [מִיָּדָיו] אֶת־הַלֻּחֹת וַיְשַׁבֵּר אֹתָם תַּחַת הָהָר:

20 He took the calf that they had made and burned it; he ground it to powder and strewed it upon the water and so made the Israelites drink it.

כ וַיִּקַּח אֶת־הָעֵגֶל אֲשֶׁר עָשׂוּ וַיִּשְׂרֹף בָּאֵשׁ וַיִּטְחַן עַד אֲשֶׁר־דָּק וַיִּזֶר עַל־פְּנֵי הַמַּיִם וַיַּשְׁקְ אֶת־בְּנֵי יִשְׂרָאֵל:

21 *Moshe* said to *Aharon*, "What did this people do to you that you have brought such great sin upon them?"

כא וַיֹּאמֶר מֹשֶׁה אֶל־אַהֲרֹן מֶה־עָשָׂה לְךָ הָעָם הַזֶּה כִּי־הֵבֵאתָ עָלָיו חֲטָאָה גְדֹלָה:

22 *Aharon* said, "Let not my lord be enraged. You know that this people is bent on evil.

כב וַיֹּאמֶר אַהֲרֹן אַל־יִחַר אַף אֲדֹנִי אַתָּה יָדַעְתָּ אֶת־הָעָם כִּי בְרָע הוּא:

32:13 To possess forever With this verse, *Moshe* attempts to convince *Hashem* to spare the Jewish nation, despite the egregious sin of the golden calf. He pleads with God to remember his oath to *Avraham*, *Yitzchak* and *Yaakov* that their progeny will inherit *Eretz Yisrael*. *Moshe* is concerned that if *Hashem* is to destroy the Nation and re-create a great nation from him alone, the promise of the Holy Land made to the Patriarchs would be lost. He therefore pleads with God to spare the people despite their transgressions.

The Holy Land, a view of the Galilee

23 They said to me, 'Make us a god to lead us; for that man *Moshe*, who brought us from the land of Egypt – we do not know what has happened to him.'

24 So I said to them, 'Whoever has gold, take it off!' They gave it to me and I hurled it into the fire and out came this calf!"

25 *Moshe* saw that the people were out of control – since *Aharon* had let them get out of control – so that they were a menace to any who might oppose them.

26 *Moshe* stood up in the gate of the camp and said, "Whoever is for *Hashem*, come here!" And all the *Leviim* rallied to him.

27 He said to them, "Thus says *Hashem*, the God of *Yisrael*: Each of you put sword on thigh, go back and forth from gate to gate throughout the camp, and slay brother, neighbor, and kin."

28 The *Leviim* did as *Moshe* had bidden; and some three thousand of the people fell that day.

29 And *Moshe* said, "Dedicate yourselves to *Hashem* this day – for each of you has been against son and brother – that He may bestow a blessing upon you today."

30 The next day *Moshe* said to the people, "You have been guilty of a great sin. Yet I will now go up to *Hashem*; perhaps I may win forgiveness for your sin."

31 *Moshe* went back to *Hashem* and said, "Alas, this people is guilty of a great sin in making for themselves a god of gold.

32 Now, if You will forgive their sin [well and good]; but if not, erase me from the record which You have written!"

33 But *Hashem* said to *Moshe*, "He who has sinned against Me, him only will I erase from My record.

34 Go now, lead the people where I told you. See, My angel shall go before you. But when I make an accounting, I will bring them to account for their sins."

35 Then *Hashem* sent a plague upon the people, for what they did with the calf that *Aharon* made.

כג וַיֹּאמְרוּ לִי עֲשֵׂה־לָּנוּ אֱלֹהִים אֲשֶׁר יֵלְכוּ לְפָנֵינוּ כִּי־זֶה מֹשֶׁה הָאִישׁ אֲשֶׁר הֶעֱלָנוּ מֵאֶרֶץ מִצְרַיִם לֹא יָדַעְנוּ מֶה־הָיָה לֽוֹ:

כד וָאֹמַר לָהֶם לְמִי זָהָב הִתְפָּרָקוּ וַיִּתְּנוּ־לִי וָאַשְׁלִכֵהוּ בָאֵשׁ וַיֵּצֵא הָעֵגֶל הַזֶּֽה:

כה וַיַּרְא מֹשֶׁה אֶת־הָעָם כִּי פָרֻעַ הוּא כִּי־פְרָעֹה אַהֲרֹן לְשִׁמְצָה בְּקָמֵיהֶֽם:

כו וַיַּעֲמֹד מֹשֶׁה בְּשַׁעַר הַמַּחֲנֶה וַיֹּאמֶר מִי לַֽיהֹוָה אֵלָי וַיֵּאָסְפוּ אֵלָיו כָּל־בְּנֵי לֵוִֽי:

כז וַיֹּאמֶר לָהֶם כֹּה־אָמַר יְהֹוָה אֱלֹהֵי יִשְׂרָאֵל שִׂימוּ אִישׁ־חַרְבּוֹ עַל־יְרֵכוֹ עִבְרוּ וָשׁוּבוּ מִשַּׁעַר לָשַׁעַר בַּֽמַּחֲנֶה וְהִרְגוּ אִישׁ־אֶת־אָחִיו וְאִישׁ אֶת־רֵעֵהוּ וְאִישׁ אֶת־קְרֹבֽוֹ:

כח וַיַּעֲשׂוּ בְנֵי־לֵוִי כִּדְבַר מֹשֶׁה וַיִּפֹּל מִן־הָעָם בַּיּוֹם הַהוּא כִּשְׁלֹשֶׁת אַלְפֵי אִֽישׁ:

כט וַיֹּאמֶר מֹשֶׁה מִלְאוּ יֶדְכֶם הַיּוֹם לַֽיהֹוָה כִּי אִישׁ בִּבְנוֹ וּבְאָחִיו וְלָתֵת עֲלֵיכֶם הַיּוֹם בְּרָכָֽה:

ל וַיְהִי מִמָּחֳרָת וַיֹּאמֶר מֹשֶׁה אֶל־הָעָם אַתֶּם חֲטָאתֶם חֲטָאָה גְדֹלָה וְעַתָּה אֶעֱלֶה אֶל־יְהֹוָה אוּלַי אֲכַפְּרָה בְּעַד חַטַּאתְכֶֽם:

לא וַיָּשָׁב מֹשֶׁה אֶל־יְהֹוָה וַיֹּאמַר אָנָּא חָטָא הָעָם הַזֶּה חֲטָאָה גְדֹלָה וַיַּעֲשׂוּ לָהֶם אֱלֹהֵי זָהָֽב:

לב וְעַתָּה אִם־תִּשָּׂא חַטָּאתָם וְאִם־אַיִן מְחֵנִי נָא מִסִּפְרְךָ אֲשֶׁר כָּתָֽבְתָּ:

לג וַיֹּאמֶר יְהֹוָה אֶל־מֹשֶׁה מִי אֲשֶׁר חָטָא־לִי אֶמְחֶנּוּ מִסִּפְרִֽי:

לד וְעַתָּה לֵךְ נְחֵה אֶת־הָעָם אֶל אֲשֶׁר־דִּבַּרְתִּי לָךְ הִנֵּה מַלְאָכִי יֵלֵךְ לְפָנֶיךָ וּבְיוֹם פָּקְדִי וּפָקַדְתִּי עֲלֵהֶם חַטָּאתָֽם:

לה וַיִּגֹּף יְהֹוָה אֶת־הָעָם עַל אֲשֶׁר עָשׂוּ אֶת־הָעֵגֶל אֲשֶׁר עָשָׂה אַהֲרֹֽן:

לג א

33 1 Then *Hashem* said to *Moshe*, "Set out from here, you and the people that you have brought up from the land of Egypt, to the land of which I swore to *Avraham, Yitzchak,* and *Yaakov,* saying, 'To your offspring will I give it'

וַיְדַבֵּ֨ר יְהֹוָ֤ה אֶל־מֹשֶׁה֙ לֵ֣ךְ עֲלֵ֣ה מִזֶּ֔ה אַתָּ֣ה וְהָעָ֔ם אֲשֶׁ֥ר הֶעֱלִ֖יתָ מֵאֶ֣רֶץ מִצְרָ֑יִם אֶל־הָאָ֗רֶץ אֲשֶׁ֣ר נִ֠שְׁבַּ֠עְתִּי לְאַבְרָהָ֨ם לְיִצְחָ֤ק וּֽלְיַעֲקֹב֙ לֵאמֹ֔ר לְזַרְעֲךָ֖ אֶתְּנֶֽנָּה׃

vai-da-BAYR a-do-NAI el mo-SHEH LAYKH a-LAY mi-ZEH a-TAH v'-ha-AM a-SHER he-e-LEE-ta may-E-retz mitz-RA-yim el ha-A-retz a-SHER nish-BA-tee l'-av-ra-HAM l'-yitz-KHAK ul-ya-a-KOV lay-MOR l'-zar-a-KHA e-t'-NE-nah

2 I will send an angel before you, and I will drive out the Canaanites, the Amorites, the Hittites, the Perizzites, the Hivites, and the Jebusites

ב וְשָׁלַחְתִּ֥י לְפָנֶ֖יךָ מַלְאָ֑ךְ וְגֵֽרַשְׁתִּי֙ אֶת־הַֽכְּנַעֲנִי֙ הָֽאֱמֹרִ֔י וְהַֽחִתִּי֙ וְהַפְּרִזִּ֔י הַֽחִוִּ֖י וְהַיְבוּסִֽי׃

3 a land flowing with milk and honey. But I will not go in your midst, since you are a stiffnecked people, lest I destroy you on the way."

ג אֶל־אֶ֛רֶץ זָבַ֥ת חָלָ֖ב וּדְבָ֑שׁ כִּי֩ לֹ֨א אֶֽעֱלֶ֜ה בְּקִרְבְּךָ֗ כִּ֤י עַם־קְשֵׁה־עֹ֙רֶף֙ אַ֔תָּה פֶּן־אֲכֶלְךָ֖ בַּדָּֽרֶךְ׃

4 When the people heard this harsh word, they went into mourning, and none put on his finery.

ד וַיִּשְׁמַ֣ע הָעָ֗ם אֶת־הַדָּבָ֥ר הָרָ֖ע הַזֶּ֑ה וַיִּתְאַבָּ֑לוּ וְלֹא־שָׁ֛תוּ אִ֥ישׁ עֶדְי֖וֹ עָלָֽיו׃

5 *Hashem* said to *Moshe,* "Say to *B'nei Yisrael,* 'You are a stiffnecked people. If I were to go in your midst for one moment, I would destroy you. Now, then, leave off your finery, and I will consider what to do to you.'"

ה וַיֹּ֨אמֶר יְהֹוָ֜ה אֶל־מֹשֶׁ֗ה אֱמֹ֤ר אֶל־בְּנֵֽי־יִשְׂרָאֵל֙ אַתֶּ֣ם עַם־קְשֵׁה־עֹ֔רֶף רֶ֧גַע אֶחָ֛ד אֶֽעֱלֶ֥ה בְקִרְבְּךָ֖ וְכִלִּיתִ֑יךָ וְעַתָּ֗ה הוֹרֵ֤ד עֶדְיְךָ֙ מֵֽעָלֶ֔יךָ וְאֵדְעָ֖ה מָ֥ה אֶֽעֱשֶׂה־לָּֽךְ׃

6 So the Israelites remained stripped of the finery from Mount Horeb on.

ו וַיִּֽתְנַצְּל֧וּ בְנֵֽי־יִשְׂרָאֵ֛ל אֶת־עֶדְיָ֖ם מֵהַ֥ר חוֹרֵֽב׃

7 Now *Moshe* would take the Tent and pitch it outside the camp, at some distance from the camp. It was called the Tent of Meeting, and whoever sought *Hashem* would go out to the Tent of Meeting that was outside the camp.

ז וּמֹשֶׁה֩ יִקַּ֨ח אֶת־הָאֹ֜הֶל וְנָֽטָה־ל֣וֹ ׀ מִח֣וּץ לַֽמַּחֲנֶ֗ה הַרְחֵק֙ מִן־הַֽמַּחֲנֶ֔ה וְקָ֥רָא ל֖וֹ אֹ֣הֶל מוֹעֵ֑ד וְהָיָה֙ כָּל־מְבַקֵּ֣שׁ יְהֹוָ֔ה יֵצֵא֙ אֶל־אֹ֣הֶל מוֹעֵ֔ד אֲשֶׁ֖ר מִח֥וּץ לַֽמַּחֲנֶֽה׃

8 Whenever *Moshe* went out to the Tent, all the people would rise and stand, each at the entrance of his tent, and gaze after *Moshe* until he had entered the Tent.

ח וְהָיָ֗ה כְּצֵ֤את מֹשֶׁה֙ אֶל־הָאֹ֔הֶל יָק֙וּמוּ֙ כָּל־הָעָ֔ם וְנִ֨צְּב֔וּ אִ֖ישׁ פֶּ֣תַח אָֽהֳל֑וֹ וְהִבִּ֙יטוּ֙ אַֽחֲרֵ֣י מֹשֶׁ֔ה עַד־בֹּא֖וֹ הָאֹֽהֱלָה׃

9 And when *Moshe* entered the Tent, the pillar of cloud would descend and stand at the entrance of the Tent, while He spoke with *Moshe.*

ט וְהָיָ֗ה כְּבֹ֤א מֹשֶׁה֙ הָאֹ֔הֱלָה יֵרֵד֙ עַמּ֣וּד הֶֽעָנָ֔ן וְעָמַ֖ד פֶּ֣תַח הָאֹ֑הֶל וְדִבֶּ֖ר עִם־מֹשֶֽׁה׃

Ascending a mountain in the Negev desert

א **33:1 Set out from here** The Hebrew for 'set out from here' is *lech, aleh mizeh* (לֵךְ עֲלֵה מִזֶּה). The word *lech* means 'go' or 'set out,' and the word *aleh* means 'ascend.' It seems that it would have been enough for *Hashem* to simply tell *Moshe lech mizeh,* set out from here, and head to "the land of which I swore …' What is

added by the word *aleh,* 'ascend'? *Rashi* finds a beautiful message in this seemingly extraneous word. He quotes the Talmud (*Zevachim* 54b) which teaches a precious lesson regarding the role of *Eretz Yisrael.* In a spiritual sense, the Holy Land is "the highest of all places on Earth" which is why the *Torah* uses an extra word, "to ascend."

לך עלה מזה

10 When all the people saw the pillar of cloud poised at the entrance of the Tent, all the people would rise and bow low, each at the entrance of his tent.

11 *Hashem* would speak to *Moshe* face to face, as one man speaks to another. And he would then return to the camp; but his attendant, *Yehoshua* son of *Nun*, a youth, would not stir out of the Tent.

12 *Moshe* said to *Hashem*, "See, You say to me, 'Lead this people forward,' but You have not made known to me whom You will send with me. Further, You have said, 'I have singled you out by name, and you have, indeed, gained My favor.'

13 Now, if I have truly gained Your favor, pray let me know Your ways, that I may know You and continue in Your favor. Consider, too, that this nation is Your people."

14 And He said, "I will go in the lead and will lighten your burden."

15 And he said to Him, "Unless You go in the lead, do not make us leave this place.

16 For how shall it be known that Your people have gained Your favor unless You go with us, so that we may be distinguished, Your people and I, from every people on the face of the earth?"

17 And *Hashem* said to *Moshe*, "I will also do this thing that you have asked; for you have truly gained My favor and I have singled you out by name."

18 He said, "Oh, let me behold Your Presence!"

19 And He answered, "I will make all My goodness pass before you, and I will proclaim before you the name *Hashem*, and the grace that I grant and the compassion that I show.

20 But," He said, "you cannot see My face, for man may not see Me and live."

21 And *Hashem* said, "See, there is a place near Me. Station yourself on the rock

22 and, as My Presence passes by, I will put you in a cleft of the rock and shield you with My hand until I have passed by.

י וְרָאָה כָל־הָעָם אֶת־עַמּוּד הֶעָנָן עֹמֵד פֶּתַח הָאֹהֶל וְקָם כָּל־הָעָם וְהִשְׁתַּחֲוּוּ אִישׁ פֶּתַח אָהֳלוֹ:

יא וְדִבֶּר יְהוָה אֶל־מֹשֶׁה פָּנִים אֶל־פָּנִים כַּאֲשֶׁר יְדַבֵּר אִישׁ אֶל־רֵעֵהוּ וְשָׁב אֶל־הַמַּחֲנֶה וּמְשָׁרְתוֹ יְהוֹשֻׁעַ בִּן־נוּן נַעַר לֹא יָמִישׁ מִתּוֹךְ הָאֹהֶל:

יב וַיֹּאמֶר מֹשֶׁה אֶל־יְהוָה רְאֵה אַתָּה אֹמֵר אֵלַי הַעַל אֶת־הָעָם הַזֶּה וְאַתָּה לֹא הוֹדַעְתַּנִי אֵת אֲשֶׁר־תִּשְׁלַח עִמִּי וְאַתָּה אָמַרְתָּ יְדַעְתִּיךָ בְשֵׁם וְגַם־מָצָאתָ חֵן בְּעֵינָי:

יג וְעַתָּה אִם־נָא מָצָאתִי חֵן בְּעֵינֶיךָ הוֹדִעֵנִי נָא אֶת־דְּרָכֶךָ וְאֵדָעֲךָ לְמַעַן אֶמְצָא־חֵן בְּעֵינֶיךָ וּרְאֵה כִּי עַמְּךָ הַגּוֹי הַזֶּה:

יד וַיֹּאמַר פָּנַי יֵלֵכוּ וַהֲנִחֹתִי לָךְ:

טו וַיֹּאמֶר אֵלָיו אִם־אֵין פָּנֶיךָ הֹלְכִים אַל־תַּעֲלֵנוּ מִזֶּה:

טז וּבַמֶּה יִוָּדַע אֵפוֹא כִּי־מָצָאתִי חֵן בְּעֵינֶיךָ אֲנִי וְעַמֶּךָ הֲלוֹא בְּלֶכְתְּךָ עִמָּנוּ וְנִפְלֵינוּ אֲנִי וְעַמְּךָ מִכָּל־הָעָם אֲשֶׁר עַל־פְּנֵי הָאֲדָמָה:

יז וַיֹּאמֶר יְהוָה אֶל־מֹשֶׁה גַּם אֶת־הַדָּבָר הַזֶּה אֲשֶׁר דִּבַּרְתָּ אֶעֱשֶׂה כִּי־מָצָאתָ חֵן בְּעֵינַי וָאֵדָעֲךָ בְּשֵׁם:

יח וַיֹּאמַר הַרְאֵנִי נָא אֶת־כְּבֹדֶךָ:

יט וַיֹּאמֶר אֲנִי אַעֲבִיר כָּל־טוּבִי עַל־פָּנֶיךָ וְקָרָאתִי בְשֵׁם יְהוָה לְפָנֶיךָ וְחַנֹּתִי אֶת־אֲשֶׁר אָחֹן וְרִחַמְתִּי אֶת־אֲשֶׁר אֲרַחֵם:

כ וַיֹּאמֶר לֹא תוּכַל לִרְאֹת אֶת־פָּנָי כִּי לֹא־יִרְאַנִי הָאָדָם וָחָי:

כא וַיֹּאמֶר יְהוָה הִנֵּה מָקוֹם אִתִּי וְנִצַּבְתָּ עַל־הַצּוּר:

כב וְהָיָה בַּעֲבֹר כְּבֹדִי וְשַׂמְתִּיךָ בְּנִקְרַת הַצּוּר וְשַׂכֹּתִי כַפִּי עָלֶיךָ עַד־עָבְרִי:

23 Then I will take My hand away and you will see My back; but My face must not be seen."

כג וַהֲסִרֹתִי֙ אֶת־כַּפִּ֔י וְרָאִ֖יתָ אֶת־אֲחֹרָ֑י וּפָנַ֖י לֹ֥א יֵרָאֽוּ׃

4 1 Hashem said to Moshe: "Carve two tablets of stone like the first, and I will inscribe upon the tablets the words that were on the first tablets, which you shattered.

לד א וַיֹּ֤אמֶר יְהֹוָה֙ אֶל־מֹשֶׁ֔ה פְּסׇל־לְךָ֛ שְׁנֵֽי־לֻחֹ֥ת אֲבָנִ֖ים כָּרִאשֹׁנִ֑ים וְכָתַבְתִּי֙ עַל־הַלֻּחֹ֔ת אֶת־הַדְּבָרִ֔ים אֲשֶׁ֥ר הָי֛וּ עַל־הַלֻּחֹ֥ת הָרִאשֹׁנִ֖ים אֲשֶׁ֥ר שִׁבַּֽרְתָּ׃

2 Be ready by morning, and in the morning come up to Har Sinai and present yourself there to Me, on the top of the mountain.

ב וֶהְיֵ֥ה נָכ֖וֹן לַבֹּ֑קֶר וְעָלִ֤יתָ בַבֹּ֙קֶר֙ אֶל־הַ֣ר סִינַ֔י וְנִצַּבְתָּ֥ לִ֛י שָׁ֖ם עַל־רֹ֥אשׁ הָהָֽר׃

3 No one else shall come up with you, and no one else shall be seen anywhere on the mountain; neither shall the flocks and the herds graze at the foot of this mountain."

ג וְאִישׁ֙ לֹא־יַעֲלֶ֣ה עִמָּ֔ךְ וְגַם־אִ֥ישׁ אַל־יֵרָ֖א בְּכׇל־הָהָ֑ר גַּם־הַצֹּ֤אן וְהַבָּקָר֙ אַל־יִרְע֔וּ אֶל־מ֖וּל הָהָ֥ר הַהֽוּא׃

4 So Moshe carved two tablets of stone, like the first, and early in the morning he went up on Har Sinai, as Hashem had commanded him, taking the two stone tablets with him.

ד וַיִּפְסֹ֡ל שְׁנֵֽי־לֻחֹ֨ת אֲבָנִ֜ים כָּרִאשֹׁנִ֗ים וַיַּשְׁכֵּ֨ם מֹשֶׁ֤ה בַבֹּ֙קֶר֙ וַיַּ֙עַל֙ אֶל־הַ֣ר סִינַ֔י כַּאֲשֶׁ֛ר צִוָּ֥ה יְהֹוָ֖ה אֹת֑וֹ וַיִּקַּ֣ח בְּיָד֔וֹ שְׁנֵ֖י לֻחֹ֥ת אֲבָנִֽים׃

5 Hashem came down in a cloud; He stood with him there, and proclaimed the name Hashem.

ה וַיֵּ֤רֶד יְהֹוָה֙ בֶּֽעָנָ֔ן וַיִּתְיַצֵּ֥ב עִמּ֖וֹ שָׁ֑ם וַיִּקְרָ֖א בְשֵׁ֥ם יְהֹוָֽה׃

6 Hashem passed before him and proclaimed: "Hashem! Hashem! a Hashem compassionate and gracious, slow to anger, abounding in kindness and faithfulness,

ו וַיַּעֲבֹ֨ר יְהֹוָ֥ה ׀ עַל־פָּנָיו֮ וַיִּקְרָא֒ יְהֹוָ֣ה ׀ יְהֹוָ֔ה אֵ֥ל רַח֖וּם וְחַנּ֑וּן אֶ֥רֶךְ אַפַּ֖יִם וְרַב־חֶ֥סֶד וֶאֱמֶֽת׃

7 extending kindness to the thousandth generation, forgiving iniquity, transgression, and sin; yet He does not remit all punishment, but visits the iniquity of parents upon children and children's children, upon the third and fourth generations."

ז נֹצֵ֥ר חֶ֙סֶד֙ לָאֲלָפִ֔ים נֹשֵׂ֥א עָוֺ֛ן וָפֶ֖שַׁע וְחַטָּאָ֑ה וְנַקֵּה֙ לֹ֣א יְנַקֶּ֔ה פֹּקֵ֣ד ׀ עֲוֺ֣ן אָב֗וֹת עַל־בָּנִים֙ וְעַל־בְּנֵ֣י בָנִ֔ים עַל־שִׁלֵּשִׁ֖ים וְעַל־רִבֵּעִֽים׃

8 Moshe hastened to bow low to the ground in homage,

ח וַיְמַהֵ֖ר מֹשֶׁ֑ה וַיִּקֹּ֥ד אַ֖רְצָה וַיִּשְׁתָּֽחוּ׃

9 and said, "If I have gained Your favor, O Hashem, pray, let Hashem go in our midst, even though this is a stiffnecked people. Pardon our iniquity and our sin, and take us for Your own!"

ט וַיֹּ֡אמֶר אִם־נָא֩ מָצָ֨אתִי חֵ֤ן בְּעֵינֶ֙יךָ֙ אֲדֹנָ֔י יֵֽלֶךְ־נָ֥א אֲדֹנָ֖י בְּקִרְבֵּ֑נוּ כִּ֤י עַם־קְשֵׁה־עֹ֙רֶף֙ ה֔וּא וְסָלַחְתָּ֛ לַעֲוֺנֵ֥נוּ וּלְחַטָּאתֵ֖נוּ וּנְחַלְתָּֽנוּ׃

10 He said: I hereby make a covenant. Before all your people I will work such wonders as have not been wrought on all the earth or in any nation; and all the people who are with you shall see how awesome are Hashem's deeds which I will perform for you.

י וַיֹּ֗אמֶר הִנֵּ֣ה אָנֹכִי֮ כֹּרֵ֣ת בְּרִית֒ נֶ֤גֶד כׇּל־עַמְּךָ֙ אֶעֱשֶׂ֣ה נִפְלָאֹ֔ת אֲשֶׁ֛ר לֹא־נִבְרְא֥וּ בְכׇל־הָאָ֖רֶץ וּבְכׇל־הַגּוֹיִ֑ם וְרָאָ֣ה כׇל־הָ֠עָ֠ם אֲשֶׁר־אַתָּ֨ה בְקִרְבּ֜וֹ אֶת־מַעֲשֵׂ֤ה יְהֹוָה֙ כִּֽי־נוֹרָ֣א ה֔וּא אֲשֶׁ֥ר אֲנִ֖י עֹשֶׂ֥ה עִמָּֽךְ׃

Exodus

11 Mark well what I command you this day. I will drive out before you the Amorites, the Canaanites, the Hittites, the Perizzites, the Hivites, and the Jebusites.

יא שְׁמָר־לְךָ אֵת אֲשֶׁר אָנֹכִי מְצַוְּךָ הַיּוֹם הִנְנִי גֹרֵשׁ מִפָּנֶיךָ אֶת־הָאֱמֹרִי וְהַכְּנַעֲנִי וְהַחִתִּי וְהַפְּרִזִּי וְהַחִוִּי וְהַיְבוּסִי:

12 Beware of making a covenant with the inhabitants of the land against which you are advancing, lest they be a snare in your midst.

יב הִשָּׁמֶר לְךָ פֶּן־תִּכְרֹת בְּרִית לְיוֹשֵׁב הָאָרֶץ אֲשֶׁר אַתָּה בָּא עָלֶיהָ פֶּן־יִהְיֶה לְמוֹקֵשׁ בְּקִרְבֶּךָ:

13 No, you must tear down their altars, smash their pillars, and cut down their sacred posts;

יג כִּי אֶת־מִזְבְּחֹתָם תִּתֹּצוּן וְאֶת־מַצֵּבֹתָם תְּשַׁבֵּרוּן וְאֶת־אֲשֵׁרָיו תִּכְרֹתוּן:

14 for you must not worship any other god, because *Hashem*, whose name is Impassioned, is an impassioned God.

יד כִּי לֹא תִשְׁתַּחֲוֶה לְאֵל אַחֵר כִּי יְהֹוָה קַנָּא שְׁמוֹ אֵל קַנָּא הוּא:

15 You must not make a covenant with the inhabitants of the land, for they will lust after their gods and sacrifice to their gods and invite you, and you will eat of their sacrifices.

טו פֶּן־תִּכְרֹת בְּרִית לְיוֹשֵׁב הָאָרֶץ וְזָנוּ אַחֲרֵי אֱלֹהֵיהֶם וְזָבְחוּ לֵאלֹהֵיהֶם וְקָרָא לְךָ וְאָכַלְתָּ מִזִּבְחוֹ:

16 And when you take wives from among their daughters for your sons, their daughters will lust after their gods and will cause your sons to lust after their gods.

טז וְלָקַחְתָּ מִבְּנֹתָיו לְבָנֶיךָ וְזָנוּ בְנֹתָיו אַחֲרֵי אֱלֹהֵיהֶן וְהִזְנוּ אֶת־בָּנֶיךָ אַחֲרֵי אֱלֹהֵיהֶן:

17 You shall not make molten gods for yourselves.

יז אֱלֹהֵי מַסֵּכָה לֹא תַעֲשֶׂה־לָּךְ:

18 You shall observe the festival of *Pesach* – eating unleavened bread for seven days, as I have commanded you – at the set time of the month of Abib, for in the month of Abib you went forth from Egypt.

יח אֶת־חַג הַמַּצּוֹת תִּשְׁמֹר שִׁבְעַת יָמִים תֹּאכַל מַצּוֹת אֲשֶׁר צִוִּיתִךָ לְמוֹעֵד חֹדֶשׁ הָאָבִיב כִּי בְּחֹדֶשׁ הָאָבִיב יָצָאתָ מִמִּצְרָיִם:

19 Every first issue of the womb is Mine, from all your livestock that drop a male as firstling, whether cattle or sheep.

יט כָּל־פֶּטֶר רֶחֶם לִי וְכָל־מִקְנְךָ תִּזָּכָר פֶּטֶר שׁוֹר וָשֶׂה:

20 But the firstling of an ass you shall redeem with a sheep; if you do not redeem it, you must break its neck. And you must redeem every first-born among your sons. None shall appear before Me empty-handed.

כ וּפֶטֶר חֲמוֹר תִּפְדֶּה בְשֶׂה וְאִם־לֹא תִפְדֶּה וַעֲרַפְתּוֹ כֹּל בְּכוֹר בָּנֶיךָ תִּפְדֶּה וְלֹא־יֵרָאוּ פָנַי רֵיקָם:

21 Six days you shall work, but on the seventh day you shall cease from labor; you shall cease from labor even at plowing time and harvest time.

כא שֵׁשֶׁת יָמִים תַּעֲבֹד וּבַיּוֹם הַשְּׁבִיעִי תִּשְׁבֹּת בֶּחָרִישׁ וּבַקָּצִיר תִּשְׁבֹּת:

22 You shall observe the festival of *Shavuot,* of the first fruits of the wheat harvest; and the Feast of Ingathering at the turn of the year.

כב וְחַג שָׁבֻעֹת תַּעֲשֶׂה לְךָ בִּכּוּרֵי קְצִיר חִטִּים וְחַג הָאָסִיף תְּקוּפַת הַשָּׁנָה:

23 Three times a year all your males shall appear before the Sovereign *Hashem*, the God of *Yisrael*.

כג שָׁלֹשׁ פְּעָמִים בַּשָּׁנָה יֵרָאֶה כָּל־זְכוּרְךָ אֶת־פְּנֵי הָאָדֹן יְהֹוָה אֱלֹהֵי יִשְׂרָאֵל:

24 I will drive out nations from your path and enlarge your territory; no one will covet your land when you go up to appear before *Hashem* your God three times a year.

כד כִּי־אוֹרִישׁ גּוֹיִם מִפָּנֶיךָ וְהִרְחַבְתִּי אֶת־גְּבוּלֶךָ וְלֹא־יַחְמֹד אִישׁ אֶת־אַרְצְךָ בַּעֲלֹתְךָ לֵרָאוֹת אֶת־פְּנֵי יְהוָה אֱלֹהֶיךָ שָׁלֹשׁ פְּעָמִים בַּשָּׁנָה:

kee o-REESH go-YIM mi-pa-NE-kha v'-hir-khav-TEE et g'-vu-LE-kha v'-lo yakh-MOD EESH et ar-tz'-KHA ba-a-lo-t'-KHA lay-ra-OT et p'-NAY a-do-NAI e-lo-HE-kha sha-LOSH p'-a-MEEM ba-sha-NAH

25 You shall not offer the blood of My sacrifice with anything leavened; and the sacrifice of the festival of *Pesach* shall not be left lying until morning.

כה לֹא־תִשְׁחַט עַל־חָמֵץ דַּם־זִבְחִי וְלֹא־יָלִין לַבֹּקֶר זֶבַח חַג הַפָּסַח:

26 The choice first fruits of your soil you shall bring to the house of *Hashem* your God. You shall not boil a kid in its mother's milk.

כו רֵאשִׁית בִּכּוּרֵי אַדְמָתְךָ תָּבִיא בֵּית יְהוָה אֱלֹהֶיךָ לֹא־תְבַשֵּׁל גְּדִי בַּחֲלֵב אִמּוֹ:

27 And *Hashem* said to *Moshe*: Write down these commandments, for in accordance with these commandments I make a covenant with you and with *Yisrael*.

כז וַיֹּאמֶר יְהוָה אֶל־מֹשֶׁה כְּתָב־לְךָ אֶת־הַדְּבָרִים הָאֵלֶּה כִּי עַל־פִּי הַדְּבָרִים הָאֵלֶּה כָּרַתִּי אִתְּךָ בְּרִית וְאֶת־יִשְׂרָאֵל:

28 And he was there with *Hashem* forty days and forty nights; he ate no bread and drank no water; and he wrote down on the tablets the terms of the covenant, the Ten Commandments.

כח וַיְהִי־שָׁם עִם־יְהוָה אַרְבָּעִים יוֹם וְאַרְבָּעִים לַיְלָה לֶחֶם לֹא אָכַל וּמַיִם לֹא שָׁתָה וַיִּכְתֹּב עַל־הַלֻּחֹת אֵת דִּבְרֵי הַבְּרִית עֲשֶׂרֶת הַדְּבָרִים:

29 So *Moshe* came down from *Har Sinai*. And as *Moshe* came down from the mountain bearing the two tablets of the Pact, *Moshe* was not aware that the skin of his face was radiant, since he had spoken with Him.

כט וַיְהִי בְּרֶדֶת מֹשֶׁה מֵהַר סִינַי וּשְׁנֵי לֻחֹת הָעֵדֻת בְּיַד־מֹשֶׁה בְּרִדְתּוֹ מִן־הָהָר וּמֹשֶׁה לֹא־יָדַע כִּי קָרַן עוֹר פָּנָיו בְּדַבְּרוֹ אִתּוֹ:

vai-HEE b'-RE-det mo-SHEH may-HAR see-NAI ush-NAY lu-KHOT ha-ay-DUT b'-yad mo-SHEH b'-rid-TO min ha-HAR u-mo-SHEH lo ya-DA KEE ka-RAN OR pa-NAV b'-da-b'-RO i-TO

30 *Aharon* and all the Israelites saw that the skin of *Moshe*'s face was radiant; and they shrank from coming near him.

ל וַיַּרְא אַהֲרֹן וְכָל־בְּנֵי יִשְׂרָאֵל אֶת־מֹשֶׁה וְהִנֵּה קָרַן עוֹר פָּנָיו וַיִּירְאוּ מִגֶּשֶׁת אֵלָיו:

31 But *Moshe* called to them, and *Aharon* and all the chieftains in the assembly returned to him, and *Moshe* spoke to them.

לא וַיִּקְרָא אֲלֵהֶם מֹשֶׁה וַיָּשֻׁבוּ אֵלָיו אַהֲרֹן וְכָל־הַנְּשִׂאִים בָּעֵדָה וַיְדַבֵּר מֹשֶׁה אֲלֵהֶם:

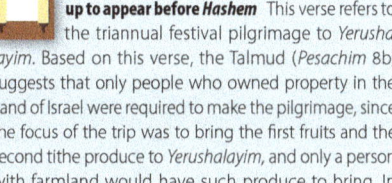

34:24 No one will covet your land when you go up to appear before *Hashem* This verse refers to the triannual festival pilgrimage to *Yerushalayim*. Based on this verse, the Talmud (*Pesachim* 8b) suggests that only people who owned property in the Land of Israel were required to make the pilgrimage, since the focus of the trip was to bring the first fruits and the second tithe produce to *Yerushalayim*, and only a person with farmland would have such produce to bring. In practice, however, everyone was required to make the journey. The pilgrimage was a joyous occasion, a celebration of thanks to God for the land and the rain that had provided the farmer with a harvest. To this day, Jews continue to make a point of visiting *Yerushalayim* and the site of the *Beit Hamikdash* during the three festivals: *Pesach*, *Shavuot* and *Sukkot*.

Praying at the Western Wall on *Sukkot*

32 Afterward all the Israelites came near, and he instructed them concerning all that *Hashem* had imparted to him on *Har Sinai*.

לב וְאַחֲרֵי־כֵן נִגְּשׁוּ כָּל־בְּנֵי יִשְׂרָאֵל וַיְצַוֵּם אֵת כָּל־אֲשֶׁר דִּבֶּר יְהֹוָה אִתּוֹ בְּהַר סִינָי:

33 And when *Moshe* had finished speaking with them, he put a veil over his face.

לג וַיְכַל מֹשֶׁה מִדַּבֵּר אִתָּם וַיִּתֵּן עַל־פָּנָיו מַסְוֶה:

34 Whenever *Moshe* went in before *Hashem* to speak with Him, he would leave the veil off until he came out; and when he came out and told the Israelites what he had been commanded,

לד וּבְבֹא מֹשֶׁה לִפְנֵי יְהֹוָה לְדַבֵּר אִתּוֹ יָסִיר אֶת־הַמַּסְוֶה עַד־צֵאתוֹ וְיָצָא וְדִבֶּר אֶל־בְּנֵי יִשְׂרָאֵל אֵת אֲשֶׁר יְצֻוֶּה:

35 the Israelites would see how radiant the skin of *Moshe*'s face was. *Moshe* would then put the veil back over his face until he went in to speak with Him.

לה וְרָאוּ בְנֵי־יִשְׂרָאֵל אֶת־פְּנֵי מֹשֶׁה כִּי קָרַן עוֹר פְּנֵי מֹשֶׁה וְהֵשִׁיב מֹשֶׁה אֶת־הַמַּסְוֶה עַל־פָּנָיו עַד־בֹּאוֹ לְדַבֵּר אִתּוֹ:

35 1 *Moshe* then convoked the whole Israelite community and said to them: These are the things that *Hashem* has commanded you to do:

ה א וַיַּקְהֵל מֹשֶׁה אֶת־כָּל־עֲדַת בְּנֵי יִשְׂרָאֵל וַיֹּאמֶר אֲלֵהֶם אֵלֶּה הַדְּבָרִים אֲשֶׁר־צִוָּה יְהֹוָה לַעֲשֹׂת אֹתָם:

2 On six days work may be done, but on the seventh day you shall have a *Shabbat* of complete rest, holy to *Hashem*; whoever does any work on it shall be put to death.

ב שֵׁשֶׁת יָמִים תֵּעָשֶׂה מְלָאכָה וּבַיּוֹם הַשְּׁבִיעִי יִהְיֶה לָכֶם קֹדֶשׁ שַׁבַּת שַׁבָּתוֹן לַיהֹוָה כָּל־הָעֹשֶׂה בוֹ מְלָאכָה יוּמָת:

3 You shall kindle no fire throughout your settlements on the *Shabbat* day.

ג לֹא־תְבַעֲרוּ אֵשׁ בְּכֹל מֹשְׁבֹתֵיכֶם בְּיוֹם הַשַּׁבָּת:

4 *Moshe* said further to the whole community of Israelites: This is what *Hashem* has commanded:

ד וַיֹּאמֶר מֹשֶׁה אֶל־כָּל־עֲדַת בְּנֵי־יִשְׂרָאֵל לֵאמֹר זֶה הַדָּבָר אֲשֶׁר־צִוָּה יְהֹוָה לֵאמֹר:

5 Take from among you gifts to *Hashem*; everyone whose heart so moves him shall bring them – gifts for *Hashem*: gold, silver, and copper;

ה קְחוּ מֵאִתְּכֶם תְּרוּמָה לַיהֹוָה כֹּל נְדִיב לִבּוֹ יְבִיאֶהָ אֵת תְּרוּמַת יְהֹוָה זָהָב וָכֶסֶף וּנְחֹשֶׁת:

6 blue, purple, and crimson yarns, fine linen, and goats' hair;

ו וּתְכֵלֶת וְאַרְגָּמָן וְתוֹלַעַת שָׁנִי וְשֵׁשׁ וְעִזִּים:

7 tanned ram skins, dolphin skins, and acacia wood;

ז וְעֹרֹת אֵילִם מְאָדָּמִים וְעֹרֹת תְּחָשִׁים וַעֲצֵי שִׁטִּים:

8 oil for lighting, spices for the anointing oil and for the aromatic incense;

ח וְשֶׁמֶן לַמָּאוֹר וּבְשָׂמִים לְשֶׁמֶן הַמִּשְׁחָה וְלִקְטֹרֶת הַסַּמִּים:

9 lapis lazuli and other stones for setting, for the ephod and the breastpiece.

ט וְאַבְנֵי־שֹׁהַם וְאַבְנֵי מִלֻּאִים לָאֵפוֹד וְלַחֹשֶׁן:

10 And let all among you who are skilled come and make all that *Hashem* has commanded:

י וְכָל־חֲכַם־לֵב בָּכֶם יָבֹאוּ וְיַעֲשׂוּ אֵת כָּל־אֲשֶׁר צִוָּה יְהֹוָה:

11 the *Mishkan*, its tent and its covering, its clasps and its planks, its bars, its posts, and its sockets;

יא אֶת־הַמִּשְׁכָּן אֶת־אָהֳלוֹ וְאֶת־מִכְסֵהוּ אֶת־קְרָסָיו וְאֶת־קְרָשָׁיו אֶת־בְּרִיחָו אֶת־עַמֻּדָיו וְאֶת־אֲדָנָיו:

12 the ark and its poles, the cover, and the curtain for the screen;

יג אֶת־הָאָרֹן וְאֶת־בַּדָּיו אֶת־הַכַּפֹּרֶת וְאֵת פָּרֹכֶת הַמָּסָךְ׃

13 the table, and its poles and all its utensils; and the bread of display;

יג אֶת־הַשֻּׁלְחָן וְאֶת־בַּדָּיו וְאֶת־כָּל־כֵּלָיו וְאֵת לֶחֶם הַפָּנִים׃

14 the *menorah* for lighting, its furnishings and its lamps, and the oil for lighting;

יד וְאֶת־מְנֹרַת הַמָּאוֹר וְאֶת־כֵּלֶיהָ וְאֶת־נֵרֹתֶיהָ וְאֵת שֶׁמֶן הַמָּאוֹר׃

15 the *Mizbayach* of incense and its poles; the anointing oil and the aromatic incense; and the entrance screen for the entrance of the *Mishkan*;

טו וְאֶת־מִזְבַּח הַקְּטֹרֶת וְאֶת־בַּדָּיו וְאֵת שֶׁמֶן הַמִּשְׁחָה וְאֵת קְטֹרֶת הַסַּמִּים וְאֶת־מָסַךְ הַפֶּתַח לְפֶתַח הַמִּשְׁכָּן׃

16 the *Mizbayach* of burnt offering, its copper grating, its poles, and all its furnishings; the laver and its stand;

טז אֵת מִזְבַּח הָעֹלָה וְאֶת־מִכְבַּר הַנְּחֹשֶׁת אֲשֶׁר־לוֹ אֶת־בַּדָּיו וְאֶת־כָּל־כֵּלָיו אֶת־הַכִּיֹּר וְאֶת־כַּנּוֹ׃

17 the hangings of the enclosure, its posts and its sockets, and the screen for the gate of the court;

יז אֵת קַלְעֵי הֶחָצֵר אֶת־עַמֻּדָיו וְאֶת־אֲדָנֶיהָ וְאֵת מָסַךְ שַׁעַר הֶחָצֵר׃

18 the pegs for the *Mishkan*, the pegs for the enclosure, and their cords;

יח אֶת־יִתְדֹת הַמִּשְׁכָּן וְאֶת־יִתְדֹת הֶחָצֵר וְאֶת־מֵיתְרֵיהֶם׃

19 the service vestments for officiating in the sanctuary, the sacral vestments of *Aharon* the *Kohen* and the vestments of his sons for priestly service.

יט אֶת־בִּגְדֵי הַשְּׂרָד לְשָׁרֵת בַּקֹּדֶשׁ אֶת־בִּגְדֵי הַקֹּדֶשׁ לְאַהֲרֹן הַכֹּהֵן וְאֶת־בִּגְדֵי בָנָיו לְכַהֵן׃

20 So the whole community of the Israelites left *Moshe*'s presence.

כ וַיֵּצְאוּ כָּל־עֲדַת בְּנֵי־יִשְׂרָאֵל מִלִּפְנֵי מֹשֶׁה׃

21 And everyone who excelled in ability and everyone whose spirit moved him came, bringing to *Hashem* his offering for the work of the Tent of Meeting and for all its service and for the sacral vestments.

כא וַיָּבֹאוּ כָּל־אִישׁ אֲשֶׁר־נְשָׂאוֹ לִבּוֹ וְכֹל אֲשֶׁר נָדְבָה רוּחוֹ אֹתוֹ הֵבִיאוּ אֶת־תְּרוּמַת יְהוָה לִמְלֶאכֶת אֹהֶל מוֹעֵד וּלְכָל־עֲבֹדָתוֹ וּלְבִגְדֵי הַקֹּדֶשׁ׃

22 Men and women, all whose hearts moved them, all who would make an elevation offering of gold to *Hashem*, came bringing brooches, earrings, rings, and pendants – gold objects of all kinds.

כב וַיָּבֹאוּ הָאֲנָשִׁים עַל־הַנָּשִׁים כֹּל נְדִיב לֵב הֵבִיאוּ חָח וָנֶזֶם וְטַבַּעַת וְכוּמָז כָּל־כְּלִי זָהָב וְכָל־אִישׁ אֲשֶׁר הֵנִיף תְּנוּפַת זָהָב לַיהוָה׃

23 And everyone who had in his possession blue, purple, and crimson yarns, fine linen, goats' hair, tanned ram skins, and dolphin skins, brought them;

כג וְכָל־אִישׁ אֲשֶׁר־נִמְצָא אִתּוֹ תְּכֵלֶת וְאַרְגָּמָן וְתוֹלַעַת שָׁנִי וְשֵׁשׁ וְעִזִּים וְעֹרֹת אֵילִם מְאָדָּמִים וְעֹרֹת תְּחָשִׁים הֵבִיאוּ׃

24 everyone who would make gifts of silver or copper brought them as gifts for *Hashem*; and everyone who had in his possession acacia wood for any work of the service brought that.

כד כָּל־מֵרִים תְּרוּמַת כֶּסֶף וּנְחֹשֶׁת הֵבִיאוּ אֵת תְּרוּמַת יְהוָה וְכֹל אֲשֶׁר נִמְצָא אִתּוֹ עֲצֵי שִׁטִּים לְכָל־מְלֶאכֶת הָעֲבֹדָה הֵבִיאוּ׃

25 And all the skilled women spun with their own hands, and brought what they had spun, in blue, purple, and crimson yarns, and in fine linen.

כה וְכָל־אִשָּׁה חַכְמַת־לֵב בְּיָדֶיהָ טָווּ וַיָּבִיאוּ מַטְוֶה אֶת־הַתְּכֵלֶת וְאֶת־הָאַרְגָּמָן אֶת־תּוֹלַעַת הַשָּׁנִי וְאֶת־הַשֵּׁשׁ׃

Exodus

26 And all the women who excelled in that skill spun the goats' hair.

וְכָל־הַנָּשִׁים אֲשֶׁר נָשָׂא לִבָּן אֹתָנָה בְּחָכְמָה טָווּ אֶת־הָעִזִּים: כו

27 And the chieftains brought lapis lazuli and other stones for setting, for the ephod and for the breastpiece;

וְהַנְּשִׂאִם הֵבִיאוּ אֵת אַבְנֵי הַשֹּׁהַם וְאֵת אַבְנֵי הַמִּלֻּאִים לָאֵפוֹד וְלַחֹשֶׁן: כז

28 and spices and oil for lighting, for the anointing oil, and for the aromatic incense.

וְאֶת־הַבֹּשֶׂם וְאֶת־הַשָּׁמֶן לְמָאוֹר וּלְשֶׁמֶן הַמִּשְׁחָה וְלִקְטֹרֶת הַסַּמִּים: כח

29 Thus the Israelites, all the men and women whose hearts moved them to bring anything for the work that *Hashem*, through *Moshe*, had commanded to be done, brought it as a freewill offering to *Hashem*.

כָּל־אִישׁ וְאִשָּׁה אֲשֶׁר נָדַב לִבָּם אֹתָם לְהָבִיא לְכָל־הַמְּלָאכָה אֲשֶׁר צִוָּה יהוה לַעֲשׂוֹת בְּיַד־מֹשֶׁה הֵבִיאוּ בְנֵי־יִשְׂרָאֵל נְדָבָה לַיהוה: כט

kol EESH v'-i-SHAH a-SHER na-DAV li-BAM o-TAM l'-ha-VEE l'-khol ha-m'-la-KHAH a-SHER tzi-VAH a-do-NAI la-a-SOT b'-YAD mo-SHEH hay-VEE-u v'-nay yis-ra-AYL n'-da-VAH la-do-NAI

30 And *Moshe* said to the Israelites: See, *Hashem* has singled out by name *Betzalel*, son of *Uri* son of *Chur*, of the tribe of *Yehuda*.

וַיֹּאמֶר מֹשֶׁה אֶל־בְּנֵי יִשְׂרָאֵל רְאוּ קָרָא יהוה בְּשֵׁם בְּצַלְאֵל בֶּן־אוּרִי בֶן־חוּר לְמַטֵּה יְהוּדָה: ל

31 He has endowed him with a divine spirit of skill, ability, and knowledge in every kind of craft

וַיְמַלֵּא אֹתוֹ רוּחַ אֱלֹהִים בְּחָכְמָה בִּתְבוּנָה וּבְדַעַת וּבְכָל־מְלָאכָה: לא

32 and has inspired him* to make designs for work in gold, silver, and copper,

וְלַחְשֹׁב מַחֲשָׁבֹת לַעֲשֹׂת בַּזָּהָב וּבַכֶּסֶף וּבַנְּחֹשֶׁת: לב

33 to cut stones for setting and to carve wood – to work in every kind of designer's craft

וּבַחֲרֹשֶׁת אֶבֶן לְמַלֹּאת וּבַחֲרֹשֶׁת עֵץ לַעֲשׂוֹת בְּכָל־מְלֶאכֶת מַחֲשָׁבֶת: לג

34 and to give directions. He and *Oholiav* son of *Achisamach* of the tribe of *Dan*

וּלְהוֹרֹת נָתַן בְּלִבּוֹ הוּא וְאָהֳלִיאָב בֶּן־אֲחִיסָמָךְ לְמַטֵּה־דָן: לד

35 have been endowed with the skill to do any work – of the carver, the designer, the embroiderer in blue, purple, crimson yarns, and in fine linen, and of the weaver – as workers in all crafts and as makers of designs.

מִלֵּא אֹתָם חָכְמַת־לֵב לַעֲשׂוֹת כָּל־מְלֶאכֶת חָרָשׁ וְחֹשֵׁב וְרֹקֵם בַּתְּכֵלֶת וּבָאַרְגָּמָן בְּתוֹלַעַת הַשָּׁנִי וּבַשֵּׁשׁ וְאֹרֵג עֹשֵׂי כָּל־מְלָאכָה וְחֹשְׁבֵי מַחֲשָׁבֹת: לה

36 1 Let, then, *Betzalel* and *Oholiav* and all the skilled persons whom *Hashem* has endowed with skill and ability to perform expertly all the tasks connected with the service of the sanctuary carry out all that *Hashem* has commanded.

וְעָשָׂה בְצַלְאֵל וְאָהֳלִיאָב וְכֹל אִישׁ חֲכַם־לֵב אֲשֶׁר נָתַן יהוה חָכְמָה וּתְבוּנָה בָּהֵמָּה לָדַעַת לַעֲשֹׂת אֶת־כָּל־מְלֶאכֶת עֲבֹדַת הַקֹּדֶשׁ לְכֹל אֲשֶׁר־צִוָּה יהוה: א

* "has inspired him" moved up from v. 34 for clarity

35:29 Whose hearts moved them The *Mishkan* is a glorious structure decorated with precious metals, tapestries and intricate designs. The raw materials for its constructions are donated by the nation itself, by every man and woman "whose hearts moved them" to give of themselves and their belongings to *Hashem*. Since this structure is meant to foster deep, meaningful relationships between man and God, it stands to reason that the construction materials were taken from those who donated with this highest of intentions.

Model of the *Mishkan* in Timna Park

Exodus

2 *Moshe* then called *Betzalel* and *Oholiav*, and every skilled person whom *Hashem* had endowed with skill, everyone who excelled in ability, to undertake the task and carry it out.

3 They took over from *Moshe* all the gifts that the Israelites had brought, to carry out the tasks connected with the service of the sanctuary. But when these continued to bring freewill offerings to him morning after morning,

4 all the artisans who were engaged in the tasks of the sanctuary came, each from the task upon which he was engaged,

5 and said to *Moshe*, "The people are bringing more than is needed for the tasks entailed in the work that *Hashem* has commanded to be done."

6 *Moshe* thereupon had this proclamation made throughout the camp: "Let no man or woman make further effort toward gifts for the sanctuary!" So the people stopped bringing:

7 their efforts had been more than enough for all the tasks to be done.

8 Then all the skilled among those engaged in the work made the *Mishkan* of ten strips of cloth, which they made of fine twisted linen, blue, purple, and crimson yarns; into these they worked a design of cherubim.

> va-ya-a-SU khol kha-kham LAYV b'-o-SAY ha-m'-la-KHAH et ha-mish-KAN
> E-ser y'-ree-OT SHAYSH mosh-ZAR ut-KHAY-let v'-ar-ga-MAN v'-to-LA-at
> sha-NEE k'-ru-VEEM ma-a-SAY kho-SHAYV a-SAH o-TAM

9 The length of each cloth was twenty-eight *amot*, and the width of each cloth was four *amot*, all cloths having the same measurements.

ב וַיִּקְרָא מֹשֶׁה אֶל־בְּצַלְאֵל וְאֶל־אָהֳלִיאָב וְאֶל כָּל־אִישׁ חֲכַם־לֵב אֲשֶׁר נָתַן יְהֹוָה חָכְמָה בְּלִבּוֹ כֹּל אֲשֶׁר נְשָׂאוֹ לִבּוֹ לְקָרְבָה אֶל־הַמְּלָאכָה לַעֲשֹׂת אֹתָהּ:

ג וַיִּקְחוּ מִלִּפְנֵי מֹשֶׁה אֵת כָּל־הַתְּרוּמָה אֲשֶׁר הֵבִיאוּ בְּנֵי יִשְׂרָאֵל לִמְלֶאכֶת עֲבֹדַת הַקֹּדֶשׁ לַעֲשֹׂת אֹתָהּ וְהֵם הֵבִיאוּ אֵלָיו עוֹד נְדָבָה בַּבֹּקֶר בַּבֹּקֶר:

ד וַיָּבֹאוּ כָּל־הַחֲכָמִים הָעֹשִׂים אֵת כָּל־מְלֶאכֶת הַקֹּדֶשׁ אִישׁ־אִישׁ מִמְּלַאכְתּוֹ אֲשֶׁר־הֵמָּה עֹשִׂים:

ה וַיֹּאמְרוּ אֶל־מֹשֶׁה לֵּאמֹר מַרְבִּים הָעָם לְהָבִיא מִדֵּי הָעֲבֹדָה לַמְּלָאכָה אֲשֶׁר־צִוָּה יְהֹוָה לַעֲשֹׂת אֹתָהּ:

ו וַיְצַו מֹשֶׁה וַיַּעֲבִירוּ קוֹל בַּמַּחֲנֶה לֵּאמֹר אִישׁ וְאִשָּׁה אַל־יַעֲשׂוּ־עוֹד מְלָאכָה לִתְרוּמַת הַקֹּדֶשׁ וַיִּכָּלֵא הָעָם מֵהָבִיא:

ז וְהַמְּלָאכָה הָיְתָה דַיָּם לְכָל־הַמְּלָאכָה לַעֲשׂוֹת אֹתָהּ וְהוֹתֵר:

ח וַיַּעֲשׂוּ כָל־חֲכַם־לֵב בְּעֹשֵׂי הַמְּלָאכָה אֶת־הַמִּשְׁכָּן עֶשֶׂר יְרִיעֹת שֵׁשׁ מָשְׁזָר וּתְכֵלֶת וְאַרְגָּמָן וְתוֹלַעַת שָׁנִי כְּרֻבִים מַעֲשֵׂה חֹשֵׁב עָשָׂה אֹתָם:

ט אֹרֶךְ הַיְרִיעָה הָאַחַת שְׁמֹנֶה וְעֶשְׂרִים בָּאַמָּה וְרֹחַב אַרְבַּע בָּאַמָּה הַיְרִיעָה הָאֶחָת מִדָּה אַחַת לְכָל־הַיְרִיעֹת:

36:8 Twisted linen, blue, purple The fine threads used to weave the curtains of the *Mishkan*, and later the *Beit Hamikdash*, were surely remarkable and unmistakable. In *Megillat Esther*, read on the holiday of *Purim* which marks the Jewish salvation from the evil Haman, the descriptions of the wall hangings in King Ahasuerus's palace are nearly identical to those of the *Mishkan*: "Hangings of white, fine cotton, and blue, bordered with cords of fine linen and purple" (Esther 1:6). This similarity prompted the Talmud (*Megillah* 12a) to understand that upon the exile from Israel after the destruction of the First *Beit Hamikdash*, the Temple's fine vessels and adornments were taken as booty, and later became part of the Persian king's treasury. It was these stolen items that were on display at King Ahasuerus's party. While most Jews ignored *Mordechai*'s warning not to participate, the Sages say that the notables fled, refusing to partake of a feast in which the holy vessels and adornments were displayed. In doing so, these Jews were declaring their loyalty to God and the fallen Temple in *Yerushalayim*.

Wool dipped in blue *techelet* dye, Kfar Adumim

Exodus

10 They joined five of the cloths to one another, and they joined the other five cloths to one another.

י וַיְחַבֵּר אֶת־חֲמֵשׁ הַיְרִיעֹת אַחַת אֶל־אֶחָת וְחָמֵשׁ יְרִיעֹת חִבַּר אַחַת אֶל־אֶחָת:

11 They made loops of blue wool on the edge of the outermost cloth of the one set, and did the same on the edge of the outermost cloth of the other set:

יא וַיַּעַשׂ לֻלְאֹת תְּכֵלֶת עַל שְׂפַת הַיְרִיעָה הָאֶחָת מִקָּצָה בַּמַּחְבָּרֶת כֵּן עָשָׂה בִּשְׂפַת הַיְרִיעָה הַקִּיצוֹנָה בַּמַּחְבֶּרֶת הַשֵּׁנִית:

12 they made fifty loops on the one cloth, and they made fifty loops on the edge of the end cloth of the other set, the loops being opposite one another.

יב חֲמִשִּׁים לֻלָאֹת עָשָׂה בַּיְרִיעָה הָאֶחָת וַחֲמִשִּׁים לֻלָאֹת עָשָׂה בִּקְצֵה הַיְרִיעָה אֲשֶׁר בַּמַּחְבֶּרֶת הַשֵּׁנִית מַקְבִּילֹת הַלֻּלָאֹת אַחַת אֶל־אֶחָת:

13 And they made fifty gold clasps and coupled the units to one another with the clasps, so that the *Mishkan* became one whole.

יג וַיַּעַשׂ חֲמִשִּׁים קַרְסֵי זָהָב וַיְחַבֵּר אֶת־הַיְרִיעֹת אַחַת אֶל־אַחַת בַּקְּרָסִים וַיְהִי הַמִּשְׁכָּן אֶחָד:

14 They made cloths of goats' hair for a tent over the *Mishkan*; they made the cloths eleven in number.

יד וַיַּעַשׂ יְרִיעֹת עִזִּים לְאֹהֶל עַל־הַמִּשְׁכָּן עַשְׁתֵּי־עֶשְׂרֵה יְרִיעֹת עָשָׂה אֹתָם:

15 The length of each cloth was thirty *amot*, and the width of each cloth was four *amot*, the eleven cloths having the same measurements.

טו אֹרֶךְ הַיְרִיעָה הָאַחַת שְׁלֹשִׁים בָּאַמָּה וְאַרְבַּע אַמּוֹת רֹחַב הַיְרִיעָה הָאֶחָת מִדָּה אַחַת לְעַשְׁתֵּי עֶשְׂרֵה יְרִיעֹת:

16 They joined five of the cloths by themselves, and the other six cloths by themselves.

טז וַיְחַבֵּר אֶת־חֲמֵשׁ הַיְרִיעֹת לְבָד וְאֶת־שֵׁשׁ הַיְרִיעֹת לְבָד:

17 They made fifty loops on the edge of the outermost cloth of the one set, and they made fifty loops on the edge of the end cloth of the other set.

יז וַיַּעַשׂ לֻלָאֹת חֲמִשִּׁים עַל שְׂפַת הַיְרִיעָה הַקִּיצֹנָה בַּמַּחְבָּרֶת וַחֲמִשִּׁים לֻלָאֹת עָשָׂה עַל־שְׂפַת הַיְרִיעָה הַחֹבֶרֶת הַשֵּׁנִית:

18 They made fifty copper clasps to couple the Tent together so that it might become one whole.

יח וַיַּעַשׂ קַרְסֵי נְחֹשֶׁת חֲמִשִּׁים לְחַבֵּר אֶת־הָאֹהֶל לִהְיֹת אֶחָד:

19 And they made a covering of tanned ram skins for the tent, and a covering of dolphin skins above.

יט וַיַּעַשׂ מִכְסֶה לָאֹהֶל עֹרֹת אֵלִים מְאָדָּמִים וּמִכְסֵה עֹרֹת תְּחָשִׁים מִלְמָעְלָה:

20 They made the planks for the *Mishkan* of acacia wood, upright.

כ וַיַּעַשׂ אֶת־הַקְּרָשִׁים לַמִּשְׁכָּן עֲצֵי שִׁטִּים עֹמְדִים:

21 The length of each plank was ten *amot*, the width of each plank an *amah* and a half.

כא עֶשֶׂר אַמֹּת אֹרֶךְ הַקָּרֶשׁ וְאַמָּה וַחֲצִי הָאַמָּה רֹחַב הַקֶּרֶשׁ הָאֶחָד:

22 Each plank had two tenons, parallel to each other; they did the same with all the planks of the *Mishkan*.

כב שְׁתֵּי יָדֹת לַקֶּרֶשׁ הָאֶחָד מְשֻׁלָּבֹת אַחַת אֶל־אֶחָת כֵּן עָשָׂה לְכֹל קַרְשֵׁי הַמִּשְׁכָּן:

23 Of the planks of the *Mishkan*, they made twenty planks for the south side,

כג וַיַּעַשׂ אֶת־הַקְּרָשִׁים לַמִּשְׁכָּן עֶשְׂרִים קְרָשִׁים לִפְאַת נֶגֶב תֵּימָנָה:

24 making forty silver sockets under the twenty planks, two sockets under one plank for its two tenons and two sockets under each following plank for its two tenons;

כד וְאַרְבָּעִים אַדְנֵי־כֶסֶף עָשָׂה תַּחַת עֶשְׂרִים הַקְּרָשִׁים שְׁנֵי אֲדָנִים תַּחַת־הַקֶּרֶשׁ הָאֶחָד לִשְׁתֵּי יְדֹתָיו וּשְׁנֵי אֲדָנִים תַּחַת־הַקֶּרֶשׁ הָאֶחָד לִשְׁתֵּי יְדֹתָיו:

25 and for the other side wall of the *Mishkan*, the north side, twenty planks,

כה וּלְצֶלַע הַמִּשְׁכָּן הַשֵּׁנִית לִפְאַת צָפוֹן עָשָׂה עֶשְׂרִים קְרָשִׁים:

26 with their forty silver sockets, two sockets under one plank and two sockets under each following plank.

כו וְאַרְבָּעִים אַדְנֵיהֶם כָּסֶף שְׁנֵי אֲדָנִים תַּחַת הַקֶּרֶשׁ הָאֶחָד וּשְׁנֵי אֲדָנִים תַּחַת הַקֶּרֶשׁ הָאֶחָד:

27 And for the rear of the *Mishkan*, to the west, they made six planks;

כז וּלְיַרְכְּתֵי הַמִּשְׁכָּן יָמָּה עָשָׂה שִׁשָּׁה קְרָשִׁים:

28 and they made two planks for the corners of the *Mishkan* at the rear.

כח וּשְׁנֵי קְרָשִׁים עָשָׂה לִמְקֻצְעֹת הַמִּשְׁכָּן בַּיַּרְכָתָיִם:

29 They matched at the bottom, but terminated as one at the top into one ring; they did so with both of them at the two corners.

כט וְהָיוּ תוֹאֲמִם מִלְּמַטָּה וְיַחְדָּו יִהְיוּ תַמִּים אֶל־רֹאשׁוֹ אֶל־הַטַּבַּעַת הָאֶחָת כֵּן עָשָׂה לִשְׁנֵיהֶם לִשְׁנֵי הַמִּקְצֹעֹת:

30 Thus there were eight planks with their sockets of silver: sixteen sockets, two under each plank.

ל וְהָיוּ שְׁמֹנָה קְרָשִׁים וְאַדְנֵיהֶם כֶּסֶף שִׁשָּׁה עָשָׂר אֲדָנִים שְׁנֵי אֲדָנִים שְׁנֵי אֲדָנִים תַּחַת הַקֶּרֶשׁ הָאֶחָד:

31 They made bars of acacia wood, five for the planks of the one side wall of the *Mishkan*,

לא וַיַּעַשׂ בְּרִיחֵי עֲצֵי שִׁטִּים חֲמִשָּׁה לְקַרְשֵׁי צֶלַע־הַמִּשְׁכָּן הָאֶחָת:

32 five bars for the planks of the other side wall of the *Mishkan*, and five bars for the planks of the wall of the *Mishkan* at the rear, to the west;

לב וַחֲמִשָּׁה בְרִיחִם לְקַרְשֵׁי צֶלַע־הַמִּשְׁכָּן הַשֵּׁנִית וַחֲמִשָּׁה בְרִיחִם לְקַרְשֵׁי הַמִּשְׁכָּן לַיַּרְכָתַיִם יָמָּה:

33 they made the center bar to run, halfway up the planks, from end to end.

לג וַיַּעַשׂ אֶת־הַבְּרִיחַ הַתִּיכֹן לִבְרֹחַ בְּתוֹךְ הַקְּרָשִׁים מִן־הַקָּצֶה אֶל־הַקָּצֶה:

34 They overlaid the planks with gold, and made their rings of gold, as holders for the bars; and they overlaid the bars with gold.

לד וְאֶת־הַקְּרָשִׁים צִפָּה זָהָב וְאֶת־טַבְּעֹתָם עָשָׂה זָהָב בָּתִּים לַבְּרִיחִם וַיְצַף אֶת־הַבְּרִיחִם זָהָב:

35 They made the curtain of blue, purple, and crimson yarns, and fine twisted linen, working into it a design of cherubim.

לה וַיַּעַשׂ אֶת־הַפָּרֹכֶת תְּכֵלֶת וְאַרְגָּמָן וְתוֹלַעַת שָׁנִי וְשֵׁשׁ מָשְׁזָר מַעֲשֵׂה חֹשֵׁב עָשָׂה אֹתָהּ כְּרֻבִים:

36 They made for it four posts of acacia wood and overlaid them with gold, with their hooks of gold; and they cast for them four silver sockets.

לו וַיַּעַשׂ לָהּ אַרְבָּעָה עַמּוּדֵי שִׁטִּים וַיְצַפֵּם זָהָב וָוֵיהֶם זָהָב וַיִּצֹק לָהֶם אַרְבָּעָה אַדְנֵי־כָסֶף:

37 They made the screen for the entrance of the Tent, of blue, purple, and crimson yarns, and fine twisted linen, done in embroidery;

לז וַיַּעַשׂ מָסָךְ לְפֶתַח הָאֹהֶל תְּכֵלֶת וְאַרְגָּמָן וְתוֹלַעַת שָׁנִי וְשֵׁשׁ מָשְׁזָר מַעֲשֵׂה רֹקֵם:

38 and five posts for it with their hooks. They overlaid their tops and their bands with gold; but the five sockets were of copper.

לח וְאֶת־עַמּוּדָיו חֲמִשָּׁה וְאֶת־וָוֵיהֶם וְצִפָּה רָאשֵׁיהֶם וַחֲשֻׁקֵיהֶם זָהָב וְאַדְנֵיהֶם חֲמִשָּׁה נְחֹשֶׁת׃

37 1 *Betzalel* made the ark of acacia wood, two and a half *amot* long, an *amah* and a half wide, and an *amah* and a half high.

לז א וַיַּעַשׂ בְּצַלְאֵל אֶת־הָאָרֹן עֲצֵי שִׁטִּים אַמָּתַיִם וָחֵצִי אָרְכּוֹ וְאַמָּה וָחֵצִי רָחְבּוֹ וְאַמָּה וָחֵצִי קֹמָתוֹ׃

2 He overlaid it with pure gold, inside and out; and he made a gold molding for it round about.

ב וַיְצַפֵּהוּ זָהָב טָהוֹר מִבַּיִת וּמִחוּץ וַיַּעַשׂ לוֹ זֵר זָהָב סָבִיב׃

3 He cast four gold rings for it, for its four feet: two rings on one of its side walls and two rings on the other.

ג וַיִּצֹק לוֹ אַרְבַּע טַבְּעֹת זָהָב עַל אַרְבַּע פַּעֲמֹתָיו וּשְׁתֵּי טַבָּעֹת עַל־צַלְעוֹ הָאֶחָת וּשְׁתֵּי טַבָּעוֹת עַל־צַלְעוֹ הַשֵּׁנִית׃

4 He made poles of acacia wood, overlaid them with gold,

ד וַיַּעַשׂ בַּדֵּי עֲצֵי שִׁטִּים וַיְצַף אֹתָם זָהָב׃

5 and inserted the poles into the rings on the side walls of the ark for carrying the ark.

ה וַיָּבֵא אֶת־הַבַּדִּים בַּטַּבָּעֹת עַל צַלְעֹת הָאָרֹן לָשֵׂאת אֶת־הָאָרֹן׃

6 He made a cover of pure gold, two and a half *amot* long and an *amah* and a half wide.

ו וַיַּעַשׂ כַּפֹּרֶת זָהָב טָהוֹר אַמָּתַיִם וָחֵצִי אָרְכָּהּ וְאַמָּה וָחֵצִי רָחְבָּהּ׃

7 He made two cherubim of gold; he made them of hammered work, at the two ends of the cover:

ז וַיַּעַשׂ שְׁנֵי כְרֻבִים זָהָב מִקְשָׁה עָשָׂה אֹתָם מִשְּׁנֵי קְצוֹת הַכַּפֹּרֶת׃

8 one cherub at one end and the other cherub at the other end; he made the cherubim of one piece with the cover, at its two ends.

ח כְּרוּב־אֶחָד מִקָּצָה מִזֶּה וּכְרוּב־אֶחָד מִקָּצָה מִזֶּה מִן־הַכַּפֹּרֶת עָשָׂה אֶת־הַכְּרֻבִים מִשְּׁנֵי קצוותו [קְצוֹתָיו]׃

9 The cherubim had their wings spread out above, shielding the cover with their wings. They faced each other; the faces of the cherubim were turned toward the cover.

ט וַיִּהְיוּ הַכְּרֻבִים פֹּרְשֵׂי כְנָפַיִם לְמַעְלָה סֹכְכִים בְּכַנְפֵיהֶם עַל־הַכַּפֹּרֶת וּפְנֵיהֶם אִישׁ אֶל־אָחִיו אֶל־הַכַּפֹּרֶת הָיוּ פְּנֵי הַכְּרֻבִים׃

10 He made the table of acacia wood, two *amot* long, one *amah* wide, and an *amah* and a half high;

י וַיַּעַשׂ אֶת־הַשֻּׁלְחָן עֲצֵי שִׁטִּים אַמָּתַיִם אָרְכּוֹ וְאַמָּה רָחְבּוֹ וְאַמָּה וָחֵצִי קֹמָתוֹ׃

11 he overlaid it with pure gold and made a gold molding around it.

יא וַיְצַף אֹתוֹ זָהָב טָהוֹר וַיַּעַשׂ לוֹ זֵר זָהָב סָבִיב׃

12 He made a rim of a hand's breadth around it and made a gold molding for its rim round about.

יב וַיַּעַשׂ לוֹ מִסְגֶּרֶת טֹפַח סָבִיב וַיַּעַשׂ זֵר־זָהָב לְמִסְגַּרְתּוֹ סָבִיב׃

13 He cast four gold rings for it and attached the rings to the four corners at its four legs.

יג וַיִּצֹק לוֹ אַרְבַּע טַבְּעֹת זָהָב וַיִּתֵּן אֶת־הַטַּבָּעֹת עַל אַרְבַּע הַפֵּאֹת אֲשֶׁר לְאַרְבַּע רַגְלָיו׃

14 The rings were next to the rim, as holders for the poles to carry the table.

יד לְעֻמַּת הַמִּסְגֶּרֶת הָיוּ הַטַּבָּעֹת בָּתִּים לַבַּדִּים לָשֵׂאת אֶת־הַשֻּׁלְחָן׃

15 He made the poles of acacia wood for carrying the table, and overlaid them with gold.

טו וַיַּעַשׂ אֶת־הַבַּדִּים עֲצֵי שִׁטִּים וַיְצַף אֹתָם זָהָב לָשֵׂאת אֶת־הַשֻּׁלְחָן׃

16 The utensils that were to be upon the table – its bowls, ladles, jugs, and jars with which to offer libations – he made of pure gold.

טז וַיַּעַשׂ אֶת־הַכֵּלִים אֲשֶׁר עַל־הַשֻּׁלְחָן אֶת־קְעָרֹתָיו וְאֶת־כַּפֹּתָיו וְאֵת מְנַקִּיֹּתָיו וְאֶת־הַקְּשָׂוֺת אֲשֶׁר יֻסַּךְ בָּהֵן זָהָב טָהוֹר׃

17 He made the *menorah* of pure gold. He made the *menorah* – its base and its shaft – of hammered work; its cups, calyxes, and petals were of one piece with it.

יז וַיַּעַשׂ אֶת־הַמְּנֹרָה זָהָב טָהוֹר מִקְשָׁה עָשָׂה אֶת־הַמְּנֹרָה יְרֵכָהּ וְקָנָהּ גְּבִיעֶיהָ כַּפְתֹּרֶיהָ וּפְרָחֶיהָ מִמֶּנָּה הָיוּ׃

va-YA-as et ha-m'-no-RAH za-HAV ta-HOR mik-SHAH
a-SAH et ha-m'-no-RAH y'-ray-KHAH v'-ka-NAH g'-vee-E-ha
kaf-to-RE-ha uf-ra-KHE-ha mi-ME-nah ha-YU

18 Six branches issued from its sides: three branches from one side of the *menorah*, and three branches from the other side of the *menorah*.

יח וְשִׁשָּׁה קָנִים יֹצְאִים מִצִּדֶּיהָ שְׁלֹשָׁה קְנֵי מְנֹרָה מִצִּדָּהּ הָאֶחָד וּשְׁלֹשָׁה קְנֵי מְנֹרָה מִצִּדָּהּ הַשֵּׁנִי׃

19 There were three cups shaped like almond-blossoms, each with calyx and petals, on one branch; and there were three cups shaped like almond-blossoms, each with calyx and petals, on the next branch; so for all six branches issuing from the *menorah*.

יט שְׁלֹשָׁה גְבִעִים מְשֻׁקָּדִים בַּקָּנֶה הָאֶחָד כַּפְתֹּר וָפֶרַח וּשְׁלֹשָׁה גְבִעִים מְשֻׁקָּדִים בְּקָנֶה אֶחָד כַּפְתֹּר וָפָרַח כֵּן לְשֵׁשֶׁת הַקָּנִים הַיֹּצְאִים מִן־הַמְּנֹרָה׃

20 On the *menorah* itself there were four cups shaped like almond-blossoms, each with calyx and petals:

כ וּבַמְּנֹרָה אַרְבָּעָה גְבִעִים מְשֻׁקָּדִים כַּפְתֹּרֶיהָ וּפְרָחֶיהָ׃

21 a calyx, of one piece with it, under a pair of branches; and a calyx, of one piece with it, under the second pair of branches; and a calyx, of one piece with it, under the last pair of branches; so for all six branches issuing from it.

כא וְכַפְתֹּר תַּחַת שְׁנֵי הַקָּנִים מִמֶּנָּה וְכַפְתֹּר תַּחַת שְׁנֵי הַקָּנִים מִמֶּנָּה וְכַפְתֹּר תַּחַת־שְׁנֵי הַקָּנִים מִמֶּנָּה לְשֵׁשֶׁת הַקָּנִים הַיֹּצְאִים מִמֶּנָּה׃

22 Their calyxes and their stems were of one piece with it, the whole of it a single hammered piece of pure gold.

כב כַּפְתֹּרֵיהֶם וּקְנֹתָם מִמֶּנָּה הָיוּ כֻּלָּהּ מִקְשָׁה אַחַת זָהָב טָהוֹר׃

37:17 He made the *menorah* of pure gold The *menorah*, made of "pure gold," was lit with pure olive oil and gave off a radiant light. The light of the *menorah* is symbolic of the Jewish Nation's duty to spread the light of *Torah* and God's will. The pure gold and olive oil are reflective of the pure intentions necessary to influence the nations of the world for the sake of Heaven. Today, the *menorah* is the official symbol of the State of Israel, which represents the eternity of the Jewish People. The bronze *menorah*, located across from the Knesset, Israel's parliament in *Yerushalayim*, was modeled after the *menorah* of the Temple. The six side branches are engraved with depictions of events from the Bible, as well as the Jews in exile. The center branch of this impressive *menorah* tells the story of the return to *Eretz Yisrael*, up until the establishment of the State of Israel. Now that the People of Israel have returned home, they can again work together to spread light to the rest of the world.

Knesset Menorah in Yerushalayim

94

23 He made its seven lamps, its tongs, and its fire pans of pure gold.

כג וַיַּעַשׂ אֶת־נֵרֹתֶיהָ שִׁבְעָה וּמַלְקָחֶיהָ וּמַחְתֹּתֶיהָ זָהָב טָהוֹר:

24 He made it and all its furnishings out of a *kikar* of pure gold.

כד כִּכָּר זָהָב טָהוֹר עָשָׂה אֹתָהּ וְאֵת כָּל־כֵּלֶיהָ:

25 He made the incense *Mizbayach* of acacia wood, an *amah* long and an *amah* wide – square – and two *amot* high; its horns were of one piece with it.

כה וַיַּעַשׂ אֶת־מִזְבַּח הַקְּטֹרֶת עֲצֵי שִׁטִּים אַמָּה אָרְכּוֹ וְאַמָּה רָחְבּוֹ רָבוּעַ וְאַמָּתַיִם קֹמָתוֹ מִמֶּנּוּ הָיוּ קַרְנֹתָיו:

26 He overlaid it with pure gold: its top, its sides round about, and its horns; and he made a gold molding for it round about.

כו וַיְצַף אֹתוֹ זָהָב טָהוֹר אֶת־גַּגּוֹ וְאֶת־קִירֹתָיו סָבִיב וְאֶת־קַרְנֹתָיו וַיַּעַשׂ לוֹ זֵר זָהָב סָבִיב:

27 He made two gold rings for it under its molding, on its two walls – on opposite sides – as holders for the poles with which to carry it.

כז וּשְׁתֵּי טַבְּעֹת זָהָב עָשָׂה־לוֹ מִתַּחַת לְזֵרוֹ עַל שְׁתֵּי צַלְעֹתָיו עַל שְׁנֵי צִדָּיו לְבָתִּים לְבַדִּים לָשֵׂאת אֹתוֹ בָּהֶם:

28 He made the poles of acacia wood, and overlaid them with gold.

כח וַיַּעַשׂ אֶת־הַבַּדִּים עֲצֵי שִׁטִּים וַיְצַף אֹתָם זָהָב:

29 He prepared the sacred anointing oil and the pure aromatic incense, expertly blended.

כט וַיַּעַשׂ אֶת־שֶׁמֶן הַמִּשְׁחָה קֹדֶשׁ וְאֶת־קְטֹרֶת הַסַּמִּים טָהוֹר מַעֲשֵׂה רֹקֵחַ:

38 1 He made the *Mizbayach* for burnt offering of acacia wood, five *amot* long and five *amot* wide – square – and three *amot* high.

ח א וַיַּעַשׂ אֶת־מִזְבַּח הָעֹלָה עֲצֵי שִׁטִּים חָמֵשׁ אַמּוֹת אָרְכּוֹ וְחָמֵשׁ־אַמּוֹת רָחְבּוֹ רָבוּעַ וְשָׁלֹשׁ אַמּוֹת קֹמָתוֹ:

2 He made horns for it on its four corners, the horns being of one piece with it; and he overlaid it with copper.

ב וַיַּעַשׂ קַרְנֹתָיו עַל אַרְבַּע פִּנֹּתָיו מִמֶּנּוּ הָיוּ קַרְנֹתָיו וַיְצַף אֹתוֹ נְחֹשֶׁת:

3 He made all the utensils of the *Mizbayach* – the pails, the scrapers, the basins, the flesh hooks, and the fire pans; he made all these utensils of copper.

ג וַיַּעַשׂ אֶת־כָּל־כְּלֵי הַמִּזְבֵּחַ אֶת־הַסִּירֹת וְאֶת־הַיָּעִים וְאֶת־הַמִּזְרָקֹת אֶת־הַמִּזְלָגֹת וְאֶת־הַמַּחְתֹּת כָּל־כֵּלָיו עָשָׂה נְחֹשֶׁת:

4 He made for the *Mizbayach* a grating of meshwork in copper, extending below, under its ledge, to its middle.

ד וַיַּעַשׂ לַמִּזְבֵּחַ מִכְבָּר מַעֲשֵׂה רֶשֶׁת נְחֹשֶׁת תַּחַת כַּרְכֻּבּוֹ מִלְּמַטָּה עַד־חֶצְיוֹ:

5 He cast four rings, at the four corners of the copper grating, as holders for the poles.

ה וַיִּצֹק אַרְבַּע טַבָּעֹת בְּאַרְבַּע הַקְּצָוֹת לְמִכְבַּר הַנְּחֹשֶׁת בָּתִּים לַבַּדִּים:

6 He made the poles of acacia wood and overlaid them with copper;

ו וַיַּעַשׂ אֶת־הַבַּדִּים עֲצֵי שִׁטִּים וַיְצַף אֹתָם נְחֹשֶׁת:

7 and he inserted the poles into the rings on the side walls of the *Mizbayach*, to carry it by them. He made it hollow, of boards.

ז וַיָּבֵא אֶת־הַבַּדִּים בַּטַּבָּעֹת עַל צַלְעֹת הַמִּזְבֵּחַ לָשֵׂאת אֹתוֹ בָּהֶם נְבוּב לֻחֹת עָשָׂה אֹתוֹ:

8 He made the laver of copper and its stand of copper, from the mirrors of the women who performed tasks at the entrance of the Tent of Meeting.

ח וַיַּעַשׂ אֵת הַכִּיּוֹר נְחֹשֶׁת וְאֵת כַּנּוֹ נְחֹשֶׁת בְּמַרְאֹת הַצֹּבְאֹת אֲשֶׁר צָבְאוּ פֶּתַח אֹהֶל מוֹעֵד:

va-YA-as AYT ha-kee-YOR n'-KHO-shet v'-AYT ka-NO n'-KHO-shet
b'-mar-OT ha-TZO-v'-OT a-SHER tza-v'-U PE-takh O-hel mo-AYD

9 He made the enclosure: On the south side, a hundred *amot* of hangings of fine twisted linen for the enclosure

ט וַיַּעַשׂ אֶת־הֶחָצֵר לִפְאַת נֶגֶב תֵּימָנָה קַלְעֵי הֶחָצֵר שֵׁשׁ מָשְׁזָר מֵאָה בָּאַמָּה:

10 with their twenty posts and their twenty sockets of copper, the hooks and bands of the posts being silver.

י עַמּוּדֵיהֶם עֶשְׂרִים וְאַדְנֵיהֶם עֶשְׂרִים נְחֹשֶׁת וָוֵי הָעַמֻּדִים וַחֲשֻׁקֵיהֶם כָּסֶף:

11 On the north side, a hundred *amot* – with their twenty posts and their twenty sockets of copper, the hooks and bands of the posts being silver.

יא וְלִפְאַת צָפוֹן מֵאָה בָאַמָּה עַמּוּדֵיהֶם עֶשְׂרִים וְאַדְנֵיהֶם עֶשְׂרִים נְחֹשֶׁת וָוֵי הָעַמּוּדִים וַחֲשֻׁקֵיהֶם כָּסֶף:

12 On the west side, fifty *amot* of hangings – with their ten posts and their ten sockets, the hooks and bands of the posts being silver.

יב וְלִפְאַת־יָם קְלָעִים חֲמִשִּׁים בָּאַמָּה עַמּוּדֵיהֶם עֲשָׂרָה וְאַדְנֵיהֶם עֲשָׂרָה וָוֵי הָעַמֻּדִים וַחֲשׁוּקֵיהֶם כָּסֶף:

13 And on the front side, to the east, fifty *amot*:

יג וְלִפְאַת קֵדְמָה מִזְרָחָה חֲמִשִּׁים אַמָּה:

14 fifteen *amot* of hangings on the one flank, with their three posts and their three sockets,

יד קְלָעִים חֲמֵשׁ־עֶשְׂרֵה אַמָּה אֶל־הַכָּתֵף עַמּוּדֵיהֶם שְׁלֹשָׁה וְאַדְנֵיהֶם שְׁלֹשָׁה:

15 and fifteen *amot* of hangings on the other flank – on each side of the gate of the enclosure – with their three posts and their three sockets.

טו וְלַכָּתֵף הַשֵּׁנִית מִזֶּה וּמִזֶּה לְשַׁעַר הֶחָצֵר קְלָעִים חֲמֵשׁ עֶשְׂרֵה אַמָּה עַמֻּדֵיהֶם שְׁלֹשָׁה וְאַדְנֵיהֶם שְׁלֹשָׁה:

16 All the hangings around the enclosure were of fine twisted linen.

טז כָּל־קַלְעֵי הֶחָצֵר סָבִיב שֵׁשׁ מָשְׁזָר:

17 The sockets for the posts were of copper, the hooks and bands of the posts were of silver, the overlay of their tops was of silver; all the posts of the enclosure were banded with silver.

יז וְהָאֲדָנִים לָעַמֻּדִים נְחֹשֶׁת וָוֵי הָעַמּוּדִים וַחֲשֻׁקֵיהֶם כֶּסֶף וְצִפּוּי רָאשֵׁיהֶם כָּסֶף וְהֵם מְחֻשָּׁקִים כֶּסֶף כֹּל עַמֻּדֵי הֶחָצֵר:

18 The screen of the gate of the enclosure, done in embroidery, was of blue, purple, and crimson yarns, and fine twisted linen. It was twenty *amot* long. Its height – or width – was five *amot*, like that of the hangings of the enclosure.

יח וּמָסַךְ שַׁעַר הֶחָצֵר מַעֲשֵׂה רֹקֵם תְּכֵלֶת וְאַרְגָּמָן וְתוֹלַעַת שָׁנִי וְשֵׁשׁ מָשְׁזָר וְעֶשְׂרִים אַמָּה אֹרֶךְ וְקוֹמָה בְרֹחַב חָמֵשׁ אַמּוֹת לְעֻמַּת קַלְעֵי הֶחָצֵר:

38:8 From the mirrors of the women who performed tasks The women of the nation donate their mirrors to provide copper for the laver. The medieval commentator *Rashi* teaches that in Egypt, the women would use these mirrors to make themselves beautiful, in order to enliven the spirits of their husbands upon returning from the day's slave labor. These righteous women never lost faith in *Hashem* and in His promised redemption, and ensured the continuity of the Jewish people with these same mirrors. It is due to the merit of the righteous women in the generation of the exodus that their mirrors are used to construct a vessel in the holy *Mishkan*.

Women of the IDF

96

19 The posts were four; their four sockets were of copper, their hooks of silver; and the overlay of their tops was of silver, as were also their bands.

וְעַמֻּדֵיהֶם אַרְבָּעָה וְאַדְנֵיהֶם אַרְבָּעָה נְחֹשֶׁת וָוֵיהֶם כֶּסֶף וְצִפּוּי רָאשֵׁיהֶם וַחֲשֻׁקֵיהֶם כָּסֶף: יט

20 All the pegs of the *Mishkan* and of the enclosure round about were of copper.

וְכָל־הַיְתֵדֹת לַמִּשְׁכָּן וְלֶחָצֵר סָבִיב נְחֹשֶׁת: כ

21 These are the records of the *Mishkan*, the *Mishkan* of the Pact, which were drawn up at *Moshe*'s bidding – the work of the *Leviim* under the direction of *Itamar* son of *Aharon* the *Kohen*.

אֵלֶּה פְקוּדֵי הַמִּשְׁכָּן מִשְׁכַּן הָעֵדֻת אֲשֶׁר פֻּקַּד עַל־פִּי מֹשֶׁה עֲבֹדַת הַלְוִיִּם בְּיַד אִיתָמָר בֶּן־אַהֲרֹן הַכֹּהֵן: כא

22 Now *Betzalel*, son of *Uri* son of *Chur*, of the tribe of *Yehuda*, had made all that *Hashem* had commanded *Moshe*;

וּבְצַלְאֵל בֶּן־אוּרִי בֶן־חוּר לְמַטֵּה יְהוּדָה עָשָׂה אֵת כָּל־אֲשֶׁר־צִוָּה יְהֹוָה אֶת־מֹשֶׁה: כב

23 at his side was *Oholiav* son of *Achisamach*, of the tribe of *Dan*, carver and designer, and embroiderer in blue, purple, and crimson yarns and in fine linen.

וְאִתּוֹ אָהֳלִיאָב בֶּן־אֲחִיסָמָךְ לְמַטֵּה־דָן חָרָשׁ וְחֹשֵׁב וְרֹקֵם בַּתְּכֵלֶת וּבָאַרְגָּמָן וּבְתוֹלַעַת הַשָּׁנִי וּבַשֵּׁשׁ: כג

24 All the gold that was used for the work, in all the work of the sanctuary – the elevation offering of gold – came to 29 *kikarot* and 730 *shekalim* by the sanctuary weight.

כָּל־הַזָּהָב הֶעָשׂוּי לַמְּלָאכָה בְּכֹל מְלֶאכֶת הַקֹּדֶשׁ וַיְהִי זְהַב הַתְּנוּפָה תֵּשַׁע וְעֶשְׂרִים כִּכָּר וּשְׁבַע מֵאוֹת וּשְׁלֹשִׁים שֶׁקֶל בְּשֶׁקֶל הַקֹּדֶשׁ: כד

25 The silver of those of the community who were recorded came to 100 *kikarot* and 1,775 *shekalim* by the sanctuary weight:

וְכֶסֶף פְּקוּדֵי הָעֵדָה מְאַת כִּכָּר וְאֶלֶף וּשְׁבַע מֵאוֹת וַחֲמִשָּׁה וְשִׁבְעִים שֶׁקֶל בְּשֶׁקֶל הַקֹּדֶשׁ: כה

26 a *beka* a head, half a *shekel* by the sanctuary weight, for each one who was entered in the records, from the age of twenty years up, 603,550 men.

בֶּקַע לַגֻּלְגֹּלֶת מַחֲצִית הַשֶּׁקֶל בְּשֶׁקֶל הַקֹּדֶשׁ לְכֹל הָעֹבֵר עַל־הַפְּקֻדִים מִבֶּן עֶשְׂרִים שָׁנָה וָמַעְלָה לְשֵׁשׁ־מֵאוֹת אֶלֶף וּשְׁלֹשֶׁת אֲלָפִים וַחֲמֵשׁ מֵאוֹת וַחֲמִשִּׁים: כו

27 The 100 *kikarot* of silver were for casting the sockets of the sanctuary and the sockets for the curtain, 100 sockets to the 100 *kikarot*, a *kikar* a socket.

וַיְהִי מְאַת כִּכַּר הַכֶּסֶף לָצֶקֶת אֵת אַדְנֵי הַקֹּדֶשׁ וְאֵת אַדְנֵי הַפָּרֹכֶת מְאַת אֲדָנִים לִמְאַת הַכִּכָּר כִּכָּר לָאָדֶן: כז

28 And of the 1,775 *shekalim* he made hooks for the posts, overlay for their tops, and bands around them.

וְאֶת־הָאֶלֶף וּשְׁבַע הַמֵּאוֹת וַחֲמִשָּׁה וְשִׁבְעִים עָשָׂה וָוִים לָעַמּוּדִים וְצִפָּה רָאשֵׁיהֶם וְחִשַּׁק אֹתָם: כח

29 The copper from the elevation offering came to 70 *kikarot* and 2,400 *shekalim*.

וּנְחֹשֶׁת הַתְּנוּפָה שִׁבְעִים כִּכָּר וְאַלְפַּיִם וְאַרְבַּע־מֵאוֹת שָׁקֶל: כט

30 Of it he made the sockets for the entrance of the Tent of Meeting; the copper *Mizbayach* and its copper grating and all the utensils of the *Mizbayach*;

וַיַּעַשׂ בָּהּ אֶת־אַדְנֵי פֶּתַח אֹהֶל מוֹעֵד וְאֵת מִזְבַּח הַנְּחֹשֶׁת וְאֶת־מִכְבַּר הַנְּחֹשֶׁת אֲשֶׁר־לוֹ וְאֵת כָּל־כְּלֵי הַמִּזְבֵּחַ: ל

31 the sockets of the enclosure round about and the sockets of the gate of the enclosure; and all the pegs of the *Mishkan* and all the pegs of the enclosure round about.

וְאֶת־אַדְנֵי הֶחָצֵר סָבִיב וְאֶת־אַדְנֵי שַׁעַר הֶחָצֵר וְאֵת כָּל־יִתְדֹת הַמִּשְׁכָּן וְאֶת־כָּל־יִתְדֹת הֶחָצֵר סָבִיב: לא

39 1 Of the blue, purple, and crimson yarns they also made the service vestments for officiating in the sanctuary; they made *Aharon*'s sacral vestments – as *Hashem* had commanded *Moshe*.

לט א וּמִן־הַתְּכֵלֶת וְהָאַרְגָּמָן וְתוֹלַעַת הַשָּׁנִי עָשׂוּ בִגְדֵי־שְׂרָד לְשָׁרֵת בַּקֹּדֶשׁ וַיַּעֲשׂוּ אֶת־בִּגְדֵי הַקֹּדֶשׁ אֲשֶׁר לְאַהֲרֹן כַּאֲשֶׁר צִוָּה יְהֹוָה אֶת־מֹשֶׁה:

2 The ephod was made of gold, blue, purple, and crimson yarns, and fine twisted linen.

ב וַיַּעַשׂ אֶת־הָאֵפֹד זָהָב תְּכֵלֶת וְאַרְגָּמָן וְתוֹלַעַת שָׁנִי וְשֵׁשׁ מָשְׁזָר:

3 They hammered out sheets of gold and cut threads to be worked into designs among the blue, the purple, and the crimson yarns, and the fine linen.

ג וַיְרַקְּעוּ אֶת־פַּחֵי הַזָּהָב וְקִצֵּץ פְּתִילִם לַעֲשׂוֹת בְּתוֹךְ הַתְּכֵלֶת וּבְתוֹךְ הָאַרְגָּמָן וּבְתוֹךְ תּוֹלַעַת הַשָּׁנִי וּבְתוֹךְ הַשֵּׁשׁ מַעֲשֵׂה חֹשֵׁב:

4 They made for it attaching shoulder-pieces; they were attached at its two ends.

ד כְּתֵפֹת עָשׂוּ־לוֹ חֹבְרֹת עַל־שְׁנֵי קְצוֹותָו [קְצוֹתָיו] חֻבָּר:

5 The decorated band that was upon it was made like it, of one piece with it; of gold, blue, purple, and crimson yarns, and fine twisted linen – as *Hashem* had commanded *Moshe*.

ה וְחֵשֶׁב אֲפֻדָּתוֹ אֲשֶׁר עָלָיו מִמֶּנּוּ הוּא כְּמַעֲשֵׂהוּ זָהָב תְּכֵלֶת וְאַרְגָּמָן וְתוֹלַעַת שָׁנִי וְשֵׁשׁ מָשְׁזָר כַּאֲשֶׁר צִוָּה יְהֹוָה אֶת־מֹשֶׁה:

6 They bordered the lazuli stones with frames of gold, engraved with seal engravings of the names of the sons of *Yisrael*.

ו וַיַּעֲשׂוּ אֶת־אַבְנֵי הַשֹּׁהַם מֻסַבֹּת מִשְׁבְּצֹת זָהָב מְפֻתָּחֹת פִּתּוּחֵי חוֹתָם עַל־שְׁמוֹת בְּנֵי יִשְׂרָאֵל:

7 They were set on the shoulder-pieces of the ephod, as stones of remembrance for the Israelites – as *Hashem* had commanded *Moshe*.

ז וַיָּשֶׂם אֹתָם עַל כִּתְפֹת הָאֵפֹד אַבְנֵי זִכָּרוֹן לִבְנֵי יִשְׂרָאֵל כַּאֲשֶׁר צִוָּה יְהֹוָה אֶת־מֹשֶׁה:

8 The breastpiece was made in the style of the ephod: of gold, blue, purple, and crimson yarns, and fine twisted linen.

ח וַיַּעַשׂ אֶת־הַחֹשֶׁן מַעֲשֵׂה חֹשֵׁב כְּמַעֲשֵׂה אֵפֹד זָהָב תְּכֵלֶת וְאַרְגָּמָן וְתוֹלַעַת שָׁנִי וְשֵׁשׁ מָשְׁזָר:

9 It was square; they made the breastpiece doubled – a *zeret* in length and a *zeret* in width, doubled.

ט רָבוּעַ הָיָה כָּפוּל עָשׂוּ אֶת־הַחֹשֶׁן זֶרֶת אָרְכּוֹ וְזֶרֶת רָחְבּוֹ כָּפוּל:

10 They set in it four rows of stones. The first row was a row of carnelian, chrysolite, and emerald;

י וַיְמַלְאוּ־בוֹ אַרְבָּעָה טוּרֵי אָבֶן טוּר אֹדֶם פִּטְדָה וּבָרֶקֶת הַטּוּר הָאֶחָד:

11 the second row: a turquoise, a sapphire, and an amethyst;

יא וְהַטּוּר הַשֵּׁנִי נֹפֶךְ סַפִּיר וְיָהֲלֹם:

12 the third row: a jacinth, an agate, and a crystal;

יב וְהַטּוּר הַשְּׁלִישִׁי לֶשֶׁם שְׁבוֹ וְאַחְלָמָה:

13 and the fourth row: a beryl, a lapis lazuli, and a jasper. They were encircled in their mountings with frames of gold.

יג וְהַטּוּר הָרְבִיעִי תַּרְשִׁישׁ שֹׁהַם וְיָשְׁפֵה מוּסַבֹּת מִשְׁבְּצוֹת זָהָב בְּמִלֻּאֹתָם:

14 The stones corresponded [in number] to the names of the sons of *Yisrael*: twelve, corresponding to their names; engraved like seals, each with its name, for the twelve tribes.

יד וְהָאֲבָנִים עַל־שְׁמֹת בְּנֵי־יִשְׂרָאֵל הֵנָּה שְׁתֵּים עֶשְׂרֵה עַל־שְׁמֹתָם פִּתּוּחֵי חֹתָם אִישׁ עַל־שְׁמוֹ לִשְׁנֵים עָשָׂר שָׁבֶט:

15 On the breastpiece they made braided chains of corded work in pure gold.

טו וַיַּעֲשֹׂוּ עַל־הַחֹשֶׁן שַׁרְשְׁרֹת גַּבְלֻת מַעֲשֵׂה עֲבֹת זָהָב טָהוֹר:

16 They made two frames of gold and two rings of gold, and fastened the two rings at the two ends of the breastpiece,

טז וַיַּעֲשֹׂוּ שְׁתֵּי מִשְׁבְּצֹת זָהָב וּשְׁתֵּי טַבְּעֹת זָהָב וַיִּתְּנוּ אֶת־שְׁתֵּי הַטַּבָּעֹת עַל־שְׁנֵי קְצוֹת הַחֹשֶׁן:

17 attaching the two golden cords to the two rings at the ends of the breastpiece.

יז וַיִּתְּנוּ שְׁתֵּי הָעֲבֹתֹת הַזָּהָב עַל־שְׁתֵּי הַטַּבָּעֹת עַל־קְצוֹת הַחֹשֶׁן:

18 They then fastened the two ends of the cords to the two frames, attaching them to the shoulder-pieces of the ephod, at the front.

יח וְאֵת שְׁתֵּי קְצוֹת שְׁתֵּי הָעֲבֹתֹת נָתְנוּ עַל־שְׁתֵּי הַמִּשְׁבְּצֹת וַיִּתְּנֻם עַל־כִּתְפֹת הָאֵפֹד אֶל־מוּל פָּנָיו:

19 They made two rings of gold and attached them to the two ends of the breastpiece, at its inner edge, which faced the ephod.

יט וַיַּעֲשֹׂוּ שְׁתֵּי טַבְּעֹת זָהָב וַיָּשִׂימוּ עַל־שְׁנֵי קְצוֹת הַחֹשֶׁן עַל־שְׂפָתוֹ אֲשֶׁר אֶל־עֵבֶר הָאֵפֹד בָּיְתָה:

20 They made two other rings of gold and fastened them on the front of the ephod, low on the two shoulder-pieces, close to its seam above the decorated band.

כ וַיַּעֲשֹׂוּ שְׁתֵּי טַבְּעֹת זָהָב וַיִּתְּנֻם עַל־שְׁתֵּי כִתְפֹת הָאֵפֹד מִלְּמַטָּה מִמּוּל פָּנָיו לְעֻמַּת מֶחְבַּרְתּוֹ מִמַּעַל לְחֵשֶׁב הָאֵפֹד:

21 The breastpiece was held in place by a cord of blue from its rings to the rings of the ephod, so that the breastpiece rested on the decorated band and did not come loose from the ephod – as *Hashem* had commanded *Moshe*.

כא וַיִּרְכְּסוּ אֶת־הַחֹשֶׁן מִטַּבְּעֹתָיו אֶל־טַבְּעֹת הָאֵפֹד בִּפְתִיל תְּכֵלֶת לִהְיֹת עַל־חֵשֶׁב הָאֵפֹד וְלֹא־יִזַּח הַחֹשֶׁן מֵעַל הָאֵפֹד כַּאֲשֶׁר צִוָּה יְהוָֹה אֶת־מֹשֶׁה:

22 The robe for the ephod was made of woven work, of pure blue.

כב וַיַּעַשׂ אֶת־מְעִיל הָאֵפֹד מַעֲשֵׂה אֹרֵג כְּלִיל תְּכֵלֶת:

23 The opening of the robe, in the middle of it, was like the opening of a coat of mail, with a binding around the opening, so that it would not tear.

כג וּפִי־הַמְּעִיל בְּתוֹכוֹ כְּפִי תַחְרָא שָׂפָה לְפִיו סָבִיב לֹא יִקָּרֵעַ:

24 On the hem of the robe they made pomegranates of blue, purple, and crimson yarns, twisted.

כד וַיַּעֲשֹׂוּ עַל־שׁוּלֵי הַמְּעִיל רִמּוֹנֵי תְּכֵלֶת וְאַרְגָּמָן וְתוֹלַעַת שָׁנִי מָשְׁזָר:

25 They also made bells of pure gold, and attached the bells between the pomegranates, all around the hem of the robe, between the pomegranates:

כה וַיַּעֲשֹׂוּ פַעֲמֹנֵי זָהָב טָהוֹר וַיִּתְּנוּ אֶת־הַפַּעֲמֹנִים בְּתוֹךְ הָרִמֹּנִים עַל־שׁוּלֵי הַמְּעִיל סָבִיב בְּתוֹךְ הָרִמֹּנִים:

26 a bell and a pomegranate, a bell and a pomegranate, all around the hem of the robe for officiating in – as *Hashem* had commanded *Moshe*.

כו פַּעֲמֹן וְרִמֹּן פַּעֲמֹן וְרִמֹּן עַל־שׁוּלֵי הַמְּעִיל סָבִיב לְשָׁרֵת כַּאֲשֶׁר צִוָּה יְהוָֹה אֶת־מֹשֶׁה:

27 They made the tunics of fine linen, of woven work, for *Aharon* and his sons;

כז וַיַּעֲשֹׂוּ אֶת־הַכָּתְנֹת שֵׁשׁ מַעֲשֵׂה אֹרֵג לְאַהֲרֹן וּלְבָנָיו:

28 and the headdress of fine linen, and the decorated turbans of fine linen, and the linen breeches of fine twisted linen;

כח וְאֵת הַמִּצְנֶפֶת שֵׁשׁ וְאֶת־פַּאֲרֵי הַמִּגְבָּעֹת שֵׁשׁ וְאֶת־מִכְנְסֵי הַבָּד שֵׁשׁ מָשְׁזָר:

29 and sashes of fine twisted linen, blue, purple, and crimson yarns, done in embroidery – as *Hashem* had commanded *Moshe*.

כט וְאֶת־הָאַבְנֵט שֵׁשׁ מָשְׁזָר וּתְכֵלֶת וְאַרְגָּמָן וְתוֹלַעַת שָׁנִי מַעֲשֵׂה רֹקֵם כַּאֲשֶׁר צִוָּה יְהוָה אֶת־מֹשֶׁה:

30 They made the frontlet for the holy diadem of pure gold, and incised upon it the seal inscription: "Holy to *Hashem*."

ל וַיַּעֲשׂוּ אֶת־צִיץ נֵזֶר־הַקֹּדֶשׁ זָהָב טָהוֹר וַיִּכְתְּבוּ עָלָיו מִכְתַּב פִּתּוּחֵי חוֹתָם קֹדֶשׁ לַיהוָה:

31 They attached to it a cord of blue to fix it upon the headdress above – as *Hashem* had commanded *Moshe*.

לא וַיִּתְּנוּ עָלָיו פְּתִיל תְּכֵלֶת לָתֵת עַל־הַמִּצְנֶפֶת מִלְמָעְלָה כַּאֲשֶׁר צִוָּה יְהוָה אֶת־מֹשֶׁה:

32 Thus was completed all the work of the *Mishkan* of the Tent of Meeting. The Israelites did so; just as *Hashem* had commanded *Moshe*, so they did.

לב וַתֵּכֶל כָּל־עֲבֹדַת מִשְׁכַּן אֹהֶל מוֹעֵד וַיַּעֲשׂוּ בְּנֵי יִשְׂרָאֵל כְּכֹל אֲשֶׁר צִוָּה יְהוָה אֶת־מֹשֶׁה כֵּן עָשׂוּ:

33 Then they brought the *Mishkan* to *Moshe*, with the Tent and all its furnishings: its clasps, its planks, its bars, its posts, and its sockets;

לג וַיָּבִיאוּ אֶת־הַמִּשְׁכָּן אֶל־מֹשֶׁה אֶת־הָאֹהֶל וְאֶת־כָּל־כֵּלָיו קְרָסָיו קְרָשָׁיו בְּרִיחוֹ [בְּרִיחָיו] וְעַמֻּדָיו וַאֲדָנָיו:

34 the covering of tanned ram skins, the covering of dolphin skins, and the curtain for the screen;

לד וְאֶת־מִכְסֵה עוֹרֹת הָאֵילִם הַמְאָדָּמִים וְאֶת־מִכְסֵה עֹרֹת הַתְּחָשִׁים וְאֵת פָּרֹכֶת הַמָּסָךְ:

35 the *Aron HaBrit* and its poles, and the cover;

לה אֶת־אֲרוֹן הָעֵדֻת וְאֶת־בַּדָּיו וְאֵת הַכַּפֹּרֶת:

36 the table and all its utensils, and the bread of display;

לו אֶת־הַשֻּׁלְחָן אֶת־כָּל־כֵּלָיו וְאֵת לֶחֶם הַפָּנִים:

37 the pure *menorah*, its lamps – lamps in due order – and all its fittings, and the oil for lighting;

לז אֶת־הַמְּנֹרָה הַטְּהֹרָה אֶת־נֵרֹתֶיהָ נֵרֹת הַמַּעֲרָכָה וְאֶת־כָּל־כֵּלֶיהָ וְאֵת שֶׁמֶן הַמָּאוֹר:

38 the *Mizbayach* of gold, the oil for anointing, the aromatic incense, and the screen for the entrance of the Tent;

לח וְאֵת מִזְבַּח הַזָּהָב וְאֵת שֶׁמֶן הַמִּשְׁחָה וְאֵת קְטֹרֶת הַסַּמִּים וְאֵת מָסַךְ פֶּתַח הָאֹהֶל:

39 the copper *Mizbayach* with its copper grating, its poles and all its utensils, and the laver and its stand;

לט אֵת מִזְבַּח הַנְּחֹשֶׁת וְאֶת־מִכְבַּר הַנְּחֹשֶׁת אֲשֶׁר־לוֹ אֶת־בַּדָּיו וְאֶת־כָּל־כֵּלָיו אֶת־הַכִּיֹּר וְאֶת־כַּנּוֹ:

40 the hangings of the enclosure, its posts and its sockets, the screen for the gate of the enclosure, its cords and its pegs – all the furnishings for the service of the *Mishkan*, the Tent of Meeting;

מ אֵת קַלְעֵי הֶחָצֵר אֶת־עַמֻּדֶיהָ וְאֶת־אֲדָנֶיהָ וְאֶת־הַמָּסָךְ לְשַׁעַר הֶחָצֵר אֶת־מֵיתָרָיו וִיתֵדֹתֶיהָ וְאֵת כָּל־כְּלֵי עֲבֹדַת הַמִּשְׁכָּן לְאֹהֶל מוֹעֵד:

41 the service vestments for officiating in the sanctuary, the sacral vestments of *Aharon* the *Kohen*, and the vestments of his sons for priestly service.

מא אֶת־בִּגְדֵי הַשְּׂרָד לְשָׁרֵת בַּקֹּדֶשׁ אֶת־בִּגְדֵי הַקֹּדֶשׁ לְאַהֲרֹן הַכֹּהֵן וְאֶת־בִּגְדֵי בָנָיו לְכַהֵן:

42 Just as *Hashem* had commanded *Moshe*, so the Israelites had done all the work.

מב כְּכֹל אֲשֶׁר־צִוָּה יְהוָה אֶת־מֹשֶׁה כֵּן עָשׂוּ בְּנֵי יִשְׂרָאֵל אֵת כָּל־הָעֲבֹדָה:

Exodus

43 And when *Moshe* saw that they had performed all the tasks – as *Hashem* had commanded, so they had done – *Moshe* blessed them.

מג וַיַּרְא מֹשֶׁה אֶת־כָּל־הַמְּלָאכָה וְהִנֵּה עָשׂוּ אֹתָהּ כַּאֲשֶׁר צִוָּה יְהוָה כֵּן עָשׂוּ וַיְבָרֶךְ אֹתָם מֹשֶׁה:

va-YAR mo-SHEH et kol ha-m'-la-KHAH v'-hi-NAY a-SU o-TAH ka-a-SHER tzi-VAH a-do-NAI KAYN a-SU vai-VA-rekh o-TAM mo-SHEH

40 1 And *Hashem* spoke to *Moshe*, saying:

מ א וַיְדַבֵּר יְהוָה אֶל־מֹשֶׁה לֵּאמֹר:

2 On the first day of the first month you shall set up the *Mishkan* of the Tent of Meeting.

ב בְּיוֹם־הַחֹדֶשׁ הָרִאשׁוֹן בְּאֶחָד לַחֹדֶשׁ תָּקִים אֶת־מִשְׁכַּן אֹהֶל מוֹעֵד:

3 Place there the *Aron HaBrit*, and screen off the ark with the curtain.

ג וְשַׂמְתָּ שָׁם אֵת אֲרוֹן הָעֵדוּת וְסַכֹּתָ עַל־הָאָרֹן אֶת־הַפָּרֹכֶת:

4 Bring in the table and lay out its due setting; bring in the *menorah* and light its lamps;

ד וְהֵבֵאתָ אֶת־הַשֻּׁלְחָן וְעָרַכְתָּ אֶת־עֶרְכּוֹ וְהֵבֵאתָ אֶת־הַמְּנֹרָה וְהַעֲלֵיתָ אֶת־נֵרֹתֶיהָ:

5 and place the gold *Mizbayach* of incense before the *Aron HaBrit*. Then put up the screen for the entrance of the *Mishkan*.

ה וְנָתַתָּה אֶת־מִזְבַּח הַזָּהָב לִקְטֹרֶת לִפְנֵי אֲרוֹן הָעֵדֻת וְשַׂמְתָּ אֶת־מָסַךְ הַפֶּתַח לַמִּשְׁכָּן:

6 You shall place the *Mizbayach* of burnt offering before the entrance of the *Mishkan* of the Tent of Meeting.

ו וְנָתַתָּה אֵת מִזְבַּח הָעֹלָה לִפְנֵי פֶּתַח מִשְׁכַּן אֹהֶל־מוֹעֵד:

7 Place the laver between the Tent of Meeting and the *Mizbayach*, and put water in it.

ז וְנָתַתָּ אֶת־הַכִּיֹּר בֵּין־אֹהֶל מוֹעֵד וּבֵין הַמִּזְבֵּחַ וְנָתַתָּ שָׁם מָיִם:

8 Set up the enclosure round about, and put in place the screen for the gate of the enclosure.

ח וְשַׂמְתָּ אֶת־הֶחָצֵר סָבִיב וְנָתַתָּ אֶת־מָסַךְ שַׁעַר הֶחָצֵר:

9 You shall take the anointing oil and anoint the *Mishkan* and all that is in it to consecrate it and all its furnishings, so that it shall be holy.

ט וְלָקַחְתָּ אֶת־שֶׁמֶן הַמִּשְׁחָה וּמָשַׁחְתָּ אֶת־הַמִּשְׁכָּן וְאֶת־כָּל־אֲשֶׁר־בּוֹ וְקִדַּשְׁתָּ אֹתוֹ וְאֶת־כָּל־כֵּלָיו וְהָיָה קֹדֶשׁ:

10 Then anoint the *Mizbayach* of burnt offering and all its utensils to consecrate the *Mizbayach*, so that the *Mizbayach* shall be most holy.

י וּמָשַׁחְתָּ אֶת־מִזְבַּח הָעֹלָה וְאֶת־כָּל־כֵּלָיו וְקִדַּשְׁתָּ אֶת־הַמִּזְבֵּחַ וְהָיָה הַמִּזְבֵּחַ קֹדֶשׁ קָדָשִׁים:

11 And anoint the laver and its stand to consecrate it.

יא וּמָשַׁחְתָּ אֶת־הַכִּיֹּר וְאֶת־כַּנּוֹ וְקִדַּשְׁתָּ אֹתוֹ:

12 You shall bring *Aharon* and his sons forward to the entrance of the Tent of Meeting and wash them with the water.

יב וְהִקְרַבְתָּ אֶת־אַהֲרֹן וְאֶת־בָּנָיו אֶל־פֶּתַח אֹהֶל מוֹעֵד וְרָחַצְתָּ אֹתָם בַּמָּיִם:

39:43 As *Hashem* had commanded Upon the completion of the building of the *Mishkan* and its vessels, *Moshe* inspects the work and rejoices, because it has been done exactly as *Hashem* has commanded. Many commentators note that particularly following the sin of the golden calf, when the nation initiated a new form of worship that was not in accordance with God's will, it was vital that the construction of the *Mishkan* followed the instructions down to the most minute detail. By doing so, the nation demonstrates its understanding that God's will is unchanging and does not yield to the interpretation of individuals.

Man reading from the Torah, the book of God's commands, at the Western Wall

13 Put the sacral vestments on *Aharon*, and anoint him and consecrate him, that he may serve Me as *Kohen*.

יג וְהִלְבַּשְׁתָּ֙ אֶֽת־אַהֲרֹ֔ן אֵ֖ת בִּגְדֵ֣י הַקֹּ֑דֶשׁ וּמָשַׁחְתָּ֥ אֹת֛וֹ וְקִדַּשְׁתָּ֥ אֹת֖וֹ וְכִהֵ֥ן לִֽי׃

14 Then bring his sons forward, put tunics on them,

יד וְאֶת־בָּנָ֖יו תַּקְרִ֑יב וְהִלְבַּשְׁתָּ֥ אֹתָ֖ם כֻּתֳּנֹֽת׃

15 and anoint them as you have anointed their father, that they may serve Me as *Kohanim*. This their anointing shall serve them for everlasting priesthood throughout the ages.

טו וּמָשַׁחְתָּ֣ אֹתָ֗ם כַּֽאֲשֶׁ֤ר מָשַׁ֙חְתָּ֙ אֶת־אֲבִיהֶ֔ם וְכִהֲנ֖וּ לִ֑י וְ֠הָיְתָ֠ה לִֽהְיֹ֨ת לָהֶ֧ם מָשְׁחָתָ֛ם לִכְהֻנַּ֥ת עוֹלָ֖ם לְדֹֽרֹתָֽם׃

16 This *Moshe* did; just as *Hashem* had commanded him, so he did.

טז וַיַּ֖עַשׂ מֹשֶׁ֑ה כְּ֠כֹ֠ל אֲשֶׁ֨ר צִוָּ֧ה יְהֹוָ֛ה אֹת֖וֹ כֵּ֥ן עָשָֽׂה׃

17 In the first month of the second year, on the first of the month, the *Mishkan* was set up.

יז וַיְהִ֞י בַּחֹ֧דֶשׁ הָֽרִאשׁ֛וֹן בַּשָּׁנָ֥ה הַשֵּׁנִ֖ית בְּאֶחָ֣ד לַחֹ֑דֶשׁ הוּקַ֖ם הַמִּשְׁכָּֽן׃

18 *Moshe* set up the *Mishkan*, placing its sockets, setting up its planks, inserting its bars, and erecting its posts.

יח וַיָּ֨קֶם מֹשֶׁ֜ה אֶת־הַמִּשְׁכָּ֗ן וַיִּתֵּן֙ אֶת־אֲדָנָ֔יו וַיָּ֙שֶׂם֙ אֶת־קְרָשָׁ֔יו וַיִּתֵּ֖ן אֶת־בְּרִיחָ֑יו וַיָּ֖קֶם אֶת־עַמּוּדָֽיו׃

19 He spread the tent over the *Mishkan*, placing the covering of the tent on top of it – just as *Hashem* had commanded *Moshe*.

יט וַיִּפְרֹ֤שׂ אֶת־הָאֹ֙הֶל֙ עַל־הַמִּשְׁכָּ֔ן וַיָּ֜שֶׂם אֶת־מִכְסֵ֤ה הָאֹ֙הֶל֙ עָלָ֖יו מִלְמָ֑עְלָה כַּֽאֲשֶׁ֛ר צִוָּ֥ה יְהֹוָ֖ה אֶת־מֹשֶֽׁה׃

20 He took the Pact and placed it in the ark; he fixed the poles to the ark, placed the cover on top of the ark,

כ וַיִּקַּ֞ח וַיִּתֵּ֤ן אֶת־הָֽעֵדֻת֙ אֶל־הָ֣אָרֹ֔ן וַיָּ֥שֶׂם אֶת־הַבַּדִּ֖ים עַל־הָֽאָרֹ֑ן וַיִּתֵּ֧ן אֶת־הַכַּפֹּ֛רֶת עַל־הָֽאָרֹ֖ן מִלְמָֽעְלָה׃

21 and brought the ark inside the *Mishkan*. Then he put up the curtain for screening, and screened off the *Aron HaBrit* – just as *Hashem* had commanded *Moshe*.

כא וַיָּבֵ֣א אֶת־הָֽאָרֹן֮ אֶל־הַמִּשְׁכָּן֒ וַיָּ֗שֶׂם אֵ֚ת פָּרֹ֣כֶת הַמָּסָ֔ךְ וַיָּ֕סֶךְ עַ֖ל אֲר֣וֹן הָֽעֵד֑וּת כַּֽאֲשֶׁ֛ר צִוָּ֥ה יְהֹוָ֖ה אֶת־מֹשֶֽׁה׃

22 He placed the table in the Tent of Meeting, outside the curtain, on the north side of the *Mishkan*.

כב וַיִּתֵּ֤ן אֶת־הַשֻּׁלְחָן֙ בְּאֹ֣הֶל מוֹעֵ֔ד עַ֛ל יֶ֥רֶךְ הַמִּשְׁכָּ֖ן צָפֹ֑נָה מִח֖וּץ לַפָּרֹֽכֶת׃

23 Upon it he laid out the setting of bread before *Hashem* – as *Hashem* had commanded *Moshe*.

כג וַיַּֽעֲרֹ֥ךְ עָלָ֛יו עֵ֥רֶךְ לֶ֖חֶם לִפְנֵ֣י יְהֹוָ֑ה כַּֽאֲשֶׁ֛ר צִוָּ֥ה יְהֹוָ֖ה אֶת־מֹשֶֽׁה׃

24 He placed the *menorah* in the Tent of Meeting opposite the table, on the south side of the *Mishkan*.

כד וַיָּ֤שֶׂם אֶת־הַמְּנֹרָה֙ בְּאֹ֣הֶל מוֹעֵ֔ד נֹ֖כַח הַשֻּׁלְחָ֑ן עַ֛ל יֶ֥רֶךְ הַמִּשְׁכָּ֖ן נֶֽגְבָּה׃

25 And he lit the lamps before *Hashem* – as *Hashem* had commanded *Moshe*.

כה וַיַּ֥עַל הַנֵּרֹ֖ת לִפְנֵ֣י יְהֹוָ֑ה כַּֽאֲשֶׁ֛ר צִוָּ֥ה יְהֹוָ֖ה אֶת־מֹשֶֽׁה׃

26 He placed the *Mizbayach* of gold in the Tent of Meeting, before the curtain.

כו וַיָּ֛שֶׂם אֶת־מִזְבַּ֥ח הַזָּהָ֖ב בְּאֹ֣הֶל מוֹעֵ֑ד לִפְנֵ֖י הַפָּרֹֽכֶת׃

27 On it he burned aromatic incense – as *Hashem* had commanded *Moshe*.

כז וַיַּקְטֵ֥ר עָלָ֖יו קְטֹ֣רֶת סַמִּ֑ים כַּֽאֲשֶׁ֛ר צִוָּ֥ה יְהֹוָ֖ה אֶת־מֹשֶֽׁה׃

28 Then he put up the screen for the entrance of the *Mishkan*.

כח וַיָּ֛שֶׂם אֶת־מָסַ֥ךְ הַפֶּ֖תַח לַמִּשְׁכָּֽן׃

Exodus

29 At the entrance of the *Mishkan* of the Tent of Meeting he placed the *Mizbayach* of burnt offering. On it he offered up the burnt offering and the meal offering – as *Hashem* had commanded *Moshe*.

כט וְאֵת מִזְבַּח הָעֹלָה שָׂם פֶּתַח מִשְׁכַּן אֹהֶל־מוֹעֵד וַיַּעַל עָלָיו אֶת־הָעֹלָה וְאֶת־הַמִּנְחָה כַּאֲשֶׁר צִוָּה יְהֹוָה אֶת־מֹשֶׁה:

30 He placed the laver between the Tent of Meeting and the *Mizbayach*, and put water in it for washing.

ל וַיָּשֶׂם אֶת־הַכִּיֹּר בֵּין־אֹהֶל מוֹעֵד וּבֵין הַמִּזְבֵּחַ וַיִּתֵּן שָׁמָּה מַיִם לְרָחְצָה:

31 From it *Moshe* and *Aharon* and his sons would wash their hands and feet;

לא וְרָחֲצוּ מִמֶּנּוּ מֹשֶׁה וְאַהֲרֹן וּבָנָיו אֶת־יְדֵיהֶם וְאֶת־רַגְלֵיהֶם:

32 they washed when they entered the Tent of Meeting and when they approached the *Mizbayach* – as *Hashem* had commanded *Moshe*.

לב בְּבֹאָם אֶל־אֹהֶל מוֹעֵד וּבְקָרְבָתָם אֶל־הַמִּזְבֵּחַ יִרְחָצוּ כַּאֲשֶׁר צִוָּה יְהֹוָה אֶת־מֹשֶׁה:

33 And he set up the enclosure around the *Mishkan* and the *Mizbayach*, and put up the screen for the gate of the enclosure. When *Moshe* had finished the work,

לג וַיָּקֶם אֶת־הֶחָצֵר סָבִיב לַמִּשְׁכָּן וְלַמִּזְבֵּחַ וַיִּתֵּן אֶת־מָסַךְ שַׁעַר הֶחָצֵר וַיְכַל מֹשֶׁה אֶת־הַמְּלָאכָה:

34 the cloud covered the Tent of Meeting, and the Presence of *Hashem* filled the *Mishkan*.

לד וַיְכַס הֶעָנָן אֶת־אֹהֶל מוֹעֵד וּכְבוֹד יְהֹוָה מָלֵא אֶת־הַמִּשְׁכָּן:

35 *Moshe* could not enter the Tent of Meeting, because the cloud had settled upon it and the Presence of *Hashem* filled the *Mishkan*.

לה וְלֹא־יָכֹל מֹשֶׁה לָבוֹא אֶל־אֹהֶל מוֹעֵד כִּי־שָׁכַן עָלָיו הֶעָנָן וּכְבוֹד יְהֹוָה מָלֵא אֶת־הַמִּשְׁכָּן:

36 When the cloud lifted from the *Mishkan*, the Israelites would set out, on their various journeys;

לו וּבְהֵעָלוֹת הֶעָנָן מֵעַל הַמִּשְׁכָּן יִסְעוּ בְּנֵי יִשְׂרָאֵל בְּכֹל מַסְעֵיהֶם:

37 but if the cloud did not lift, they would not set out until such time as it did lift.

לז וְאִם־לֹא יֵעָלֶה הֶעָנָן וְלֹא יִסְעוּ עַד־יוֹם הֵעָלֹתוֹ:

38 For over the *Mishkan* a cloud of *Hashem* rested by day, and fire would appear in it by night, in the view of all the house of *Yisrael* throughout their journeys.

לח כִּי עֲנַן יְהֹוָה עַל־הַמִּשְׁכָּן יוֹמָם וְאֵשׁ תִּהְיֶה לַיְלָה בּוֹ לְעֵינֵי כָל־בֵּית־יִשְׂרָאֵל בְּכָל־מַסְעֵיהֶם:

KEE a-NAN a-do-NAI al ha-mish-KAN yo-MAM v'-AYSH tih-YEH
LAI-lah bo l'-ay-NAY khol bayt yis-ra-AYL b'-KHOL mas-ay-HEM

The Israeli flag waiving in a cloudy sky

40:38 A cloud of *Hashem* rested by day, and fire would appear in it by night The pillars of cloud and fire that accompanied the nation upon their exodus from Egypt now reposition themselves by hovering above the *Mishkan* at its completion. This manifestation of God's presence accompanies the Jews throughout their travels in the desert, reminding them that He continuously dwells in their midst. Similarly, when the *Beit Hamikdash* is built by King *Shlomo*, God's glory fills the Temple in the form of a cloud (I Kings 8:10–11), and a fire comes down from heaven (II Chronicles 7:1). Again, His presence among the people is manifest, this time in the holy city of *Yerushalayim*.

List of Transliterated Words in *The Israel Bible*

The following is a list of nouns which have been transliterated into Hebrew in the English translation and commentary of *The Israel Bible*:

Hebrew Name	English Name	Pronunciation	Hebrew
Achan	Achan	a-KHAN	עָכָן
Achav	Ahab	akh-AV	אַחְאָב
Achaz	Ahaz	a-KHAZ	אָחָז
Achazyahu	Ahaziah	a-khaz-YA-hu	אֲחַזְיָהוּ
Achiezer	Ahiezer	a-khee-E-zer	אֲחִיעֶזֶר
Achihud	Ahihud	a-khee-HUD	אֲחִיהוּד
Achikam	Ahikam	a-khee-KAM	אֲחִיקָם
Achilud	Ahilud	a-khee-LUD	אֲחִילוּד
Achimelech	Ahimelech	a-khee-ME-lekh	אֲחִימֶלֶךְ
Achira	Ahira	a-khee-RA	אֲחִירַע
Achisamach	Ahisamach	a-khee-sa-MAKH	אֲחִיסָמָךְ
Achitofel	Ahithophel	a-khee-TO-fel	אֲחִיתֹפֶל
Achituv	Ahitub	a-khee-TUV	אֲחִיטוּב
Achiya	Ahijah	a-khi-YAH	אֲחִיָּה
Adam	Adam	a-DAM	אָדָם
Adar	Adar	a-DAR	אֲדָר
Adoniyahu	Adonijah	a-do-ni-YA-hu	אֲדֹנִיָּהוּ
Adulam	Adullam	a-du-LAM	עֲדֻלָּם
Agur	Agur	a-GUR	אָגוּר
Aharon	Aaron	a-ha-RON	אַהֲרֹן
Amasa	Amasa	a-ma-SA	עֲמָשָׂא
Amatzya	Amaziah	a-matz-YAH	אֲמַצְיָה
Amen	Amen	a-MAYN	אָמֵן
Amiel	Ammiel	a-mee-AYL	עַמִּיאֵל
Aminadav	Amminadab	a-mee-na-DAV	עַמִּינָדָב
Amitai	Amittai	a-mi-TAI	אֲמִתַּי
Amnon	Amnon	am-NON	אַמְנֹן

Hebrew Name	English Name	Pronunciation	Hebrew
Amon	Amon	a-MON	אָמוֹן
Amos	Amos	a-MOS	עָמוֹס
Amotz	Amoz	a-MOTZ	אָמוֹץ
Amram	Amram	am-RAM	עַמְרָם
Anatot	Anathoth	a-na-TOT	עֲנָתוֹת
Aron	Ark	a-RON	אָרוֹן
Aron HaBrit	Ark of the Covenant	a-RON ha-b'-REET	אָרוֹן הַבְּרִית
Arpachshad	Arpachshad	ar-pakh-SHAD	אַרְפַּכְשַׁד
Asa	Asa	a-SA	אָסָא
Asael	Asahel	a-sah-AYL	עֲשָׂהאֵל
Asaf	Asaph	a-SAF	אָסָף
Ashdod	Ashdod	ash-DOD	אַשְׁדּוֹד
Asher	Asher	a-SHAYR	אָשֵׁר
Ashkelon	Ashkelon	ash-k'-LON	אַשְׁקְלוֹן
Atalya	Athaliah	a-tal-YAH	עֲתַלְיָה
Avdon	Abdon	av-DON	עַבְדּוֹן
Avichayil	Abihail	a-vee-KHA-yil	אֲבִיחַיִל
Avidan	Abidan	a-vee-DAN	אֲבִידָן
Avigail	Abigail	a-vee-GA-yil	אֲבִיגַיִל
Avihu	Abihu	a-vee-HU	אֲבִיהוּא
Avimelech	Abimelech	a-vee-ME-lekh	אֲבִימֶלֶךְ
Avinadav	Abinadab	a-vee-na-DAV	אֲבִינָדָב
Aviram	Abiram	a-vee-RAM	אֲבִירָם
Avishai	Abishai	a-vee-SHAI	אֲבִישַׁי
Aviya	Abijah	a-vi-YAH	אֲבִיָּה
Aviyam	Abijam	a-vi-YAM	אֲבִיָּם
Avner	Abner	av-NAYR	אַבְנֵר
Avraham	Abraham	av-ra-HAM	אַבְרָהָם
Avram	Abram	av-RAM	אַבְרָם
Avshalom	Absalom	av-sha-LOM	אַבְשָׁלוֹם
Azarya	Azariah	a-zar-YAH	עֲזַרְיָה
Azeika	Azekah	a-zay-KAH	עֲזֵקָה
Azza	Gaza	a-ZAH	עַזָּה

Hebrew Name	English Name	Pronunciation	Hebrew
B'nei Yisrael	The Children of Israel	b'-NAY yis-ra-AYL	בְּנֵי יִשְׂרָאֵל
Barak	Barak	ba-rakh-AYL	בָּרָק
Baruch	Baruch	ba-RUKH	בָּרוּךְ
Barzilai	Barzillai	bar-zi-LAI	בַּרְזִלַּי
Basha	Baasa	ba-SHA	בַּעְשָׁא
Batsheva	Bath-sheba	bat-SHE-va	בַּת־שֶׁבַע
Be'er Sheva	Beer-sheba	b'-AYR SHE-va	בְּאֵר שֶׁבַע
Be'eri	Beeri	b'-ay-REE	בְּאֵרִי
Beit Aven	Beth-aven	bayt A-ven	בֵּית אָוֶן
Beit El	Beth-el	bayt el	בֵּית אֵל
Beit Hamikdash	Temple	bayt ha-mik-DASH	בֵּית הַמִּקְדָּשׁ
Beit Lechem	Beth-lehem	bayt LE-khem	בֵּית לָחֶם
Beit Shean	Beth-shean	bayt sh'-AN	בֵּית שְׁאָן
Beit Shemesh	Beth-shemesh	bayt SHE-mesh	בֵּית שָׁמָשׁ
Berechya	Berechiah	be-rekh-YAH	בֶּרֶכְיָה
Betzalel	Bezalel	b'-tzal-AYL	בְּצַלְאֵל
Bilha	Bilhah	bil-HAH	בִּלְהָה
Binyamin	Benjamin	bin-ya-MIN	בִּנְיָמִין
Boaz	Boaz	BO-az	בֹּעַז
Buki	Bukki	bu-KEE	בֻּקִּי
Buzi	Buzi	bu-ZEE	בּוּזִי
Carmel	Carmel	kar-MEL	כַּרְמֶל
Chachalya	Hacaliah	kha-khal-YAH	חֲכַלְיָה
Chagai	Haggai	kha-GAI	חַגַּי
Chana	Hannah	kha-NAH	חַנָּה
Chanamel	Hanamel	kha-nam-AYL	חֲנַמְאֵל
Chanani	Hanani	kha-NA-nee	חֲנָנִי
Chananya	Hananiah	kha-nan-YAH	חֲנַנְיָה
Chaniel	Hanniel	kha-nee-AYL	חַנִּיאֵל
Chanoch	Enoch	kha-NOKH	חֲנוֹךְ
Chava	Eve	kha-VAH	חַוָּה
Chavakuk	Habakkuk	kha-va-KUK	חֲבַקּוּק
Chermon	Hermon	kher-MON	חֶרְמוֹן

Hebrew Name	English Name	Pronunciation	Hebrew
Chetzron	Hezron	khetz-RON	חֶצְרוֹן
Chever	Heber	KHE-ver	חֶבֶר
Chevron	Hebron	khev-RON	חֶבְרוֹן
Chilkiyahu	Hilkiah	khil-ki-YA-hu	חִלְקִיָּהוּ
Chizkiyahu	Hezekiah	khiz-ki-YA-hu	חִזְקִיָּהוּ
Chofni	Hophni	khof-NEE	חָפְנִי
Chogla	Hoglah	khog-LAH	חָגְלָה
Chulda	Hulda	khul-DAH	חֻלְדָּה
Chur	Hur	Khur	חוּר
Dan	Dan	Dan	דָּן
Daniel	Daniel	da-ni-YAYL	דָּנִיֵּאל
Datan	Dathan	da-TAN	דָּתָן
David	David	da-VID	דָּוִד
Devora	Deborah	d'-vo-RAH	דְּבוֹרָה
Dina	Dinah	DEE-nah	דִּינָה
Doeg Ha'adomi	Doeg the Edomite	do-AYG ha-a-do-MEE	דּוֹאֵג הָאֲדֹמִי
Efraim	Ephraim	ef-RA-yim	אֶפְרַיִם
Efrat	Ephrat	ef-RAT	אֶפְרָתָה
Efrat	Ephrathah	ef-RA-tah	אֶפְרָתָה
Ehud	Ehud	ay-HUD	אֵהוּד
Eila	Elah	AY-lah	אֵלָה
Eilon	Elon	ay-LON	אֵילוֹן
Ein Gedi	En-gedi	ayn GE-dee	עֵין גֶּדִי
Elazar	Eleazar	el-a-ZAR	אֶלְעָזָר
Elchanan	Elhanan	el-kha-NAN	אֶלְחָנָן
Eli	Eli	ay-LEE	עֵלִי
Eliav	Eliab	e-lee-AV	אֱלִיאָב
Elidad	Elidad	e-lee-DAD	אֱלִידָד
Eliezer	Eliezer	e-lee-E-zer	אֱלִיעֶזֶר
Elimelech	Elimelech	e-lee-ME-lekh	אֱלִימֶלֶךְ
Elisha	Elisha	e-lee-SHA	אֱלִישָׁע
Elishama	Elishama	e-lee-sha-MA	אֱלִישָׁמָע
Elisheva	Elisheba	e-lee-SHE-va	אֱלִישֶׁבַע

Hebrew Name	English Name	Pronunciation	Hebrew
Elitzafan	Eli-zaphan	e-lee-tza-FAN	אֱלִיצָפָן
Elitzur	Elizur	e-lee-TZUR	אֱלִיצוּר
Eliyahu	Elijah	ay-li-YA-hu	אֵלִיָּהוּ
Elkana	Elkanah	el-ka-NAH	אֶלְקָנָה
Elyasaf	Eliasaph	el-ya-SAF	אֶלְיָסָף
Elyashiv	Eliashib	el-ya-SHEEV	אֶלְיָשִׁיב
Enosh	Enosh	e-NOSH	אֱנוֹשׁ
Er	Er	ayr	עֵר
Eshtaol	Eshtaol	esh-ta-OL	אֶשְׁתָּאֹל
Esther	Esther	es-TAYR	אֶסְתֵּר
Eved Melech	Ebed-melech	E-ved ME-lekh	עֶבֶד־מֶלֶךְ
Even Ha-Ezer	Eben-Ezer	E-ven ha-E-zer	אֶבֶן הָעֵזֶר
Ever	Eber	AY-ver	עֵבֶר
Evyatar	Abiathar	ev-ya-TAR	אֶבְיָתָר
Ezra	Ezra	ez-RA	עֶזְרָא
Gad	Gad	gad	גָּד
Gadi	Gaddi	ga-DEE	גַּדִּי
Gadiel	Gaddiel	ga-dee-AYL	גַּדִּיאֵל
Gamliel	Gamaliel	gam-lee-AYL	גַּמְלִיאֵל
Gedalia	Gedaliah	g'-dal-YA (hu)	גְּדַלְיָהוּ
Gedera	Gederah	g'-day-RAH	גְּדֵרָה
Gershom	Gershom	gay-r'-SHOM	גֵּרְשֹׁם
Gershon	Gershon	gay-r'-SHON	גֵּרְשׁוֹן
Geshem	Geshem	GE-shem	גֶּשֶׁם
Geuel	Geuel	g'-u-AYL	גְּאוּאֵל
Gidon	Gideon	gid-ON	גִּדְעוֹן
Gilad	Gilead	gil-AD	גִּלְעָד
Gilgal	Gilgal	gil-GAL	גִּלְגָּל
Giva	Gibeah	giv-AH	גִּבְעָה
Givon	Gibeon	giv-ON	גִּבְעוֹן
Hadassa	Hadassah	ha-da-SAH	הֲדַסָּה
Har Eival	Mount Ebal	ay-VAL	הַר עֵיבָל
Har Gerizim	Mount Gerizim	g'-ri-ZEEM	הַר גְּרִזִים

Hebrew Name	English Name	Pronunciation	Hebrew
Har HaBayit	Temple Mount	har ha-BA-yit	הַר הַבַּיִת
Har HaZeitim	the Mount of Olives	har ha-zay-TEEM	הַר הַזֵּיתִים
Hashem	Lord/God		
Hayman	Heman	hay-MAN	הֵימָן
Hoshea	Hosea	ho-SHAY-a	הוֹשֵׁעַ
Ido	Iddo	i-DO	עִדּוֹ
Imanu-El	Immanuel	i-MA-nu ayl	עִמָּנוּ אֵל
Ish-boshet	Ish-bosheth	eesh BO-shet	אִישׁ־בֹּשֶׁת
Itamar	Ithamar	ee-ta-MAR	אִיתָמָר
Itiel	Ithiel	ee-tee-AYL	אִיתִיאֵל
Ivtzan	Ibzan	iv-TZAN	אִבְצָן
Iyov	Job	i-YOV	אִיּוֹב
Kadmiel	Kadmiel	kad-mee-AYL	קַדְמִיאֵל
Kalev	Caleb	ka-LAYV	כָּלֵב
Keesh	Kish	keesh	קִישׁ
Kehat	Kohath	k'-HAT	קְהָת
Keinan	Kenan	kay-NAN	קֵינָן
Kemuel	Kemuel	k'-mu-AYL	קְמוּאֵל
Keruvim	Cherubim	k'-ru-VEEM	כְּרוּבִים
Kilyon	Chilion	kil-YON	כִּלְיוֹן
Kiryat Arba	Kiriath-arba	keer-YAT AR-bah	קִרְיַת אַרְבַּע
Kiryat Sefer	Kiriath-sepher	keer-YAT SAY-fer	קִרְיַת־סֵפֶר
Kiryat Ye'arim	Kiriath-jearim	keer-YAT y'-a-REEM	קִרְיַת יְעָרִים
Kislev	Chislev	kis-LAYV	כִּסְלֵו
Kohanim	Priests	ko-ha-NEEM	כֹּהֲנִים
Kohelet	Koheleth	ko-HE-let	קֹהֶלֶת
Kohen	Priest	ko-HAYN	כֹּהֵן
Kohen Gadol	High Priest	ko-HAYN ga-DOL	כֹּהֵן גָּדוֹל
Korach	Korah	KO-rakh	קֹרַח
Kushi	Cushi	ku-SHEE	כּוּשִׁי
Lachish	Lachish	la-KHEESH	לָכִישׁ
Leah	Leah	lay-AH	לֵאָה
Lemech	Lamech	LE-mekh	לֶמֶךְ

Hebrew Name	English Name	Pronunciation	Hebrew
Lemuel	Lemuel	l'-mu-AYL	לְמוֹאֵל
Levi	Levi	lay-VEE	לֵוִי
Leviim	Levites	l'-vee-IM	לְוִיִּם
Machla	Mahlah	makh-LAH	מַחְלָה
Machlon	Mahlon	makh-LON	מַחְלוֹן
Machseya	Mahseiah	makh-say-YAH	מַחְסֵיָה
Malachi	Malachi	mal-a-KHEE	מַלְאָכִי
Manoach	Manoah	ma-NO-akh	מָנוֹחַ
Mashiach	Messiah	ma-SHEE-akh	מָשִׁיחַ
Mefiboshet	Mephibosheth	m'-fee-VO-shet	מְפִיבֹשֶׁת
Mehalalel	Mahalalel	ma-ha-lal-AYL	מַהֲלַלְאֵל
Menachem	Menahem	m'-na-KHAYM	מְנַחֵם
Menashe	Menasseh	m'-na-SHEH	מְנַשֶּׁה
Menorah	Candlestick	m'-no-RAH	מְנֹרָה
Merari	Merari	m'-ra-REE	מְרָרִי
Metushelach	Methusaleh	m'-tu-SHE-lakh	מְתוּשָׁלַח
Micha	Micah	mee-KHAH	מִיכָה
Michael	Michael	mee-kha-AYL	מִיכָאֵל
Michaihu	Micaiah	mee-KHAI-hu	מִיכָיְהוּ
Michal	Michal	mee-KHAL	מִיכַל
Milka	Milcah	mil-KAH	מִלְכָּה
Miriam	Miriam	mir-YAM	מִרְיָם
Mishael	Mishael	mee-sha-AYL	מִישָׁאֵל
Mishkan	Tabernacle	mish-KAN	מִשְׁכַּן
Mitzpa	Mizpah	mitz-PAH	מִצְפָּה
Mizbayach	Altar	miz-BAY-akh	מִזְבֵּחַ
Mordechai	Mordecai	mor-d'-KHAI	מָרְדֳּכַי
Moriah	Moriah	mo-ri-YAH	מוֹרִיָּה
Moshe	Moses	mo-SHEH	מֹשֶׁה
Nachbi	Nahbi	nakh-BEE	נַחְבִּי
Nachor	Nahor	na-KHOR	נָחוֹר
Nachshon	Nahshon	nakh-SHON	נַחְשׁוֹן
Nachum	Nahum	na-KHUM	נַחוּם

Hebrew Name	English Name	Pronunciation	Hebrew
Nadav	Nadab	na-DAV	נָדָב
Naftali	Naphtali	naf-ta-LEE	נַפְתָּלִי
Naomi	Naomi	na-o-MEE	נָעֳמִי
Natan	Nathan	na-TAN	נָתָן
Naval	Nabal	na-VAL	נָבָל
Navi	Prophet	na-VEE	נָבִיא
Navot	Naboth	na-VAL	נָבָל
Nechemya	Nehemiah	n'-khem-YAH	נְחֶמְיָה
Negev	Negeb	NE-gev	נֶגֶב
Nerya	Neriah	nay-ri-YAH	נֵרִיָּה
Netanel	Nethanel	n'-tan-AYL	נְתַנְאֵל
Neviah	Prophetess	n'-vee-AH	נְבִיאָה
Neviim	Prophets	n'-vee-EEM	נְבִיאִים
Nisan	Nisan	nee-SAN	נִיסָן
Noa	Noah	no-AH	נֹעָה
Noach	Noah	NO-akh	נֹחַ
Nov	Nob	nov	נֹב
Nun	Nun	nun	נוּן
Oded	Oded	o-DAYD	עוֹדֵד
Ohola	Oholah	a-ho-LAH	אָהֳלָה
Oholiav	Oholiab	o-ha-lee-AV	אָהֳלִיאָב
Oholiva	Oholibah	a-ho-lee-VAH	אָהֳלִיבָה
Omri	Omri	om-REE	עָמְרִי
Onan	Onan	o-NAN	אוֹנָן
Otniel	Othniel	ot-nee-AYL	עָתְנִיאֵל
Ovadya	Obadiah	o-vad-YAH	עֹבַדְיָה
Oved	Obed	o-VAYD	עוֹבֵד
Oved Edom	Obed Edom	o-VAYD e-DOM	עוֹבֵד אֱדֹם
Pagiel	Pagiel	pag-ee-AYL	פַּגְעִיאֵל
Palti	Palti	pal-TEE	פַּלְטִי
Paltiel	Paltiel	pal-tee-AYL	פַּלְטִיאֵל
Pekach	Pekah	PE-kakh	פֶּקַח
Pedael	Pedahel	p'-da-AYL	פְּדַהְאֵל

Hebrew Name	English Name	Pronunciation	Hebrew
Pekachya	Pekahiah	p'-kakh-YAH	פְּקַחְיָה
Peleg	Peleg	PE-leg	פֶּלֶג
Penina	Peninnah	p'-ni-NAH	פְּנִנָּה
Peretz	Perez	PE-retz	פֶּרֶץ
Petuel	Pethuel	p'-tu-AYL	פְּתוּאֵל
Pinchas	Phinehas	peen-KHAS	פִּינְחָס
Rachel	Rachel	ra-KHAYL	רָחֵל
Ram	Ram	ram	רָם
Rama	Ramah	ra-MAH	רָמָה
Re'u	Reu	r'-U	רְעוּ
Rechovam	Rehoboam	r'-khav-AM	רְחַבְעָם
Reuven	Reuben	r'-u-VAYN	רְאוּבֵן
Rivka	Rebecca	riv-KAH	רִבְקָה
Rut	Ruth	rut	רוּת
Salma	Salmon/Salmah	sal-MAH	שַׂלְמָה
Salmon	Salmon	sal-MON	שַׂלְמוֹן
Sara	Sarah	sa-RAH	שָׂרָה
Sarai	Sarai	sa-RAI	שָׂרַי
Selah	Selah	SE-lah	סֶלָה
Seraya	Seraiah	s'-ra-YAH	שְׂרָיָה
Serug	Serug	s'-RUG	שְׂרוּג
Setur	Sethur	s'-TUR	סְתוּר
Shaarayim	Shaaraim	sha-a-RA-yim	שַׁעֲרַיִם
Shabbat	Sabbath	sha-BAT	שַׁבַּת
Shabbatot	Sabbaths	sha-ba-TOT	שַׁבָּתוֹת
Shafan	Shaphan	sha-FAN	שָׁפָן
Shafat	Shaphat	sha-FAT	שָׁפָט
Shalem	Salem	sha-LAYM	שָׁלֵם
Shalum	Shallum	sha-LUM	שַׁלּוּם
Shamgar	Shamgar	sham-GAR	שַׁמְגַּר
Shamua	Shammua	sha-MU-a	שַׁמּוּעַ
Shaul	Saul	sha-UL	שָׁאוּל
Shealtiel	Shealtiel	sh'-al-tee-AYL	שְׁאַלְתִּיאֵל

Hebrew Name	English Name	Pronunciation	Hebrew
Shear Yashuv	Shear-Jashub	sh'-AR ya-SHUV	שְׁאָר יָשׁוּב
Shechanya	Shecaniah	sh'-khan-YAH	שְׁכַנְיָה
Shechem	Shechem	sh'-KHEM	שְׁכֶם
Sheila	Shelah	shay-LAH	שֵׁלָה
Shelach	Shelah	SHE-lakh	שָׁלַח
Shelumiel	Shelumiel	sh'-lu-mee-AYL	שְׁלֻמִיאֵל
Shem	Shem	Shaym	שֵׁם
Shemaya	Shemaiah	sh'-ma-YAH	שְׁמַעְיָה
Sheshbatzar	Sheshbazzar	shaysh-ba-TZAR	שֵׁשְׁבַּצַּר
Shet	Seth	Shayt	שֵׁת
Shevat	Shebat	sh'-VAT	שְׁבָט
Shilo	Shiloh	shi-LOH	שִׁלֹה
Shim'i	Shimei	shim-EE	שִׁמְעִי
Shimon	Simeon	shim-ON	שִׁמְעוֹן
Shimshon	Samson	shim-SHON	שִׁמְשׁוֹן
Shlomo	Solomon	sh'-lo-MOH	שְׁלֹמֹה
Shmuel	Samuel	sh'-mu-AYL	שְׁמוּאֵל
Shofar	Horn	sho-FAR	שׁוֹפָר
Shofarot	Horns	sho-fa-ROT	שׁוֹפָרוֹת
Shomron	Samaria	sho-m'-RON	שֹׁמְרוֹן
Sivan	Sivan	see-VAN	סִיוָן
Tamar	Tamar	ta-MAR	תָּמָר
Tanakh	Hebrew Bible	ta-NAKH	תָּנָ"ךְ
Tapuach	Tappuah	ta-PU-akh	תַּפּוּחַ
Tavor	Tabor	ta-VOR	תָּבוֹר
Tekoa	Tekoa	t'-KO-a	תְּקוֹעַה
Terach	Terah	TE-rakh	תֶּרַח
Teveria	Tiberias	t'-ver-YAH	טְבֶרְיָה
Tevet	Tebeth	tay-VAYT	טֵבֵת
Tirtza	Tirzah	tir-TZAH	תִּרְצָה
Tola	Tola	to-LA	תּוֹלָע
Tzadok	Zadok	tza-DOK	צָדוֹק
Tzefanya	Zephaniah	tz'-fan-YAH	צְפַנְיָה

114

Hebrew Name	English Name	Pronunciation	Hebrew
Tzelofchad	Zelophehad	tz'-lo-f-KHAD	צְלָפְחָד
Tzeruya	Zeruiah	tz'-ru-YAH	צְרוּיָה
Tzfat	Safed	tz'-FAT	צְפַת
Tzidkiyahu	Zedekiah	tzid-ki-YA-hu	צִדְקִיָּהוּ
Tziklag	Ziklag	tzi-k'-LAG	צִקְלַג
Tzion	Zion	tzi-YON	צִיּוֹן
Tzipora	Zipporah	tzi-po-RAH	צִפֹּרָה
Tzora	Zorah	tzor-AH	צָרְעָה
Tzuriel	Zuriel	tzu-ree-AYL	צוּרִיאֵל
Ukal	Ucal	u-KAL	אֻכָל
Uri	Uri	u-REE	אוּרִי
Uriya	Uriah	u-ri-YAH	אוּרִיָּה
Utz	Uz	Utz	עוּץ
Uzziyahu	Uzziah	u-zi-YA-hu	עֻזִּיָּהוּ
Yaakov	Jacob	ya-a-KOV	יַעֲקֹב
Yachaziel	Jahaziel	ya-kha-zee-AYL	יַחֲזִיאֵל
Yael	Jael	ya-AYL	יָעֵל
Yaffo	Joppa/Jaffa	ya-FO	יָפוֹ
Yair	Jair	ya-EER	יָאִיר
Yakeh	Jakeh	ya-KEH	יָקֶה
Yarden	Jordan	yar-DAYN	יַרְדֵּן
Yarmut	Jarmuth	yar-MUT	יַרְמוּת
Yechezkel	Ezekiel	y'-khez-KAYL	יְחֶזְקֵאל
Yechiel	Jehiel	y'-khee-AYL	יְחִיאֵל
Yechonya	Jeconiah	y'-khon-YAH	יְכָנְיָה
Yedutun	Jeduthun	y'-du-TUN	יְדוּתוּן
Yehoachaz	Jehoahaz	y'-ho-a-KHAZ	יְהוֹאָחָז
Yehoash	Jehoash	y'-ho-ASH	יְהוֹאָשׁ
Yehochanan	Jehohanan	y'-ho-kha-NAN	יְהוֹחָנָן
Yehonatan	Jonathan	y'-ho-na-TAN	יְהוֹנָתָן
Yehoram	Jehoram	y'-ho-RAM	יְהוֹרָם
Yehoshafat	Jehoshaphat	y'-ho-sha-FAT	יְהוֹשָׁפָט
Yehoshavat	Jehoshabeath	y'-ho-shav-AT	יְהוֹשַׁבְעַת

Hebrew Name	English Name	Pronunciation	Hebrew
Yehosheva	Jehosheba	y-ho-SHE-va	יְהוֹשֶׁבַע
Yehoshua	Joshua	y'-ho-SHU-a	יְהוֹשֻׁעַ
Yehotzadak	Jehozadak	y'-ho-tza-DAK	יְהוֹצָדָק
Yehoyachin	Jehoiachin	y'-ho-ya-KHEEN	יְהוֹיָכִין
Yehoyada	Jehoiada	y'-ho-ya-DA	יְהוֹיָדָע
Yehoyakim	Jehoiakim	y'-ho-ya-KEEM	יְהוֹיָקִים
Yehu	Jehu	yay-HU	יֵהוּא
Yehuda	Judah	y'-hu-DAH	יְהוּדָה
Yehudi	Jew	y'-hu-DEE	יְהוּדִי
Yehudim	Jews	y'-hu-DEEM	יְהוּדִים
Yered	Jared	YE-red	יֶרֶד
Yericho	Jericho	y'-ree-KHO	יְרִיחוֹ
Yerovam	Jeroboam	ya-rov-AM	יָרָבְעָם
Yerubaal	Jerubbaal	y'-ru-BA-al	יְרֻבַּעַל
Yerushalayim	Jerusalem	y'-ru-sha-LA-yim	יְרוּשָׁלַיִם
Yeshayahu	Isaiah	y'-sha-YA-hu	יְשַׁעְיָהוּ
Yeshua	Jeshua	yay-SHU-a	יֵשׁוּעַ
Yiftach	Jephthah	yif-TAKH	יִפְתָּח
Yigal	Igal	yig-AL	יִגְאָל
Yirmiyahu	Jeremiah	yir-m'-YA-hu	יִרְמְיָהוּ
Yishai	Jesse	yi-SHAI	יִשַׁי
Yisrael	Israel	yis-ra-AYL	יִשְׂרָאֵל
Yissachar	Issachar	yi-sa-KHAR	יִשָּׂשכָר
Yitzchak	Issac	yitz-KHAK	יִצְחָק
Yizrael	Jezreel	yiz-r'-EL	יִזְרְעָאל
Yoash	Joash	yo-ASH	יוֹאָשׁ
Yoav	Joab	yo-AV	יוֹאָב
Yochanan	Johanan	yo-kha-NAN	יוֹחָנָן
Yocheved	Jochebed	yo-KHE-ved	יוֹכֶבֶד
Yoel	Joel	yo-AYL	יוֹאֵל
Yona	Jonah	yo-NAH	יוֹנָה
Yonadav	Jonadab	yo-na-DAV	יוֹנָדָב
Yonatan	Jonathan	yo-na-TAN	יוֹנָתָן

Hebrew Name	English Name	Pronunciation	Hebrew
Yoram	Joram	yo-RAM	יוֹרָם
Yosef	Joseph	yo-SAYF	יוֹסֵף
Yoshiyahu	Josiah	yo-shi-YA-hu	יֹאשִׁיָהוּ
Yotam	Jotham	yo-TAM	יוֹתָם
Yotzadak	Jozadak	yo-tza-DAK	יוֹצָדָק
Yozavad	Jozabad	yo-za-VAD	יוֹזָבָד
Zanoach	Zanoah	za-NO-akh	זָנוֹחַ
Zecharya	Zechariah	z'-khar-YAH	זְכַרְיָה
Zerach	Zerah	ZE-rakh	זֶרַח
Zerubavel	Zerubbabel	z'-ru-ba-VEL	זְרֻבָּבֶל
Zevulun	Zebulun	z'-vu-LUN	זְבוּלֻן
Zilpa	Zilpah	zil-PAH	זִלְפָּה
Zimri	Zimri	zim-REE	זִמְרִי

Jewish Holidays

Chanukah	Hanukkah	kha-nu-KAH	חֲנוּכָּה
Pesach	Passover	PE-sakh	פֶּסַח
Purim	Purim	pu-REEM	פּוּרִים
Rosh Hashana	Jewish New Year	rosh ha-sha-NAH	רֹאשׁ הַשָּׁנָה
Shavuot	Feast of Weeks	sha-vu-OT	שָׁבוּעוֹת
Shemini Atzeret	Eight Day of Assembly	sh'-mee-NEE a-TZE-ret	שְׁמִינִי עֲצֶרֶת
Sukkot	Feast of Tabernacles	su-KOT	סֻכּוֹת
Yom Kippur	Day of Atonement	yom kee-PUR	יוֹם כִּיפּוּר

Biblical Measurements

Amah	Cubit	a-MAH	אַמָּה
Amot	Cubits	a-MOT	אַמּוֹת
Bat	Bath	bat	בַּת
Batim	Baths	ba-TEEM	בַּתִּים
Beka	half-shekel	BE-ka	בֶּקַע
Chomarim	Homers	kho-ma-REEM	חֳמָרִים
Chomer	Homer	KHO-mer	חֹמֶר
Efah	Ephah	ay-FAH	אֵיפָה
Geira	Gerah	gay-RAH	גֵּרָה

Hebrew Name	English Name	Pronunciation	Hebrew
Gomed	Gomed	GO- med	גֹּמֶד
Hin	Hin	heen	הִין
Kav	kab	kav	קַב
Kesita	kesitah	k'-see-TAH	קְשִׂיטָה
Kikar	talent	ki-KAR	כִּכָּר
Kikarim	talents	ki-ka-RIM	כִּכָּרִים
Kor	kor	kor	כֹּר
Letek	lethech	LE-tek	לֶתֶךְ
Log	Log	log	לֹג
Maneh	Mina	ma-NEH	מָנֶה
Manim	Minas	ma-NEEM	מָנִים
Omer	Omer	O-mer	עֹמֶר
Pim	Pim	peem	פִּים
Se'ah	Seah	say-AH	סְאָה
Se'eem	Seahs	s'-EEM	סְאִים
Shekalim	Shekels	sh'-ka-LEEM	שְׁקָלִים
Shekel	Shekel	SHE-kel	שֶׁקֶל
Tefach	Handbreadth	TE-fakh	טֶפַח
Zeret	Span	ZE-ret	זֶרֶת

Photo Credits

1:1 PICRYL.com, **2:10** makarenko7/Shutterstock.com, **2:19** Moshe Milner, Government Press Office (Israel), **3:17** Rostislav Glinsky/Shutterstock.com, **4:22** Protasov AN/Shutterstock.com, **5:2** Protasov AN/Shutterstock.com, **6:8(1)** Jewish Content Images, Shutterstock.com, **6:8(2)** Protasov AN/Shutterstock.com, **7:17** Shabtay/Shutterstock.com, **8:15** Mark Neyman, Government Press Office (Israel), **9:1** To14go via Wikimedia Commons, **9:24** Sergei25/Shutterstock.com, **10:2** Orr Matzkin/Shutterstock.com, **11:13** Vadim Petrakov/Shutterstock.com, **12:2** S1001/Shutterstock.com, **13:4** Mark Neyman, Government Press Office (Israel), **13:5** lusubov Nizami/Shutterstock.com, **14:19** Reut Gross via Wikimedia Commons, **15:17** By Aklyuch – Original digital photo, Public Domain, https://commons.wikimedia.org/w/index .php?curid=9896237, **16:35** Mark Neyman, Government Press Office (Israel), **17:17** Valeriy Yatsun/Shutterstock.com, **18:23** By israeltourism – https://www .flickr.com/photos/visitisrael/6180275423, CC BY 2.0, https://commons .wikimedia.org/w/index.php?curid=26626207, **19:4** Teddy Brauner, Government Press Office (Israel), **20:21** Moshe Milner, Government Press Office (Israel), **21:1** Dmitry Pistrov/Shutterstock.com, **22:3** irisphoto1/Shutterstock. com, **23:11** John Theodor/Shutterstock.com, **23:30** Luciano Santandreu/Shutterstock.com, **24:4** Yan Simkin/Shutterstock.com, **25:8** graceenee/Shutterstock. com, **26:15** Mark A. Wilson via Wikimedia Commons, **27:8** Tamarah, CC BY-SA 3.0 <https://creativecommons.org/licenses/by-sa/3.0>, via Wikimedia Commons, **28:2** ArtMari/Shutterstock.com, **29:1** Ekaterina Lin/Shutterstock. com, **30:12** Roman Sigaev/Shutterstock.com, **31:17** Zoltan Kluger, Government Press Office (Israel), **32:13** John Theodor/Shutterstock.com, **33:1** Evgeny Subbotsky/Shutterstock.com, **34:24** Mark Neyman Government Press Office (Israel), **35:29** Ruk7, CC BY-SA 3.0 <https://creativecommons.org/licenses /by-sa/3.0>, via Wikimedia Commons, **36:8** The original uploader was Sputnikcccp at English Wikipedia. – Transferred from en.wikipedia to Commons by Mangostar using CommonsHelper., CC BY-SA 3.0, https:// commons.wikimedia.org/w/index.php?curid=5098869, **37:17** SA via Wikimedia Commons, **38:8** Israel Defense Forces, CC BY-SA 2.0, via Wikimedia Commons, **39:43** VenturaStock/Shutterstock.com, **40:38** Olga Mukashev/ Shutterstock.com

Map of Modern-Day Israel and its Neighbors

The following is a map of modern-day Israel and the surrounding countries

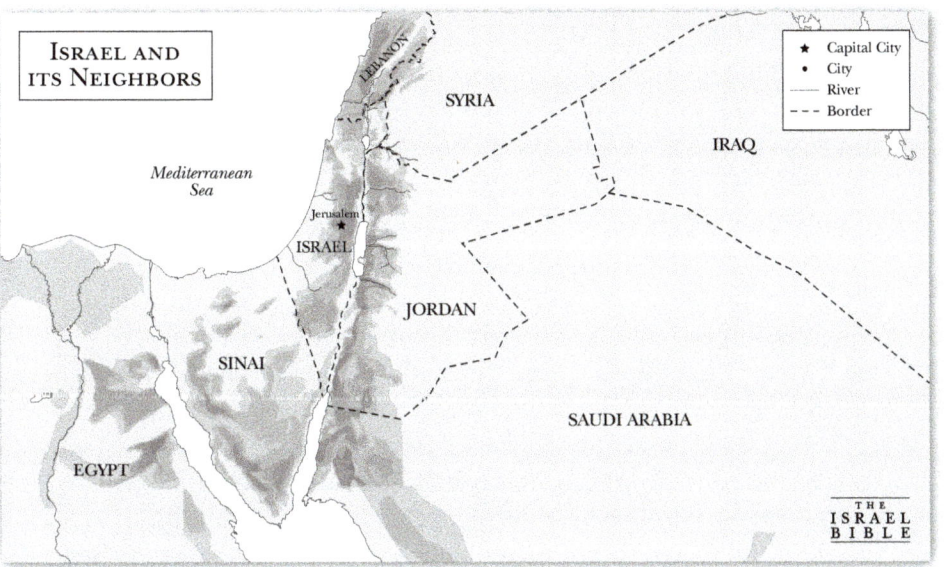

NOTES

NOTES

NOTES

NOTES

NOTES

For more inspiring commentary,
interactive maps, educational videos,
vivid photographs and more,
please visit our website

www.TheIsraelBible.com

THE
ISRAEL
BIBLE